Who Will Rescue Us?

Who Will Rescue Us?

The Story of the Jewish Children
Who Fled to France and America
During the Holocaust

LAURA HOBSON FAURE

YALE UNIVERSITY PRESS
NEW HAVEN AND LONDON

For information about this and other Yale University Press publications, please contact:
U.S. Office: sales.press@yale.edu   yalebooks.com
Europe Office: sales@yaleup.co.uk   yalebooks.co.uk

Set in Adobe Garamond Pro by IDSUK (DataConnection) Ltd
Printed in the UK using 100% renewable electricity at CPI Group (UK) Ltd

Library of Congress Control Number: 2024948092
A catalogue record for this book is available from the British Library.
Authorized Representative in the EU: Easy Access System Europe, Mustamäe tee 50, 10621 Tallinn, Estonia, gpsr.requests@easproject.com

ISBN 978-0-300-26996-3

10 9 8 7 6 5 4 3 2 1

To my children, Léo and Talia

Contents

CONTENTS

Illustrations

1. The Jewish orphanage of Frankfurt am Main, after the November 9–10, 1938 pogrom. Collection of Elfriede Schloss.
2. Andrée Salomon with a group of refugee children, c.1939–1942. Mémorial de la Shoah, OSE collection.
3. Germaine de Rothschild and Helene Papanek with refugee children in front of an OSE home, c.1939–1940. Papanek family archive.
4. Baron and Baroness Pierre and Yvonne de Gunzbourg, c.1945–1946. Courtesy of the family of the late Aline Berlin.
5. Ernst Papanek and the OSE children, c.1939–1940. Mémorial de la Shoah, OSE collection.
6. Ernst and Lida Jablonski with refugee children, c.1947. United States Holocaust Memorial Museum, courtesy of Lida Jablonski.
7. Norbert Bikales and his parents in Berlin, May 1939. United States Holocaust Memorial Museum, courtesy of Norbert Bikales.
8. Norbert Bikales and fellow refugee children with educators at the Chabannes home in August 1941. United States Holocaust Memorial Museum, courtesy of Norbert Bikales.
9. Refugee children and teens at the Château de la Guette, c.1939. Archives Nationales, Alfred and Françoise Brauner collection.
10. Thirteen-year-old Heinz Löw's diary page, September 1939. United States Holocaust Memorial Museum, courtesy of Ruth Salmon Seltzer, with permission from Carol Low.

11. A drawing by a child in La Guette, c.1939. Mémorial de la Shoah, Werner Matzdorff collection.

12. A poster of the United States Committee for the Care of European Children, c.1940–1942. United States Holocaust Memorial Museum, courtesy of the Crown Family.

13. Andrée Salomon, JDC's Herbert Katzki, and a group of children in Marseille, 1941. Mémorial de la Shoah, OSE Collection.

14. Brothers Werner and Claus Peter Gossels at the OSE's Chabannes home before leaving for the United States, c.1941. Courtesy of Nancy Lee Gossels.

15. Children and caretakers at the OSE's Chabannes home before the August 26, 1942 round-ups. United States Holocaust Memorial Museum, courtesy of Lida Jablonski.

16. Refugee children on the SS *Mouzinho*, sailing to New York from Lisbon in June 1941. United States Holocaust Memorial Museum, courtesy of Henry Schuster.

17. Elfriede Meyer Schloss, in 2016, with the photos of her family she carried to the United States in 1941. Photograph by Laura Hobson Faure with permission of Elfriede Schloss.

Abbreviations

AFSC	American Friends Service Committee
Alliance, AIU	Alliance israélite universelle
Amerose	American Committee of OSE
CAR	Comité d'assistance aux réfugiés
CIE	Comité israélite pour les enfants venant d'Allemagne et d'Europe centrale
Cimade	Comité inter-mouvements auprès des évacués
CRC	Central Refugee Committee
GJCA	German Jewish Children's Aid
JDC or Joint	American Joint Distribution Committee
LICA	Ligue internationale contre l'antisémitisme
NCC	National Coordinating Committee
NRS	National Refugee Service
ORT	Organization for Rehabilitation through Training
OSE	Union OSE
OSE-USA	American Friends and Alumni of the OSE
OZE	Obshtshestvo Zdravookraney Evrei
SHEK	Schweizer Hilfswerk für Emigrantenkinder
Secours Suisse	Schweizerische Arbeitsgemeinschaft für kriegsgeschädigte Kinder
TOZ	Polish branch of the OSE
UGIF	Union générale des Israélites de France

ABBREVIATIONS

USC	Unitarian Service Committee
USCOM	United States Committee for the Care of European Children
YMCA	Young Men's Christian Association

Acknowledgments

It is a bittersweet joy to write the acknowledgments of this book, for it means letting go of a project that has stimulated my historical imagination and enriched my life for over a decade. It is nonetheless an honor to thank the individuals and institutions that supported this book from its origins. My first note of thanks goes to Katy Hazan, historian of the Œuvre de Secours aux Enfants, who opened up a new research question by encouraging me to find out what happened to the children who immigrated to the United States during the Second World War. With the help of the American Friends and Alumna of OSE in the United States, I set out to interview as many former children as possible. Our hours together provided me with a framework for contemplating the experiences of Jewish refugee children in France and the United States. Many shared their most precious personal papers with me, taking time to explain the importance of each letter, photo, and administrative record. I remain humbled by the trust bestowed upon me and hope to have represented the diversity of the experiences with diligence and respect.

I am also extremely grateful for the institutional support from which this book has benefited. A first version of this manuscript was defended in front of a six-person jury at Sciences Po in 2018 as part of my *Habilitation à diriger des recherches*. I would like to sincerely thank my *"garant"* Claire Andrieu for her enduring support and careful reading, which illuminated my blind spots and contributed greatly to my analyses. I am also indebted to the jury members for their valuable feedback, including Laura Lee Downs, Hélène Le Dantec-Lowry, Nancy L. Green, Atina Grossmann, and Romain Huret. Writing this book would not have been possible without a research fellowship from the Centre national de la recherche scientifique (CNRS) at the Institut d'histoire du temps présent. Likewise, my research groups at the Sorbonne Nouvelle (2010–2019) and the Université Paris 1 Panthéon-Sorbonne (2019–present), the Center for Research on the English-Speaking World and the Centre d'histoire sociale des mondes contemporains, respectively, have provided an intellectual home and precious resources. More recently, a CNRS residency at the Musée d'art et d'histoire du Judaïsme allowed me to finalize the manuscript. I sincerely thank its director Paul Salmona and his team for their warm reception. This research required extensive travel which could not have been done without outside funding from the Rothschild Foundation Hanadiv Europe, the Bauman Foundation, and the European Holocaust Research Infrastructure, and a Sharon Abramson Research Grant from the Holocaust Educational Foundation.

I am also indebted to many librarians and archivists. Dominique Rotermund and a team of volunteers at the OSE, as well as Karen Taieb, Ariel Sion, Lior Smadja, and the staff at the Mémorial de la Shoah, offered their help and characteristic enthusiasm. Jean-Claude Kuperminc was a formidable guide to the Alliance israélite universelle (Alliance) archives, as was Guila Cooper. Philippe Landau and Jean-Pierre Levy of the Central Consistory Archives also merit thanks, as does Jeanne-Henriette Louis, who granted me access to the Quaker archives in Paris. Archivists, including David Pascal-Dormien at the Archives nationales and others at the Bibliothèque nationale de France, the Archives du Ministère des affaires étrangères, the Archives diploma-tiques, and the Archives départementales du Bas-Rhin and de la Creuse, have provided ample help.

Outside of France, Karin Hofmeester and the staff at the International Institute for Social History in Amsterdam inspired me with their rich archival holdings and the unparalleled beauty of their work space, overlooking the canals. In Switzerland, the staff of the State Archives of Geneva provided precious assistance. In Germany, the archivists of the Jewish Museums in Frankfurt and Berlin, as well as the Centrum Judaicum, were extremely helpful. Thank you to Aubrey Pomerance for sharing Marianne Hirsch's diary. In the United Kingdom, Juliet Carey, Catherine Taylor, and Pippa Shirley at the Waddesdon Manor went out of their way to help, as did Christine Schmidt and the staff at the Wiener Holocaust Library, providing multiple occasions to enrich this project through research and feedback. In Israel, the Oral History Division at the Avram Harmon Institute for Contemporary Jewish History at the Hebrew University of Jerusalem allowed me to benefit from their prescient work to document the history of the Second World War. Being able to listen to Andrée Salomon's oral history interview helped me, quite literally, find her voice. I also sincerely thank Eliot Nidam, Emmanuelle Moscovitz, Yael Robinson, Sharon Kangisser-Cohen, and the staff at Yad Vashem, for their warm reception and scholarly insights. Emmanuelle Moscovitz deserves a special note of thanks for sharing her own findings on Rabbi René Hirschler with me.

I am equally indebted to archivists working on the other side of the Atlantic. Ron Coleman at the United States Holocaust Memorial Museum has provided consistent help since my 2014 research trip, and generously shared his own findings with me. Linda Levi and her staff at the American Jewish Joint Distribution Committee archive in New York, especially Misha Mitsel, Jeffrey Edelstein, and Isabelle Rohr, have been instrumental to my research, providing me with access not only to their archives, but also to unlimited coffee and bagels. Likewise, the Center for Jewish History has been essential. I would like to thank Ilya Slavutskiy for his unparalleled help in May 2017, as well as the archivists of the American Jewish Historical Society. I am especially indebted to the expertise of Gunnar Berg, Ettie Goldwasser, and Leo Greenbaum at YIVO. Frank Mecklenburg of the Leo Baeck Institute not only advised me on archival holdings, he also provided help translating a poem by a refugee teen. The staff of the University of Michigan's Bentley Historical Library, as well as at the New York Public Library Rare Manuscripts division, also deserve thanks. And last but not least, I would like to thank Donald Davis at the AFSC archive in Philadelphia for his sincere help and warm welcome.

ACKNOWLEDGMENTS

In addition to the archives are the many colleagues who shared their own research materials or provided concrete assistance. Maud Mandel did me a great favor by sending me two students who were eager to learn more about historical research, Sam Bresnick and Caleigh Forbes-Cockell, whom I thank sincerely. A fortuitous conversation with Michaela Raggam-Blesch led us to realize we had "children" in common. Michaela's generous sharing of her interview with the only survivor of a group of eight teens from Vienna has allowed me to honor their memory by documenting their lives in Paris. Likewise, Pierre Goetschel has helped me learn more about Hanna Eisfelder, who merits greater attention. Filmmaker Lisa Gossels entrusted me with the interviews from her film *The Children of Chabannes*. Célia Keren has shared her vast knowledge on child refugees and important archives. I have benefited from comparing notes with Renate Hebauf on the Kindertransport children from Frankfurt. Stephanie Corazza and Erin Corber entrusted me with their unpublished dissertations. Claudia Curio sent an electronic version of her dissertation, allowing me to engage with her scholarship.

Transnational research requires multiple languages. While intimate knowledge of French and English is essential here, so is German, a language I do not yet master. I have benefited greatly from the translations of Jean-Pierre Randon, whom I thank sincerely. I also extend my gratitude to historians Alina Bothe and Patrick Farges, who helped me interpret certain passages in German. I also thank Till Lieberz-Gross and Ute Lemke for their assistance. A stranger on a train by the name of Astrid Geue spent the entire four-hour ride from Paris to Frankfurt translating one of the rare documents on the Kindertransport to France! Her interest in the fate of Jewish children attests to the sincere desire among many Germans to engage with this history. The fact that I was willing to interrupt a stranger on the train speaks volumes about my own relationship to this project.

This book engages with both my unpublished and previously published research, indicated in the endnotes, upon which I have built here to make a sustained argument on the transnational efforts to rescue Jewish child refugees. I thank the editors of these publications, as well as colleagues who heard me present this research at conferences, for their precious feedback and encouragement.

ACKNOWLEDGMENTS

I am also indebted to my colleagues who took the time to read and offer advice. Constance Pâris de Bollardière and Brian Schiff of the Georges and Irina Schaeffer Center for the Study of Genocide at the American University of Paris have nourished this research in more ways than one. Catherine Nicault, Susan Gross Solomon, and Shannon Fogg have generously provided advice on this project at each important juncture. Since our meeting in 2012, Alexandra Garbarini has become a cherished friend and dedicated reader. Our ongoing conversation on Holocaust representation has influenced my thinking and broadened the scope of this book. I am so deeply indebted to my mentor Nancy Green that it justifies thanking her twice. The same is true for Atina Grossmann. I have also benefited greatly from conversations with Daniel Lee, Susan Rubin Suleiman, Lisa Moses Leff, Deborah Dash Moore, Veerle Vanden Daelen, Jérémy Guedj, Manon Pignot, Sally Charnow, and, of course, Rebecca Clifford, whose work on child Holocaust survivors has served as an inspiration.

Thanks go to Rebecca and James McAuley for putting me in contact with Yale University Press. It has been an honor to work with its entire staff and to learn from my editor, Julian Loose. I thank him sincerely for believing in this book. Julian, Frazer Martin, and my anonymous readers have offered keen advice that has greatly improved the manuscript.

Friends and family have accompanied this book in more ways than one, offering unparalleled hospitality and support. Anjali Malhotra Roye, Meera Malhotra Marti, Karen Kurczynski, Tali and Nick Albukerk, Barbara and Norman Kravitz, Harvey Halperin and Donna Barr, Shaina Hammerman and Octavio Di Sciullo, and Nat and Julie Bender have given me a home away from home during research trips. Nat has also provided me with a steady stream of secondary sources, demonstrating his characteristic helpfulness. Closer to home, Roby Antonucci, Kevin Cassu, Ariane Jouette, and Ellen Hampton have created the happiest of support networks, lending an ear and even office space when needed. My *belle famille*, especially Brigitte Meudec Mouhica, has always offered a helping hand. My sisters Lisa, Nicole, and Jenny have provided me with ample examples of their love and encouragement. Jenny deserves a special note of thanks for the concrete help she has so generously provided. This book has given me many occasions to consider what it means to be a parent. My gratitude to my own parents, Sherry and Jim Hobson, is immense. My husband, Jérôme Faure, and our children, Léo and Talia, deserve the largest thank you of all. Thank you for creating the chaotic, joyful balance that encourages me to live in the present, with you by my side. This book is dedicated to Léo and Talia, of course.

While many individuals have helped shape this book, I alone remain responsible for any errors.

On Names

Almost all of the individuals I interviewed for this book granted me written permission to use their real names, and some even insisted upon it. However, using real names can create ethical problems, especially when associating them with children's case files. It can also lead to self-censorship on the part of the historian for fear of over-revealing the spontaneous and deeply personal thoughts expressed in interviews. I have tried, in cases of doubt, to show individuals the sections of this book that pertain to them and offered to provide a pseudonym. At times, I simply use a first name and last initial or discuss an event without naming those involved. At times I use real names. This is the imperfect solution I have found to conduct this research in the most ethical manner possible.

Introduction

In 1989, Henry Schuster was focused on the fifty-year reunion he was planning for a group of some 280 individuals who, like him, had escaped the Holocaust as children by fleeing unaccompanied to France and then to the United States. Schuster and his co-organizers had spent years tracking down fellow "children" who, like them, were among the sole survivors of their families. "The feeling was that we found a member of our lost family,"[1] Henry noted, to explain his investment. Historians estimate that only 11 percent of the Jewish children present in Europe before the Second World War survived the Holocaust.[2] Henry's story, like that of all children who survived, is by nature exceptional and significant.

Henry was originally Heinz, born in 1926 into a traditional Jewish family in Sterbfritz, Germany. His father's death in 1935 led his mother to send him to a Jewish orphanage in Frankfurt am Main.[3] After the November 9–10, 1938 country-wide pogrom, this orphanage, overrun with children, managed to send many of its wards abroad with the help of rescue committees that had emerged throughout Western Europe. Unlike the better-known British Kindertransport child evacuation scheme that saved some 10,000 children, French committees, headed by Jewish women, obtained fewer than 500 visas for unaccompanied Central European Jewish children.

Heinz Schuster arrived in Paris in March 1939 along with nine children from his orphanage and forty others from the surrounding region.

His first precarious step on the path to surviving the Holocaust was to become Henri. He was sent to one of the children's homes run by the Jewish public health organization, the Union OSE (OSE, pronounced O-zay),[4] but this placement proved temporary. After the Nazi invasion in May 1940, France, a land of refuge, turned quickly into a trap.

Across the Atlantic, a group of child-welfare activists in the United States reacted to the turn of events in Europe by establishing the United States Committee for the Care of European Children (USCOM) in July 1940. This non-sectarian organization was primarily interested in evacuating children from the United Kingdom, now under the threat of Nazi bombs. Yet when a German submarine attacked a ship transporting ninety British children in September 1940, the USCOM abandoned this evacuation scheme. It was considering dismantling when two refugees in New York who had helped Jewish child refugees in France, along with the American Jewish Joint Distribution Committee (JDC), began a campaign to convince the USCOM to redirect its efforts to occupied France. After several months of hesitation, the USCOM appointed the Quaker American Friends Service Committee (AFSC) to carry out a new evacuation scheme for refugee children in France. From June 1941 to July 1942, 5 transports left France, bringing about 320 children to the United States, about 280 of whom were Jewish.[5]

Henri had an uncle and a cousin in the United States—recent refugees—who began writing to the AFSC's American office in February 1941 to advocate for his immigration.[6] Henri was selected for the first USCOM transport and arrived in the United States on June 21, 1941. Thus began his second, permanent, exile, as Henry.

Henry's story raises many questions, but the one I will explore in this book is on rescue: who was responsible for saving Henry's life? Was it his mother, who found the strength to separate from him? Was it the Frankfurt orphanage directors, Isidor and Rosa Marx, who sought out new homes for their wards outside of Germany? Was it the French Jewish committees that advocated for visas for unaccompanied children, or the organizations in the United States—Jewish, Christian, and non-sectarian—that funded and orchestrated the evacuations? What about his uncle and cousin, whose letter-writing campaign alerted the

AFSC to Henry's situation? As seen in his many name changes, Henry also took action to adapt to his new surroundings as he moved from place to place. Could he too have played a role in his own rescue?

The notion of rescue during the Holocaust immediately evokes the righteous individuals who sought to help Jews at great personal risk. Their stories, often deemed heroic, help us cope with the magnitude of loss that occurred during the Holocaust, in which 6 million Jews, and many other victims, were murdered by Nazi Germany and its accomplices.[7] Beyond the destruction of human lives lies the stark fact that this genocide occurred in the "developed world," in places that were, just years before, industrialized democracies. When we delve deeply, we are faced with the terrifying fact that, yes, because it happened before, it can happen again. The uncertainty of the current moment heightens our sense of panic. Our search for heroes reflects our need to reassure ourselves that the Holocaust was not able to destroy our humanity.

Heroes may inspire us, yet when we glorify them, we tamper with our ability to think critically. We embrace our heroes before knowing them, we lend an intentionality to their actions based on final outcomes, without a keen understanding of how events actually unfolded. We approach their stories individually and often ignore the group contexts in which their actions took place. We recognize some, but ignore others. We forget all too easily the fact that only successful cases of rescue come to our attention, because the dead cannot tell their stories. Unsuccessful cases—in which genuine assistance was unable to stop deportation and murder—remain, for the most part, in the shadows. At the same time, tales of rescue are easily instrumentalized for political purposes, allowing contemporary societies to commemorate the Holocaust without evoking deportation and murder.[8]

This book will look not for heroes but for humans, in all their complexity. It will study individuals not alone, but in their networks and groups. And it will not argue that rescue always works. By approaching the notion critically, I hope to contribute to a growing field of research that engages with the phenomenon in historical perspective, in contrast to the philosophical and sociological approaches that probe the motivations of individual rescuers.[9] I argue in this book that we need to study the rescue process *as it unfolded* (and not based on final outcomes). To do so, I tell an integrated story: one that explores how Jews, Christians, and individuals without religious ties attempted to build productive collaborations (in the best sense) and how the latter shaped the rescue process.

Such collaborations were rarely as seamless as they now appear. Exploring them is of utmost importance to our understanding of the Holocaust because they shed light on Jews' responses to persecution and, more specifically, on the larger debate on their political acumen under Nazism. Hannah Arendt claimed that Jews did not benefit from political experience, which led them to participate in their own destruction.[10] Yosef Hayim Yerushalmi countered that Jews have a long history of political action, yet traditionally privileged "vertical alliances" with local and national powers, at the cost of establishing "horizontal alliances" with fellow subjects and citizens.[11] Here, by asking who answered Jews' calls for help, I explore to what extent they managed, in a context of increasing state persecution, to kindle horizontal alliances in order to evacuate Jewish children from Nazi territories. To do so, I take into account the question of gender, which is both new and essential, since women, due to their traditional role caring for children, became key negotiators in this process. Under certain conditions, horizontal alliances created real opportunities for rescue. I explore here how these actors emerged, what factors led them to advocate on behalf of Jewish children, and what shaped their ability to act. A comparative and transnational perspective will underscore the fact that while the actions of individuals are important, so are the groups and societies in which they operated.[12]

Finally, and perhaps most significantly, this book argues that a key actor has been altogether missing from studies of Holocaust rescue: Jews themselves. I am not referring to Jewish rescuers, who have recently and rightfully gained more historical attention but who by nature are excluded from Yad Vashem's Righteous Among the Nations award, established to honor non-Jews who saved the lives of Jews during the Holocaust.[13] I am talking about Jews, like young Henry, who needed help. In most accounts, these individuals are relegated to a passive, minor role, as they are moved from safe house to safe house, on the receiving end of the solidarity, but rarely an integral part of it. Jews' ability to assert their agency was certainly impaired by persecutions in occupied Europe, yet I argue here that their perceptions and actions were vital to the rescue process.

In this book, those in need of rescue are children, including those who self-identified as Jewish and those who were considered "non-Aryan" according to Nazi policies.[14] Their diaries, autograph books, letters, drawings, songs, and poems help me reconstruct a child-centered social history of their attempted escape from Nazi territories. Thus, in addition to telling the story of their caretakers and rescuers, this book represents an exploration of Jewish children's intimate lives and emotions as they fled from Central Europe to France and from France to the United States on the eve of, and during, the Second World War.[15] I hope to show that by looking for their agency (even if we cannot always find it), we stop thinking of Jewish children as passive victims and instead consider them as subjects and actors in the Holocaust. Indeed, when historians seek out agency, a new set of expectations emerges: we expect our subjects to have opinions, emotions, and reactions. This allows us to gain a more capacious understanding of their lived experiences, as well as their undisputable victimhood.

The Kindertransport, the term used to describe the evacuations of non-accompanied Jewish children and teens from Nazi territories, required separating children from parents. This scheme must be understood in the context of the largely unsuccessful Evian conference, convened by President Franklin Delano Roosevelt in July 1938 to aid refugees fleeing Nazism, and the more general failure of international diplomacy to protect the victims of Nazism throughout the 1930s. Allowing children to immigrate without their parents offered democratic states a symbolic solution to a delicate political problem: it served as a public gesture on behalf of the victims of Nazi violence that did not exclude a concomitant tightening of immigration restrictions. Historians thus observe that Great Britain, lauded for its acceptance of some 10,000 Kindertransport children, designed this policy in order to reduce protests on its decision to severely limit Jewish immigration to Mandatory Palestine.[16] This analysis helps us understand a paradox:

at the same moment that British child psychologists were theorizing why children should not be separated from their mothers, policymakers in this country responded to Nazism by advocating the migrations of children without their parents. It is important to recognize that, while touted as a humanitarian response, the Kindertransport required separating families. It was not a Nazi emigration policy, but one produced by democratic host societies.[17]

The large-scale nature of the British Kindertransport initiative often obscures the fact that Central European Jewish children were also sent to Mandatory Palestine, Italy, Denmark, Belgium, the Netherlands, Switzerland, and France.[18] While fewer than 500 children came to France, the study of their case represents an important analytical opportunity because it allows us to explore what happened when this land of refuge became a trap. The heightened violence of 1938, followed by the outbreak of the Second World War in September 1939 and the Nazi invasion of France in May 1940, had direct effects on Jewish children's lives, long before their actual lives were put in danger by deportation measures in 1942.

By seeking to understand who brought the children to France in 1938–1939, and who fought to evacuate them yet again to the United States in 1941–1942, I hope to paint a more complex picture of rescue that takes into account the evolving perceptions of danger among the actors, the difficulties of collective action, and their need to work across borders, transnationally. While most accounts of rescue in France focus on the period between 1942 and 1944, during which deportation measures clearly threatened Jews' lives, this study intentionally focuses on the period before this, between 1938 and 1942, in order to explore perceptions as persecutions mounted. In 1938–1939, evacuating children from Nazi Germany was not understood by all as a life-saving operation, even if some actors did indeed claim they were "saving" Jewish children and parents felt an urgent need to remove their children from harm. However, not all agreed that Jewish children needed special protection. In reality, the perception of danger and access to information varied greatly from person to person throughout the entire Holocaust, even during the 1942–1945 period, when Jewish children's lives were most threatened in Nazi Europe.[19] The problem, of course, is that rescue requires a basic consensus on who is targeted and the nature of the threat.

The earlier periodization of this study thus engages directly with the ambiguities surrounding rescue. Since flight from Nazi-occupied territories is one of the main ways Jews survived the Holocaust, I consider child evacuations as rescue operations, even if they may not have been fully understood as such at the time. What interests me in this book is to explore how the actors viewed their actions as events unfolded, which requires stepping into their shoes and, of course, paying attention to the differences between their sources from the period and those produced after the Holocaust, with full knowledge of its implications.

The important story of the Kindertransport to France has remained, until now, unnoticed and untold. The evacuations of children from France to the United States in 1941–1942 have garnered more attention, yet historians have tended to oversimplify the picture by focusing on the role of individual organizations, often attributing the role of "hero" to one organization in particular without taking into account their complex collaboration. As a result, a disjointed picture has emerged in the historiography.[20] This book will take into account the roles and relationships among the multiple actors in the evacuations, both individual and organizational, including the USCOM, the American JDC, the AFSC (known by many as "the Quakers"), and the Jewish organization Union OSE. As seen above, the children and their families are also essential to my analysis.

As seen with Heinz, who became Henri and then Henry, children crossed multiple borders to survive the Holocaust. Yet until now, historians have not really caught up with the transnational lives of children like Henry. Those working on children in the Holocaust most often focus on one place in particular, without taking into account children's migrations.[21] When they do explore children in exile, it is usually assumed that the latter experienced one, and not multiple, journeys. Furthermore, while scholars have widely explored the Holocaust in France, they have only rarely considered Jewish children's experiences as a subject of historical analysis.[22]

Parallel to historical research, a magnificent body of memoirs documents the exceptional experiences of children's survival, in France and elsewhere.[23] Nonetheless, because they focus on individual trajectories, these sources create the illusion that survival was a phenomenon experienced alone. Contemporary testimony projects often impose an individual format, also fostering the assumption of an individual survival experience. However, children rarely experienced the Holocaust alone in Western Europe: most lived in groups or families. In France, collective Jewish children's homes remained open until 1943, and in some cases even later.[24] Escape to Spain or Switzerland almost always took place in groups. Only in hiding were some Jewish children (but not all) isolated from others. In France, most were "in hiding and visible,"[25] under new identities. They were in contact with other children, new families, and/or caretakers. When listening closely to testimonies, one finds that when speaking about their experiences, most survivors provide a relational map, placing themselves within an interconnected web composed of family members, friends, and caretakers.[26]

Considering children as members of families and networks sheds new light on how they survived the Holocaust and its long aftermath, responding to deeper shifts in both the history of childhood and in Holocaust studies. In the 1990s, both fields sought to reconsider children and Jews, respectively, as subjects, rather than objects, of history.[27] In Holocaust studies, the need to document the range and depth of Jewish experiences was expressed in the years following the war.[28] Nonetheless, most historians intentionally excluded sources produced by Jews, considering them unreliable or biased. It was Saul Friedländer who convincingly argued for the need to probe Jewish sources and, more generally, for the integration of the two distinct branches of Holocaust studies: one focused on perpetrators, and the other on Jewish responses to the Holocaust.[29] Significant contributions on Jewish children's experiences during the Holocaust by Deborah Dwork (*Children with a Star*, 1991), Nicholas Stargardt (*Witnesses of War: Children's Lives under the Nazis*, 2005), and, most recently, by Rebecca Clifford (*Survivors: Children's Lives after the Holocaust*, 2020) should be understood in this dual historiographical turn in the history of childhood and Holocaust studies.[30] Building on their work, I seek to explore children's agency and actions, even in moments of powerlessness.

After the war, the children who survived the Holocaust were called "Holocaust orphans" or "war orphans."[31] They were often assumed to have been completely alone. Some certainly were, and many *felt* abandoned. Yet sometimes, these orphans still had one parent or surviving siblings and extended families. They may have been part of tightly knit friendship groups. While children's relational worlds rarely survived intact, new networks emerged during the war, at times creating surrogate families. Asking how these networks were formed allows for a new dimension of survival to come to light, revealing how children negotiated displacement, acculturation to new societies, and separation from their nuclear families.

Henry's story exemplifies the group context in which rescue occurred, as well as the emergence of its memory. As seen above, total family reunification was simply not possible for Henry and many others. His mother and two sisters were deported to Nazi camps from Frankfurt; only one of his sisters, Bertel, survived. This loss made Henry even more determined to seek out his "siblings," the term he used to describe the children with whom he had lived in Europe.[32] After growing up in foster care in a distant cousin's home, Henry joined the U.S. Army and began reaching out to other children in the United States who had been with him in the OSE homes. By the late 1970s, he had linked up with a group of other "OSE children" in California that had been meeting regularly since the mid-1950s.[33] In 1979, they celebrated the forty-year anniversary of their arrival in France.[34] In 1989, as seen above, Henry helped organize their fifty-year OSE reunion in Los Angeles. "Now I didn't have to remember alone,"[35] he explained in an interview in the Jewish press, suggesting that a weight had been lifted. This concise statement has resonated with me, inviting me to ask why, for at least some of the children who came unaccompanied to France and the United States, remembering *together* represented an important part of their story. Many historical works on the Holocaust have sought to understand the responses of Jewish individuals to Nazi persecution. Yet "not remembering alone" suggests a need to approach this history both diachronically and synchronically, by questioning the place of the individual within the group over time.[36] More generally, as I explain in the methodology essay, a transnational perspective has guided my archival research and oral history interviews, helping me reconstruct two child evacuation schemes and the experiences of those involved: first and foremost the refugee children and teens, but also their families and the adults who cared and advocated for them.

~

"You're not going to be one of those researchers who just sends a thank-you note and says goodbye, are you?" Professor Hank Greenspan asked me in 2015, over coffee in Ann Arbor. A psychologist, historian, and playwright, Greenspan has urged Holocaust scholars to "listen to survivors"[37] by encouraging multiple interviews and extended relationships. While I did write those thank-you notes, earlier training in participant observation and interviewing in various settings certainly helped me follow Greenspan's advice to embrace the messiness of human interactions.[38] After our interviews, I continued to interact with many of the "children" and their families, who remain a precious resource for my research. When in doubt, I asked follow-up questions. I have visited, made phone calls, and shared meals. I mourn their passing. I have certainly influenced the networks I have sought to study and reject the claim to neutrality that still lingers in some historical research yet has been thoroughly refuted in other disciplines. I take the position that thinking critically about my own place in my research is essential for honoring the quest for truth that defines the historical method.[39]

More than once, I have found inspiration from those I have studied. One of the refugee girls in this study, Hanna Kaiser Papanek, proves exceptional in that she obtained a PhD in social relations from Harvard in 1962. In the 1990s, she decided to turn her scholarly eye to her own past.[40] By 2006, she had completed her intensely personal "participative history" of her own family and generation, named after her parents, *Elly und Alexander*.[41] While our endeavors and personal trajectories are quite different, I share Hanna's desire "to write stories with the novelist's fullness of detail and also wanting to 'tell the truth'—the many 'truths'—about events recorded in history books, diaries, documentary films, and photographs without turning them into fictions."[42]

~

Let us return to our initial question: who rescued Henry? The answer to this question is complex. Our puzzle begins in Frankfurt at the Jewish orphanage run by Isidor and Rosa Marx, and then moves on to France. As French rescuers sought to move the children away from mounting persecutions in Central Europe, gender dynamics in the French Jewish community contributed to making this a woman's issue. While this had the advantage of bringing women into new positions of power, it also hindered their ability to fight effectively for visas in a society hostile to refugees, Jews, and women. Most likely fewer than 500 unaccompanied children came to France, and most were placed in children's homes.

Without understanding the children's experiences of exile, the puzzle remains fragmentary. Children maintained affective ties with their families and created new relationships in France, even if the fragility of their networks was exposed after France was invaded by Nazi Germany. Those who organized the Kindertransport, now targeted by Nazi and Vichy persecutions, felt a moral obligation to try to evacuate the children.

We need to cross the Atlantic to understand how some of the children managed to find refuge in the United States. Their caretakers— now refugees themselves—reached out to American Jews and child welfare experts of all backgrounds who had been working to help Jewish children in Nazi Germany since 1933, and especially since the November 1938 pogrom. They failed to change American immigration policy, but they did manage to build an intricate collaboration between Jewish, Quaker, American, and French organizations and governments to evacuate Jewish and non-Jewish refugee children from France. While this book seeks to document two little-known evacuation schemes, children remain at its center, revealing the changes in Jewish families and societies during the Holocaust. With the help of their parents and extended families, children fought to be included on the transports, showing once again their active role in the rescue process.

A historical puzzle, by nature, can never be complete. Yet we move toward greater understanding when we grasp not only what happened, but what *did not* occur when children and adults, individuals and organizations, set out to save lives—their own and those of others— during the Holocaust.

Indeed, not all were saved. In summer 1942, Nazi-Vichy authorities began targeting children for deportation in both the occupied and unoccupied zones of France. The partnerships that developed to evacuate children among Jewish and non-Jewish humanitarian organizations in the 1938–1942 period intensified as their representatives worked furiously to organize a large-scale evacuation of 5,000 Jewish children to the United States in the fall of 1942. They almost succeeded, but, ultimately, the children were not granted exit visas and remained in France, at great peril. Such failed attempts are essential to the history of rescue, allowing us a glimpse of the complex forces at play when it came to rescuing children during the Holocaust.

CHAPTER 1

Elfriede and the November 1938 Turning Point

In 1937, several months before her eleventh birthday, Elfriede Meyer's father, a German First World War veteran, died of tuberculosis. This event changed Elfriede's world, causing her and her mother to leave their home and clothing store in Mönchengladbach for Frankfurt, where her mother's family lived. Elfriede's older sister Klara, a high-level athlete, initially stayed behind to continue her schooling. In spite of her drastically altered family life, Elfriede, in her early nineties at the time of our 2016 interview, recalled feeling happy in Frankfurt. She had spent every summer there as a child and loved this city. Elfriede's mother, like many other German Jewish parents, was struggling to find emigration solutions and placed her in the Frankfurt Jewish Orphanage, at 87 Röderbergweg.[1] The home was directed by Isidor and Rosa Marx, who sought to establish a warm environment for the increasingly diverse group of children under their care. Elfriede, like the other children, referred to her new caretakers as surrogate family: "they were aunts and uncles or grandparents."[2]

The Frankfurt Jewish community—which numbered 30,000 in 1930 and 13,751 in May 1939[3]—reflected the religious diversity of German Jewish life. Frankfurt's orthodox community remained strongly attached to the teachings of Rabbi Samson Raphael Hirsch, founder of the neo-orthodox movement that emerged in the mid-nineteenth century to counter the growing influence of the reform movement.[4] The orphanage was run under orthodox auspices, and to enter it,

Elfriede's family had obtained a letter from their rabbi attesting to their orthodoxy. In reality, the Meyer family was traditional but not orthodox, although it did keep kosher. Young Elfriede was annoyed by the strict rules that dictated Shabbat. Work is forbidden on this day of rest, and at the orphanage, this included brushing her hair and teeth. But while boys were required to attend religious services, girls seemed to have more freedom.[5] Elfriede was allowed to spend Shabbat with her mother and grandparents, who lived on the other side of the Main river in Sachsenhausen. Risking expulsion for transgressing the rule of riding on Shabbat, she simply walked out of sight of the orphanage and hopped on the street car to her grandparents' house.

During this period, Elfriede's mother was working actively to send her on a Kindertransport to the United States.[6] If Elfriede chose to cast a positive light on her stay in Frankfurt in our interview, records from the period suggest it represented a more complicated moment in her life. As one of her case workers explained in October 1938, "She is dealing with the separation from her mother and sister more intellectually, than emotionally. She understands the conditions that make such a separation necessary, but it seems absurd to live in the same country as her relatives yet separately from them. She wishes to emigrate and hopes to come together again with her loved ones 'through her work and initiative.'"[7]

As the Meyer family's story shows, from 1933 onward, Jewish families in the Third Reich faced Nazi persecution—and the dilemmas it provoked—in a multiplicity of ways. While the availability of visas, financial resources, and contacts abroad influenced Jews' capacity to flee, so did their readings of the political situation. Indeed, an important yet complex element of rescue—of oneself or others—resides in how individuals perceive danger. This perception is shaped, we know, by personal history, social class, gender, educational level, past experiences with state authorities, and social networks.[8] The term "rescue" is now associated with the Kindertransport. However, it was only after the Holocaust that it became clear that removing children from Nazi territories was a life-saving operation. This was understood only by some contemporaries.

Nonetheless, initiatives to evacuate Jewish children and teens from Nazi territories emerged as early as 1933.[9] Some thought that children should be evacuated for psychological reasons, in order not to have to witness the violence against others; other activists considered there was indeed a physical threat to children. Others sought to protect Jewish children's educational opportunities in light of the April 1933 restrictions on "non-Aryan" children in German public schools. Still others sought to encourage emigration to Mandatory Palestine.[10]

To separate young children from their parents, both parents and rescuers had to overcome the deeply ingrained cultural beliefs on the family that bound young children to their parents, especially their mothers. Nevertheless, notions of the mother–child bond differed greatly according to place, generating discourses of trauma in some places that were absent in others.[11] In Germany and Austria in the years leading up to 1938, there was still debate among Jews as to whether their lives were in danger in the Third Reich. Widespread cultural notions of the innocence of women and children led many to assume the latter would be spared from Nazi violence.[12] As Andrea Hammel observes, "we certainly should not assume that the Jewish parents in Central Europe did not consider the detrimental effect emigration as unaccompanied minors might have on the child refugees. The journal of the Jewish Women's Organization carried an article as early as 1933 on the first two pages, considering exactly this question and largely coming to the conclusion that a child emigrating without parents was not desirable. By 1938 of course, Jewish parents felt such pressure from the National Socialist government that the Kindertransport was considered the lesser evil."[13]

The unprecedented violence of 1938 shifted perceptions among Jews and non-Jews alike and therefore represents a turning point. Indeed, for parents to separate from their children, for rescuers to undertake such administratively complex endeavors, and for governments to provide visas, there had to be a perception of danger and political will. The Nazi invasion of Austria in March 1938, followed by the brutal expulsion of some 16,000–18,000 Jewish men, women, and children of Polish nationality from Germany in late October 1938, and especially the November 9–10 pogrom, known by many by the Nazi term "Kristallnacht," made it clear that Jewish men, women, and children were indeed in physical danger in the Third Reich.[14] In the words of Marion Kaplan, "the November Pogrom decisively tipped the balance toward emigration."[15] As Benjamin Hirsch, a Kindertransport child, noted, many years later, "If German Jews had been under the illusion, as my father had been, that they and their families would be safe in the Third Reich, Kristallnacht dispelled that fantasy."[16]

Jewish children and their orphanages throughout Germany were not spared the violence of the pogrom. Thirteen-year-old Heinz (Stephan) Lewy experienced the events from the Auerbach Jewish orphanage in Berlin, where his father placed him at the age of six, after his mother's death. According to his memoirs, on the night of November 9, Nazis in uniform pushed the teachers and about one hundred children into the orphanage's synagogue. They then cut the gas line to the eternal light, a light fixture in all synagogues that symbolizes the divine presence, and bolted the door. Eventually, one of the older children smashed a window, and a friendly neighbor unbolted the door.[17] A contemporaneous account of these events can be found in the diary of fourteen-year-old Marianne Hirsch, who also lived in the orphanage. She also describes four officers of the Schutzstaffel (SS) entering the orphanage and destroying what they could, before opening the gas line in the synagogue, and locking the door. In her account, the SS then gave the keys to the police, who came to open the room immediately, in order to avoid an explosion.[18] While the two accounts differ slightly, what is clear is that the orphanage ceased being a safe place; both emphasize the authorities' intention to put children's lives at risk.

In the Frankfurt Jewish orphanage, where Elfriede Meyer was living, the violence was less extreme but nonetheless seared children's memories. Heinz Schuster was twelve and a half in 1938. As seen in the introduction, he had been placed in the orphanage at age ten, when his sisters and widowed mother found work in Frankfurt. "Life changed drastically in November of 1938," he wrote in his memoirs:

Why I remember this, I'll never know, but for lunch that day [November 10] we were served red cabbage and boiled potatoes. Maybe it's so indelibly printed on my memory because during the meal several Brown Shirt Nazis stormed into the dining hall looking for the two Jews who were hiding in the synagogue. Searching everywhere, they finally found them in the synagogue and dragged them by the hair to the outside of the building where they beat them bloody. Then leaving them in the street to die, they took the Safer Torahs [Torah scrolls] from the Ark, tore them to shreds and crushed them into the floor with their boots.

From the dining room, we could hear the men screaming and the sound of the Torahs being ripped to pieces. Then, suddenly, there was silence. Frozen with fear, some of the boys began to whimper quietly but stopped when the Gestapo once again burst through the dining room door, swinging clubs at anyone in their path. Herding the councilors [sic] to the far side of the room and away from the children, they arrested all the male teachers, councilors and older boys and forced them into the back of closed trucks to be taken who knew where.[19]

Heinz's account notes that orphanage director Isidor Marx was "spared because during the commotion he slid unnoticed under a table. Children standing nearby pulled the tablecloth lower to the floor concealing him as he huddled there."[20]

The day after the pogrom, members of the Gestapo and the SS visited Marx and made it clear he had been spared for a reason: they needed him to care for the numerous children who, as a result of arrests and expulsions, had almost doubled the ranks of the orphanage. Marx asked if he could contact friends abroad to send them children and was told his telegrams and phones would not be censored. He spent the night reaching out to his contacts in England, Switzerland, Holland, Belgium, France, and Palestine. He ran up a huge bill but started receiving offers to take his children within a few days.[21] An enthusiastic response came from Jewish activists in Strasbourg, France. Their efforts coincided with initiatives of Jewish women in Paris, which eventually led to a small number of visas for unaccompanied Jewish children.

Thanks to the efforts of Isidor and Rosa Marx, Elfriede, now twelve, was granted refuge in France. On the night before her departure in March 1939, she was able to leave the orphanage for a goodbye dinner at her grandparents' house.[22] There, she had a prescient moment: "I went in the attic with a big paper sack and filled it with [family] pictures," she explained. "It boggles my mind, what I was thinking. Nobody knew, I never told anybody. I carried those with me all the way there [to France] and then to get here [to the United States]. And we were not allowed, coming here . . . we were allowed a little suitcase, and I had the pictures in there and a few other things, and two prayer books that had my name on them, [. . .] a *haggadah*, a *megillah*."[23] When I met her in 2016, the family photos Elfriede had smuggled out of her grandparents' attic were hanging on the walls of her bedroom in her immaculate San Diego home (Plate 17).

Looking at what Elfriede brought with her on her journey out of Germany shows her ardent desire to remain connected to her family and the latter's hope that she would maintain her Jewish identity while far from home.[24] While in France, she received a camera from her cousins in Switzerland that allowed her to document her new friends and surroundings. It anchored her in the present, just as the promise of developing film and creating photographs provided a way to project into the future.

Elfriede kept the photos she took in France in neatly organized albums. She also shared with me a prized possession: her memory book. The book's pages are filled with signatures and messages in German, French, and Hebrew, penned by her friends and teachers over the 1938–1941 period. Such a source offers a rare glimpse at the advice children gave to one another in exile. On the eve of their first Yom Kippur in France, one fellow refugee child wrote in her native German: "You shall talk, not much but sensibly; you shall pray, not long but fervently; you shall love, not loudly but fiercely; you shall act, not quickly but firmly; you shall live, not wildly but cheerfully; You should help yourself, G—d will help you."[25] On the same occasion, another girl wrote "*Sois courageuse pour être juif*" (Be proud to be Jewish)[26] in her newly learned but still erroneous French. Alongside the occasional Hebrew phrase, one sees Elfriede's translations, suggesting that the book has remained very much alive for her, having accompanied her into the winter of her life.

"Most of us can tell the story of our lives," historian Rebecca Clifford writes, "from the beginning through to the present, because others have helped us to build the narrative. Our parents, families and communities, the collective and social context in which we live, provide the details that we cannot remember or explain, and help us to contextualize memories that we hold in our mind's eye but might otherwise struggle to interpret."[27] Child Holocaust survivors often lack the external narratives that help provide a sense of self. For Elfriede and other children in this study who lost their parents in genocide, photos, archives, and objects act as scaffolding in the absence of such narratives. They prop up and support a sense of identity, offering concrete proof of a past that, for many, still eludes explanation.

In the absence of their parents and families, some former children play this role for one another, serving as witnesses to one another's lives, and providing proof of their distant, often inaccessible past. During our interview, Elfriede received a phone call from a fellow child from the Frankfurt orphanage, Werner Dreifuss, whom I was scheduled to interview after her. When Elfriede dropped me off at his house, she referred to him as her "little brother." He keeps a photo of them on his desk from Elfriede's eightieth birthday party. As a historian, one must take into account the intensity of their relationships to their archives and fellow children, for they influence our own narratives. Elfriede's warm approval of my research helped Werner share the story of his flight from Germany, to which I will now turn.

Werner was eight years old when he came to France from Frankfurt in 1939. He arrived at the Frankfurt Jewish orphanage at the age of five, most likely, although he knows little about his past. He explained that he never learned the proper spelling of his family name and kept his own child's spelling, with an "i," throughout his adult life. One can measure the meaning of his departure by the pains taken by his caretaker, Tante Rena, who assembled a small photo album for him. The album contained a photo of his mother, Henny Dreyfuss, several images of his life before the orphanage, photos of him playing in the orphanage courtyard with his friends, and a posed portrait of Werner with Tante Rena. The album was inscribed with the loving words, "My beloved Werner, do not forget your 'Auntie' Rena."[28] Many blank pages remained, inviting young Werner to continue narrating his life story as it unfolded, far away from Germany. The first stop on this journey was France.

CHAPTER 2

From Frankfurt am Main to Strasbourg

A Widespread Mobilization

In the aftermath of the November 1938 pogrom, Frankfurt Jewish orphanage director Isidor Marx reached out to a friend who had fled to Strasbourg, looking for evacuation possibilities for his young wards. This German refugee turned to his French neighbors, Andrée and Tobie Salomon.[1] Thirty-year-old Andrée Salomon was at the heart of Strasbourg's burgeoning Zionist and youth movements. As one of the founders of the Central Fund for the East (Caisse centrale pour l'Est), an aid committee for Jewish refugees, she immediately set out to obtain visas for a group of children from Frankfurt. The first group of fifty-two arrived on December 6, 1938, less than one month after the pogrom.[2] Until the outbreak of the Second World War, many other children crossed the border alone and obtained help from the same local networks.

Shared religious affinities had linked Jews in Frankfurt with those across the Rhine, in Strasbourg, long before Germany annexed Alsace-Lorraine in 1871 after the Franco-Prussian war. Even after France regained this territory after the First World War, the linguistic and geographical proximity to Germany continued to shape the lives of Strasbourg's inhabitants, placing them on the front lines of the Central European refugee crisis. Indeed, the initiatives that developed on behalf of young Jewish refugees in Strasbourg, and for Jewish refugees from Central Europe more generally, emerged in a broader context, during what many in France deemed an immigration crisis. To understand how they emerged, it is thus necessary to consider the larger question of migration to France in the aftermath of the First World War and especially after 1933, before looking more specifically at how the local Jewish population decided to respond.

In the aftermath of the First World War, France maintained relatively open borders. The country had lost one tenth of its active male population during the war, and devastated areas needed rebuilding. Furthermore, new restrictions on immigration to the United States established a quota system, which redirected flows to France. The Russian Revolution, as well as political crises in Poland and Italy in the 1920s, also encouraged departures.[3] These factors made France a primary immigration destination for individuals, mostly from Europe but not exclusively, looking for better economic conditions and political stability.

The relatively open migration policies in 1920s France, designed to recruit laborers and, to a more limited extent, provide refuge, contrasted sharply with those that developed in reaction to the political and economic upheavals of the 1930s. The Great Depression led to record unemployment in France, as well as mobilizations to establish protectionist restrictions in key sectors of the labor market, including commerce, medicine, and law.[4] Many of the latter policies were a response to the arrival of some 25,000 Germans, most of whom were Jewish, who fled the rise of Nazism in 1933.[5] A second wave of migration from Germany followed in 1935 after the passage of the Nuremburg Laws and the Saar referendum. In the same year, in Poland, anti-Jewish violence and repression, often condoned by the state, increased exponentially after the death of its authoritarian leader Jozef Pilsudski.[6] Just a year later, in 1936, the outbreak of the Spanish Civil War further destabilized the geopolitical situation. Finally, the March 1938 German annexation of Austria, followed by the establishment of racial laws in Italy and the November pogrom, led to another peak in migrations.

Each political crisis brought new populations to France, especially families, who did not fit nicely into France's work-oriented migration model.[7] While we might easily label those who came as "refugees," it is more accurate to call them migrants or exiles, since there was little consensus on the need to provide them an official political status to grant them legal protection and some form of social rights. German exiles (but not those of other nationalities who had been living in Germany) officially obtained recognition of their refugee status under the Popular Front government in September 1936. However, as Mary D. Lewis shows, in practice, they were often denied this status by local authorities, who considered them to have come for economic reasons.[8]

In reality, Polish and German Jews made up only a tiny percentage of the migrations to France in the interwar period, yet the policies shaping their reception were influenced by larger tensions. The number of German nationals in France (Jewish and non-Jewish) had actually dropped from 71,729 individuals in 1931 to 58,138 in 1936, or about 2.6 percent of the total foreign population.[9] It remains difficult to determine the total number of German Jewish individuals who sought refuge in France: an estimation of 40,000–60,000 for the entire 1933–1939 period has been advanced, although the higher figure includes Eastern European Jews in some sources.[10] The total number of unaccompanied Central European Jewish children who came to France in the 1938–1939 period is even more difficult to determine, but, as we will see, it is most likely fewer than 500. When compared to the almost 500,000 Spanish refugees who fled to France in January 1939, and the 10,000–15,000 unaccompanied Spanish and Basque children received by France from 1936–1939, it becomes clear that the Jewish refugee crisis was simply not on the same scale.[11]

The Jewish migrations to France in the 1930s may have been insignificant in comparison to other migratory groups, but the attention these migrants received was much greater than their numbers warranted. As seen above, Central European Jewish asylum seekers, often middle-class professionals, sparked protectionist policies. Amplified in the French press and in public discourse, the growing presence of Jewish refugees served as an easily exploitable vehicle for antisemites and nativists alike.[12]

For many French and immigrant Jews living in France, the Central European refugee crisis was not a distant problem. Helping refugees provided concerned Jews in France with a concrete means of addressing the antisemitism that they too were experiencing. The centralized nature of French life made Paris the main hub for refugee aid committees, and, fittingly, most scholarly accounts of the Jewish refugee crisis focus on the aid organizations that developed there.[13] However, those on France's shared border with Germany who maintained ties to friends and family on the other side of the Rhine were hit first by the crisis. Located on France's periphery, they proved nonetheless to be crucial actors.

The efforts of Alsatian Jews in Strasbourg provided a blueprint for French Kindertransport. This administratively complex initiative required not only convincing state officials to offer visas but also finding childcare solutions in a rapidly changing political situation. Alsatian Jews in Strasbourg acted swiftly in the days that followed the November pogrom. They set an example, yet the program they devised for unaccompanied Jewish youth was in many respects unique, reflecting their longstanding religious traditions and tightly knit communities. It also seems that certain Jewish leaders benefited from local political connections that led, at least initially, to a positive response for the children's visas.

If Paris had progressively become the center of French Jewish life over the course of the nineteenth century, Alsace remained home to a vibrant and interconnected network of Jewish communities. Jewish life in Alsace was unique due to restrictions, imposed on Jews until their political emancipation in 1791, that prevented them from living in cities. This led them to settle in villages throughout the region, where they occupied an essential role in the rural economy, often working as cattle traders or grain or wine dealers. To avoid consanguinity, marriages were usually arranged between members of different villages.[14] This practice created kin networks throughout the region, linking Jews in a tightly knit web. When the region was ceded to Imperial Germany after the Franco-Prussian war in 1871, many Jews migrated westwards to remain French. By the 1930s, Strasbourg was yet again part of France. The city had a sizable Jewish population, with over 10,000 individuals (of the 15,000–20,000 in the Alsace region).[15]

Alsatian Jews were not the only ones in the region with strong familial and cultural ties to Germany, however. The geographic and linguistic proximity to the Third Reich gave all Alsatians access to

German radio stations and Nazi propaganda, leading to a significant jump in antisemitism in the 1930s. The increase was not only a German importation, but the result of the internal French political and economic context. The high-profile role of Prime Minister Léon Blum during the Popular Front fed antisemitic tropes about Jews' power and increased the number of attacks against Jews and their property in Alsace and Lorraine. Likewise, fear over the secularization of the educational curricula—a particularly sensitive issue in the region—led to antisemitic outpourings in the region's Catholic press on the "foul-smelling Jewish bargaining" and "the hands of a Jewish atheist removing the crucifixes from our schools."[16] In the 1938–1939 period, the extreme right proved especially active, circulating tens of thousands of "*papillons*" (butterflies), little slips of paper designed to fly everywhere, full of antisemitic slogans.[17]

In the years leading up to the war, the atmosphere became, in the words of one Jewish contemporary, "unbreathable."[18] The region's Jewish newspaper, La Tribune Juive, shows the local Jewish population closing ranks to fight against two scourges: antisemitism and assimilation. At first glance, these phenomena seem unrelated. Yet at the time, for Jews who could do little about the increasing hostility, fighting assimilation represented a more feasible fight. Helping Jewish refugees, especially youth and children, was a means of responding to both antisemitism and assimilation, since it created an opportunity to strengthen communal bonds and educate the youth on the need to remain Jewish.

One finds Andrée Salomon (née Sulzer) at the center of these efforts. It is important, for epistemological reasons, to note that Salomon survived the Holocaust. The significant role she played saving children throughout the occupation led historians to solicit her after the war in order to document her work.[19] Others, such as René Hirschler, a young rabbi from Marseille who studied in Paris and was assigned to the Alsatian town of Mulhouse in 1929, took similar risks yet did not survive, leaving important gaps in our knowledge. Like a missing photo in an album, we must acknowledge the absence of his testimony, which diminishes my ability to reconstruct his role. Salomon always took pains in her postwar accounts to name those who worked alongside her, including Hirschler. While it is important to note that she did not act alone, it is nonetheless safe to consider her a central actor in French Kindertransport.

Salomon can be considered an example of what historian Edoardo Grendi called the "exceptional normal."[20] In most respects, her life reflected the bourgeois aspirations that shaped Jewish life in her native Alsace. Almost imperceptibly, though, her actions deviated from the traditional "home, family, synagogue"[21] triumvirate, making her a respectable counter-model for other young French Jewish women who, during the occupation, would play a crucial role in the Jewish resistance.[22]

Born into a traditional Jewish family in the village of Grussenheim in 1908, Andrée Sulzer was the fourth of six children of Jonas Sulzer and Marie Geismar, a butcher and a seamstress. A small detail set her apart from her family: she looked different. With her long dark hair and black eyes, her family often told her she was a "gypsy," teasing her that she must have fallen off a passing buggy.[23] Growing up with this label may have emboldened her to take a different path, or perhaps given her more freedom from the strictures of tradition. Salomon embraced Zionism in her early teens, even before leaving her village. Her political activism set her apart from the rest of her Francophile family, which, now safely back under French auspices after almost fifty years of German rule, saw no reason to dream of an elsewhere.[24] When her father died in 1915, the family's financial situation worsened. Each of the four Sulzer sisters had to leave school at fourteen or fifteen to find work in Strasbourg. Andrée left for the city at the age of fourteen,[25] and boarded at the Jewish Girls' Home (Home de jeunes filles israélites), established by Laure Weil. Andrée's mastery of both French and German helped her find work as a secretary for a Strasbourg lawyer.

In Strasbourg, Andrée Sulzer's path continued to diverge from that of her sisters, who had accepted arranged marriages. In many ways, their differences were generational. Andrée came of age in the aftermath of the First World War. Faced with seemingly unprecedented destruction, religious and political groups throughout Europe focused their energies on a recently discovered category of the population: adolescents. Youth movements, especially scouting, were seen as a means of rehabilitating postwar societies by encouraging greater contact with nature and physical activity. Among Jews, this trend helped foster new forms of Jewish identity that, depending on the organization, reinforced religious practices, yet also legitimated secular or political Jewish forms of belonging. This represented a break with the Franco-Jewish tradition, forged over the course of the nineteenth century, that had sought to frame Judaism as a strictly religious identity. Many of the youth organizations, following a new generation of Jewish writers such as André Spire and Edmond Fleg, embraced a word that had been shunned by French Jews since the early nineteenth century. Instead of the term "*Israélite*," considered more refined, these writers proudly reappropriated the word "Jew," assigning a positive meaning to the pejorative term.[26]

From the perspective of the 1920s, many Jews were indeed "*heureux comme Dieu en France*" (happy like God in France), to cite a common expression in the Yiddish-speaking world. The rehabilitation of Capitaine Alfred Dreyfus in 1906 cast a positive light on the affair, and Jews had, thanks to their participation in the First World War, become one of France's "spiritual families," even the antisemite Maurice Barrès seemed to agree.[27] Youth movements taught teens that it was possible to affirm both a Jewish and a French identity. Furthermore, they allowed for greater interaction among Jews of different backgrounds, creating new ties between French and immigrant Jews.[28]

These trends ring especially true for Andrée Sulzer. Her arrival in Strasbourg corresponded with the development of new forms of engagement for youth, such as the establishment in 1917 of the German Zionist youth organization, Blau-Weiss, which changed its name to Hatikva (Hope) in 1923. According to Salomon's nephew, it was there that Andrée met her future husband, Tobie Salomon, a young chemist affiliated with the University of Strasbourg who had been born in Galicia. In 1928–1929, Andrée Sulzer, along with a group of friends, helped establish Strasbourg's branch of the Jewish scouting movement, the Éclaireurs Israélites de France, which put her in close contact with Jewish youth.[29]

In 1931, Andrée Sulzer married Salomon, breaking with family tradition not only by marrying out of love, but by marrying a Zionist. Even worse, in her family's eyes, Tobie Salomon was considered a Polish Jew, even though he had lived most of his life in France.[30] After this bout of rebellion, Andrée quickly stepped back in line, leaving her job and volunteering for the Consistory's Jewish aid committee, the Comité de bienfaisance israélite de Strasbourg.

While Andrée Salomon seemed to embrace bourgeois gender norms for married women, the Central European refugee crisis brought her into a new, more political and public role. From June 1933 onward, French Zionists established agricultural training centers (*hachsharot*) for German Jewish teenagers on their way to Mandatory Palestine, which led to veritable emigration solutions for German youth.[31] Salomon belonged to a Zionist women's group named Ghalei, which was one of several organizations setting up *hachsharot* for this purpose. Since the British limited immigration certificates to Palestine, the group didn't hesitate to organize false marriages in order to double the allotted number.[32] In this precursor to the Kindertransport, Salomon took on an advocacy role, helping the young refugees with their immigration applications. During this period, she also served as Strasbourg's delegate to the Zionist organization Hehaloutz, a commitment that brought her to Paris regularly.

Salomon was not alone in her activism. Her former housemothers from the Jewish Girls' Home (Home de jeunes filles israélites), Laure Weil and Fanny Schwab, served as role models, providing refuge to approximately thirty young German Jewish women in 1933.[33] At the end of the year, Weil formally requested the prolongation of their stay from local officials at the Bas-Rhin Prefecture, but the minister of foreign affairs refused, citing the negative public reaction to German refugees in Alsace.[34] The city's Polish Jewish synagogue, Adath Israel, attended by 20 percent of Strasbourg's Jewish population, was also actively helping young Jewish refugees.[35] In 1937, Salomon, as well as the Head Rabbi of Strasbourg and the Lower Rhin, Isaïe Schwartz, and Mulhouse Rabbi René Hirschler, created the Central Fund for the East.[36] This committee helped support Jewish refugee families in the region. Clearly, Alsatian Jews were willing to open their homes and wallets to help refugees.

Youth remained central to communal life, yet with the growing persecution, the optimism of the 1920s faded, and the celebrated symbiosis between French and Jewish identities seemed more fraught. As one Jewish Scout leader wrote to Rabbi René Hirschler before speaking at an event in 1938: "It is important to show them that there is no rupture between Jewish and French life, that the feeling of fraternity they must feel toward fellow Jews does not change their feeling of love for the country, and that remaining affiliated [*attaché*] with Jewish life does not make them less French. These ideas, obvious to us, can be a source of intense questioning for the youth."[37]

In response to what must have appeared to be a passing storm, Strasbourg's Jews unified on behalf of the community's youngest members. Along with other local leaders, including Dr. Joseph Weil, Andrée Salomon helped found a community center, the Merkaz Hanoar, in 1938 for Jewish youth of all backgrounds and ideological tendencies.[38] As scholars of the French Jewish resistance have shown, this work paid off during the occupation, creating a cohort of engaged young people, prepared to take exceptional risks on behalf of others, at times at the cost of their own lives.[39]

With the help of Rabbi René Hirschler,[40] Andrée Salomon turned to these local aid networks when she received the news about the children in the Frankfurt orphanage from her neighbor Simon Marx in November 1938. Her recollection of this moment, in a 1965 interview, mirrors Isidor Marx's account:

> The day after Kristallnacht, hospitals were burned, orphanages were burned, so in the Frankfurt area, which was the closest, in terms of "Jewish spirit"—because Strasbourg was known as a traditional community, and Frankfurt was strictly observant—The director, Mr. [Isidor] Marx, of the Frankfurt orphanage, telephoned a friend (also named Marx), who was a former benefactor of the Frankfurt orphanage but had long since emigrated to Strasbourg, to say "I'm overwhelmed and I don't know what to do. Every day, children are brought to me whose fathers are interned in Dachau, the small institutions have been burnt down, decimated, I have three times as many children as I have beds. I've obtained the agreement of the Basel orphanage to take in a certain number of children. They're going to take the necessary steps to get permission to bring them to Basel—what can you do for me in France?"[41]

Salomon then explained the chain reaction her neighbor's visit set off: "He came to see me, and we immediately held a meeting the same day and decided to apply as quickly as possible to the Prefecture to obtain an entry permit for the children, knowing full well that in Alsace, as everywhere else in France, once the habit is formed, the chain can continue."[42]

It is quite likely that it was Rabbi René Hirschler who obtained the visas for Frankfurt children from the Bas-Rhin Prefecture.[43] Here I must advance a hypothesis, since, as seen above, Rabbi Hirschler was murdered during the Holocaust, and did not live to document his extensive work on behalf of others, as rabbi then *Grand Rabbin* of Strasbourg and the Lower Rhin, and then as head of the chaplaincy, where he assisted those interned in French camps until his own deportation. Hirschler's wife was also murdered, yet their three children survived in hiding. The latter managed to save some of his papers from the 1936–1938 period, which reveal the rabbi's work on behalf of Jewish causes, including religious instruction for girls, and his deep ties to French civil society. Amid the guilt-ridden letters from parents explaining their child's absence from Hebrew school, one finds quite a few letters from local authorities, responding to Hirschler's numerous queries on behalf of individual refugees. The letters suggest that Hirschler was highly respected by local authorities, who usually heeded his advice.[44] This is the reason why it is plausible to assume that it was Hirschler who reached out to his local contacts to obtain the visas. While I could not find the archival trace,[45] the fact that the local Jewish press published an article on the transport confirms that the initiative received the blessing of the authorities.

On the occasion of the children's arrival on December 6, 1938, a certain "A.S.," most likely Andrée Salomon, penned an article in the *Tribune Juive* noting "the indescribable happiness of the children" upon their arrival. She continued:

> Surrounded in this way, they had, I'm sure, forgotten that they had just left their parents, teachers and friends to adapt to a new life. The stay in France, even if it is only a short one for many of them,

will have its influence on these young minds, on these tiny souls, and we feel great gratitude for the governmental and administrative authorities, whose generous collaboration has ensured a new life of peace and trust for this group of children.[46]

This short article shows how the Kindertransport came to be seen as a viable option for parents and rescuers alike. First, it suggests that the children were capable of forgetting their recent separation from their parents. It then emphasizes their malleability and capacity to adapt to their new settings. It also shows that the organizers assumed that France would be a safe environment for the children, and that their refuge would be temporary. If the article reveals the mindset and strategies of Strasbourg's Kindertransport organizers, it also points to a progressive shift in women's roles. By publishing an article in the Strasbourg Jewish press, Andrée Salomon had, perhaps unwittingly, moved squarely into a public position in French Jewish life.[47]

Andrée Salomon and a few other women received the children, who were accompanied by a nurse from the Frankfurt orphanage.[48] The organizers decided that half of the children would be placed in local Jewish families. Indeed, Strasbourg's Jews showed a clear preference for foster care: "We continue to believe that the family circle is the most beneficial for these children. It is there that they forget their worries most quickly, and it is there that they most appreciate the Jewish environment that is offered to them and that we must give them in life as their most solid support."[49] The other half would go into the long-established Jewish orphanages in Haguenau and Strasbourg. The youngest in the group were cared for in a Jewish structure called Le Nid (The Nest).[50]

Not all of the children who arrived on the transport came from the Frankfurt orphanage, and not all of them stayed in Strasbourg. The orthodox Hirsch family, from Frankfurt, learned about the December 1938 transport through their French cousin, Marcus Cohn, who happened to be a friend of Andrée Salomon's from Strasbourg.[51] In the early 1930s, the parents had placed two of their children at the Frankfurt orphanage when one of their other children was suffering from a contagious illness. On November 9, 1938, Dr. Hirsch was arrested and sent to Buchenwald. Even though her husband had expressed the conviction that the family should not be separated, Mathilda Hirsch signed up all seven of their children for Kindertransport. At the last minute, however, she was unable to part with her two youngest children, Werner-Shmuel Moshe and Roselene-Shoshanna, born respectively in 1937 and 1938. They remained with her. The five oldest Hirsch siblings were sent on the first Kindertransport from Frankfurt to Strasbourg, and then on to Paris, where they were dispersed among their French relatives. The youngest sibling Benjamin's placement with an uncle fell through, however, and he was sent alone to an orthodox family from his uncle's synagogue.[52]

Other children were placed near Strasbourg. Fourteen-year-old Ernst (later Ernest) Stock and his sister Lotte were also from Frankfurt. Like that of the Hirsch siblings, their case also shows how private relationships led to real emigration solutions. After the November pogrom, family friends from Frankfurt, now living in Thann, a small village in the Vosges, offered to open their home to the Stock children. Young Ernst made a lasting impression on Andrée Salomon when they met at the station. Before sending the children to Thann, she gave Ernst her contact information and encouraged him to write in case he needed anything. Stock did not speak French, which kept him from attending the local high school. Isolated, he wrote to Salomon, telling her he knew refugee children had to pursue a trade, and he had decided to become a photographer. Salomon sent for Stock to learn this profession in Strasbourg, where he attended the Jewish community's École de travail (vocational training school) and obtained an apprenticeship with a photographer. Ernst lived with Salomon and her husband for several days, then with her mother, attending Shabbat lunches at the home of Yetty Weill, Salomon's sister. In Strasbourg, Andrée encouraged the Jewish Scouts to help care for the German children and teach them French. Some of the refugee teens, like Ernst Stock, attended summer camp in Brittany in summer 1939. Salomon served as an anchor for the Stock children throughout their exile in France. While the children were very much alone, she provided them with precious help, and they eventually managed to immigrate on their own to the United States. The case of Ernst and Lotte Stock shows the deep personal engagement behind Salomon's brand of social work.[53]

The Strasbourg group requested a second transport of forty children in early 1939; most likely permission was granted, since Salomon refers to the arrival of the second group of approximately fifty children in 1939, as well as another one hundred who came independently across the border (see Appendices, Table 1).[54] Salomon crossed the Kehl bridge several times in 1939 to pick up children, linking up with Frankfurt orphanage director Isidor Marx's brother and sister-in-law, Rabbi Sigmund Marx and Berthel Marx from Ludwigshafen, who accompanied children and provided lists of future candidates.[55] As the number of children arriving in Strasbourg grew, the Central Fund for the East multiplied its requests for help to readers of the Jewish press, asking for household goods, cash donations, and hospitality for the children. "Help us bring the light back to you," they insisted, during Chanuka, the Jewish festival of lights.[56] Each additional foster family, they explained, liberated another Jewish child from Germany.[57]

As the movement in eastern France gathered momentum, Andrée Salomon reached out to Jews in Paris. They, too, were working to bring German and Austrian Jewish children to France, relying upon a complex infrastructure of French and international Jewish organizations.

CHAPTER 3

Parisian Initiatives for Jewish Children

Women's Work?

Andrée Salomon's activism in Strasbourg on behalf of Jewish children fit into a larger pattern that was also playing out in Paris. Women were disproportionately involved in the networks that French Jews developed to bring Elfriede and other Jewish and "non-Aryan" children to France. Indeed, as a result of the refugee crisis that began in 1933 and especially the November 9–10, 1938 pogrom, an almost imperceptible shift was underway in French Jewish circles. Women's public roles were evolving from taking care of children and the needy—a form of non-threatening "women's work"—to leading a highly political (yet behind-the-scenes) initiative to bring Jewish children into a society hostile to refugees and Jews.

Women's accomplishments certainly deserve recognition, but it is equally important to comprehend the gender dynamics at play here because they tell us more about how Jews responded to Nazi persecutions on the eve of the war. Rescue was in large part the result of Jews asking for help from civil society. This behavior co-existed with Jews' tendency, honed over centuries of vulnerability and dependence on princes and kings, to privilege the establishment of vertical alliances with political authorities over horizontal alliances with fellow subjects and citizens.[1] The latter observation helps explain Jewish responses to persecution, but it is based on the assumption that all Jewish actors were males. If we move women out of the historical blind spot, we can glean an altogether different understanding of Jews' political behavior in Western societies on the eve of the Holocaust. Indeed, because their work of caring for others was deemed unthreatening and often went unnoticed (and not only by historians!), Jewish women had room to maneuver. In the name of helping others, they attempted to negotiate alliances, both horizontal and vertical, with members of civil society and state authorities. Working at times from the margins, and at times from within the establishment, they did not hesitate to ask for help on behalf of Jewish children in Central Europe. Gender dynamics in French society thus shaped the outcomes of Kindertransport, just as the latter led to new leadership roles for women in French Jewish life and, eventually, to some fruitful outcomes in the form of visas. Nothing shows this better than the situation in Paris, where Jewish organizations and their primarily male leaders had been working since 1933 to address the Central European Jewish refugee crisis.

Parisian Jews from both immigrant and native circles had been confronting the Central European refugee crisis since 1933. Jewish immigrant organizations were the first to provide aid for refugees. Both the left-oriented Ligue internationale contre l'antisémitisme (LICA), established in 1928 by Bernard Lacache, the son of Eastern European immigrants, and the Fédération des sociétés juives de France, which represented middle-class immigrant Jews and their mutual aid societies, organized rallies against Nazism and in favor of aid for refugees.[2] Leaders of the native Jewish establishment, often board members of the Alliance and the Central and Paris Consistory, also set up committees, eventually establishing the Comité national français de secours aux réfugiés allemands victimes de l'antisémitisme (National Committee).[3] This committee, led by the Baron Robert de Rothschild and Jacques Helbronner, was endorsed by several non-Jewish politicians and presented itself as a non-sectarian body.[4] From 1933 until its dissolution in 1935, the National Committee was the principal aid provider for Jewish refugees and was recognized by the French government as the official committee of French Jews. However, it was never the only source of aid for refugees, and by the spring of 1933 in Paris alone there were at least fifteen committees sponsored by both Jewish and non-Jewish groups.[5]

By late 1933, however, French Jews' enthusiasm was already beginning to wane. Not only were native French and immigrant Jews alike critical of the German Jewish refugees in the Jewish press (seen as too German by the French, too arrogant by the Eastern European immigrants), but the economic depression led the refugees to increasingly be seen as a threat, especially by middle-class professionals who organized successfully to fight for labor market restrictions against foreigners.[6] Faced with these internal and external tensions, the conservative leadership of the National Committee sought to dispel accusations of a double allegiance that would place solidarity with fellow Jews over national interests. Jacques Helbronner was especially influential. Not only was he a member of the French Conseil d'État, he also served as one of France's delegates on the League of Nation's High Commission for Refugees. In his official capacities, Helbronner fought to implement the most restrictive refugee policy possible, including closing France's borders.[7] Unfortunately for the refugees, this attitude came to characterize the work of the National Committee. Until its decision to close its doors in 1935, the National Committee refused to consider France as anything more than a stopover for the refugees.[8]

French Jews did not face the crisis alone, however. The rise of Nazism in Germany forced several international Jewish organizations to leave Berlin for Paris. One of the most influential was the American Jewish organization, the JDC.[9] The "Joint," as it is still known in European Jewish communities, was established during the First World War in New York to centralize American Jewish aid for victims on the front. It established extensive aid programs in the interwar period, especially in Poland and the Soviet Union. The JDC's role in France was quite limited until early 1933, when it moved its European headquarters to Paris. Its overseas director, Dr. Bernard Kahn, had extensive ties to German Jewish life and was an ardent Zionist.[10] His first-hand knowledge of German Jews made him a strong advocate for this population in France.

The JDC represented first and foremost a source of funding, both for French Jewish aid committees and the international Jewish organizations that fled Berlin alongside the JDC.[11] British Jews also sent funds to France through the Central British Fund for German Jewry, established in April 1933. By February 1934, this committee had raised more than American Jews had been able to raise during the same period.[12] Nonetheless, it was the JDC that played the most influential role in the French refugee crisis, due to its hands-on role in French Jewish life.

Indeed, in summer 1936, JDC overseas director Bernard Kahn approached French Jewish leaders with the hope of establishing a new refugee aid committee, building on the political victory of the Popular Front in May 1936.[13] In exchange for JDC funding, Kahn imposed a new set of conditions, demanding vocational training for refugees, and, more importantly, sought out a new cohort of pro-refugee leaders.[14] Kahn's pro-refugee stance was reinforced by representatives from immigrant and refugee organizations, including the Zionist Israel Jefroykin, as well as—*chose rare*—a woman, the feminist journalist Louise Weiss.[15] This marked a new era, ushering in the Comité d'assistance aux réfugiés (CAR), which played an important role in French Jewish welfare throughout the Second World War. The historiography on the Central European refugee crisis, in large part thanks to Vicki Caron, now emphasizes the diverse political responses of Jews in France and French society in general. However, the scholarship has neglected another ever-present variable, at times as salient as political ideology: gender.

Jewish leaders in France may have endorsed a diverse set of political views on the refugee crisis, yet they were united by a common denominator: the decision-makers were almost all men. Women, while not altogether absent, have gone unnoticed since they were acting in their traditional "helper" capacity. In this respect, the refugee crisis reflected gender roles, yet at the same time, it caused them to evolve by facilitating women's emergence into new leadership positions.[16] Indeed, moved by the gravity of the situation, Jewish women's help became, by nature, more political.

More research is needed on the lives of Jewish women in France to fully grasp their political intercession at this moment.[17] Looking back over the course of the nineteenth century, one sees a slow evolution of their status. As Jews entered the middle class across Central and Western Europe, they adopted bourgeois norms that increasingly called for a stricter differentiation between men and women's roles, as well as a distinct separation between private and public spaces. Relegated to the home, middle- and upper-class women were increasingly considered the responsible party for transmitting Judaism to the next generation, and became easy targets when modernity led to "too much" assimilation.[18] Some historians have argued that a "third sphere" emerged for women in the second half of the nineteenth century, allowing them access to public life through philanthropy and social welfare. In the words of Derek Penslar, "The feminine, or more accurately 'maternal,' sphere encompassed both domestic and public space. Philanthropic activity comprised a liminal zone between intimacy and publicity, between home economics and political economy. Middle-class women inhabited overlapping and amorphous spheres that could embrace municipal and even national government so long as their activity could be seen as an extension of maternalist nurturing of the family."[19]

With a few exceptions, to find Jewish women in nineteenth-century and even early-twentieth-century French Jewish public life, one must seek out the caregivers.[20] Women were active in the non-threatening work of caring for children and the poor, as well as running social activities in synagogues. The expectation to care for others was not reserved to the upper classes, who comprised the philanthropic elite. Women from middle and lower classes also gave their time to help others, caring for the sick, the destitute, and children, although the historiography has yet to consider fully their actions in France.[21] Women's voices sometimes emerged and advocated for change, as seen in the movement to reform French Judaism at the end of the nineteenth century or during the Dreyfus Affair.[22] French Jewish women also engaged with the political movements of larger French society and were among the reformers of the Third Republic, especially among the leaders of the French feminist movement.[23] These reformist networks, woven as women fought (in vain) to obtain the right to vote, carried over into the Jewish communal world, to help refugees.

Indeed, the massive arrival of German refugees in 1933, followed by new waves after the Nuremburg Laws in 1935 and the November pogrom in 1938, mobilized Jewish women from across the ideological spectrum. It is not surprising to find women with Jewish backgrounds who had already crossed into the public sphere as feminists among the Parisian leaders in the early stages of the refugee crisis. Before becoming the under-secretary of state at the ministry of education in Léon Blum's government, Cécile Brunschvicg (1877–1946) was active in the organization that later became the National Committee. As head of its social work department, she ran a staff of 45 people, 70 percent of them women from the "Jewish bourgeoisie."[24] Brunschvicg initially sought to keep her role strictly philanthropic. However, by the end of 1933, she suggested creating a committee to monitor the growing antisemitism in the French press. A few years later, as a member of Blum's cabinet, she was targeted by the very antisemitism she had denounced.[25]

A rival of Cécile Brunschvicg, feminist journalist Louise Weiss (1893–1983) had a more powerful role as the only woman on the board of the newly established CAR.[26] Yet even before this, she had cultivated an exceptional image. Weiss was one of the rare women in France to obtain the *agrégation*, a highly competitive exam, in 1914. In addition to her university studies in France, she studied for one year at Oxford.[27] After the First World War, Weiss became active in pacifist and feminist circles, founding and running the weekly publication *L'Europe nouvelle* from 1918 to 1934. An outspoken public figure, she published her first memoirs in 1937, in which she openly discussed her Jewish mother and Protestant father. Her parents' upper-class Alsatian families chose to remain French in 1871, and a portrait of Robespierre hung in their anti-clerical household.[28] It seems as if the identity that mattered most to Weiss herself was not religious in nature, but political.

Weiss's own distinct background seems, nonetheless, to have allowed her to bridge vastly different groups, even if her writings suggest her distance from Judaism. A comical example can be found in one of her notes from the period: "Semitic agricultural workers have settled at the farm of Chenehutte-les-Tuffo [sic], in Maine & Loire. The local butcher is furious with them because they go as far as Tours to get their Koschner [sic] meat. They don't eat pork, but they want to present a beautiful pig at the agricultural fair in Angers."[29] Weiss's misspelling of the word "kosher" is curious: she had passed the *agrégation*, after all, and her mother was from a Jewish family. The account hints at an impatience with Jewish ritual. Thus, while she could have claimed a Jewish identity, it seems as if she put forward her secular (or even anti-clerical) views and perhaps her Protestant identity: one contemporary described her as "Protestant and quite unbearable."[30] The pragmatic leaders of the JDC most likely turned to Weiss not as a fellow Jew, but as a well-connected, pro-refugee advocate. Her fluent English certainly helped the male JDC leadership overlook her gender.

This feminist clearly did not leave others indifferent. Her reputation was surely influenced by the fact that Weiss considered herself a free agent. According to her biographer, she had affairs with several politicians, including Foreign Affairs Minister Georges Bonnet and Minister of Public Health Marc Rucart.[31] I provide this detail here only because it helps explain how Weiss could have, according to her own account, forced Bonnet to establish a committee on refugees in late 1938: "Snatched is the word. Since October [1938], I had been assaulting him in the ministry for this purpose, once or twice a week."[32] Her undated notes allude to her relationship with Bonnet and provide greater detail, suggesting it was the September 1938 Munich agreement and not the November pogrom that pushed her to take action: "Mr. Georges Bonnet had complained to me about my harsh remarks on the Munich disaster. I pointed out to him that they could have been even harsher and in writing, because many newspapers had asked for my collaboration on this subject." Explaining why she decided to refrain from publicly criticizing the French government for "its weakness, even its cowardice toward Hitler," she stated that her "long and affectionate relations with him [one assumes, Bonnet] made me scrupulous about criticizing him for a negotiation that I considered a French disaster."

In compensation for this "friendly silence," she asked Bonnet to "take responsibility for the persecuted and form a committee which would represent the greatest honor to France and to him, because our indifference to the sufferings of these unfortunate people was an object of blame and international shame."[33]

Bonnet is not known for his political courage. As minister of foreign affairs, he orchestrated France's appeasement policy at Munich, attended Vom Rath's funeral, and held a dinner for his Nazi homologue von Ribbentrop in Paris in early December 1938, without inviting the Jewish members of the government. And let us not forget, in the aftermath of the November pogrom, the Daladier government continued to restrict immigration, passing *décret* laws that provided the French government with the right to detain "undesirable foreigners" who could not be expelled in "special centers."[34] During the Vichy Regime, Bonnet chose to support Pétain and served as a member of Vichy's Conseil National. Bonnet's postwar autobiographical writings must therefore be read with this context in mind. In serious need of rehabilitating his reputation, he emphasized his generous stance on refugees and suggested that the idea for the committee had been his own.[35]

Known as the Bonnet Committee or the Central Refugee Committee (Comité central des réfugiés, CRC), it was announced in late December 1938 and included Protestant, Jewish, and Catholic clergy members, including the Cardinal Verdier, Pastor Marc Boegner, and Head Rabbi of Paris Israël Lévi, and prominent members of civil society such as François Mauriac and Georges Risler, as well as Bonnet's political allies and friends, including Henry Bérenger, Jean Mistler, and Jacques Helbronner. Under the guidance of Louise Weiss, its secretary general, the committee played a role in the Kindertransport initiatives.[36]

Bonnet was not the only man Weiss had to deal with to work effectively on behalf of Jewish refugees. She had to face the conservative French Jewish leadership, who did not share her pro-refugee views. In the early days of the committee, she was invited to lunch by Bonnet's friend Jacques Helbronner, who happened to be a relative through marriage. Weiss's notes on their encounter show her disgust, and even flirted with antisemitic tropes. According to Weiss, this "representative of the Rothschilds, devoured by ambition and needy, in spite of his apparent wealth" would "plead against the refugees as the representative of a Consistory elected by 400 rich Jews [*israëlites*, sic]".[37] Weiss felt Helbronner was sabotaging the committee, and even tried to get her removed from it.

Weiss also had to contend with the Baron Robert de Rothschild, head of the French Jewish establishment. She claims she befriended him by inviting him to lunch, proposing a menu that displayed her wit: each dish represented a play on words to evoke helping the needy.[38] Rothschild, in turn, invited Weiss to a more extravagant lunch, in his home. Weiss, never worried about creating enemies, describes the lunch in her later memoirs, regaling her readers with details on the "incomparable roast" that "transformed [. . .] the business climate in this den of the Stock Exchange into one more fitting of private quarters." She then explained her indifference as "the baron changed his tone," in an attempt to both seduce her and put her in her place:

—O my crazy mistress! O my beloved filly [*bourrique*]! . . . he exclaimed between gluttonous mouthfuls.
Two certain untruths! He continued:
—Once and for all, you must understand that it is up to your Committee to decide certain questions of principle of an internal nature, and that it is up to me to act for the rest. Of course, I'm speaking a language that is incomprehensible for a woman. But I will make myself less abstract . . .

Weiss concluded: "He wanted to be the uncontested ruler of Zion. There was no point in arguing with this monarch. I crunched a third mint while, swearing like a coachman, he signed a royal check—for the Joint perhaps."[39]

Armed with a sharp pen and an even sharper wit, Weiss seems to have thrived on transgressing barriers of all sorts. There is no way to corroborate her account, clearly designed to entertain.[40] Nonetheless, her anecdote points to the political tensions among the leaders of the refugee crisis. In this context, gender never went unnoticed, and women were indeed actors. Not all of them, however, were as flamboyant as Louise Weiss.

Even before Louise Weiss convinced Georges Bonnet to create the CRC in late 1938, two women, most likely recent refugees themselves, discreetly decided to take action. Indeed, it was a Viennese woman living in the ninth arrondissement of Paris named Nathalie Lourié (née Wahl, born most likely in the 1870s) who unwittingly changed the nature of French aid for German and Austrian Jews by suggesting that children be brought to France in the summer of 1938.[41] Lourié was carrying out an initiative started by another Viennese refugee, Dr. Vita Stein, who had stopped in Paris on her way to the United States, where she continued her work with the blind.[42]

Few details can be found about Lourié, other than the fact that she was married to Dr. Alexander Lourié, had three children around the turn of the twentieth century, and was living in Vienna during the First World War and its aftermath.[43] Lourié contributed regularly to a charity run by Zionist Anita Cohen-Müller for Galician refugees in Vienna.[44] According to her friend, Vita Stein, Lourié had worked closely with the Institute for the Blind and the Charlotte Merores-Itzeles Jewish Girls' Orphanage in Vienna. She was perhaps a doctor herself.[45] Lourié's husband died in Vienna in 1924, followed by her son, Martin, two years later, in 1926.[46] It is possible these personal losses caused her to move to Paris, but what is more likely is that, like many other affluent Viennese Jews, she fled after Nazis invaded her city in March 1938.

What is clear is that, by summer 1938, Lourié was in Paris and her own situation was stable enough for her to help others. It was at this moment that she took on the project to bring girls from the Merores Jewish Girls' orphanage in Vienna to the Rothschild orphanage in Paris. Lourié clearly knew people in Paris and Vienna, and she indicated in her correspondence that she was in contact with the Baroness Germaine de Rothschild (née Halphen), as had been her friend, Vita Stein.[47] Lourié's request to send eight girls to the Rothschild orphanage was granted immediately, in mid-July 1938.[48] By the end of the month, the Baroness de Rothschild herself had agreed to accept another group of twenty girls who would be enrolled in apprenticeship programs and fully supported by her organization, Beneï Israël–Centres sociaux pour la jeunesse juive (Children of Israel–Social Centers for Jewish Youth) until they were self-sufficient.[49] In August 1938, Minister of Foreign Affairs Georges Bonnet granted authorization to allow the eight teens to travel to France.[50] Lourié continued to serve as the go-between between the Austrian Jewish community emigration bureau, the Merores, and the Rothschild orphanages until the arrival of six of the eight girls, accompanied by their instructor from the Merores orphanage, Lizzie Landau, on December 27, 1938. At least six other Austrian and German girls followed.[51] More than 138 letters were exchanged between Paris and Vienna over an eight-month period to evacuate the girls, indicating the complexity and time-consuming nature of the endeavor.

Lourié's personal connections with Jewish individuals and organizations in Vienna and Paris, coupled with the Baroness de Rothschild's contacts in the French government, allowed for this small accomplishment. It is important, nonetheless, to put this "success" in perspective: all but one of the eight Viennese girls were deported from France and perished in Nazi camps. The only one who survived did so by returning, in great peril, to Vienna in 1943.[52] The historian and the reader have the advantage of hindsight. The activists on the ground did not. They could not know they were leading children into a trap.

In late 1938, the hour was nonetheless grave: many felt that war was inevitable. If the costume balls, lotteries, and evening gowns belonged to a different era, philanthropy continued to represent an essential part of upper-class Jewish women's identities.[53] As seen above, the Rothschild women and a handful of other Jewish women still played an important role in Jewish charities.[54] With nannies, nurses, and staff to care for their children and relieve them of household duties, these women had time to dedicate to their philanthropic and artistic endeavors. It is thus fitting that two particularly prominent women, the Baroness Germaine de Rothschild (1884–1975) and the Baroness Yvonne de Gunzbourg (1882–1969) could be found heading initiatives to assist German and Austrian Jewish children. As Jewish nobility, they belonged to a tightly knit network, connected through multi-generational bonds of marriage, business, and philanthropy. It was also no coincidence, then, that the two women were first cousins.[55]

The Baroness Germaine de Rothschild was the daughter of Émile Halphen and Louise Halphen (née Fould).[56] According to her daughter, Germaine Halphen's mother opposed her marriage in 1905 to the Baron Edouard de Rothschild, with whom she would have four children, due to the fact that he was Jewish. Her mother, while also Jewish, preferred her daughters to marry Christians to "complete" their assimilation into French society.[57] It is quite possible that Germaine de Rothschild had a rebellious streak that manifested itself through her choice in marriage and her continued dedication to Jewish causes at a moment when other Jewish philanthropists were progressively drawn to helping the general public.[58] One can also imagine that perpetuating the Rothschild family's charitable traditions was a gendered expectation of wives and surely a means of consolidating power within her *belle famille*.[59]

This lesson may have been learned from Germaine de Rothschild's own mother, Louise Halphen. In 1914, the latter established the Émile Halphen Foundation to fight infant mortality in the name of her late husband. In 1922, she created the Infant Protection Society (La Protection du Nourrisson), which provided medical care to women and infants in the Seine Department.[60] "My mother also initiated me to philanthropy," Louise Halphen wrote in her memoirs. "I started to get involved in charitable work, which was for me an ever-growing passion."[61] Halphen included her daughter Germaine in her endeavors, putting her on the board of directors of the Infant Protection Society. Yet there appears to have been a slight variation between Halphen's philanthropy and her daughter's charity: the mother's non-sectarian philanthropy seems to have been part of her larger assimilatory project; Germaine de Rothschild, however, remained active in Jewish causes.[62]

Many women members of the Jewish elite wrote their memoirs, often for private circulation among their descendants. Germaine de Rothschild's mother did so, as did her daughter, Jacqueline. It is quite possible that Germaine de Rothschild wrote her life story as well.[63] However, this text, if it does exist, has remained in private hands. In the absence of her own voice, one can find extremely different portraits of Germaine de Rothschild in her children's respective memoirs. Her daughter Jacqueline Piatigorsky painted her mother as a self-assured socialite: "She could make any decision. She had no fears and believed nothing could go wrong" and "indulged in a flashy social life, ordering many new dresses and decorating them with beautiful jewelry. She fluttered from one party to another and enjoyed it when men turned around to look at her as she passed."[64] Her son, Guy de Rothschild, asserted the importance of his mother's role in his life and her engagements for others:

> My mother was a virtuous woman with a generous heart. Mindful of her obligations, she considered it only natural to help others. Throughout her life, she employed a social worker, who investigated

needy cases and advised her in finding ways to aid them. Every Thursday, she visited the Rothschild Foundation's children's home in Nogent-sur-Marne, distributing gifts and playing with the children, who smothered her with hugs and kisses and called her Germaine.[65]

If one child described her as a socialite and the other as a committed mother and philanthropist, both considered her a confident and competent woman. Those who met her in the context of her activism on behalf of refugees concur, vouching for her genuine interest in the lives of those she sought to assist.[66] In the words of one contemporary, "She was an intelligent woman, quite charming, very capable of creating human, personal relationships, much more so than her husband, who was rather stiff and unsociable."[67]

Germaine de Rothschild appeared to be in complete harmony with the expectations imposed upon her as a female member of the Jewish elite. Yet, instead of embracing a life of leisure, she became deeply involved in the Jewish refugee crisis. She hired a team of five or six social workers, as well as a head social worker, to provide aid to thirty Central European refugee families.[68] She also helped run Beneï Israël–Centres sociaux pour la jeunesse juive, the Rothschild orphanage, and the Union of Jewish Youth Organizations for Physical Education (Union des œuvres de la jeunesse israélite pour l'éducation physique), and perhaps other charitable endeavors.[69] It is therefore not a coincidence that Viennese émigrés Vita Stein and Nathalie Lourié turned to Germaine de Rothschild when looking for a solution for the Viennese girls. According to Lourié, in summer 1938, the Baroness was already trying to bring Jewish children from an orphanage in Germany to Paris to place them in families.[70] By December 1938, she decided to take her advocacy on behalf of German and Austrian Jewish families to a new level by seeking permission for fifty children to enter France under her sponsorship.[71] Her actions echoed, and were perhaps inspired by, those of her friend and confidante in England, Dorothy de Rothschild, the wife of James de Rothschild, with whom she corresponded regularly. Like Germaine, Dorothy was helping evacuate Central European Jewish children. Her efforts led to the arrival of thirty boys from a Frankfurt Jewish boy's home to Waddesdon, the Rothschilds' sumptuous country house.[72]

As efforts emerged to bring children to France, the question of their care arose. In December 1938, Germaine de Rothschild's cousin, Baroness Yvonne Fanny de Gunzbourg, developed a second initiative, designed to address this issue. Even less can be said about Yvonne de Gunzbourg than Germaine de Rothschild: her children and grandchildren have not published autobiographies, nor have they shared her correspondence.[73] Yvonne was the daughter of Émile and Louise Deutsch de la Meurthe, and a member of the French Jewish elite. Her marriage to Baron Pierre de Gunzbourg, son of Horace de Gunzburg, was followed by the birth of four children.[74] Like her cousin, Yvonne de Gunzbourg embraced the philanthropic endeavors of her husband's family, who had settled in Paris from Russia. Even though she was a product of French Israelite society, Yvonne de Gunzbourg became active in two Russian Jewish organizations in France, Obchestvo Rasprostranienia Truda (Organization for Rehabilitation through Training, ORT) and Union OSE (OSE).

Like the Gunzbourg family, both ORT and OSE originated in St. Petersburg. In 1880, ORT was established by Yvonne's father-in-law, the Baron Horace de Gunzburg, and other Jewish notables to promote manual trades and agriculture for Jews as part of the larger Jewish productivist movement.[75] In France, ORT had a small fundraising committee in the 1920s. However, in 1934, it transferred its headquarters from Berlin to Paris.[76] The Gunzbourg family continued its support of ORT in France throughout the 1930s and thereafter.

Thirty-two years after the creation of ORT, a group of Jewish doctors in St. Petersburg founded Obshtshestvo Zdravookraney Evrei (OZE) to address public health problems among the Jewish populations of the Russian Empire. Ten years later, in 1922, OZE was forced out of the Soviet Union and transferred its headquarters to Berlin. Like ORT, it created an umbrella organization in Berlin in 1923, the Union OSE, to coordinate its multiple branches in Eastern Europe. In 1933, the Union OSE fled Berlin, moving its headquarters to Paris and Geneva. While it had been raising funds in Paris since the early 1920s, the Union OSE officially set up a French branch in 1934.[77]

Under the patronage of the Baron and Baroness Pierre de Gunzbourg, the French section of OSE, as it was sometimes called, ran several clinics in Paris, caring for needy and disabled Jewish children.[78] It created a summer colony for children in June 1934 that moved to Montmorency, just north of Paris, and became a year-round institution in 1936.[79] By 1938, OSE had made inroads into French society, having obtained the support of Senator Justin Godart and other French public figures, while Yvonne de Gunzbourg presided over its ladies' auxiliary committee and financed its day center for disadvantaged children in Montmorency in 1935.[80] Nonetheless, OSE's leadership remained Eastern European, and, with one exception, consisted of male doctors.[81]

As in other Jewish organizations in France, the November pogrom caused OSE leaders to reevaluate their activism on behalf of Central European Jews. Yvonne de Gunzbourg took the lead and organized OSE's efforts to care for Austrian and German Jewish children in France. By the end of December 1938, she had raised 1 million francs and assembled a twenty-five-person committee, comprised of OSE's Russian-Polish leadership and prominent French personalities. The committee's goal was to provide "medical and educational care" as well as homes for Central European refugee children between the ages of three and seven years old. A special sub-committee, led by the well-known pediatrician Dr. Benjamin Weill-Hallé, oversaw its work.[82] In the end, the Gunzbourg couple bore a great deal of the costs of opening the homes. Austrian pedagogue Ernst Papanek, hired to run one of OSE's children's programs, noted in his memoirs the Baroness's initial grant of 40,000 francs, with the warning "you'll never get another penny out of me." Papanek recalled: "It was really very funny. The Baroness was an imposing woman, with hatchetlike [sic] features that she refused to make the slightest attempt to pretty over, and a warm, beautiful heart that she was always trying to hide."[83] His account suggests Yvonne de Gunzbourg had internalized the ambivalent views of her milieu toward Jewish philanthropy, seen by many as too restrictive. She "wanted us to understand that she was a completely assimilated Frenchwoman who wasn't giving us the money because the children were Jewish but only because they were children who happened to be in danger." According to Papanek, her resistance soon faded:

"Before the year was over, she had bought castles for us all over France at a cost of more than a million francs and was serving very actively as the chairman of our Board."[84]

Nonetheless, for all her generosity, neither the Baroness de Gunzbourg nor the OSE initially planned on organizing actual evacuations of children. Instead, their program was designed to care for refugee children once in France. By December 1938, the men of the Alliance had made it clear that negotiating to bring Jewish children to France would be their domain, exclusively.

~

Before closing, let us return to the question of the alliances, both horizontal and vertical, that developed to bring Jewish children to France. To what extent was the French Kindertransport an exclusively Jewish endeavor? To whom did French Jews turn for help? It is hard to say whether the feminist Louise Weiss—a woman with multiple religious backgrounds and a staunchly secular identity—was unconsciously playing out a well-established Jewish political tradition when she sought out a vertical alliance with the state in order to create the CRC.

One also sees Jewish women turning to one another for help, firmly anchored within Jewish circles. There is some evidence, however, that horizontal alliances between Jewish and non-Jewish individuals and organizations did exist. According to an article in the Jewish press, the French chapter of Save the Children International (Comité français de secours aux enfants) created a sponsorship program to send money and support to Jewish children in Central Europe, most likely in 1939, yet did not have a satisfactory number of sponsors.[85] Furthermore, long before its arrival in France, the Union OSE became affiliated with the international children's advocacy group Save the Children International. The OSE did not hesitate to turn to the international organization for help when efforts to evacuate Jewish children from Germany to France became complicated in February 1939.[86] After the outbreak of the war, in February 1940, the OSE asked Save the Children International to intercede directly with Nazi Germany and with neutral states for visas with the hope of evacuating all Jewish children from Nazi Germany, which it felt were in danger of "death from hunger and cold."[87] The organization's response was negative, judged unrealistic by its leadership.[88]

The archival documentation is unfortunately scarce, but it suggests that Jewish individuals and organizations in France did indeed turn to help from non-Jews, with limited results. However, with a few exceptions, the French Kindertransport scheme was a primarily Jewish affair. The question remained: if women started the process, would they also take the lead? Or would the established communal leaders—all men— take over?

CHAPTER 4

Centralization and Action

January–September 1939

I n early January 1939, Andrée Salomon boarded a train from Strasbourg to Paris with the hope of unifying the multiple initiatives to
evacuate Jewish children from Nazi territories. She was not the only person travelling. By the end of the same month, almost 500,000 Spanish
republican refugees had crossed the French border, looking for safety as
the Spanish Civil War drew to an end. Surely, some of these individuals
were the parents of the 10,000–15,000 children who had been granted
refuge in France during the conflict.[1] The unfolding Spanish refugee
crisis would serve as a critical lesson to French officials, providing them
with an easy justification for turning down requests to bring Jewish children to France. Yet in December and early January 1939, those working
on behalf of Jewish children were hopeful, and they launched an initiative to bring thousands of Jewish children to France.

Andrée Salomon was well aware of Germaine de Rothschild's efforts
on behalf of Central European children, but her sights were set on the
more established organization, the Alliance israélite universelle, with
the hope that its well-connected leaders might produce a better
outcome. The Alliance, established in Paris in 1860, had been working
since its origins to defend Jewish civil rights throughout the world.
Children were central to both its history and mission, since its creation
was sparked by the 1858 Mortara affair, the kidnapping by papal
authorities of a six-year-old Jewish child in Bologna who had been
secretly baptized by his nanny.[2] Frustrated and outraged by Jews'

50

inability to retrieve the child, a small group of French Jews founded the Alliance in 1860. In addition to its advocacy work, the organization developed a network of schools for Jewish children in the French colonial empire and the Levant, partaking actively in the French "civilizing mission."[3] Such schools, along with the Alliance's teacher training programs in Paris, created new educational and professional opportunities for girls and women, leading historians to laud its emancipatory role.[4]

This said, the Alliance's Parisian headquarters, where key decisions were made, was a masculine space. Only one woman served on the Alliance's central committee in the 1930s, which was otherwise comprised of men with strong ties to the state and civil society.[5] While its central committee members espoused a range of political beliefs and took variegated stances as individuals during the Central European refugee crisis, the Alliance avoided challenging state policies. Historians suggest that a leadership crisis, provoked by the death of several of its leaders in a short time span, clouded the Alliance's ability to act decisively. Catherine Nicault also sees deeper, political reasons for its inaction: "Disheartened by the growing influence of Zionism in the Jewish world, stubborn in its bias toward discretion, trapped in a traditional conception of its mission, the Alliance seemed to be struck by both a lack of vision and visibility."[6] Concerned about its diminishing status in Jewish affairs, the Alliance remained on the sidelines of the Central European refugee crisis throughout the 1930s.

Nonetheless, the November 1938 pogrom sparked a wave of concern among French Jews and their organizations, and the Alliance was no exception. It held an emergency meeting on November 12 and met again four days later, on November 16. It was at this meeting that Central Committee member Pierre Dreyfus, the son of Captain Alfred Dreyfus and a staunch advocate of Central European refugees in France, asked one of the Alliance's two vice-presidents, Georges Leven, to present a proposal that would lead the organization toward a more active role in the crisis.[7] Dreyfus suggested that the Alliance, along with the "Jewish community of Paris," request the entry of "several thousand" Jewish children to France, where they would be cared for until reaching the age of majority.[8] Dreyfus and Leven took pains to frame this initiative as beneficial to France when presenting it to their peers. Stressing the malleability of the children, they also mobilized older French tropes on the need to regenerate Jews into "useful" citizens by suggesting the opening of several rural centers for the children: "From these children we would make farmers, workers, and above all good Frenchmen who would increase the vital forces of France at a time when the birth rate is declining."[9] Dreyfus had already approached the Minister of Interior Albert Sarraut, as well as the Minister of Foreign Affairs Georges Bonnet for visas.[10] Alliance committee members expressed concern over the cost of the program, as well as the political stability of France. Some felt it might be wiser, in light of the impending conflict, to receive the children on a temporary basis and then redirect them to other countries. Nonetheless, taking pains to note that the Alliance would obtain permission from the proper French authorities,[11] the Alliance's Central Committee approved Dreyfus's proposition.

By December 7, Dreyfus's plan had become more concrete: the children would not be cared for in families. Instead, they would be sent to Jewish institutions, including the École Maïmonide in Paris, as well as the children's organization For Our Children (Pour Nos Enfants), which ran a children's summer camp in the seaside town of Berck Plage, as well as other vacation colonies.[12] The Rothschild Hospital made forty beds available for the children for medical screening upon arrival. Committee members questioned the length of the children's stay in France, as well as the challenge of caring for children from diverse social classes, and suggested that advice be sought from Jewish and non-Jewish organizations that had experience with children. Others suggested the Alliance contact its members in London and Amsterdam, since they, too, were setting up initiatives to evacuate Central European children.[13] Indeed, as seen in the previous chapter with Germaine de Rothschild in France and Dorothy de Rothschild in England, French Jews were quite aware of the efforts of Jews in other European countries on behalf of German and Austrian children. Their transnational vision, the result of overlapping social and kin networks, certainly influenced their decision to take action.

Perhaps most tellingly, Dreyfus proposed that the Alliance include in its efforts a "professional orientation center" that would study the labor market for the refugee children and other youth. While clearly inappropriate for young children, this idea shows to what extent larger discussions about refugee employability and national interests shaped the Alliance's initiative. On December 7, the Central Committee approved the funding for the project. On December 30, the Jewish press in France (and even in Austria) announced the establishment of the Alliance's Central Reception Bureau for Children (Bureau central d'accueil aux enfants).[14] The articles specified that the Bureau was created on November 16, 1938. In a display of its respect for the government, the Alliance most likely preferred to wait until Foreign Affairs Minister Georges Bonnet announced the creation of the CRC, which also appeared in the *Journal Officiel* on December 30.[15] As seen in the previous chapter, the creation of Bonnet's committee represented an important step in the refugee crisis, serving not only as a bridge between the state and the multiple associations involved with the care of refugees, but also as an ecumenical, pro-refugee force in an increasingly xenophobic moment.

Dreyfus's initiative was taking the Alliance into new, somewhat uncomfortable territory. The organization had a limited scope of action in metropolitan France and sought to maintain, as seen above, a neutral position toward the French government. Creating a professional orientation center for refugee children shows the Alliance's concern for national interests, and perhaps a somewhat outdated vision of children as economic actors. But gender seems also to have been an issue: even though the Alliance ran schools for children throughout the world, undertaking a large program for refugee children in metropolitan France represented a new initiative for the Alliance's exclusively male leadership. This is why committee leaders suggested that a "Ladies' Committee" be created to help run the Reception Bureau, all while specifying that the women's group should not be considered part of the Alliance.[16] Indeed, women were needed as helpers, but would have to be kept separate. The initiative to bring German and Austrian children was therefore asking a great deal of the Alliance's leadership: it threatened to complicate not only its relationship with the French government, but also the gendered order of French Jewish life.

Andrée Salomon's intervention before the Alliance's central committee on January 4, 1939 brought these tensions to a head. It started well enough, with Salomon thanking the Alliance on behalf of Alsatian Jews for its decision to intervene. Yet she quickly turned critical, alluding to "the concerns that the project's slow execution had raised among them. Mrs. Salomon insisted on the tragic situation of the children who must be saved from the national-socialist hell and expressed the wish that a close and daily collaboration among all men of good will and all the committees, with the hope that for the good of the children, they would surpass all the difficulties."[17] The committee put a swift end to her presentation: "The president thanked Mrs. Salomon [. . .] and asked her to assure Alsatian Jewry of the Alliance's willingness to do everything possible for the benefit of Jewish children in Germany."[18]

After Salomon's short intervention, the committee went on to discuss its plan to bring children to France in minute detail. She was not allowed to stay for this part of the meeting, despite her proven experience in this work.[19] Expecting a collaboration, she was instead told that the Alliance was "doing everything possible."[20] This encounter left her with a bitter recollection. After the war, she described how Rabbi Maurice Liber, a member of the Alliance's central committee, "immediately destroyed the case by saying: 'It does not interest us, it is a private matter, it does not concern us, it does not concern the Alliance.' This could have become a very good thing, carried out in a much more effective way if these gentlemen had understood; but only two or three understood."[21] Contrary to her recollection, however, Rabbi Liber was not at the meeting, leading historians Katy Hazan and Georges Weill to conclude that this exchange may have occurred with Head Rabbi of Paris Julien Weill, who was indeed present and who had shocked French Jews just several weeks earlier by accepting an interview in the extreme right daily *Le Matin* in the aftermath of the November pogrom. While his words were most likely twisted by the editors, the rabbi's message was two-fold: France could not receive any more refugees, and peace with Germany should take priority over Jewish needs.[22] Salomon may have had an exchange with Liber at a different moment during her trip and incorrectly situated this declaration at the Alliance board meeting. Yet also underlying Salomon's expedited (and unsatisfactory) reception was the fact that she transgressed a gendered boundary: not only was Salomon the only woman to attend a central committee meeting in the entire 1937–1939 period, she also expressed criticism over their slow reaction.[23]

Had Salomon been able to stay, she would have learned that the Alliance leadership wasn't quite satisfied with the direction their program was taking. Already in late December, it had become clear that Pierre Dreyfus's goal of bringing thousands of children was unrealistic. Foreign Affairs Minister Georges Bonnet had indeed agreed to provide 5,000 entry visas. However, his counterpart, Minister of the Interior Albert Sarraut, was "categorically refus[ing] to let German children enter France, motivating this refusal by the bad experience with Spanish children and the fear of seeing the parents who remained in Germany follow one day."[24] By early January, it was becoming clear that Bonnet would not grant collective visas for children, but only "for those individual cases on which a broad investigation will have been conducted beforehand."[25] Morris Troper, the representative of the American JDC in Paris, was also privy to the negotiations, and he commented in late January on the negative results with some bitterness:

> In the meantime I understand permission has been granted to bring in 500 Spanish children and it is of importance to point out that the whole children's situation and the German and Austrian refugee situation in general is today sadly influenced by events in Spain. It is anticipated almost daily that hordes of Spanish refugees may come over the Western frontier and this will certainly create a serious condition in France, and one from which the refugees from Germany will suffer.[26]

Observing the concomitant political crises in Spain and Germany, Jewish leaders in France noted their impotence.

There was one initiative, however, that was making some minor inroads. In December 1938, Minister of the Interior Sarraut granted Germaine de Rothschild visas for fifty children under her personal guarantee, on an exceptional basis.[27] In early January, Alliance committee member Jacques Sée suggested that the Baroness might create an embarrassing situation by engaging in "an area of action in which the Alliance was already involved."[28]

Nonetheless, he noted (and not without rhetorical prowess) that this would relieve the Alliance of the financial burden of such a program: "Assigning the upkeep of the children to the members of the Rothschild family means finding an important guarantee of which we should be proud."[29] Jacques Helbronner, one of the most conservative French Jewish leaders and a personal friend of Foreign Affairs Minister Georges Bonnet,[30] was also present at the meeting. He explained that Bonnet, inspired by former prime minister Lord Baldwin in England, had decided to establish a French Committee to bring Jewish children to France. He was referring, of course, to the CRC, the organization established at the urging of Louise Weiss, of which he was a member. According to Helbronner, Germaine de Rothschild would wait until Bonnet publicly announced his committee before officially constituting her own.[31] Helbronner therefore seconded Sée, suggesting "in the interest of the children themselves, the Alliance should make the gesture of entrusting [confier] to the Baroness de Rothschild the task she has started. [. . .] The Alliance will be associated with the new Committee and will continue to benefit from her initiative."[32] Helbronner and Sée's arguments held sway, and the Alliance decided to withdraw from its own initiative in favor of Germaine de Rothschild's committee. Exit Alliance, enter Baroness.

Foreign Affairs Minister Georges Bonnet and Louise Weiss held the first meeting of the CRC on January 14, 1939, after which the Baroness announced the creation of her Comité israélite pour les enfants venant d'Allemagne et d'Europe centrale (Jewish Committee for Children from Germany and Central Europe, CIE).[33] The CIE leadership included Germaine de Rothschild as president, as well as the Alliance's Pierre Dreyfus and Claude de Rothschild (née Dupont) as vice-presidents, French feminist and member of the ministry of public health Susanne Schreiber-Crémieux as general secretary, and the Baroness's son, Guy de Rothschild, as treasurer.[34] Once established, Jewish communal organizations put their weight behind the CIE: the word of the moment was centralization. In late January, the Alliance reported in the Jewish press that the CIE would take over its initiative.[35] American JDC representatives also noted that the Baroness was at the head of the "Reception Bureau for Children," which it considered the "central institution for dealing with the government on questions relating to the reception of children in France."[36] The JDC provided a one-time grant of $5,000 to help cover the costs of bringing the children to France and setting up homes for them.[37]

~

It is no small irony of history that the fight to bring Jewish children to France established its headquarters at 38 Rue Mont Thabor, Paris. While the name of the street refers to the Napoleonic battle of 1799, it also harkens back to the one waged by the prophetess Deborah against the Canaanites in the Book of Judges. In the late nineteenth century, the same location had served as the place from which the notorious antisemite Marquis de Morès published his defamatory pamphlet 'Rothschild, Ravachol et Cie' in 1892. After his death, the Rothschilds may have acquired his property as a form of retroactive vengeance.[38]

The small staff that ran the CIE office, open initially in the mornings, three days a week, was most likely unaware of their symbolically charged location.[39] The Baroness employed a thirty-year-old Jewish lawyer, Robert Jablonski (changed later to Jablon), to run its operations. Jablonski was actually born in Paris to German Jewish parents in 1909, but he had to return to Germany as a result of the First World War. After 1933, he joined the left-wing anti-Nazi coalition Neu Beginnen. He fled Germany in 1935 for Prague and arrived in France in March 1936. With his legal training and experience in international patent law, as well as his fluency in German and French, Jablonski had the skill set needed to navigate the complex bureaucracy involved in bringing unaccompanied children across borders.[40] Nonetheless, as a recent refugee himself, Jablonski was in a precarious situation. During this period, he was trying, initially without success, to retrieve his French nationality. Not only was he considered a foreigner and most likely spoke French with an accent, he also lacked contacts in official circles.[41] Although Pierre Dreyfus and Suzanne Schreiber-Crémieux helped him obtain meetings with French officials, Jablonski's own refugee status certainly didn't help the cause of the children.[42]

The archives of both the CIE and the CRC, most likely looted by the Germans or destroyed, have not been located.[43] However, the scarce archival evidence does show the two groups working hand in hand on behalf of children.[44] The CIE paperwork had both committees' names on it, for example, yet they remained independent and seem to have led parallel negotiations with the French authorities.[45] Robert Jablonski recalls negotiating with Minister of the Interior Sarraut and the director of the foreigners' police (*police des étrangers*) Yves Fourcade on behalf of the CIE as he set out to obtain a legal status for the children that would grant the CIE parental authority in case of war.[46] At the same time, a note written by Louise Weiss, dated January 24, 1939, shows her own repeated attempts to pressure Bonnet: "Last Friday, January 20, I tried in vain to get an appointment with Bonnet. The bailiffs, witnessing my distress, promised me to contact him. They called me to say that I must contact him on Saturday morning at 9:30 am by telephone. On Saturday I followed through, but did not obtain an answer. I telephoned the bailiffs again who, because of their fondness for me, told me to hurry." She finally did see Bonnet but "found a man absolutely undecided who did not want to decide, nor to entrust the decisions to LEGER [Alexis Léger, general secretary of the Ministry of Foreign Affairs], and from whom I managed to get an appointment for Wednesday 25, at 4pm." A chain of communication emerges here, based on social networks: Germaine de Rothschild via Helbronner contacts Weiss, who in turn dealt with Bonnet: "On Monday morning, given the urgency of the situation and the desperate phone calls I received from the Baroness de Rothschild, through the intermediary of Jacques Helbronner, I decided to start again. Here is the note I sent to M.G. Bonnet."[47]

Inserted in Weiss's papers, on the same page, was a hand-written note, most likely the one to which she referred: "My dear Minister, I beg you to consider the fact that there are 1200 beds here to receive children who are dying because of a decision that would take you but one minute. Since you will not be making your speech until Thursday, could you please settle the outstanding issues at the end of the intergovernmental conference with [Henry] Bérenger this afternoon."[48]

Weiss's January 24 note concludes, "He gave me a response: 'Find a solution with LEGER, while 3 days before he did not want me to find a solution with LEGER.'"[49] She must have been effective, because several days after her intervention, on January 31, 1939, the CIE obtained visas for 200 children.[50]

Weiss may have fought for the reception of the children, but she remained extremely critical of the Rothschild family, including Germaine de Rothschild. Between the lines of her notes, one can read class and political tensions but also, perhaps, some ambivalent feelings about Judaism, as she twists the Baroness's desire to respect the children's religious identities into a more sinister accusation: "You get the impression that refugee relief is their [the Rothschild's] big toy—nobody is allowed to touch it," she wrote. "No one will be helped or rescued without one. Baroness Edouard—very queen in Israel [*très reine en Israël*]—wants the refugee children to continue to be brought up in the Jewish religion. Whether consciously or not, she wants to extend her kingdom and continue to be the undisputed queen of her subjects."[51]

With 200 visas secured, the selection of the children could begin.[52] Jablonski was in contact with the youth emigration departments of the German and Austrian Jewish institutions, Reichsvertretung der Juden in Deutschland and the Israelitische Kultusgemeinde, which centralized the increasing number of Kindertransport requests in Central Europe.[53] Eligibility for the transports was based on religion, age, and health. Trude Frankl, a Vienna-based social worker, noted in her April 1939 report that the CIE defined "Jewish" loosely and did not distinguish between children who were partially Jewish, without a declared confession, or non-Aryan Christians.[54] To come to France, the children had to be under the age of fifteen, yet there was a preference for those who were fourteen and under. In both Germany and Austria, the children went through extensive medical exams to screen out those with disabilities or illness. Children in collective Jewish institutions, such as orphanages, were given priority, as were stateless children or those who had been left on their own due to the arrest or expulsion of their parents.[55]

Descriptions of children, sent to France in early January, were clearly written to convince the French committee of the children's merit and incite pity. One read: "Born in 1925 in Vienna, stateless, the child has been in the orphanage for the past six years. She is very nice, intelligent and remarkably lively for her age. Her father was a clerk, yet he passed away years ago. The mother [. . .] lives in great poverty."[56] Such descriptions are not numerous in the archives, however, suggesting that German and Austrian aid workers took over the selection process.

As seen above, unaccompanied children began arriving in France in groups as early as December 1938. The children sponsored by the CIE began arriving in March 1939. Archival records are scarce, leaving a great deal of uncertainty surrounding the figures, especially regarding those who came independently (and not on an organized transport).[57] After years of extensive research, I found only the transports lists from Vienna, but not those from the other cities. Cobbling together multiple sources on the Kindertransport children in France, my nominative database currently includes 292 children.[58] A 1939 report of the CRC states it obtained 418 visas for children.[59] While it is impossible to know exactly how many unaccompanied Jewish children migrated to France on the eve of the war, it is possible to estimate that between 400 and 500 came under official auspices in groups or were provided visas through the CIE once in France.[60] Indeed, in April 1939, the French government temporarily halted all group transports.[61] In response, the CIE worked to obtain visas for children with relatives in France who were willing to sponsor them. Thanks to Andrée Salomon, a collaboration was set up in April 1939 with a Jewish summer camp in Schirmeck, 50 kilometers west of Strasbourg, where some children were able to spend the summer months of 1939.[62]

The centralization of the Kindertransport through the CIE allowed for greater coordination. Andrée Salomon continued to oversee the arrivals of children in Alsace and Lorraine, while working closely with Parisian committees. Her passport suggests she went to Germany in January, April, and twice in July 1939 to pick up children.[63] The growing sense of urgency caused the Central Fund for the East to expand throughout Eastern France. By May 1939, there were 120 communities affiliated with the organization, with branches in Strasbourg, Mulhouse, Dijon, Troyes, Metz, Colmar, Nancy, Épinal, and Besançon.[64] By late July 1939, *La Tribune Juive* reported that the Central Fund for the East was caring for ninety refugee children.[65] Salomon mentions her close collaboration with OSE during this period, noting that the Lower Rhin prefecture was extremely strict. When a refugee child could not obtain legal status in Strasbourg, Salomon would send the child to OSE in Paris.[66]

In addition to caring for refugee children in their homes and children's institutions, Alsatian and Lorraine Jews served as impromptu welcome committees for the youth from Austria and Germany who passed through Strasbourg or Metz in spring 1939. Accounts published in *La Tribune Juive* emphasize the last-minute nature of these encounters and the sense of excitement they brought. Between the lines, one notes their conviction that, through a warm reception, French Jews could ease the children's pain. When a group of fifty children passed through Metz in March 1939, the paper proudly reported: "Although informed only an hour before the convoy's arrival, the leaders of the Central Fund and the Ladies' society were in position and waiting on the platform. The 50 children, aged 9 to 13, were taken to the station buffet where they were served a hot drink. Then they got acquainted with the old city of Metz, during a walk through the city." The article also presented the unrealistic hope that a family's love could somehow be substituted: "The youngest ones were happy to be in a country as hospitable as ours, where thoughts can be expressed freely. The older ones, looking sad and serious, were aware of their new situation which, although better than on the other side of the Rhine, nonetheless tears them away from their families in which they found the tenderness that they will miss, but that our co-religionists try their best to replace."[67]

In April 1939, a group of seventy-two Czech youth on their way to Palestine came through Strasbourg on the second day of Passover and found a similar welcome. According to the *Tribune Juive*, forty young Jews from Strasbourg, who had learned about the transport the night before, showed up to greet them at the station early in the morning, providing the refugees with ample Matzah, baked goods and fruit for the holiday.[68] One individual wrote to complain to the editor, asking why the transports were so poorly organized that they forced young people to travel on the Jewish holiday.[69] Nonetheless, such accounts show French Jews' pride in being able to do something concrete to help the victims of Nazism.

~

The hold on collective transports was eventually lifted, at least for one last group. On July 4, 1939, a transport of forty boys from Berlin, primarily from the Auerbach Jewish orphanage, arrived in Paris. At this point, it is quite possible that neither the OSE homes nor Germaine de

Rothschild's Château de la Guette, which we will soon discover, had enough space to receive more children. A solution was found by placing the children under the auspices of a non-Jewish organization, the Aid Committee for Refugee Children (Comité de secours aux enfants réfugiés).[70] The committee was headed by the Protestant Count Hubert Conquéré de Monbrison and his mistress, the Russian Princess Irène Paley, who operated a boarding school for young Russian girls in the town of Quincy-sous-Sénart, about 50 kilometers outside of Paris. The Count, however, was married to Renée Cahen d'Anvers, a member of a prominent Jewish family.[71] Renée de Monbrison converted to Protestantism and espoused her husband's commitment to social Christianity, becoming a leader in the efforts to bring Spanish children to France during the civil war. The Monbrisons' activism led the Princess Irène Paley to accept fifteen Spanish refugee girls in her Russian boarding school in 1937, to the shock of the staunchly anti-communist Russian exile community.[72] In July 1939, the arrival of forty Jewish boys from Berlin represented yet another group of refugee children under the care of the Count and the Princess's organization.

What factors allowed for a group of Jewish children to be assigned to the care of a non-Jewish organization? In spite of years of searching, I have not found more than a few archival traces on this group. Oral history interviews filled in some blanks, as did some sheer luck in seemingly unrelated archives, which provided a crucial hint.[73] Nonetheless, while I can advance several hypotheses, there is no way of knowing what really transpired.

What can be said with certainty: in 1939–1940, the Countess Renée de Monbrison was serving as general secretary of the Commission to aid Spanish refugee children in France (Commission d'aide aux enfants espagnols réfugiés en France), whose headquarters was at the same location as Bonnet and Weiss's CRC, on 102 rue de l'Université, in Paris.[74] This is certainly not a coincidence: "shared affinities," both personal and political, had long united Jews and Protestants in France, and, as seen here, merit even greater study.[75] It is quite possible that Renée de Monbrison and Louise Weiss, who could both claim Jewish and Protestant identities, knew one another and had exchanged about their work on behalf of refugees in their organizations' respective headquarters. On May 1, 1939, Countess Renée de Monbrison represented Christian and secular organizations at a meeting held by the Jewish Coordination Group (Groupement de Coordination), designed to unite the diverse efforts for refugees.[76]

Yet there are other connections, in fact, so many that one starts to see the contours of an elite Protestant–Jewish circle. Hubert de Monbrison's first wife, Marguerite Léonino, was the niece of Baron Robert de Rothschild, a major figure in the Central European refugee crisis. Furthermore, Monbrison was an avid polo player, having played for France in the 1924 Olympic games, and attended the same polo club as Robert de Rothschild. The Monbrison family was also very close friends with its pediatrician, Gaston Lévy, who became quite active in the OSE during the occupation. According to the Count's son, Christian de Monbrison, the Lévys were so close to the Monbrison family that they offered their tickets to the United States to the Count's two eldest sons in the early phases of the occupation.[77]

Finally, the Count somehow knew and sought advice from Dr. Hanna Eisfelder-Grunewald, a recent Jewish refugee from Berlin who established a clinic for German refugee children in Paris, Medical Assistance for Refugee Children (Assistance médicale aux enfants de réfugiés).[78] Eisfelder managed to secure funding from an impressive set of international organizations for her clinic and to send groups of refugee children from Paris to Switzerland for the summer, including Save the Children International, the British Save the Children Fund and the Swiss organization SHEK (Schweizer Hilfswerk für Emigrantenkinder). These groups may have turned to Eisfelder when the possibility of sending the forty boys to France arose, and since many were prominent Protestants in their respective countries, they may have connected her to Monbrison, who was active in both pacifist and Protestant circles. Finally, it is also quite possible (and perhaps most likely) that Eisfelder, having attended and worked in a Berlin Jewish orphanage in her youth, initiated the transport herself through her own contacts.[79] There are therefore many ways that the Count and Countess de Monbrison, as well as the Princess Irène Paley, may have heard about the Jewish children's transports and been incited to offer their hospitality.

The gaps in the archives leave many questions, yet one can nonetheless find visual proof that the children arrived in France. The Count was an amateur cinematographer and filmed them as they hopped off the bus at his Château in Quincy-sous-Sénart.[80] This transport, most likely the last Kindertransport to France, shows a rare moment of overlap between the Spanish and Central European refugee crises, establishing what was, to my knowledge, the only case of a non-Jewish organization caring for Central European Jewish children in France in the period preceding the Second World War. At the same time, it is quite possible, in light of the behind-the-scenes role played by Renée de Monbrison, that the non-Jewish nature of the committee was barely noticed by French Jews.[81] Even though she had converted to Protestantism, she may have remained Jewish in the eyes of the other Jews and their organizations, and she was certainly strongly connected to her Jewish family.

Writing a social history of the Kindertransport to France is complicated by the plunder and loss of archives in France during the Second World War and its aftermath. In light of the gaps in our knowledge, we can still apprehend its general contours and significance. When compared to England's large-scale Kindertransport scheme, or the French efforts to take in Spanish child refugees, which triggered a strong response from disparate factions of French society, including workers, Catholic clergy, and society women, the French efforts to evacuate Jewish children from Central Europe appear extremely modest.[82] Most likely, fewer than 500 unaccompanied Jewish children were brought to France between December 1938 and September 1939, although it is possible that more came illegally or informally, through family contacts or alone.

It is important to question why the French Kindertransport scheme was limited in scope. It appears that in the eyes of contemporaries, the Nazi persecutions of Jews in the 1933–1938 period simply could not be compared to the bombings and murders of civilian children during the Spanish Civil War. Jewish and "non-Aryan" children in Germany simply did not spark the broad base of support in French civil society that the Spanish refugee children inspired. Even French Jews refrained from mobilizing until the 1938 November pogrom. Only two non-Jewish committees, the CRC and the Aid Committee for Refugee Children, helped bring Jewish children to France, although others may have assisted. Finally, the conjuncture with the end of the Spanish Civil War must be noted. The upheaval provoked by the arrival of 400,000–500,000 Spanish refugees in early 1939 provided French authorities with the perfect excuse to refuse Jewish initiatives.

The meager French Kindertransport program can also be explained by factors within French Jewish communal organizations. Faced with a leadership crisis, and concerned about the cost of such an initiative and its relationship to the state, the Alliance in France chose to sit on the sidelines, contrary to its branches in other European countries, such as the Netherlands and Belgium, which actively sought to bring children to their countries. Gender, while not the only factor, also proved decisive. As seen in this and the previous chapter, women, in their caretaking capacities, became central figures in the fight to evacuate children to France. This advocacy role nudged women into new roles in French Jewish life, challenging the strictly male communal hierarchy. As seen in the decision to entrust the initiative to Germaine de Rothschild's CIE or Salomon's initiatives through the Central Fund for the East, French Jewish leaders put their faith in women. However, this simply reflected, and did not challenge, the deeply seated cultural notions that bound women to children. While the Alliance was in the business of educating Jewish youth outside of France, it is quite possible that its central committee did not know how it would handle large groups of young children in Paris. The Alliance's decision to renege on its leadership role proved decisive. Andrée Salomon cast judgement in a 1965 oral history interview: "If this action had been in the hands of the Alliance israélite, it could have led to a Jewish policy that was directed in a different way, instead of the personal initiative led by Baroness Edouard de Rothschild, who could only, based on the way she worked, follow very closely the prohibitions of the police and the very small openings of authorizations."[83] Instead of the well-connected leaders of the Alliance, it was Louise Weiss and a talented yet young German refugee, Robert Jablonski, who ended up leading the negotiations for visas. An equally young Andrée Salomon, while fiercely determined, failed to convince the Alliance to organize a large-scale evacuation.

The significance of French Kindertransport lies not in the number of children sent, but elsewhere, for it allows us to observe the lives of a small group of refugee youth in a rapidly changing political situation. As we will see next, some desperate parents were unable to find a place for their children on a Kindertransport and turned to distant family for help.

CHAPTER 5

Ruth

Crossing the Border Alone

From her dining room table in California, eighty-eight-year-old Ruth[1] began our interview by discussing her family, which was forced apart just days before her tenth birthday. In late October 1938, her father, along with 18,000 other Jews of Polish nationality, was expelled from Germany to Poland as part of the Nazi scheme to "repatriate" Polish Jews.[2] According to Ruth, her father was highly respected in their neighborhood, to the extent that when the police came to arrest him they "apologized to him because they liked him so much."[3] Looking closely at Ruth's family shows its agency in a context of forced migrations. Indeed, states and organizations may have initiated the Kindertransport, but families made the decision to send their children abroad, often as part of larger strategies to flee persecution. In Ruth's case, the family sent two of their children to France illegally, without visas.

Ruth's family placed a great deal of importance on the study of the Torah and the Talmud.[4] Reflecting on her father's orthodoxy helped Ruth situate herself among her six siblings: "He [my father] was a great student of Rashi, and he had these unbelievably beautiful books, really big books. [. . .] And he loved them. He taught this to our brothers. Every week they had to come and study Torah with him and also Talmud. And the girls were not particularly . . . they didn't need to do that, but the boys did. They really didn't like it very much, but they did it. And one day when I was sitting in on it [the lesson], he did let me sit in on it—I was very close to my dad—I knew the answer to a question that he asked them, because we had just learned it in school. And he said: 'Look, your little sister knows the answers and you don't even know the answer.' I think it was one of the proudest moments of my life at the time."[5] Studying Jewish texts provided Ruth with an opportunity to connect with her father and, in turn, find a place in her large family. Her gratitude to him, as well as her sense of loss, are palpable to this day.

Ruth attributes a certain prescience to her father, who went to France in 1932, where his brother was living, to explore the idea of moving the family there:

> When he went to France, it didn't work out apparently, because of the seven children. I don't know if it was because his brother didn't want him to come there and have the burden of having to take care of a family with seven kids. I don't know. I was too young to know. But anyway, he did send all of his Talmuds [sic] there because it was important to get them out of Germany. That's how much he loved his religion, and he lived his life according to religion.[6]

The many volumes of the family's Talmud were sent to France for safe keeping. After the father's expulsion from Germany in October 1938, Ruth's mother considered doing the same for her children. After the November 1938 pogrom, the family was forced to move from their home into a cramped apartment. Soon thereafter, Ruth's mother arranged for her twelve-year-old daughter Miriam and a niece to cross illegally into France, where their uncle lived. However, when the girls reached the border, they didn't see him. They panicked and returned home.

In March 1939, a new opportunity to send the children to France arose.[7] Mrs. S., the wife of a French orthodox rabbi, came to Germany to visit her own father. The S. family was related to Ruth's family through marriage, which led Mrs. S. to pay them a visit. "I know she came to visit my mother," Ruth explained. "And my mother at that time begged her to please take her children to France with her and send them to my uncle. So, she said, well, she couldn't take the chance of taking all of us, but she would take two of them [sic]. Because she had four children of her own, and she would take us as her children."

At the time, children traveled on their parents' passports, which allowed for Mrs. S. to consider substituting her own children with those of Ruth's family. This was not an isolated case: while it is impossible to know how many mothers used their passports to bring Central European Jewish children to France, the practice was widespread enough to be noted in postwar accounts.[8] Ruth continued:

> She was wondering, you know, who would fit the bill on the passport. She had twins who were seven, a daughter who was nine, and a son who was twelve, almost Bar Mitzvah age. And at first it was going to be my brother and myself, I don't know why. I was always the one who was going to go. And my little sister was only six, so my mother wouldn't have sent her. And she would have been too young, I think, anyway, for any of her children. But then my mother said she really wants my brother to stay there. [. . .] So, it was decided that Miriam and I would go. This was on a Thursday. We were leaving on Sunday. So, I didn't go back to school on Friday because my mother was worried that I would tell everybody I was going to go, which I probably wouldn't have.

Both the past and the present are embedded in Ruth's description of leaving Germany for France, as she oscillates between how she felt as a child and her adult reading of the events:

> I think kids are really, they know, they just *know*. I mean I wasn't that young. I was ten years old. At ten you're pretty sophisticated already. If not sophisticated, you have good instincts. [. . .] The only thing that she taught us was *je m'appelle Charlotte* [my name is Charlotte]. I was Charlotte. Miriam was Suzanne. We went at night so . . . she thought it would be better. We went through Belgium because they said those borders are easier. And we were in a compartment, and she said for us to lie down. Miriam was tall for her age. She was twelve at the time and really did look like a young lady. And

I was supposed to lie on her legs so they wouldn't see how tall she was, you know, at the borders. [. . .]

My mother took us to the train station, but she didn't come to the train itself. And Miriam was quite hysterical when she was leaving, I guess because she remembered what had happened the last time when she was at the border. I'm not sure. And also saying goodbye to my mother. And she's more emotional, I think, than I am. [. . .] Madame S. said, "if somebody comes into the compartment, just act like you're asleep." So I did wake up, but I acted like I was asleep. And I'm sure we couldn't have passed if he would've asked us "what's your name?" Would I have understood? No. So anyway, it worked. We made it into France.[9]

Through the eyes of Ruth and other children, the following chapters will explore how Jewish children experienced flight from Nazi persecution and exile in France and how they adapted to their new settings. How did families maintain ties after separation and to what extent did children form new networks, or surrogate families, in exile? We will also consider the complexities of caring for the children and the role their caretakers played in the lives of the children.

Ruth's account provides an entry point, illustrating some of the profound reconfigurations experienced by Jewish families that resulted from Nazi persecution. First and foremost, the consequences of persecution were not contained behind borders; they were felt transnationally. As persecution scattered families in Central (and later Western) Europe, a new and at times unbearable weight was placed on extended family members, some of whom had emigrated long before the rise of Nazism. Indeed, as anthropologist Jonathan Boyarin points out: "the family as a conceptual unit has become smaller, more private, more of an affective unit and less of an economic unit, at least in the West, over the past few centuries. A more dramatic way to put this is that the rich ties, practical and affective, that characterized members of extended families across generations and through successive 'levels' of cousinship in earlier times have fundamentally broken down, in Jewish as in other lifeworlds."[10] In Ruth's case, after her father's expulsion to Poland, the family obtained help from its farthest extremities—relatives through marriage—placing an unprecedented burden on bonds that, even in the best of times, can prove superficial and weak. Nonetheless, sociologists have argued that there can be a great deal of strength in weak bonds; acquaintances or distant family can provide access to new information and real solutions to vital problems.[11] Such weak bonds provided needed affidavits for immigration to the United States and, as seen with Ruth and Miriam, the creative use of a French passport.

Distant relatives were sometimes expected to act as replacement families for displaced kin, especially children. Often, though, they were unable or unwilling to withstand the considerable and very real responsibilities of caring for distant family. Many of the children in this study expressed, as adults, a profound disappointment at the failure of these weak bonds to transform into affective and durable ones. Six-year-old Benjamin Hirsch, for example, was sent to France with his older siblings from Frankfurt in December 1938. After his placement with his uncle fell through, he was sent to a stranger's home on his own, while his four older siblings were dispatched, two by two, to other relatives. Benjamin would later briefly reunite with his siblings in an OSE children's home, yet he experienced most of his time in France alone.[12] As we will soon see, Ruth experienced a similar fate.

Children and parents maintained their relationships, albeit deeply transformed as a result of the distance. As Deborah Dwork and Robert Jan van Pelt put it, "loved ones become letters."[13] In addition to writing home, children devised creative ways of getting their letters to Germany after postal service became less reliable. Others followed their parents' advice to keep diaries: "It was Mutti, who had herself kept a journal of my childhood from the day I was born, who made the suggestion, relayed by Papa, that I keep a diary," wrote Ernest Stock, who left Frankfurt for Strasbourg at age fourteen with his younger sister, Lotte, in December 1938. Stock's diary writing was a method for coping with separation, allowing him to project into a future in which he could tell his parents about their time spent apart: "Mutti's purpose in asking me to keep a diary was to let her and Papa later share our experiences during the separation, which she was sure would soon come to an end."[14] Diary writing, at least for the Stocks, had long been a family affair, reflecting German bourgeois women's writing practices.[15] As seen above, Stock's mother,

Julie, had recorded her son's daily life since his birth. On his wedding day, she presented her son's wife with the diary. Stock later published his and his mother's diaries side by side in a common volume, in their native German.[16] Few parents lived to reunite with their children, making the Stock's parallel documentation of their separation appear quite unique, when in fact this practice may have been more widespread.

Sources generated by children, both contemporaneous and retrospective, present a unique set of challenges. Nicholas Stargardt has explored the difficulties of capturing children's experiences through their wartime sources, including letters, diaries, autograph books, and drawings. Yet children under a certain age, approximately ten, did not produce written sources, nor did they all have access to writing materials.[17] Likewise, as Boaz Cohen and Rita Horváth convincingly argue, "Holocaust testimonies were not given in a vacuum."[18] They note that children's testimonies emerged only under specific conditions, usually at the prompting of adults. Such conditions require analysis in their own right.

We will also see that children influenced each other's writing practices. Indeed, while often assumed to be an intimate, individual experience, diary writing was at times a collective activity in Jewish children's homes. One particularly gifted twelve-year-old from Vienna, Paul Peter Porges, who later became a well-known cartoonist, illustrated his friend Heinz Löw's diary, capturing in great detail Heinz's painful separation from his grandmother. Others wrote in their diaries simultaneously, as shown by the diary of twelve-year-old Susi Hilsenrath, who mentioned, in July 1941: "Just now I am sitting with three, Helga, Edith and I, and all of us are writing in our diary. We just spoke about the diaries and when we can show them. Maybe when we are grown up. Maybe. Maybe I will show it to my 15-year-old daughter."[19] Fellow refugee children clearly sparked one another's desire to document their lives. As one older teen, Ursula Matzdorff, wrote on November 19, 1942, just after escaping France for Switzerland: "It's a new fad to have a diary and I'm going to try too. I'm going to try to tell all of the outcomes and impressions of these last months, since really, they are worth telling."[20]

72

Children's contemporaneous sources provide, in the words of Alexandra Garbarini, "near-sighted vision," reflecting the emotions and the scope of possibilities perceived by their young authors as events unfolded. They are strikingly different from their later retrospective sources, produced in the aftermath of the Holocaust, which offer "far-sighted vision" of the same events.[21] Oral history interviews, as well as unpublished and published writings, revisit events, which take on new meaning in light of the older author's knowledge of the Holocaust and distance from the events. They also benefit from the lapse of time: secrets too shocking to reveal at the time do not burn as ardently fifty years later. For each period and place under discussion here, I try to juxtapose contemporaneous and retrospective perspectives. However, for reasons that merit some discussion, certain places are over-represented in contemporaneous sources, while others are discussed more in retrospective sources, leaving me at times fully dependent upon one type of source, at times produced exclusively by one gender. For example, I located six diaries kept by Central European Jewish refugee children in France during the period under study, in addition to a collective diary written in an OSE children's home, correspondence between several children and their parents, and children's writings, produced during the war or immediately afterwards, as well as short autobiographies and newspaper articles.

While these materials reflect the experiences of children in several homes, the Château de la Guette, which became home to the least religious Kindertransport children primarily over the age of ten, looms large in my sources with four of the six diaries having been written by its wards.[22] Interestingly, diary writing was not a gendered activity at the Château de la Guette: two were written by boys and two by girls. Most parent–child correspondence is also from the collection on La Guette, as are the children's autobiographies and their newspapers. As we will see, the age of the children and the distinct pedagogy in the home can help explain this overrepresentation. Of equal importance is the memory work done by one former La Guette child, Werner Matzdorff. The latter was ineligible for the transports for the United States and thus remained in France after the deportations of Jewish children began. In August 1942, he and two other La Guette children were arrested and sent to Le Vénissieux internment camp. With the help of their teachers and other members of the Resistance, they were evacuated from the camp, just barely escaping deportation.[23] Was it Matzdorff's close brush with deportation that fueled his memory work? He began reaching out to other La Guette children in the mid-1980s with the goal of gathering information for a historical study, building on their transnational efforts to reunite.[24] His collection was instrumental for the 1990 documentary by Andrea Morgenthaler, *Le Voyage des Enfants de la Guette*, as well as the publication of *Les enfants de La Guette*, a short book on the home and its young inhabitants.[25]

Younger children, as well as those from religious families, were sent to homes run by the OSE. These children may have written less due to their younger ages, even if their educators encouraged the practice of writing to parents.[26] It would be presumptuous to draw broader conclusions on writing practices and pedagogy in the homes based on my archival findings, yet it is nonetheless interesting to note that several individuals from this group discussed their autograph or memory books with me, rather than diaries. Keeping such books may have been a gendered practice: now grown women, four former children, including two from OSE's home for orthodox children in Eaubonne, spoke to me about their autograph books. These objects remain intimate and active memorial documents. One book, shared by two sisters during the war, is now in the possession of one of the sister's daughters. While I asked multiple times if I could photograph it for use in this study, I stopped insisting when I came to understand that this document was simply too personal to share. Another woman's book had been given to her by an older teen in her home. She kept it in her nightstand drawer for years, until losing it in a move.[27] Still another child's autograph book was found in the ceiling of a police station in France in the 1990s, along with a trove of her family's papers, having been stashed there by a member of the family after their arrest in August 1942. The entire family was deported and murdered in Auschwitz.[28] Only one person shared her memory book with me: Elfriede Meyer. As seen above, it contains poems, rhymes, and advice provided by fellow children, as well as notes from educators. In addition to autograph books, a collective diary was produced in an OSE home in 1941 as a pedagogical project to commemorate the two-year anniversary of the home.[29]

Furthermore, several OSE children wrote about their experiences in children's homes soon after arriving in the United States, during the war or in its direct wake, perhaps for school assignments or with the hope of publication.[30] These documents show us what Jewish children were thinking and feeling during the war years—what they longed for and expected.

Retrospective sources on the war years must be read in light of the rise of Holocaust consciousness and the memory work it sparked. By the late 1970s, many of the former children were seeking to rekindle old networks and establish new ones in order to commemorate their arrival in France. By the 1990s, this led to several reunions and commemorations and the creation of the American Friends and Alumni of the OSE in 1994 (OSE-USA). My oral history interviews certainly reflect (and reinforced) the children's reestablished networks.[31] Memoirs and oral histories help fill in the gaps in contemporaneous sources. While they are just as authentic as wartime sources, they are not unproblematic. In addition to the bonds they seek to foster, there are real issues of gender representation. While both men and women who lived as refugee children in France wrote memoirs, only a handful were published by women.[32] The reasons, explored in the methodology essay, are linked to the children's highly gendered experiences as refugees in the United States. University study among women was rarer than among men.

Taking these epistemological questions into account, I hope to shed light on children's experiences in France by delving deeply into their sources, while maintaining the messiness inherent in how humans describe the past and make it usable. While all sources are a product of mediation, dependent upon place and context, I am convinced that looking for the children's voices brings us closer to grasping the breadth of their experiences. By listening closely, we will see that children participate actively in the process of becoming refugees. This brings us back to Ruth's account of her first weeks in France.

The arrival of ten-year-old Ruth and her older sister Miriam came as a surprise to their rescuer's husband, Rabbi S. The latter was active in the Central European refugee crisis in Paris, yet did not have a solution for the sisters.[33] He immediately called his brother-in-law, the girls' uncle in

Alsace, who did not invite the girls to stay with him. After one week, Rabbi S. sent Ruth to his sister's home in Paris, keeping Miriam with them. The new host family, Ruth explained, "tried very hard to be nice to me, but in the evenings, they went out every night. And that was the first time I ever was alone by myself. And I think that was the first time I really started feeling homesick. I started realizing that . . . I'm not sure what I realized. I really don't know. I don't know what my feelings were, except I was very lonesome."[34]

The unanticipated arrival of the children into the homes and lives of distant relatives tested the bonds of the extended family. Social convention called for solidarity and hospitality, but the obligation of caring for distant relatives' children weighed heavily on daily routines. Ruth's feelings of loneliness were certainly linked to her recent separation from her father, then her mother and siblings, then, one week after her arrival in Paris, from her older sister. Yet being alone was also a very real part of Ruth's life in her new surroundings.

Ruth's host parents had no children of their own and didn't have a childcare solution for this young German-speaking illegal refugee. French public school was certainly not an option. The couple still had to go to work in their clothing store. Before work, they simply dropped Ruth off at the nearest park with a picnic lunch. Today, Ruth expresses her shock at having been left to her own devices: "The only thing they did, when I look back on it—that I even survived—they put me in the park with a bag so that I could have lunch, so that I could have something to eat, and again, I didn't speak French. All kinds of things could have happened to me. I could have been kidnapped, or God knows what else." Ruth's anxiety remains with her to this day, explaining: "But the worst part was going to the bathroom, because the toilets were in the ground. [. . .] I really didn't know what to do. It was terrible. I really didn't know what to do. I don't know how long that lasted. I don't think it really lasted for a long time. But there I was, in the park in France all by myself. And then they picked me up after work and took me home."[35]

This improvised solution continued for several weeks, at least through Passover, which took place in April 1939. It was at this holiday that young Ruth expressed her resistance to the situation: "I know I stayed with them through Passover, because I wouldn't say the four questions." Considering her refusal to partake in the centuries-old ritual in which the youngest at the seder recites four questions on the meaning of the holiday, Ruth surmised, "I must have been very stubborn at that time, not very cooperative. They probably would have kept me if I would have been a cooperative child. But I was never a bad child, you know, just stubborn. So, when they asked me to do the four questions, and we were at somebody else's house, I wouldn't do it, you know. And I knew it [the four questions], because I went to a Jewish school."[36]

Ruth seems to have internalized the idea that she did something wrong, but her "stubbornness" had nothing to do with the end of her placement with the family. During this same period, Rabbi S. was actively fundraising for the OSE to help it establish a children's home for orthodox children. Finding a sustainable placement for Ruth and Miriam certainly provided him additional motivation. Located just north of Paris in the town of Eaubonne, the home opened in May 1939, providing a solution for the sisters, as well as other children, such as Elfriede Meyer and Heinz Schuster, who came from the orthodox children's orphanage in Frankfurt in March 1939.[37] As we will now see, the home was one of several structures established to care for the increasing number of unaccompanied Jewish youth in France.

CHAPTER 6

Accidental Republics

Caring for Jewish Refugee Children

Whether they came on organized Kindertransports or crossed the border on their own, the young refugees required care. In the aftermath of November 1938, Jewish organizations anticipated their arrival by establishing children's homes and, more rarely, family placements. As we will see, there was a great deal of improvisation as to who would take responsibility for the children, and how.

Caretakers and the pedagogical worlds they created greatly influenced the children's ability to maintain ties to their parents and siblings and create new bonds in exile. As others have also observed, children's homes grouped together individuals with similar characteristics under a single authority, representing what sociologist Erving Goffman conceptualized as "total institutions."[1] With some minor exceptions, the children had little contact with the outside world, since almost all of their activities took place within the homes.[2] Many caretakers were attracted to progressive pedagogy as part of their commitment to left-wing political movements. Under their auspices, the homes served as utopian experiments in which children played a central role. Indeed, in many homes, caretakers created children's republics, in which children elected their peers to co-administrate the homes, allowing for an exploration of democracy at a moment when this concept was most threatened.

Exploring the pedagogical underpinnings of the homes—the result of the accidental encounter of French Jewish philanthropists, Eastern European OSE leaders, and Central European caretakers—is essential for understanding the children's experiences in their new environment. French Jewish philanthropists had long embraced collective childcare models for their *colonies de vacances*. Some were even interested in the new pedagogical methods that grew popular throughout Europe in the aftermath of the First World War. Nonetheless, the children's homes required German-speaking staff, and the OSE and Germaine de Rothschild's Château de la Guette hired from the growing pool of Central European refugees, some recently arrived from Spain, where they assisted the republican cause during the civil war. These individuals brought their own *savoir faire* to France, inspired by socialist and communist pedagogical models. French philanthropy thus unwittingly took a progressive turn.

Looking at France in comparative perspective provides an interesting vantage point to begin a discussion on the Kindertransport children's care.[3] At the same moment that those in France were opening homes for unaccompanied Jewish children, activists in the United Kingdom were working frantically to find foster families for just under 10,000 Jewish and "non-Aryan" refugee children. The large-scale nature of their mobilization created a need for foster care that surpassed the reception capacity of the United Kingdom's Jewish communities. Furthermore, placing the children in Jewish families was not a priority for all of the activists, who came from multiple religious backgrounds. As a result, Jewish children sent to the United Kingdom were cared for primarily in Christian homes, at times in stark contrast to the Jewish children's identities, sparking a lively debate in British Jewish orthodox circles on the ethics of their care.[4] At the same moment, in the United States, it was firmly asserted that the Jewish refugee children sent there would be cared for under Jewish auspices. This perhaps had roots in the racialized nature of child welfare in the United States, as seen in the Supreme Court decision following the 1904 scandal over Irish Catholic orphans who were sent to Mexican-American Catholic homes. In this case, race trumped religion. However, to many Americans in the 1930s, including Jews themselves, Jews represented a separate race.[5] Like the British, Americans also preferred foster care, which was recognized as a superior method to institutional care in the early twentieth century.[6] By the 1930s, the American social work establishment was firmly under Freudian influence. According to social workers' interpretation of Freudian theory, it was in a family setting, or in foster care, that children would develop properly.[7]

France thus stands in interesting contrast to the Kindertransport programs in other countries due to the choice of collective homes. Furthermore, it is interesting to note the absence of debate in the Jewish press—the only remaining source in light of the paucity of organizational archives—about where the children would go once they arrived, whether they would be cared for under Jewish auspices or not, and whether they would stay in families or collective homes. Kindertransport activists in France, it seems, improvised solutions, building on local and imported traditions. Children ended up being cared for in collective homes, but also in foster families, under primarily Jewish, but also non-Jewish, auspices.

Determining how to care for refugee children was not just a practical problem for French Kindertransport organizers, it also touched on communities' own self-perception. A poem entitled "The Jewish Month of May" by a fourteen-year-old Gertrud Gewürz, published in German in Strasbourg's bilingual *La Tribune Juive*, provides a window into one child's mindset several months after her arrival in France:

May is here now, everything gains new courage
Only one doesn't, the Jew.
He is like a lamb taken from his mother,
He was not touched by the merry month of May.
He cannot rejoice inwardly like the others
He has to keep going, he must always wander,
Feels always tied in chains . . .
But one day, one day G–d shall save him:
Only when he arrives in his own land,
Which he'll cultivate with his own hands,
Then he will be able to say: this is the month of May,
Where I feel fresh and free!

Gertrud Gewürz, 14 1/2 ans.[8]

This poem was accompanied by an equally telling request, in French, that local children and parents "read it closely and that as they read, they think about the children separated from their families who live here [in France], and of those who are still in the German hell, which is worse. A fraternal bond unites us, all of us."[9] A shared belief in "fraternal bonds," enduring family ties linking Jewish families on either side of the Rhine, as well as the largely middle-class status of Alsace's tightly knit Jewish community,[10] created a setting in which children could be cared for in private homes, without significant fear of deviant or irresponsible behavior toward the children. (This is *not* to say that these things didn't happen.) As a result of this shared set of assumptions, roughly half of the children cared for in Alsace were placed in local Jewish families, while the others were cared for in Jewish orphanages in Strasbourg and Haguenau or in a smaller structure for the youngest children called Le Nid. While research is silent on the question, it is quite possible that older childcare traditions in this region influenced the choice of foster care. As Alsace was one of France's only rural areas with a considerable Jewish population, local Jews may have opened their homes in the summertime to Jewish children in need of both fresh air and kosher food.[11] Whether Strasbourg's Jews were building on past traditions or not, the very fact that the local paper printed a poem by this child, expressing her feelings of collective persecution and nascent Zionism, suggests that refugee children were playing an important function in the region. Not only did they give local Jews an occasion to respond to Nazi persecution, they also helped reinforce communal cohesion and provided a strong argument in favor of Zionism. Fittingly, the foster care method reinforced their ideals of communal trust and took on an important symbolic value for the group.

In Paris, the situation was altogether different. As the center of French Jewish life, it had a Jewish population that was considerably larger and more ideologically diverse, reflecting the geographical, political, class, and religious divisions that characterized life in the capital. As city dwellers in an immigration hub, Jews in Paris were less likely to claim that "fraternal bonds" linked them to other Jews, especially those outside their immediate circles. The refugee children may have sparked the interest of a small number of activists, but, as seen earlier, they did not inspire the community-wide mobilization seen in the east of France.

The refugee children's care reflects these dynamics. While some family placements were set up privately by German and Austrian families with their French relatives, as seen in young Ruth's case, large-scale foster care for the refugee children was most likely never considered a viable option. Instead, children were sent to collective children's homes, including those established by the OSE, the Rothschild's Château de la Guette, or the Monbrison's Château Leroy in Quincy-sous-Sénart.

For Germaine de Rothschild and other Parisian Jews—immigrant and native alike—establishing children's homes for the refugee children was most likely viewed as a natural solution. Collective children's homes, in the form of vacation colonies (*colonies de vacances*), became a prevalent model in France during the early years of the Third Republic. As Laura Lee Downs has shown, summertime placements with rural families remained an inexpensive solution to fortify urban youth throughout the 1930s and into the years of the Second World War. Yet over time, concern over the hygienic conditions in rural homes and a desire for better supervision of the children grew. Likewise, Republican teachers sought to replicate the school environment and its collective pedagogy. By the 1930s, this had led to a decided preference for collective models over family placements.[12]

Parisian Jews had followed national trends and organized their own *colonies de vacances* since the late nineteenth century. The history of the Œuvre israélite de séjours à la campagne is especially significant. Even more than Protestant or Catholic *colonies*, this French Jewish program, founded in 1899, required a collective model because it sought to maintain a "Jewish environment," even if its organizers didn't exactly define this mission precisely.[13] While it had long been a collective structure, the organization had been housed since 1926 at the Château de Maubuisson in Saint-Ouen-l'Aumône,[14] which belonged to Edmond de Rothschild. It is quite likely that Germaine de Rothschild was closely associated with the program in the interwar period.[15] On the eve of the children's arrival in France, Noémie Halphen de Rothschild offered her cousin Germaine de Rothschild the Château de Maubuisson as a reception center.[16] In the meantime, with Robert Jablonski taking care of the bureaucratic details, Germaine de Rothschild was free to transform another Rothschild property, the Château de la Guette in Villeneuve-Saint-Denis, into a spectacular children's home.

The Count Hubert de Monbrison's Château in Quincy-sous-Sénart was also an outgrowth of the French "Château du social"[17] tradition, in that it had been serving as a boarding school for White Russian girls. As seen earlier, the Count purchased the Château for his mistress, Princess Irène Paley. The spacious Château Leroy provided room for the folk dances, music concerts, and sporting competitions that nourished her dream of preserving Czarist Russia. By the late 1930s, however, the political atmosphere at the school had changed, as seen in its change of name to the Aid Committee for Refugee Children.[18] After receiving Spanish refugee girls, the school accepted forty Jewish boys from Berlin who arrived in July 1939, reflecting the major upheavals of the twentieth century.

If caring for the Central European children in children's homes drew upon well-established French philanthropic traditions, it was also an obvious choice for the Russian-Jewish OSE. The OSE was surely influenced by its French patroness, Yvonne de Gunzbourg, who, like her cousin, Germaine de Rothschild, would have seen a collective model as an obvious solution for refugee children. Yet this care policy also reflects trends beyond France's borders, imported from Eastern and Central Europe. Significantly, the decision to establish homes for the refugee children was discussed at an April 1939 conference in Paris that gathered OSE's leadership from Eastern, Central, and Western Europe. The policy was thus international in its scope, intended for each country where OSE was operating. OSE leaders justified the collective homes by taking into account the broader historical and political context. Their first argument focused on the German origins of the children: "German Judaism has played a leading role in Jewish life over the past two centuries and has also enriched general European culture enormously. These children, who are without help or protection, are the heirs of a branch of the Jewish people which is perhaps, from the spiritual point of view, the most important." This argument reflects the historical tensions between Eastern European "Ostjuden" and German Jews, the former typically looked down upon by the latter. The rise of Nazism turned the tables on these intra-group dynamics: now it was an Eastern European Jewish committee, previously operating in Berlin to help Ostjuden, that was in a position to help German Jewish families.[19] In framing itself as the protector of young German Jews, the OSE found a new and powerful justification for its existence.

It also based its policy on the expectation that its wards would eventually be reunited with their parents:

> It should not be forgotten that most of these children have parents and hope to be reunited with their families sooner or later. It is therefore not a rational solution to give them to families who are prepared to adopt them. On the other hand, the distribution of children between families where they suddenly fall into a completely different cultural environment is fraught with all sorts of difficulties. It is, as we see, a *sui generis* case, and the experiences acquired until now in the field of child protection are not all valid here.[20]

As this citation makes clear, the OSE leaders—who had survived the upheavals of the First World War, the Russian Revolution, and the rise of Nazism—viewed the situation on the eve of the Second World War as a moment of rupture, calling for entirely new rules. Yet it is also quite possible that they were influenced by collective childcare models circulating in interwar Eastern and Central Europe. Despite efforts to privilege foster care, most Jewish First World War orphans in Eastern Europe were cared for in collective homes, some of which had become sites for pedagogical innovation.[21]

OSE leaders were expecting traumatized children: "The horrors and the constant fear through which they lived in Germany have left a lasting impression on their physical and mental condition."[22] As foreigners themselves, they also anticipated that France would represent a "new and strange environment" for the children, leading to a difficult adaptation process. This logic justified the choice of collective homes and caretakers "who know the language of the children and intimately understand their mentality."[23] This contrasts with attitudes expressed in the Strasbourg Jewish press, which posited that children might forget their pasts if they were received with warmth and enough hot chocolate.

Viennese social worker Trude Frankl escorted Austrian Jewish children throughout Europe once Kindertransport measures began, with the hope of finding new homes for her wards.[24] The Rothschild's Château de la Guette made a lasting impression on this external observer, who quickly obtained a pan-European vision of child welfare. In her April 1939 report, she noted:

> The magnificent historical castle, which was generously transformed by the Baroness de Rothschild into a modern boarding school, is the place of accommodation for children over 10 years of age. The four-story castle is located in the middle of an immense park and high and wide windows let in air and light. The interior of the house is decorated in delicate pastel colors, there are bright flowery fabrics everywhere, each room has luxurious central heating and the wash-basins are equipped with cold and hot water.

She focused her observations on the home's material comforts but also mentioned the "two proper light-colored classrooms with all the current equipment, a workshop and in a small annex building [i.e. an outbuilding of the castle], a housekeeping school *en miniature* [sic] which is run by a qualified housekeeping teacher. The staff is composed of young and excellent teachers, a young doctor, a nurse providing care and training in hygiene and first aid."[25]

If the Baroness de Rothschild had thrown herself into this spectacular renovation project, it was not (only) out of a penchant for redecorating. The Château design actually reflected an openness to *éducation nouvelle*. Indeed, a set of progressive ideals on education emerged in France in the early days of the Third Republic that sought to break with anti-Republican authoritarianism. In the aftermath of the First World War, left-leaning pedagogues renewed their mission to shape society through educational methods that sought to make children more active in the learning process. In this moment of transnational exchange, French *éducation nouvelle* methods drew upon a diverse set of thinkers, including but not limited to Belgian Jean-Ovide Decroly, Italian Maria Montessori, Soviet-Ukrainian Anton Makarenko, American John Dewey, and, of course, France's own Célestin Freinet.[26] This is not to say that these pedagogical philosophies were interchangeable. As Laura Lee Downs notes in her discussion of scouting movements, "Each of these drew its coherence as a movement from its own distinctive and over-arching worldview that linked a particular understanding of human and child nature with a vision of society as it is or as it may be." Nonetheless, she asserts, "In terms of method and technique, the different forms of scouting shared a great deal with each other, and with the international movement for *éducation nouvelle*: an emphasis on the importance of concrete experience, versus abstract discourse, in children's learning process, and a common conviction that the game constitutes a privileged arena for learning, thanks to its status as spontaneous and universal childhood activity."[27]

The fact that the Château de la Guette had a workshop and a miniature home-economics department suggests that Germaine de Rothschild was drawn to innovative social work and educational methods. A second clue on the Baroness's progressive views on education can be found in *Mes 126 Gosses*, a fictional work published in 1938 by Juliette Pary, who was active in Jewish children's initiatives. In the book, the narrator encounters a woman at a dinner party with whom she shares her passion for "education, Montessori, Jean-Jacques [Rousseau], and an atmosphere of freedom for children."[28] This conversation leads her to be considered for a position working for a "Countess" who ran a patronage for poor children from Belleville (a character most likely based on the Baroness, who did indeed run a patronage for poor children in Belleville). When the narrator explained she had never actually worked with children, the Countess exclaimed: "What is important is to love the poor little ones and to devote yourself to them as if on a mission."[29] When the narrator explained that what she really wanted was to create an "atmosphere" for the children, the Countess enthusiastically responded: "An atmosphere, exactly! We want an atmosphere!"[30] The tone here mocks the Countess's naïve enthusiasm. Hannah Arendt, who worked for Germaine de Rothschild during her Paris exile, shared a similar critique of her employer. Nonetheless, both the philosopher and the Baroness "lost their heads as far as children were concerned."[31]

The OSE homes in Montmorency also reflected an openness to progressive educational methods and left a positive, if less memorable, impression on Trude Frankl: "Designed in the spirit of Montessori, these children's homes offer a charming vision with all their small colorful furniture and walls painted with funny childlike scenes."[32] As Frankl's observations indicate, a commitment to *éducation nouvelle* played a large role in the physical conception of the homes. Yet more important, of course, were the caretakers who were selected to work with the children. The Central European refugee crisis had the effect of diversifying the pool of applicants and, with it, the pedagogical influences within the homes.

Caretakers at both the Château de la Guette and in the OSE's children's homes established children's republics. Designed to foster children's participation in the governance of their homes, the method was pioneered in the United States by John Dewey in the early twentieth century. It grew popular among Eastern European pedagogues in the aftermath of the First World War, as well as in children's homes throughout Spain during the civil war.[33] By the 1930s, the method had made its way into France through the writings of Soviet pedagogue Moisei Pistrak, whose work appeared in French as early as 1925, and thanks to the abovementioned Juliette Pary, who translated Makarenko's book *The Road to Life* on the Gorky Colony, a children's republic in Soviet Ukraine, into French.[34] In France, the Red Falcons, a socialist youth group that counted as many as 2,000 members during the Popular Front, organized children's republics in their summer camps.[35] The children's republic in 1930s France was thus an innovative method, resolutely associated with left-wing politics. Germaine de Rothschild was perhaps unaware of the political implications of these pedagogical initiatives. The Russian and Polish leadership of the OSE in France was comprised primarily of non-practicing Jews and bundists,[36] yet they seemed staunchly traditional and conservative to one of the educators they hired.[37] Likewise, while progressive on educational matters, it is difficult to assess Germaine de Rothschild's political views, even if she most likely shared the conservative orientation of her milieu.[38]

Indeed, if the design of the Château de la Guette reflected the Baroness's openness to new methods, her staffing decisions did show some ideological inconsistencies. She apparently placed an advertisement in a newspaper to find German-speaking educators to work with the refugee children.[39] Twenty-year-old Willy Katz, a member of the Jewish scouting movement Éclaireurs Israélites de France, was initially selected to direct the institution. Perhaps due to his inexperience, he arrived accompanied by his mother![40] The Baroness then recruited three other couples as educators and medical staff: Ernst and Lida (Hellman) Jablonski, Alfred and Fritzi (Riesel) Brauner, and Harry and Irene (Goldin) Spiegel.

The latter, deeply engaged in progressive political and pedagogical circles, brought their distinct views to the children's homes. Ernst Jablonski (1913–1988), who during the war became Ernest Jouhy, was a German Jewish refugee. He was not related to Germaine de Rothschild's personal secretary, Robert Jablonski, but apparently it was their shared last name that allowed his and his wife's job application for the Œuvre de la Guette to stand out.[41] It was not Jablonski's Jewish origins but his affiliation to the Communist party that had caused him to flee Berlin for France, most likely in 1933.[42] Before his exclusion from the Humboldt University of Berlin for communist activities, Jablonski had studied sociology, history, and psychology. Since 1930, he had been involved with the progressive Odenwaldschule in Heppenheim, although it is not clear in what capacity.[43] Founded by Paul Geheeb in 1910, this boarding school encouraged gender and ethnic equality as well as self-government among the students. Hierarchical relationships and religious practice were not tolerated. Furthermore, its director encouraged "air baths" (i.e. running naked outdoors).[44]

Upon arrival in France, Jablonski worked at Citroën while writing a dissertation under the direction of child psychologist Henri Wallon at the Sorbonne. It was at a friend's house in Paris that he met his future wife, Lida Hillman (1911–?), a native of Riga who came to France in 1931 to study comparative literature. Interviewed numerous times about her husband, little has been written about her. According to one historian, Lida had spent time in Belgium before coming to France, where she encountered the pedagogy of Ovide Decroly, which placed an equal emphasis on intellectual and manual activities.[45] The Château de la Guette was the perfect place to apply these principles.

Like other left-leaning pedagogues, Ernst Jablonski was especially attracted to Austrian psychologist Alfred Adler's individual psychology, which he had studied under Professor Alexander Neuer, either in Germany or in France.[46] Adler's individual psychology positioned itself as a theoretical and political critique of Freud. Adler considered Freud's focus on biological urges as authoritarian, and instead emphasized the role of the group or community in shaping the individual.[47] In the words of Ernst Papanek, who would become the director of the OSE homes and an emissary of Adlerian psychology once in the United States: "Adler saw the inferiority feeling in every human being. We can hinder the tendency to strive for power by promoting and developing the innate potentiality of social emotion. Cooperativeness cannot be taught by moral preaching, it can only be achieved by cooperative living."[48] A belief in the therapeutic power of groups thus provided common ground in the children's homes, allowing for an exciting pedagogical opportunity.

The Jablonskis were joined by Alfred and Fritzi (later Françoise) Brauner, a couple who had just returned to France from the Spanish Civil War. The couple had met in Vienna, where Fritzi Riesel (1911–2000) was born and had obtained a doctorate in medicine. Alfred Brauner (1910–2002) was born in France, yet his family was Austrian. Brauner had spent part of his childhood in Vienna, where he had obtained a doctorate on the notion of unanimism in the work of Jules Romains from the University of Vienna in 1934. His intellectual interest in the power of the collective may have been a result of his exposure to Adler's individual psychology. Brauner's uncle was the prominent psychologist Erwin Wexberg, a disciple of both Freud and Adler. According to his son, Brauner was well acquainted with the psychoanalytical theories of the interwar period, having regularly read his uncle's publications.[49] While in Vienna, Brauner had also spent time at the Kaiser-Ebersdorf school, working with delinquent children.[50]

Brauner characterized himself as a "social democrat" in the interwar period, describing his politics as "anti-communist, yet very leftwing, further left than socialists ever were."[51] Little is known about Fritzi Brauner's political views, and while her entourage was clearly left-wing, it should not be assumed that she shared her husband's exact worldview.

The couple's engagement in Spain was initially practical: Brauner had to return to France from Austria for his military service, but Fritzi was not licensed to work as a doctor in France. Instead, she went to Spain, where she worked as a surgery assistant. After completing his military service, Alfred joined her, producing fundraising propaganda for the children's homes set up by the International Brigades. This is where he discovered and began his collection of children's drawings, which later brought the couple considerable recognition.[52]

The Brauners' engagement in Spain caused the Baroness to view their candidacy with some suspicion. Alfred Brauner explained in a later interview: "Relations said, here are child specialists and here are children from Germany, it was an interfaith committee and money from the Rothschilds, a Baroness de Rothschild and Edouard de Rothschild who received me with a lot of suspicion, because I came from red Spain but in the end they didn't have any better."[53]

The two couples were joined by a Viennese musician, Harry Spiegel (1910), and his wife, Mabel Irene Goldin (1910), a nurse from Brooklyn.[54] As communists, they had signed up for the International Brigades independently and met in a military hospital in Mataro, Spain. The couple married in 1938 and arrived in France in 1939. It is possibly the Brauners who introduced them to the Château de la Guette, where Irene joined Fritzi's medical team and Harry organized a choir.

Perhaps the best way to get a sense of the educators is through a child's eyes. Fourteen-year-old Minnie Engel from Germany described her educators in her wartime diary, showing her affective ties to this diverse bunch:

I was first in the B class where we had classes with Ernst Jablonsky [sic]. He was a Berliner. An incredible guy. He was tall, broad-shouldered and slim. An interesting and friendly face. His wife, Lida, was relatively small and petite. She was very nice and I liked her a lot. She was the teacher of class A, that is, the little ones. Class C was taught by Fred Brauner, a Viennese [sic]. He too was tall and slim, temperamental, with bulging eyes. I don't understand how anyone could dislike him. He romped around with us all day long. I liked him very much. His wife, Fritzi, was our doctor. She was very athletic, like Ernst and Fred. Besides that, she is also very good at her job.

In the meantime, Willy Katz left "la Guette." And for some time, Miss Bernheim, a lady from the committee, became our director. This worked well. Whether old or young, everyone admired her. Fred was the teacher of class C, i.e. the older children. Shortly thereafter a new educator arrived, a friend of Fred's, Harry Spiegel. He had just been injured in Spain and had arrived from there. A few days later his wife, Irene, also arrived. She had a petite figure and beautiful big eyes. She is American and was our nurse. Her German was very broken, which amused us a lot.[55]

This child's description of her educators, one can notice, is in the past tense: she most likely wrote this passage after the dissolution of the home, in the period after June 1940 but before her later, dated entries from September 1944. She was thus writing in a period of uncertainty or danger, fondly remembering the moments before the Nazi invasion of France. Yet one can also note that she only gives a physical description of the individuals she appreciated. Their physical details are accompanied by descriptions of their personalities. Minnie Engel provides no information on the Jewish identities or political views of her educators. Her silence suggests either indifference to these matters or the idea that these identities were so obvious that they did not need mentioning.

Indeed, the Baroness had hired a group of leftists to educate the Jewish refugee children. While all of the educators were, in the words of Lida Jablonski, "fiercely secular" (*farouchement laïcs*),[56] evidence suggests they all had Jewish backgrounds.[57]

In questioning the Jewish origins of individuals who clearly did not embrace a Jewish identity, it is not my intention to challenge or disrespect their choices, but rather to consider the multiple implications of Jewishness in interwar Austrian, German, and French societies. Scholars have analyzed "non-Jewish Jews" and explored what Leora Auslander has called the "boundaries of Jewishness."[58] As Lisa Silverman argues, "Studies of Jewish history that restrict their inquiry to explicit manifestations of Jewish culture, or to works that Jews themselves called 'Jewish,' severely limit the depths to which we can probe these processes as they occurred on stages and in courtrooms, were narrated in fiction and in essays, and were revealed in the choices people made in their everyday lives about where to live, work and entertain themselves."[59] Building on Judith Butler's work on gender, Silverman considers Jewishness as a "performative identity," whose expression varies according to place, period, and situation.[60] This scholarship argues that even when individuals chose not to identify as Jews, this category of difference still could shape or influence their lives.

While these observations would have infuriated the caretakers, they do help contextualize their profiles. Indeed, there is something to be said about the social conditions in Central Europe that allowed for the fertile encounter of left-wing politics, alternative pedagogy and youth of Jewish origin. Individuals from Jewish backgrounds were disproportionately represented in left-wing movements, enticed by the promise of a better world for all, even if engaging in these circles may have marked them as Jewish against their own wishes. It is not a coincidence that the Odenwald school, which had influenced Jablonski, was labeled by local conservatives as a "communist Jew school."[61]

The couples' strong political identities also say a great deal about the French Jews who hired them. Germaine de Rothschild's commitment to establishing a "Jewish" children's home was assuaged by holding a Passover seder and sending a "very liberal"[62] rabbi to the Château de la Guette to instruct the children in Jewish history. The food served there was not kosher. A "staunchly secular" or even anti-religious staff was not a deal breaker. The Parisian situation thus stands in striking contrast with Strasbourg's more traditional Jewish community. As we will soon see, Strasbourg's Zionist youth leaders would later join the left-wing educators in the children's homes, creating a somewhat explosive encounter.

If the caretakers at Château de la Guette were determined to establish a secular children's republic, a more moderate yet equally engaged pedagogy emerged in the OSE homes through the work of Ernst Papanek. Ten years older than the educators at La Guette, Papanek (1900–1973) was a well-known pedagogue in interwar Vienna. A graduate of the Pedagogical Institute in Vienna, he took part in post-First World War street-play experiments and ran programs for delinquent children. In 1932, he was elected to Vienna's city council, and in 1933, to head the Socialist Youth International. Even more than Ernst

Jablonski and Alfred Brauner, Papanek was directly engaged in Adlerian circles. An anecdote from his daughter-in-law and former OSE child Hanna Kaiser Papanek shows his proximity to the Viennese psychological establishment:

> During his university studies, first in medicine and then in pedagogy, he came to reject the psychoanalytical approach of Sigmund Freud (1856–1939), whose seminar he attended but with whom he came to disagree. To illustrate his differences with Freud, he often talked about the day when a big May Day demonstration, red flags flying, marched past the building where the seminar group met. Freud closed the big windows facing the street, turned his back to the marchers, and said angrily: "Politics is unimportant!" For Ernst, that was the end of studying with Freud.

Alfred Adler provided an alternative to Freud for those, like Papanek, with a "profound commitment to Democratic Socialism; for him [Papanek], the political and educational strands were inseparable."[63]

As Hanna emphasizes, a commitment to socialism shaped Papanek's personal identity and his pedagogical methods. He does not mention his own background in his autobiographical writings and only indicates that his wife Helene (born Goldstern) was a member of a prominent Jewish family.[64] Nonetheless, like the La Guette educators, Ernst Papanek was indeed from a Jewish family. According to one of his sons, Papanek was observant until his teens, when he discovered Marxism and became an atheist.[65] The Papaneks did not give their two sons a Jewish education, and, according his sons, the boys discovered their Jewish background only after the Nazi annexation of Austria. They did, however, transmit a strong political identity to their children: their sons' middle names, Otto and Fritz, were given in homage to Otto Bauer and Fritz Adler, leaders of the Austrian Socialist movement.[66]

Papanek's deep ties to Austrian socialism forced him into exile when the Austrian Social Democratic Party was outlawed on February 12, 1934.[67] After flight to Prague, Papanek circulated around Europe and eventually went to Spain, where he served as the ambassador of the Social Democratic International to the Spanish Republicans.[68] After the

Nazi annexation of Austria, his wife Helene, a doctor, and their two children fled Vienna for France. That summer, the couple ran a summer camp together on the Atlantic coast. The family had visas for the United States and was intending on leaving for New York when OSE leader Dr. Aron Lourié, a relative of Helene's, offered Papanek the job directing the OSE homes.[69] Papanek indicates in his memoirs that he was not enthusiastic about working with this group of men, whom he considered conservative, nor with Jewish refugee children, per se: "I couldn't have been less enthusiastic. I wasn't interested in Russian or Jewish refugee children as such. My concern had always been with youth and human misery wherever they were found."[70] However, in the days following the Munich conference, Papanek felt it was not the moment to flee Hitler. Plus, he needed the money. He accepted the position.

The children's homes presented these socialist and communist educators with an irresistible opportunity to put their politics into action. As Château de la Guette educator Lida Jablonski recalled in a postwar account, "The Baroness was very interested in the home and came often, yet gave us complete freedom in the educational domain."[71] As a result, the educators were free to create a laboratory in which they could enact their political ideals:

> Full of youthful enthusiasm (we were all between 25 and 30 years old), we put into practice our revolutionary pedagogical ideas at the time: we created a "Children's Republic," wrote a Constitution, elected a Parliament . . . All the work was administered by the children and paid in Francs-Guette convertible into Francs. Co-responsible for the running of the house, the children had to devote a lot of time to administrative tasks; they also helped in the kitchen, in the household, in the garden. They built a large sports field . . . A children's court operated for cases of dispute or infringement of the rules. A general assembly was held every day at the evening meal.[72]

Ernst Papanek seems to have encountered slightly more resistance to his methods, but nonetheless states that he too obtained "carte blanche" from the OSE's administration to implement his pedagogy and set up a children's republic in each OSE home.[73] Yet, contrary to the La Guette educators, Papanek was opposed to creating a strictly secular environment for children who came from religious families. This created some tension with Yvonne de Gunzbourg and Guy de Rothschild, the philanthropists behind the OSE homes, who were against providing "special privileges" for orthodox children. Ironically, it was Papanek, who had been nicknamed "the Goy" by OSE board members, who insisted that religious children should be presented with the opportunity to have a bar mitzvah, kosher food, and a separate children's home where Jewish rituals would be respected.[74] The fact that this special home was created for the orthodox children in Eaubonne at the Villa La Chesnaie in May 1939 can be considered a result of Papanek's insistence and, of course, the fundraising efforts of orthodox Jews such as Ruth's uncle.[75]

If the educators and caretakers learned how to negotiate with their employers, their innovative pedagogical methods created a new source of resistance, from the children themselves. The children's exile in France was not only a rupture with home and family: it was also the discovery of a set of political ideals that were both unfamiliar and radical to many of them. The children seemed to embrace these pedagogical experiments wholeheartedly, yet they also pushed back and learned how to assert their own opinions. As we will see next, this encounter naturally led to divisions, between the children and their caretakers, but also among the children themselves.

CHAPTER 7

An Enchanted Parenthesis

In contrast to life in Nazi Germany and Austria, the first months in France during the spring and summer of 1939 felt like a joyful liberation for many of the Jewish refugee children. As one La Guette child wrote in his diary: "It is wonderful."[1] As if in summer camp, children spent their days on the premises of their respective homes and began with exercises, followed by classes and group activities. Music was an important part of children's daily routines, and this helped Ruth find her place. Having left her distant relatives for OSE's home for observant children, the ten-year-old child who had refused to recite the four questions at the Passover seder seemed to bloom. Ruth was reunited with her older sister in the home, yet her counselors seemed to play an even larger role in her life. The latter taught her several songs, including "*Ich bin ein kleiner Halutizm*" (I'm a little pioneer).

The busy life in the homes masked, however, a deep longing for home and family. After observing the children's first eight days in France, one caretaker noted: "The children, with one exception, were not homesick (*Heimweh*), but extremely worried (*Sorge*) about their parents' and siblings' well-being and possibilities of emigration."[2] The distance from home weighed especially heavy on Shabbat in OSE's home for religious children. In addition to organizing services, the children gathered to listen to little Ruth sing "*Das Herz einer Mutter*" (The heart of a mother), the German version of the 1925 Yiddish ballad "*A Yiddishe Momme*."[3] The song made them weep, allowing for a weekly catharsis.[4] At the Château de la Guette, a resolutely less religious environment, the children also sang. It is hard to imagine dry eyes as they intoned the words of "*Alles schweiget*" (All is silent), the lullaby whose lyrics evoke "tears in eyes" and "a heaviness in one's heart."[5]

Between the joy of discovering a new place and longing for home, we will explore the children's experiences during their first months of exile in France to question how displacement was experienced on the individual level and what changes it provoked in their collective lives and networks. We will see that the children, while unable to dictate the decisions that shaped their everyday lives, continually employed strategies to maximize their control over their environment and maintain bonds with those they loved. Probing sources produced by the children as the events unfolded, as well as their later accounts, allows us to apprehend their experiences through a more nuanced and complex prism than the trope of victimhood. The children were indeed victims of Nazi, and later Vichy, persecution, yet they deserve a more complex treatment in the historical record: their drawings and writings remind us they were also boys and girls, friends and siblings, and, very simply, humans, trying their best to maintain control and stability in an ever-changing environment.

As the children arrived and sought to adapt to life in France without their parents, groups emerged among them along geographic, political, and religious lines. Such sociological divisions remain salient decades later and are reflected in the networks I encountered as I sought to document their experiences. Some children had lived together in Jewish orphanages in Germany, yet, for the majority, France represents a sort of "ground zero" for understanding the formation of their friendships.

As seen above with young Ruth and her counselors, one coping technique the children developed during the war years was to form new relationships in exile. For historian Joachim Schlör, creating surrogate families was a key part of the migration experience for those fleeing Nazi Germany:

Acting as a scout, they meet people in their new surroundings who have comparable experiences and use this circle to create a network of contacts and exchange, which those who "stay behind" cannot understand as they cannot know what is going on "outside." For many emigrants the journey by ship, either to Palestine or the United States, is especially symbolic of this experience of transition, not least because during the passage they can strike up important social relationships.[6]

Building on Carlos Sluzki's concept of "ship brothers and sisters," Schlör emphasizes the importance of the individuals encountered in transit: "'Ship brothers and ship sisters' [. . .] become a replacement family, to the chagrin of their real family."[7] For most of the children in this book, France represented a period of transit between two destinations, and while it is not surprising that children developed surrogate families in exile—this is a noted theme in survivor testimonies on hiding and Nazi camps—historians have rarely considered this question from the perspective of the children themselves.[8] Paying attention to children's relationships with others shows to what extent flight from Nazi Germany was a collective experience, shaped by the increasingly important bonds with friends and siblings. Studying children in a group context, synchronically, therefore tells a different story from the individualized survival narratives that emerged in contemporary video and written testimonies after the Holocaust.

Before their departure from Germany and Austria, the children faced an onslaught of medical visits and appointments to secure a coveted place on a transport. While some certainly grasped the significance of their departure, their contemporaneous accounts do not dwell on the emotion of saying goodbye. Their postwar writings, however, linger on this moment, which represents for many the last time they saw their parents.[9]

Minnie Engel, born in 1925 in Schönlanke, West Prussia, wrote down her experiences in France in a notebook. Writing primarily in her native German, she did not state what sparked her desire to write, and she only dated the last entry (September 8, 1944). However, her detailed accounts suggest she was recalling recent events. Her notebook, given to her former educator after the war, provides a rare contemporaneous account of the children's arrivals in France.[10]

Like Minnie, other children made the decision to write about their lives in France. Twelve-year-old Heinz Lonnerstädter, who left Berlin with his brother Walter, received the parting gift of a notebook from his friend Eva, who promised to "do everything possible to assure the friendship between [them] will remain."[11] Viennese thirteen-year-old Heinz Löw also began a diary, six months after his arrival.[12] Heinz Löw arrived first, from Vienna. One week later, Minnie Engel and Heinz Lonnerstäder followed, from Berlin. What was it like to leave one's home for France? How did children perceive their caretakers and fellow children? All three of their first diary entries explore these questions.

Unlike the other children, Heinz Löw starts his account on the day Nazi Germany invaded Poland, which prompted him to reflect upon his recent past. The Nazi annexation of Austria was a natural starting point for his narrative. "Hitler occupied Austria in 1938 and bad times started for Jews. From all of Austria, Jews emigrated," he wrote. I initially thought he was referring to his own parents, but I eventually learned that this hypothesis was incorrect: both of his parents had committed suicide, most likely in 1937.[13] This explains why it was his grandmother and his older sister Klara who helped him leave the country:

My grandmother, since I had no parents anymore, and my sister, tried very hard to send me to a foreign land; they tried in pain for a long time and one day a letter came from the Kultusgemeinde that I had the opportunity to leave Austria in mid 1939, possibly to France. There was great anxiety in my family. A few days later I had to have a physical and shortly after we heard that I would have to leave on March 14, 1939 for France.

Unlike the other children's accounts, Heinz Löw alludes to the pain of departure:

We went shopping, packed, went to the Kultusgemeinde etc. and the 14th of March was approaching fast . . . and was here! I had to be at the West train station at 11:30 pm. Grandma, Klara and a few friends came with me. I received many gifts and mementos. The farewell was very hard on me, but it had to be. At 12:15 am the train departed.[14]

This diary is also unique in that it represents a collaboration: his friend Paul Peter Porges, a fellow child from Vienna, illustrated several passages, which provides a second window into Heinz's narrative. This passage is accompanied by a drawing of a woman and child on a busy train platform (Plate 10). The couple, assumedly Heinz and his grandmother, is embracing. Looking closer, one can read the hour on the station clock: 11:20 p.m. In addition, in the background, the artist has added another child and adult. This child most likely is also saying goodbye, yet the pair is not embracing. By creating a juxtaposition between the two couples, the young artist managed to communicate Heinz's feelings about departure. To emphasize his message, he quoted the diary: "The Farewell was very hard on me."[15] The illustration, one teen's attempt to document another's pain, attests to the collective nature of diary writing and, of course, their ability to cope with displacement by sharing their emotions.

Fourteen-year-old Minnie Engel's account avoids her farewells entirely. Eschewing all mention of parents, she jumps ahead to the station and focuses on the other teens with whom she traveled:

We left on March 20, 1939 at ten pm, about 46 young people, from the Potsdam station. We were dispatched into different compartments. In mine, there was Susi and Eva Guttmann, Trautchen Feith, Eveline Fuchs, Manfred Fuchs and Gerda Einbinder. Gustl Kranzler, a travel companion, was with us all the time since it seems like he was in love with Susi.

Minnie's first impression of France was not positive:

After a night of travelling, we arrived at the station in Metz where we were received by some of the ladies from the Comité. At the station buffet, we received our lunch. There was soup, a big piece of bread (which I didn't know what to do with), an orange and a small piece of cheese that I swallowed with difficulty. Since we had an hour's stop, we visited the city. Then our journey continued and we arrived on March 21 in the evening in a Parisian station of which I keep a bad impression, as of Paris too.

Her account also shows that Germaine de Rothschild was no stranger to the children. From the Rothschild hospital they were taken to the Château de Maubuisson, which served as a triage center:

> The Baroness came to pick us up and we were taken by bus to the Rothschild Hospital. We spent 3 days playing and letting off steam in the garden. And apart from that we were thoroughly examined. We were treated very well. Then on to Maubuisson, an old château of the Baroness [sic]. The reception was terrible. [. . .] It was Pesach [Passover] at that time and we were preparing a great celebration. The room was well decorated. A young rabbi came from Paris for the evening of the Seder.[16] It was nice and pleasant. We had among other things visits from the gentlemen of the Committee as well as from the Baroness who wanted to know if we were orthodox, what we were learning etc. Afterwards we were divided up, the little ones, with the exception of those who had sisters and brothers, went to Montmorency [OSE homes], the religious went to an Orthodox house, and the rest of us went to the Château de la Guette. We were once again divided into two groups on April 6. One group stayed there for a few more days and the other group, to which I belonged, left for their new home.
>
> As we knew each other well, the goodbyes were difficult. We finally got on the bus and left. We all thought we were going to an old house. At each stop, we were gripped with fear.[17]

Minnie doesn't hesitate to discuss her emotions, especially her fear over where they would live. Heinz Lonnerstädter, also from Berlin, describes his arrival and departure more succinctly:

> On Monday 20 March 1939 we left Berlin. We left from the Potsdam train station. We went through Magdeburg, Frankfurt and arrived at the border [. . .]. We reached Strasbourg at 5 o'clock. In Metz we were welcomed by a committee. We were taken to a hotel. For the first meal we had soup which contained a big piece of white bread. Then we continued to Paris. Here we were met by a bus which brought us to a Hospital for two days. After two days again

we went by bus to Château Maubuisson, which was a children's home. Here we met Viennese children. The Château was not very nice and was located opposite a cloister built in the 14th century. French lessons here were very poor. We spent the whole day lying on the lawn. Finally after three weeks, we were taken to Château de la Guette. This was our final destination. It is *prima* (superb) here.[18]

The children's first writings on France give precious clues on the policies dictating their care, including the length of stay of children at the Château de Maubuisson and the policy of placing siblings together, in spite of established age limits for each home.

Yet beyond these key facts, these diaries show adolescents' perspectives on being on the receiving end of such angst-ridden philanthropy. Indeed, the division between the world of adults and that of children in Minnie Engel's diary is palpable. This teenager's tale, like Heinz Lonnerstäder's, begins on the train, making no allusion to those she left behind. Instead, she focuses on life inside the train: her friends and, perhaps, sexual tensions with caretakers. Heinz seems to be noting what he saw when he looked out the window, suggesting he was in a more introspective mood.

While the women of Metz proudly described their reception of these children in the pages of *La Tribune Juive*, as seen earlier, the adolescents provide a slightly different version of the same events. Minnie emphasized the difficulty she had swallowing the food the women had so enthusiastically provided them. Both teens noted their surprise over French bread. And no one seemed to care for the Château de Maubuisson. Minnie qualified the reception at the Château de Maubuisson as "horrid." Heinz Lonnerstadter stated the Château was "not very nice" and Heinz Löw concurred, noting: "There it didn't go too well for us."[19] Minnie expresses more emotion, addressing her increasing fear as she approached the Château de la Guette. Perhaps even more significantly, her account focuses on the difficulty of separating from her friends as they were being dispatched to their children's homes, not from her parents.

Not all children were old enough to produce written sources. Photography leaves some clues as to how younger children and their families grappled with the departure. Family photos, taken in the weeks or days before the children left, suggest that even if families didn't realize their separation would be permanent, they did grasp its significance. This is evident in the case of ten-year-old Norbert Bikales. His father, Salomon Bikales, as well as his eldest brother were expelled from Germany to Poland in October 1938. However, Salomon was allowed to return to Berlin for several weeks in order to liquidate his assets in spring 1939, at which point he and his wife found a place on a Kindertransport for their youngest son, Norbert.[20] The family took the time in this rushed and surely panicked moment to pose for a photo (Plate 7). The image shows Norbert kneeling beside his mother, brushing his arm and hand against her own. She does not reciprocate his touch and instead stares stoically toward the camera, as does her husband. Norbert's parents were forced to leave for Poland in June 1939, before their son's departure. In a cruel role reversal, it was Norbert who took his parents to the station. He remembers running along the train as they waved goodbye.[21] Norbert left several weeks later for France on the transport from Berlin that arrived in Quincy-sous-Sénart on July 4, 1939.

Contemporaneous accounts and images are grounded in the period itself. They show that parents and children felt the need to document a moment they deemed significant. Children's writings, in particular, also serve as reminders that the children were in the midst of an unprecedented adventure. Separation from parents and families is one theme among others. The young teens seem more interested in the scenery, their travelling companions, the strange new foods, and how they were treated by others.

Such accounts stand in stark contrast to retrospective accounts by the adult children, who, with full knowledge of the Holocaust, probe their final moments with their parents. Ernst Valfer, who left his native Frankfurt in March 1939, recalled this moment concisely in our 2016 interview: "My father took me to the train. My mother couldn't go; it was too heart-wrenching for her. She smiled as I left, but I'm sure the moment I walked out the door she broke down. My father courageously took me but cried all the way."[22]

Young Berliner Stephan Lewy, who was reunited with both his father and stepmother in the United States in 1942, described his farewell in his 2015 memoir:

I did not feel I had a full grasp of what was happening, when my parents, on July 7 [3], 1939, took me to the railroad station similar to other families who were thinking of their children's safety. They were sending me, their fourteen year old son, to a refuge in France on a children's convoy [. . .]. At the train station I could hear the adults joking and laughing as they kissed their children goodbye. It seemed more or less as if we were being sent off to a picnic.

I noticed most of the parents smiled, joked, and promised, "We will see you soon" – "in a little while." – "Be good children." Were they trying to avoid upsetting their children? I am old enough to realize some parents were trying to hide any signs of sadness or fear.

As the train pulled out of the station, I drew three x's with my finger in the dust on the last window of the train. This was a German superstition, signifying I would never return.[23]

Unlike Stephan Lewy, Benjamin Hirsch was not reunited with his parents, who perished in the Holocaust. The latter left Germany at age six with four of his older siblings on the transport from Frankfurt in December 1938. His retrospective account of his departure focuses almost entirely on his mother:

When Mom told us we would be going to Paris, I could hardly hold back the excitement I felt. I was too young to grasp why we would be going to Paris. Actually, I had thought we were preparing for a pleasure trip from which we would return soon. I remember being impressed at the care that my mother took in packing my suitcase for me. Everything was so neatly placed. With every item she would put in, a tear drop would fall from her face. Her sadness, and that of my older siblings, was apparent and, at the same time, very confusing to me.

Indeed, Benjamin's account emphasizes his inability to grasp the nature of their separation:

When the day finally came, Mom found someone to watch Werner and Roselene [the two youngest siblings, who remained behind] while she took us to the *Bahnhof*, the Frankfurt train station. She saw to it that each of us had our own luggage and the little lunch bags she packed for us. [. . .] I still had no clue as to what was going on. I saw Asher, Flo and Sarah [siblings] holding on to Mom, all of them weeping, yet I still was unable to fathom a reason for all the sadness, especially since we would be embarking on a short pleasure trip to Paris, the "City of Lights." Actually, no one told me the trip would be a short one; I must have assumed that on my own. We boarded the train, waved and blew kisses to our mother and we were on our way. It was a blessing that I didn't realize that we wouldn't see Mom or the little ones for a long time, or, as it turned out, forever. I don't think I would have been able to handle the separation.[24]

As these retrospective accounts show, the departures took on new meaning after the Holocaust, when the children, as adults, processed these experiences with the realization that they were their last exchanges with their parents. Retrospective sources provide adults' narratives about the past, just as they reveal what they, as children, kept to themselves. This can also be seen in their accounts of how they presented themselves upon their arrival in France.

Discussions with the adult children about their early moments in France highlight the actions they took to maximize their control over their lives in the uncertain hours and days after arriving. They may have been separated from their parents, but family identities and advice followed them to France. At the same time, they were also free from the parental gaze and may have seized this occasion to fashion a new identity. For refugee children, the problem of the presentation of self is particularly acute, as they have to read and interpret the codes of the adult world, without having mastered the language or culture of their new environment.[25]

This difficulty can be seen in how children negotiated the selection process at the Château de Maubuisson, where most of the children were sent upon arrival. As they tried to grasp the expectations of their new caretakers and follow parental advice, the children twisted their family backgrounds and individual prerogatives into new identities. The CIE and OSE had determined that children over the age of ten or eleven who did not keep kosher would be sent to the Château de la Guette, whereas OSE would specialize in younger children, as well as those who came from orthodox families, for whom they opened a home in May 1939. Siblings, as seen above, were to be kept together, meaning the Château de la Guette had some children under eleven, while OSE cared for a group of (primarily orthodox) teenagers. While adults set the rules, the youth clearly sought to determine their own placements.

La Guette educators Alfred and Françoise Brauner wrote in the late 1990s that most of the La Guette children were from families of Jewish *origin*, many of whom had been shocked to discover that they were Jewish: "All of these children were profoundly German in their behavior and even in their physical attitudes, and many of them were blond and blue-eyed; very few could have been identified as 'Semites.' Moreover, most often, these children had learned of their Jewish ethnicity as a result of the Nazi racial measures, and it was a shock to them. They suddenly learned that they were 'enemies' of the German people."[26] This assessment of the children's Jewish identities was perhaps accurate for some of them, yet it most likely served to justify the Brauners' own secular methods.

It also contradicts the children's accounts. As seen above, celebrating Passover was not a new experience for young Minnie Engel, who used the Hebrew name for this holiday in her notebook. In a retrospective account from 1987, she described, in French, the experience of watching her family's synagogue burn down during the November pogrom: "The Synagogue was burning, and everything around it was destroyed. [. . .] In front of the window, the wall of ashes of this house of God, where we had spent so many beautiful hours inside and playing on the lawn [sic]."[27] While one cannot know with certainty how fourteen-year-old Minnie defined herself, it is clear that she was not as estranged from Judaism as her educators thought. Likewise, Herbert Feuerstein, another La Guette child from Vienna, described his upbringing in our 2015 interview as "moderately religious. We happened to have a Kosher house, not because of religion that much, because my mother wanted the kids to grow up knowing what they are. And then the kitchen makes the decision. And High Holidays and other holidays we went to synagogue, but we were not religious orthodox."[28]

It is difficult, even for adults, to define orthodox Judaism, since this concept has different meanings, depending on place and period. Asking a group of foreign children to define their religiosity was thus guaranteed to lead to mix-ups. The above examples of children with a Jewish upbringing in La Guette, including at least one from a kosher home, suggest that the selection process may have been disorganized, or fraught with comprehension problems. It is also possible that the children's own desires may have led them to downplay a traditional background in order to enter a less religious environment.

Selection for OSE's home in Eaubonne for orthodox children proved equally elusive. Retrospective accounts from its former children show the lengths to which they went to determine their place of landing. Fourteen-year-old Ernst Valfer's mother managed to get him a spot on the March 1939 transport from Frankfurt as donors to Frankfurt's orthodox orphanage. The family rarely attended synagogue, except for the High Holidays. Even then, it did not belong to one particular synagogue and alternated where it went each year. This is not to say, however, that the family was indifferent to its Jewish identity: before leaving, young Ernst had his bar mitzvah at one of Frankfurt's liberal synagogues. Still, Ernst received a strange parting gift from his mother, Frieda: "She gave me a prayer shawl to wear daily, as orthodox children wore under their clothing. And she said, 'The orthodox have taken you out, you stay with them and you do what they do.' So for all my time in Paris, I was orthodox. [. . .] My mother said, 'Look, you stay with the orthodox group, you'll stay safe.' So I did. I learned a lot."[29]

Frieda Valfer's assumption that her son would be safer with the orthodox is intriguing. She and her husband were both raised in orthodox homes, so perhaps her parting advice reflects a deeper desire to transmit this identity on the eve of her son's departure. It may have also been a token of gratitude to the orthodox orphanage for evacuating her son. More likely, though, Ernst's mother thought he would be safer among the orthodox because the latter would feel bound by Jewish law to care for him. The Talmud makes it clear that "all Israel is responsible for one another,"[30] while the five books of Moses and the Talmud provide multiple injunctions to care for orphans.[31] While Frieda Valfer could not anticipate her and her husband's deportation and murder, this mother certainly understood the gravity of their situation and may have felt that orthodox Jews would be less likely to ignore these sacred prescriptions. As a result, young Ernst adopted orthodoxy in France, choosing to live in the Eaubonne home for orthodox children, and he remains to this day committed to his daily prayers.

Susi K., who was also cared for in the orthodox Eaubonne home, recounted a telling anecdote about her religious identity in our 2015 interview. Her family history shows the diversity of Jewish families in interwar Europe and the acute difficulties atypical families faced when migrating. After the death of her father, when she was three years old, Susi went to live with an aunt and uncle in Deutsch Eylau, a small town in East Prussia. However, her adoption by the couple was never made official. When her adoptive parents' visas for the United States arrived just after the November pogrom, Susi was not able to leave with them. In the panicked moments before departure, Susi's adoptive father managed to find a place for his eleven-year-old daughter on a Kindertransport. The parents had to leave for the United States before their child's transport, forcing her to return to her birth mother for her final days in Germany. In this strange family reunion, Susi rekindled her relationship with her brother, who had remained with their birth mother after their father's death. For young Susi, leaving Germany meant not only losing home and separation from the parents who had raised her. It also forced her back into a family that, in her eyes, had rejected her but not her brother.

Susi's departure story reflects her confusion over her destination and anxiety over having to depend on her birth mother:

I thought I was going to Palestine. I thought I was going to end up in Palestine and, but, the irony of the whole thing was that I stayed with my real mother, whom I really didn't know and didn't want to know because I considered, you know, my adoptive parents, they were my parents. But I had to stay with her for three days [. . .]. My adoptive parents left for America. I had three days with strict instructions [. . .] that I was to go to the railroad train station and to remind my birth mother not to forget to take me. And that was all I remember. I got on the train, and I got off the train. Of course, I didn't realize I wasn't in Palestine, but it was Paris.[32]

In Paris, Susi's new caretakers asked about her religious background. In reality, Susi had been raised with some Jewish practice, but her family was definitely not orthodox: "I think, I think my mother always lit Shabbat candles. We weren't kosher. And we were just cultural Jews, you know, German Jews were not particularly religious Jews. If you were really religious, the German Jews would think we were Polish," she said, alluding to the historical tensions between German and Eastern European Jews. Nonetheless, she continued, "when they asked me 'Do you come from an orthodox home,' I said: 'Yes.' I said my father was a rabbi because I was afraid they wouldn't accept me. And someone said to me: 'Tell him your father was a rabbi.' So I had to learn a lot of stuff there, you know. We did the prayers."[33] A fear of not being accepted, part of this eleven-year-old's family history in Germany, had accompanied her to France. She simply pretended to be orthodox and learned the prayers.

Such "crossover" children, who migrated directly from their parents' homes, were most likely a minority, yet they found themselves with children who had been cared for in the Frankfurt and Berlin (Auerbach) Jewish orphanages, which were run under orthodox auspices. The young wards of these German Jewish institutions had faced major adjustments to their religious practices long before coming to France. Heinz Schuster, for example, came from a traditional Jewish family, yet he wrote, of his arrival in the Frankfurt orphanage, "One of the most significant adjustments I had to make was living in a more strictly orthodox environment than I had ever experienced."[34] Elfriede Meyer, it should be recalled from Chapter 1, was not orthodox when she entered the Frankfurt Jewish orphanage and rebelled against the rules of Shabbat by hopping on the tramway to go see her grandparents. But by the time they arrived in Paris, the children from the Frankfurt orphanage constituted a tightly knit group. While Elfriede could have asked to be placed in a less religious home, she did not do so. It is quite possible that she wanted to stay with the children who were familiar to her. The Frankfurt group was surely reminded of their shared bond just after their arrival in France, when they received a letter from Isidor Marx, the director of the orphanage who had sent them to France. Marx wrote to them during one of his quick trips to Strasbourg, on the occasion of Passover 1939, referring to himself as "Vati" (Papa) and to his wife, Rosa, as "Mutti" (Mama) and sharing with the children news about the difficult conditions in the orphanage since their departure.[35] Marx continued to escort children out of Germany, while his wife, Rosa, remained behind to care for the growing number of wards. One group of thirty-five boys, Marx explained in his letter, would leave for Palestine in late April 1939. The Frankfurt children in France must have been overjoyed to receive an account of their voyage from Germany to Palestine in a letter from Joseph (Seppel) Einhorn to Fritz Strauss, who noted the presence of girls on the train. A second letter followed, describing their new life in their youth village for religious children, Kfar Hanoar Hadati, near Haifa: "The girls from the orphanage are not as coy as they used to be—and write to each other. Oh, my dear boy [*Männecken*], it's a pity you aren't here."[36] Such correspondence reinforced the children's shared geographical bonds, even if their religiosity seemed challenged by their hormones.

Looking more closely at Eaubonne's young inhabitants, one sees that those who were truly from "orthodox" families (a concept that requires continual redefinition), such as Ruth and her sister Miriam or Benjamin Hirsch and his siblings, were actually fewer in number than the children suggested. Such identity reconfiguration, which began for some in the German children's orphanages, would continue throughout the children's exile in France and with each step of their migratory path. Adults may have imposed structures and selection criteria, but children negotiated around them, interpreting their new settings to their best ability. The arrival of the children into the homes led to new confrontations and friendships, shedding light on surprising differences which in turn caused the children to further question their identities.

Through this adult-dictated, child-mediated selection process, the Château de la Guette soon had 130 children under its care from Berlin,

Mannheim, Frankfurt, and Vienna. In March 1939, the OSE had 109 Kindertransport children, in addition to 40 children who arrived in France on their own and who, according to OSE, had been imprisoned due to lack of visas.[37] Due to the unstable political situation, new groups of refugee children continually arrived in the OSE homes. As a result of these new arrivals, by September 1939 the OSE was responsible for 307 children in its four homes. [38]

The children in the OSE homes represented a diverse bunch. As we will later see, they stemmed from extremely different political and religious backgrounds and built durable bonds according to their shared affinities. In some respects, the La Guette children were comparatively more homogeneous. All of the children in this home had come to France unaccompanied and shared a sense of anxiety regarding the fate of their siblings and parents in Central Europe. Nonetheless, they, too, established different social groups. At La Guette, geographical origin seemed to be the most salient factor determining the children's social networks. According to a retrospective testimony from former educator Lida Jablonski:

These three groups were very different from each other: the Berliners and the Viennese had such a different mentality, despite the same social background (families of rather well-to-do intellectuals: doctors, engineers) that at the beginning they felt violently opposed (e.g. a 10-year-old Austrian girl cried her eyes out when she learned that she had to share her room with "German girls"!) Among the Austrians, there were many Zionists, while the Berliners were mostly from assimilated backgrounds. Those from the Palatinate came from very small towns and were in most cases from comfortable, middle-class homes (cattle merchants, etc.) yet were quite rustic. They kept out of the quarrels between the Viennese and the Berliners.[39]

According to Lida Jablonski, the geographic divisions stemmed from very real linguistic barriers among the children:

The Viennese and those from the Palatinate generally spoke their own dialects, which the Berliners did not understand. I remember a baroque scene in which a Viennese boy, who could speak '*Hochdeutsch*' (literary German), had to translate what was being said between a girl from Berlin and a boy from Austria who could only speak in dialect.[40]

The educators had initially planned on mixing up the geographical groups by placing German and Austrian children of the same age together in "packs" (*meutes*), the term they used for their shared bedrooms. Each pack had been named after an animal (for boys) or a flower (for girls) by the home's first director, twenty-year-old Willy Katz, to the great annoyance of Alfred and Fritzi Brauner, who found this infantilizing. The educators quickly gave up on the idea of grouping their wards by age group and ended up rooming the children by geographic origin.[41]

Children's contemporaneous sources make reference to these tensions yet do not dwell on them. Minnie Engel, for example, describes the feeling of walking into the Château de Maubuisson: "Without giving us time to take off our coats and hats, nor wipe off the dust from the trip, we were led to a table where other boys and girls were already seated, staring at us very curiously. It was, as we would later learn, a Viennese transport. We did not get along at all. There were arguments and fights. Afterwards, however, things got better."[42]

Nonetheless, if tensions did ease, we see Minnie's description of her friendships focus on her roommates from the "Sunflower Pack," all of whom, like her, came from Berlin or its surroundings:

I was first on the 4th floor with girls I didn't like. I would have preferred to be with Lotte, Susi etc. And that's how we got to the *Tourne-Sol* (Sunflower). All the girls' rooms were on the first floor and were named after flowers. [. . .] I liked it much better at the *Tourne au Sol* (Sun Flower) [sic]. We were good friends and got along very well despite the age differences. [. . .] Among us, there were no Viennese. Later on, Ursula Matzdorff was added, whom we didn't like at first, but who adapted well. There was a competition between the rooms for decoration and cleanliness.[43]

As Minnie shows, regional identities were maintained at La Guette through room assignments, and it also seems that educators cultivated a friendly competition among the "packs" to foster group belonging, in keeping with the teachings of Alfred Adler.

Boys at La Guette describe similar divisions. Heinz Löw, from Vienna, mentions in his diary that he became friends with Luz Scheucher, from Berlin. Yet his closest friends appear to have been other boys from Vienna, including Fritz David (Duft'l), Ernst Appenzeller, and Maurice Horowitz (Mundi). He mentions the "Viennese gang" that was "quite rowdy" in an entry of September 4, 1939: "We irked the new educator, ran up to the 2nd story, and made a lot of noise and banged our dressers."[44] On November 1, Heinz remembered, his group had a "fight scheduled with the Eagle group; they were very cowardly by beating Mundi up."[45] Contrary to the "Viennese gang," the Eagle Pack was composed of German teens, mostly from Berlin. Heinz Lonnerstädter, from Berlin, was more concise. His diary entries rarely extend beyond one or two lines, but we learn from him that on September 24, there was a "grand soccer match. Berlin and Vienna vs. Palatinate."[46]

Regional differences thus mattered most in contemporaneous testimonies about La Guette, perhaps more than in OSE homes, where the testimonies point to divisions stemming from politics, religious practice, and social class. The nature of the sources and period in which they were written matter: I have in my possession primarily retrospective sources for the OSE homes; as adults, the former OSE children may have realized that what had divided them had been, in fact, political, religious, and class orientations, especially after reading Ernst Papanek's posthumous memoir.[47] At the time, however, they may have considered differences solely in terms of geography, just as the contemporaneous sources on La Guette describe.

Understanding the dividing lines between children is important because they reveal the criteria the children themselves used to form their friendship networks. These durable yet changing groups, in the absence of direct family, may have come to feel like surrogate family to some. Children's relationships did not, however, develop in a vacuum:

the larger pedagogical project in the homes was essential for cultivating their bonds. The children's republics in the OSE homes and the Château de la Guette opened children's social worlds, shaping their relationships with other children and their educators.

The refugee children began learning French upon their arrival in Spring 1939 but were not yet able, for the most part, to attend French public schools. The educators, as seen earlier, had their own pedagogical agenda that gave them an ulterior motive for schooling the children in the homes. As the OSE homes' director Ernst Papanek explained: "To take the children away for the better part of every day would be bad enough. To take them away and turn them over to a school system which was run along the strict authoritarian lines of the French school system would be to undercut me completely."[48] Similarly, the adolescents at the Château de la Guette continued their schooling with Alfred Brauner and Ernst and Lida Jablonski, who encouraged the children to write and draw about their experiences of persecution and to build confidence through sports.[49] They, too, were driven by a larger agenda, both political and intellectual. As he wrote in his 1946 book:

> Their [the children's] attitude toward politics had to be corrected without bias. We sought to give them what they lacked most: the spirit of solidarity. They were a mass of small, selfish individuals who could not see beyond the limits of family interest. We tried to create a community within the framework of our house by creating a newspaper, an artistic group, an open atmosphere, and we succeeded so well that within four months a collective feeling had arisen, encompassing the entire house.[50]

Many of the children encountered progressive pedagogy for the first time in the homes. If the Château de la Guette made some of the children feel they had entered a castle straight out of a fairy tale, it was the establishment of the children's republic, most likely on May 1, 1939, that confirmed this idea.[51] Two diaries of La Guette children mention the important day on which their republic was declared, although they do not give the same dates.[52] Minnie Engel provides the most detail:

> Now, a very important chapter, the republic: it was proclaimed on July 3 [sic]. It was not only a game, as many of us said, it was a very good idea thought up by our educators who wanted to raise us as independent individuals, with our own opinions and ideals. Nothing was missing. Everything was there, everything that belongs to a real republic: the citizens of La Guette elected a parliament. There were 13 members. First a constituent assembly was held and then we had to promise (an oath) to fulfill our obligations faithfully. The rights and duties of the senate (the educators) and the citizens (the children) were discussed. At the first session of the parliament the ministers were elected: Mausi, Minister-President (Chairman of the Council), Kurt Pauker, Minister of the Interior, Fee, Minister of Finance, Lore Shapira, Minister of Health, Georg Wozaseck, Director of the Bank, Harry Rotenberg, Minister of Sports, Hans Denes, Minister of Education (the one who conducts discussions in French), Heinz Berger, Minister of Public Works. Whenever there was something important to discuss, the parliament and the ministerial cabinet met.[53]

Once established, the republic seemed to wear down the regional barriers among the children, creating a new set of leaders, even if the children from the Palatinate were underrepresented among its ministers.[54] As members of a republic, the children had an official voice, plus a newspaper and their own currency, les Guettes. Alongside the political goal of restoring democracy for the young victims of Nazism and the therapeutic goal of healing traumatized children was the ideal of collective play. This is what the children emphasize in their accounts. Writing during the Nazi occupation, after the dissolution of the home, Minnie Engel noted that the choir organized by Harry Spiegel was her "most beautiful memory"[55] of La Guette. Yet she also wrote about their garden, in which each "pack" had a section.[56]

Minnie's perceptions of life in the Château de la Guette are echoed in an unsigned drawing from a fellow child, most likely from July 1939. On the top of the drawing (Plate 11), in a before-and-after sequence, one sees the children fighting in their different "packs," but then lining up and working in the garden. The lower part of the image then depicts a child pledging, most likely in the context of the children's republic. "I promise," she states, overlooking a table on which the French flag was spread out. One notices the word "July" written across in the lower corner, which was most likely added by Alfred Brauner. The fact that Brauner took the liberty of writing the date (yet not the names of the artists) on the children's drawings indicates he was actively studying the evolution of their art, in continuity with the collection of children's drawings he had begun in Spain. Unbeknownst to the children, Brauner was studying them as subjects. His analyses, on Spanish and Jewish children, earned him a second PhD in 1946 from the Sorbonne, which he published as a book soon after.[57]

Encouraged by adults, the drawings from La Guette cannot be considered spontaneous, child-driven sources. The children knew they had an audience, and surely tailored their art to what they thought their caretakers wanted to see. The French flag, as seen above, is an important motif in many of the children's drawings. One sees the influence of Willy Katz's short-lived directorship, with the caption: "Our oath: The spirit of la Guette is to live in us and give us new hope, like Willi [sic] said."[58] Learning to be a refugee clearly required reverence to a new flag and new symbols. Their educators seemed to be consciously instructing their wards on the importance of belonging to the French Republic. This would have been important to the patriotic Baroness de Rothschild, and possibly even the left-wing educators.[59] For the children, however, it is quite possible that the children's republic and its symbols were just another French quirk, like the white bread that had puzzled them upon arrival.

Retrospective accounts of La Guette wax nostalgic, suggesting that this period, when seen in hindsight, was an enchanted parenthesis. The artist Paul Peter Porges, when interviewed as an adult, exclaimed: "It was fantastic! But don't tell anyone!"[60] Indeed, their period in the home was sandwiched between Nazi persecution in Central Europe and the Nazi occupation of France and the ensuing Nazi-Vichy persecutions.

Werner Matzdorff, the person who would later coax his comrades into sharing their memories, recalled, in the late 1990s:

> We were grouped by age or origin, in "packs." A small store was managed by the children. We found stationery, darning thread, some sweets paid for in "guettes," our currency, which was earned not according to results but for our efforts in school. What an adventure the vaccination was, the first shower taken together, naked! Waking up early in the morning and doing gymnastics or "hebertism" in the open air. For lack of knowing better, at meals, we sometimes ate the artichokes, leaves and hay included. Childhood loves were emerged. We sang. We came and went as we pleased in the woods.[61]

As seen earlier, Werner was later arrested, in 1942, just barely escaping deportation. His older sister Ursula was forced to flee to Switzerland. The violence of these events stands in striking contrast to life at La Guette and helps explain Werner's idyllic depiction of a world without adults, in which children actually ate artichokes, leaves and all. His positive memories shed light on why, at the time of his retirement in the 1980s, he dedicated so many hours to collecting information from fellow children.

Martin Axelrad from Vienna, known in the home as "Maki," answered Werner Matzdorff's questionnaire with a detailed account, written in 1986. Adults are present in his account, providing a certain framework to his childhood experiences at La Guette:

> I remember a very satisfying group life, with more or less free or skillfully directed activities (in particular building huts in the woods, participating in two plays from "Lumpazi vagabundus" and "Chveik"). I don't remember teaching per se, but "lectures" (on Darwin, etc).
>
> A failure: while I was rather athletic (participant in an athletics and gymnastics club in Vienna, member of the soccer team of the Guette, etc.) the compulsory gymnastics after jumping out of bed managed to turn me off from sports definitively; in this case, the skill of our educators showed its limits.

Martin Axelrad points to the important role of educators at La Guette. They were the ones behind the "very satisfying collective life," the annoying morning calisthenics, and the imposed secularism that left him feeling unmoored:

> It was confirmed, on the other hand, in their attitude toward a "religious crisis" that I went through with a small group of other children. This crisis was obviously due to the attempt to cling to a "father" more powerful than mine, who had proved incapable of preventing the shipwreck of my little universe; perhaps there was also in my attitude a reaction to the secularism of the educators [. . .]. Cleverly tolerated by the latter, the crisis did not last: this "father" turned out to be just as powerless to prevent catastrophes.[62]

Martin's own religious rebellion suggests that the educators served as a model or counter-model, depending on the child, and, significantly, shows that the children felt secure enough in their environment to stand up to their educators' secularism without fear of being rejected or sent away. Such sentiments were also present in contemporaneous accounts. During the occupation, Minnie Engel wrote: "And most importantly, the educators were amazing. We could open up to them about anything and they gave us advice. They really tried to replace our parents. They never lost patience. If someone had gone too far, they would explain it to him calmly and made his mistake clear."[63]

Minnie alludes to parents in this passage, a painful topic for many children. Indeed, even if most of the children's contemporaneous and retrospective accounts describe their initial months in France as being like summer camp, at closer glance one can detect their longing for their parents. As seen above, educators played a key role not only in mediating the children's emotions about missing home through music, but also in their insistence that children write about their past lives and reach out to their parents by writing letters.[64]

Educators are also a central theme in retrospective accounts about the OSE homes. The children's republics certainly marked children's memories, but Ernst Papanek seems to have played an even more important role in making them feel they had a right to personhood.

Seventy-seven years after her stay in OSE's Eaubonne home (Plate 5), former resident Eda Pell noted:

> All these things that we did that they taught us how to do, it's pretty damn good. It's pretty amazing. But most of all Ernst [Papanek] gave us a feeling that there's a future, that we're young and we can conquer the world. At least I took him very seriously. [. . .] We had a student council, as you would call it. I mean that was very revolutionary. That was Ernst's idea. To have the kids have some power, basically. I agree. And I think that's what was so marvelous about it. And Ernst [Valfer] was the president of our student council. And we all voted for that. We were the ones who voted for it. So we knew how to vote. That was very democratic.[65]

While all of the OSE homes set up children's republics, the Eaubonne home's implementation of Papanek's pedagogy was challenging due to its orthodox orientation. In his posthumous memoir, Ernst Papanek relates his conflict with an orthodox Rabbi over whether Eaubonne would be a home for orthodox children, as Papanek wished, or an orthodox children's home: "It would be impossible to conduct a system of progressive education under such conditions [in an orthodox children's home], not only because I would be obliged to follow all the Orthodox rules and rituals but because I—and every counselor and teacher who took his authority from me—would be acting as an agent of God."[66] The two men eventually reached a compromise. Papanek oversaw the home and had authority over all educational matters, while a resident-director took responsibility for Jewish ritual and the respect of dietary laws. As seen above, fourteen-year-old Ernst Valfer had decided to pass as orthodox when he arrived in France, following his mother's advice. This did not prevent him from becoming the president of the Eaubonne home's children's republic. He shared an anecdote in our 2016 interview that reveals the complicated coexistence between orthodoxy and progressive education: "What happened is it was New Year's [Eve], and the non-orthodox in Tourelles [children's home] were allowed to have a dance. And because we were orthodox we were not allowed to participate. A: it was too late. It was boys and girls. The only time you could dance a little bit was on Purim. So, we had to leave early. They had a party, and we were angry." Ernst decided they should "do something":

It was an expression of anger. In those days I just thought it was an expression of adventure. And so, our idea was that the five of us, plus one or two from another bedroom, would don our bed sheets over our heads, flashlights, take the front off so that the bulb was exposed. We'd go in the big girls' room, shake up their beds, moan and groan.

"Like ghosts," I asked? He answered in the affirmative. Yet things did not go as planned:

Well, another thing happened, that on the way to the big girls' room, which was the biggest room, the biggest bedroom, there were something like 20 girls in it, 18 maybe. On the way was past the home, or the rooms of the *directrice,* whom we didn't like. So somebody, and it wasn't I—it wasn't in the program—stuffed some clothes together, took some clothes of hers, stuffed them, and put them on her toilet. And then we went to the girls' rooms. And the girls shrieked.

[The effigy of the *directrice* was] sitting on the toilet, as far as I remember. And the girls shrieked, naturally. We didn't see anything because we were covered. Going in there was okay, but not looking at the girls semi-naked, that we wouldn't do. And eventually after we had scared them all out of their minds, we retreated.

Victorious, the boys went back to their room, where they "had a little party" and ate some sausage. However, Ernst continued:

This became *un scandale,* and the *directrice* exaggerated, not only did we put this effigy in the bathroom, but we tore her clothes and did damage. It's probable that somebody tipped over a bottle. And the grand rabbi of Paris, maybe it wasn't the grand rabbi, who had the religious authority over us, was summoned. And he came in an army uniform. He had been conscripted already. He was a rabbi, so he had the tablets of Moses. And all the students were assembled. And they wanted to separate boys and girls. And I don't know what they wanted to do. Ernst Papanek was there. And Ernst Papanek talked them into putting us on probation. And we lost for, I forgot how long, the self-government.[67]

This account, provided over seventy years after the events, shows how vivid the children's homes remain for the former children. It also shows the importance of the children's republic in creating a new set of leaders in the home, or, in Ernst Valfer's proud words, a "president with a capital P."[68] Making an effigy of the *directrice* of their home, raiding the girls' dormitory as ghosts, eating (perhaps unkosher?) sausage, was enough to threaten the children's "student-government." Papanek describes in his book what Ernst shared, calling it "the great revolt" of the Eaubonne children.[69] Papanek served as a counterweight, defending the children. In this account, the children push back against adults. Papanek seems to have enjoyed joining them in their fight.

The "great revolt" also had significance for Henny Marks, a former Eaubonne child. She wrote to Papanek in 1965 on the occasion of his sixty-fifth birthday:

Prior to that day in 1939, when a group of us drove into Montmorency, calling an adult by his first name was a completely foreign thought to me. Being able to freely call you Ernst was possibly one of the first steps to a new kind of world, where every child in its own right was listened and talked to, and where trust and communication between people could help us overcome many doubts and inner conflicts. Do you recall the night of our revolution in Eaubonne, when an entire home of "good bourgeois children" turned into what is currently called a group of juvenile vandals? Yes, we all participated, even those of us who were only approving onlookers. You never thought of asking who or what initiated it. But the moment you had us assembled and looked at all of us, I knew, and I think we all understood, that no material punishment imposed by you, could have hit us harder than our own shame and uneasiness you confronted us with.[70]

Papanek, it seems, through his progressive pedagogy, opened a door for the children that allowed them a new sense of self, which included an ability to protest and take responsibility for their actions.

Papanek's relationships with certain children outlasted their stay in France. Their retrospective accounts suggest that Papanek became a father figure to more than one OSE child. The seeds for these relationships were planted in France, and they flourished in the United States in the postwar period. Discussions on Papanek reveal what the oral history scholar Alessandro Portelli calls "the fabula" and "the plot," the "way in which the story materials are arranged by narrators in order to tell the story."[71] Papanek represents a turning point in the "plot" of several adult children's lives: their narratives jump across the periods to explain his importance. Ernst Valfer, whose two parents were murdered in the Holocaust, explained: "He was, without question, next to my parents, the most influential person to everybody. He had this ability of dealing with every child as if he were their very best personal friend. And, as the president of the home, I dealt with him more than others. And so, I think I had a very special bond with him."[72] Ernst Valfer remained in contact with Papanek until the latter's death. After a career in engineering, he became a psychologist. When I asked Kurt Sonnenfeld, another former OSE child, what Papanek represented for him, he had one word: "Inspiration."[73] Sonnenfeld later became a social worker, specializing in youth. Like Ernst Valfer, he continued to meet with Papanek regularly throughout his adult life. Sonnenfeld's own parents survived the war. For him, Papanek was not a surrogate father but an "uncle figure."[74]

Both men, one can notice, state that, while all the children had a close relationship to Papanek, their own relationship to him was somehow special. This seems to have been the gift Ernst Papanek had with children, helping them feel "as if he were their very best personal friend."[75] Such sentiments were not shared only by boys and men. Hanna Kaiser, in marrying Gus Papanek, acquired Ernst Papanek as a father-in-law. Her decades-long dedication to preserving his intellectual and pedagogical legacy speaks volumes.[76] Papanek's wife, Helene (Lene), should not be forgotten. As the home's doctor, she had a great deal of contact with the children. Viennese girl Renée Spindel and her sister Brigitta, ten and seven years old, respectively, were aware of her presence at the Villa Helvetia. In our 2016 interview, Renée explained to me that Lene Papanek was the reason why she later became a nurse.[77]

With their educators and other children in their collective homes, many children found a sense of security, even if they longed for home. Yet even the best of educators could not keep war at bay. The enchanted parenthesis started to unravel in September 1939.

CHAPTER 8

The Meanings of War, September 1939–June 1940

The greatest circus leader in the country
It is the famous Supermedrano,
World-known are his famous artists
And his big caravan of beasts.
If he shouts in the arena that the animals should obey,
It is the lions and the bears that sway.
Yes, we are a circus of wonder,
A circus, unlike any other![1]

Thus sang the children in the OSE homes in the final act of the circus they staged in September 1939, just days after the outbreak of the Second World War. Two hundred individuals, including French officials, came to see the refugee children perform.[2] The event would be recalled by many, decades later: Ruth remembers dressing up as a cat, while her older sister performed as a "Turkish dancer." Elfriede performed as a yodeler from the Tyrols.[3] The fact that she saved the program and the words of the finale through her multiple migrations speaks to its significance. *Out of the Fire*, Ernst Papanek's posthumous memoir, also evokes the circus, especially the fact that, after the final act, the German and Austrian children sang the "Marseillaise," to the great delight of the French onlookers.

One senses that the circus served many functions: for Papanek and his collaborators, it was a means of showcasing his pedagogical methods to the doubtful OSE leadership and French officials: after only six months in France, the children had mastered enough French to put on a show and sing the "Marseillaise," even if Papanek admits it was "as close as it was possible to get to French without actually hitting upon one certifiable French word."[4] For the adult children recalling their life in the children's homes, the circus perhaps serves as a screen memory, helping them repackage the bittersweet period as a joyful one.[5] Yet it is also quite possible that the circus remains lodged in their memories because it marked the end of what many considered to be an enchanted parenthesis, the six-month period between leaving home and the outbreak of war.

The Nazi invasion of Poland on September 1, 1939 and subsequent outbreak of the Second World War had consequences throughout Europe. France officially declared war on September 3, 1939. The term "Phoney war" or "*Drôle de guerre*," used to describe the period between the declaration of war and the Nazi invasion of France in May 1940, implies that the war did not drastically impact life in France. Yet for the young refugee children, this could not be further from the truth. Even in its earliest phases, the Second World War had direct consequences on the daily lives of these young refugees.[6]

Children's republics in the Jewish children's homes established very real structures in which the children and educators could explore democracy in a larger moment of political instability. However, the declaration of war put a brutal end to the children's republic at the Château de la Guette. The children in the OSE homes continued to "co-administer" the homes yet found themselves confronted with new tensions. Communication between parents and children was greatly affected. Bomb drills and, eventually, air raids led to new anxieties. However, children were never passive wards of organizations. They continued to push back against authority and devised creative ways to communicate with their parents, despite new complications. The relationships they cultivated with others provided vital affective ties that helped them cope with the growing uncertainty.

Viennese thirteen-year-old Heinz Löw began his diary on the day Nazi Germany invaded Poland. The gravity of the hour encouraged Heinz to record his departure from Vienna and first moments in France. The war represented an important event for the young teen, but so did the model of the château he and his friends Ernst and Walter were building. He noted: "We do not have enough nails (but never fear, we'll get them somehow). Ernst [Jablonski, most likely] told us some scary news at dinner; England and France declared war against Germany. There is a real war already started. I can hardly believe it. German planes have already bombed London (hard to comprehend)." The next day, he wrote: "After lunch I went to the playhouse and started, with Ernst and Walter, to build the model of the castle; it's coming along well." On September 5, he wrote: "Nothing much to report today. Ernst [Jablonski] brought us (the Vienna gang), a large fret saw and saw blades (really nice of him)."[7] War was a significant event for Heinz. So was building the model of the château.

Tuning out the outside world could only work for so long, since the war had almost immediate consequences for the children. Most significantly, the declaration of war led La Guette's male educators to leave, putting an end to the children's republic. Alfred Brauner, a French citizen, was called up for military duty. Ernst Jablonski and Harry Spiegel, recent refugees, were interned as enemy aliens. To replace them, Germaine de Rothschild turned to the same Strasbourg-Jewish circles that would eventually replace OSE's foreign leadership. While the children's accounts mention Mademoiselle Bernheim, it was Flore Loinger (née Rosensweig, 1911–1995) who permanently took over the direction of La Guette.[8] Born in Chemnitz, Germany, to a Polish father and an Alsatian mother, she had come to France as an eight-year-old orphan. She was raised in Laure Weil's Jewish Girls' Home in Strasbourg, where Andrée Salomon, as seen earlier, had boarded after her arrival in the city. Three years apart in age, both young women were active in Strasbourg's burgeoning Zionist milieu. This is where Flore met her future husband, Georges Loinger, whose father was a well-respected antiques dealer from Galicia. The couple married in 1934 and settled in Paris. While Georges Loinger was a trained engineer, he decided to dedicate his life to the Zionist project of "regeneration through sports"[9] by obtaining a degree in physical education. He first worked with the rabbinical students at the Séminaire Israélite on the Rue Vauquelin, providing them with "twenty-minute warm-ups before their lessons."[10] During this period, Flore worked as a secretary at the Jewish Scouting movement, Éclaireurs Israélites de France. In 1935, Strasbourg native Marcus Cohn, founder of the Parisian École Maïmonide, offered the couple positions at the Parisian Jewish school which had been designed to train future rabbis and Jewish communal workers. Georges ran the sports department, and Flore worked as an administrator, supplying the boarding school with food and supplies.[11] In the summertime, Georges was popular in Jewish summer camps, working with the Jewish Scouting movement, as well as at the Belleville Patronage, which was funded by Germaine de Rothschild. This led the Baroness to ask him to direct the Château de la Guette in September 1939. However, Georges Loinger, like many others, had been called up for military duty. He mentioned that his wife Flore "would do the trick very well."[12]

From both a professional and, especially, an ideological point of view, Flore Loinger couldn't have been more different from the progressive educators who had been running La Guette. She quickly terminated the children's republic. She and Henry Pohorylès, an educator who had worked with the children at the Château de Maubuisson, immediately established Shabbat services and lessons on Zionism. Alfred Brauner's wife Fritzi was asked to leave.[13] According to Lida Jablonski, who stayed on after her husband left, Flore Loinger established "a classical system of organization and teaching and introduced, together with Henry Pohorylès (who was good with the children), a national Jewish, Zionist tendency in the House: songs, Friday night celebrations . . ."[14]

Martin Axelrad, a former La Guette resident, looked back at this transition: "After the departure of F[red], E[rnst] and H[arry] in September, the atmosphere at La Guette changed. I am unable to judge Mrs. Loinger, who took over the management at that time, objectively. In any case she was in an impossible situation; she would have had to be really extraordinary for the change not to have been perceived as a general deterioration and not arouse more or less open opposition; this, in turn, made things even more difficult for her."[15]

Indeed, by this point, the La Guette children had learned to question authority. They openly contested Flore Loinger, which some felt had serious consequences for their group. In early December 1939, twenty-five of the oldest children were selected to leave La Guette. Sixteen boys were sent to a boarding school, the Institution du Bel-Air, in the Paris suburb of Clamart. Nine girls were sent to a different boarding school, the Pensionnat du Bois, Colonie de Vacances La Vigne, in St Briac, Brittany. A member of the Baroness's staff notified the French police of the change in student body, providing them the exact list and location of the students.[16] Martin Axelrad recalled: "I was part of the group that left in November 39 to the 'Pension' in Clamart. Rightly or wrongly, (probably wrongly!) this 'exile' was perceived by the group (about twenty) sent there as a measure aimed at breaking up the anti-Loinger opposition." The austere conditions in the boarding school may have reinforced this suspicion among the children. In the words of Martin Axelrad, the boarding school in Clamart was "an infectious place from all points of view (living conditions, atmosphere, discipline, hygiene, food, etc.), especially after the 'children's republic' that we had known."[17]

It is most likely that sending the children away was not a punishment but a preparation for the war. A close look shows that the young leaders of the children's republic were, with a few exceptions, kept at La Guette. This suggests that the move was intended to better integrate the teens into their host country, which was now at war. Lida Jablonski, who had no reason to defend her husband's replacement, recalled that the children were sent away to learn French.[18] In the 1990s, Flore Loinger explained her position somewhat anachronistically: "I had a completely different perspective [from the former educators]. They [the children] should have fun, that's fine, but what was important to me was that they were ready for the life that awaited them, because I sensed that they would never see their parents again. That's why they were sent to vocational schools, and the extraordinary thing is that these schools accepted them even though they were German."[19]

The Château de la Guette thus lost a significant number of its educators and its wards, as well as its innovative pedagogy, long before the Nazi invasion of France in May 1940. The children's sources point out the effect this had on their affective lives. As seen above, Heinz Löw shared his diary with his friend Paul Peter Porges, leaving room for the latter to illustrate key passages. The two Viennese boys were separated. Heinz Löw was sent to the Clamart boarding school, while Paul Peter Porges stayed behind at La Guette. Heinz stopped writing in his diary entirely during the period between November 1, 1939 and May 26, 1940. After this date, while still writing in German, he changed his handwriting from the German *Sütterlinschrift* of its initial entries to the round cursive taught in French schools, only to switch back to *Sütterlinschrift* in late July 1940, since he "almost forgot how to write in German script."[20] There were no other illustrations, however. Allusions to friends abound in Heinz's diary, yet we cannot know if he dared share his writings with other children.

The children's republics, known as "co-administration" in the OSE's four children's homes, continued to thrive, even after the declaration of war. The war nonetheless changed their dynamics. The rapidly changing geopolitical situation announced new challenges, bringing new groups of children into the fold.

Already in June 1939, a group of children arrived in the OSE homes who had left Germany with their families on the SS *St. Louis* in May 1939, en route to Havana with the hope of eventually finding refuge in the United States. However, while all of the 907 passengers had entry permits to Cuba, they had been issued illegally by the corrupt head of immigration in Havana. In spite of the efforts of the JDC, the refugees were denied entry to Cuba. The United States also refused to accept them, and the *St. Louis* was forced to make its way back to Europe. To prevent the refugees from having to return to Nazi Germany, the head of JDC in France, Morris Troper, with the help of the French feminist Louise Weiss, encountered earlier, led negotiations with Western European governments. Two hundred and twenty-four refugees were accepted by France, where they were assigned residence outside of Paris.[21] Parents were given the option of sending their children to the OSE homes. The *St. Louis* children, most likely twenty-seven in number and of various ages, created a new group in the OSE homes and were referred to as the "*Kubaner*" (Cubans), whereas the religious children eventually came to be known as the "*Eaubonner*," since their home was located in the town of Eaubonne.[22] They were soon joined by a new group that couldn't be more different from them.

Indeed, the Nazi invasion of Poland on September 1, 1939 and France's declaration of war on September 3 led to the arrival of the offspring of the central figures of the Austrian and German labor movement, who had fled Germany and Austria in the earliest hours and had been living in exile with their parents. For some in this group, Prague had represented a first landing point. Others had fled directly from Vienna to Paris after the Nazi annexation of Austria in March 1938. The Red Falcons, a socialist youth group in Paris, provided a natural home for the refugee teens.[23]

While many of the children in this group had at least one parent with a Jewish background, their identities and sense of solidarity ran along political, not religious, lines. Hanna Kaiser fled to Paris from Prague with her non-Jewish mother, Elly Kaiser, who had worked at the Reichstag as secretary and archivist of the German Social Democratic Party. Her Jewish father, Alexander Rubenstein, known as Alexander Stein, had fled Czarist Russia in 1906. In Berlin, as a journalist and a writer, he had remained active in Menshevik and socialist circles, which had caused him to flee to Prague in 1933. Hanna was seven when she and her mother had joined him there, in April 1934. Hanna's parents were not married and had not lived together in Berlin. Exile provided the family an opportunity to live under the same roof. Hanna, eleven at the moment of her arrival in Paris, describes her Paris entourage in her book:

> Most of the members of our Paris group of Red Falcons had been between twelve and fifteen years old at the time of the German annexation of Austria, the *Anschluss*, on March 11, 1938. They went into their first exile in France a few months later, most of them together with their families. Before they left Vienna, the ones who were Jewish had suddenly been forced to transfer from their regular schools to a segregated High School set aside for Jewish children, the *Staatsgymnasium* [. . .].
>
> For some of the children, the transfer came as a surprise because their sense of identity was most clearly defined by the political

affiliations of their parents and by the neighborhoods they lived in, not their religion or ethnicity. Their families, like mine, were almost all *konfessionslos* (without a religion, secular): this had been a political decision, not a spiritual or theological one. Even though many of the leading figures in the strongly anti-clerical Austrian Socialist movement before the *Anschluss* were Jews, their children had rarely been brought up to observe religious ritual.[24]

For Hanna, the friendships formed in France would prove both durable and formative.

"My formal political education began in that Red Falcon group in Paris," she wrote. "Being from Berlin and not from Vienna mattered a lot. The other children teased me for my Berlin accent and laughed like mad when I could not pronounce words in the Viennese dialect, words like *Zwirnknäulerl*, little ball of yarn, that nobody used except as a tongue-twister. I didn't really mind being teased because it made me the focus of their attention and I liked that, liked it a lot."[25]

The group spent the summer months of 1939 together in a Red Falcons summer camp just south of Paris, in the town of Le Plessis-Robinson. At the outbreak of war, the teens were transferred to the OSE homes in Montmorency, most likely thanks to Ernst Papanek, whose own son Gustl was also in the Red Falcons. As seasoned political observers, their parents assumed the Nazis would bomb Paris in the early stages of the war and felt their children would be safer outside the city. Furthermore, as enemy aliens, the men were interned after the declaration of war on September 3, 1939. Ernst Papanek, too, was interned for a short period, first in a hippodrome in the town of Maisons-Laffitte, near Paris, and then in two other camps in Normandy. By early November, however, he was back at Montmorency.[26]

The dynamics among the children and teens show other pressing concerns. Hanna was twelve when she became one of the "*Robinsoner*," as this new group was called in the OSE homes, after the place they had spent the summer of 1939. While the orthodox children, both girls and boys, lived in the Villa La Chesnaie in Eaubonne, and the youngest lived in a special home called La Petite Colonie, the other boys and girls lived in two separate homes, in the Villa les Tourelles and the Villa Helvetia, respectively. Separation by gender sent shock waves through the progressive *Robinsoner* group, whose members were used to mixed settings. Hanna and her closest friends were placed in direct confrontation with a group she calls "The Big Girls":

> In retrospect, I see them as traditionally feminine, already well prepared for their adult roles as wives and mothers. In the photographs that survive, they sit on little chairs in the garden, sewing and mending. They returned our contempt for what we saw as their bourgeois natures with superior smiles when we invaded their rooms as sheeted ghosts, flashlights held below our chins, to see how they felt about having their beds short-sheeted, maybe even with slimy things in them. We beat them at sports but found that most of them didn't care about sports—did they think sports were only for boys? They participated reluctantly in the compulsory gymnastics each morning and in the team games that we played with a passion to win.[27]

As the two groups of girls performed their competing conceptions of femininity, they were testing and exploring their very real political differences. Hanna Papanek maintains that the animosity between these two groups was acute: "But who among us—and on which side—enshrined the antagonism in a nasty version of a then popular song about grunting savages? Only a fragment survives in one *Robinsoner's* memory: '*Menschenfressende Kubaner / fressen alte Robinsoner / Umba-Umbarassa*' ('Cuban cannibals / devour old Robinsonians. . .'). As he sang it over the telephone, it came back to me, along with the demeaning refrain meant to depict savage grunts."[28] It is possible, as Hanna's first passage suggests, that this animosity was gendered, and that it was felt more intensely among the girls due to the strikingly different conceptions of femininity each group embodied at such a key age. Indeed, the girls were confronting womanhood at the same time that they were becoming refugees, and they faced highly politicized performance choices. Would they be "tomboys" or "girly girls"?[29]

Belonging to either the *Robisoner* or *Kubaner* groups had concrete implications not only for the girls' behavior, dress, and attitudes toward boys, but also regarding Judaism. Hanna explained this in our 2015 interview: "My first understanding, or my first contact with Jewish ritual, with Jewishness came at [OSE's Villa] Helvetia [. . .] all the Jewish children at Helvetia, they, well with some exceptions, they were mostly from the *St. Louis*. So they were upper-middle class, well to do, and as *Robinsoner*, we had contempt for people who we considered bourgeois. So that got all mixed up with Jewishness."

Life in the OSE home represented Hanna's first contact with matza, eaten during Passover: "I may have written in my diary or somewhere that they taste like cardboard, but once you added butter and jam, that wasn't too bad." She also celebrated Purim, the springtime holiday to commemorate Queen Esther's successful attempt to save Jews from massacre that involves costumes and raucous reenactments:

> I had no idea what Purim meant, but we were told you [could] dress up as a boy. I dressed up as a shoemaker's apprentice with, you know, leather apron, pair of boots slung over my shoulder [. . .]. There are drawings of that, but you know, I was dressed as a boy. I was really unhappy at the beginning of the dance because my two special friends, Gus [Papanek] and Herbert, I don't know whether Herbert was there, and Gus wasn't there either. And then along in the festivities, Ernst [Papanek] said: "Attention please. I have an announcement. We have a new girl." He opens the door, and a little girl comes in, wire glasses, big ears, blondish hair, blonde braids, wearing a *dirndl*. And we screamed and yelled. [. . .] So Gus comes in with these little braids, and his wire rim glasses, and we went crazy. And I said to myself: "Ah, I'm dressed as a boy, so I get to dance with her!" So this was a big triumph.[30]

The *Robinsoner* children, especially the rebellious Hanna, it seems, were actively playing with (and protesting) the traditional gender norms they associated with the bourgeoisie. Indeed, while cross-dressing is not forbidden on Purim, most of the other girls were probably dressed as the heroine of the day, Queen Esther. And what better moment to stage a revolt than on a Jewish holiday? Cross-dressing in the name of Jewish tradition made their act of rebellion even sweeter, even if the holiday encourages transgressions. Ernst Papanek, as well as his sister, Olga, who worked in the kitchen and had helped Gus with his costume, seemed to delight in the *Robinsoner* teen's audacity. Such moments made a political statement, just as they fused children's relationships. Later, in the United States, Hanna, the shoemaker's apprentice, eventually married Gus, the girl in the dirndl.

While the boys were also facing puberty at this moment, it is possible that competing conceptions of masculinity did not come into play to the same extent as for the girls. These were boys who came of age in the shadow of Hitler Youth, in societies seeped in age-old representations of Jewish men as neurotic, overtly feminine, or sexually deviant.[31] A "muscle-Jew"[32] vision seduced Zionist youth culture in Germany and Austria at the turn of the century, competing with the bourgeois commitment to *Bildung*, with its emphasis on individual self-development through study, instruction in the classics and music. Yet after the First World War, a new commitment to renewing Jewish health encouraged all Central European Jewish boys to participate in sports and spend time outdoors in generational groupings.[33] As seen in the importance of sports in the children's homes, these ideas had also permeated French society.[34] The two *Robinsoner* boys I interviewed downplayed the conflict between the groups. Kurt Sonnenfeld stated: "So it was, so the older groups were sort of, you know, not divided, but sort of a two-group kind of thing: The *Kubaner* and *Robinsoner*, really. But we got along with each other, really."[35] Gus Papanek, the "girl" in the dirndl, recalled, "And I, at least, had a community in the *Robinsoner* group, and then in the larger children's homes, because, while there was some rivalry between us and the *Kubaner* that Ernst [Papanek] describes, we were also friends."[36]

Quite likely, these boys did not embrace fundamentally different visions of masculinity and thus could more easily develop bonds. If one looks closely at the friendships created between the children, one notes that *Eaubonner* Ernst Valfer's "best friend" was a *Kubaner*, Hans

Windmüller, who was on the SS *St. Louis*. His "second best friend" was Lutz Greve, also a *Kubaner*. What seems to have kindled Ernst's respect for Hans was their shared attachment to *Bildung*: "Hans was by far the most mature and intelligent among us. He was one or two years older than I was. [. . .] He played piano. [. . .] And I loved his piano playing."[37] While a friendship between an *Eaubonner* and a *Kubaner* seems quite plausible, especially in light of Ernst Valfer's liberal Jewish upbringing, it should be noted that Gus Papanek, a *Robinsoner*, also mentioned his long friendship with *Kubaner* Hans Windmüller.

Hanna Papanek suggests it was the presence of two distinctly different groups, the *Kubaner* and the *Robinsoner*, that allowed for the emergence of the *Eaubonner* as a group, even though these children were the first to arrive in the OSE homes. As an anthropologist, Hanna surely had Frederik Barth's work on ethnic groups and their boundaries on her mind when she made this observation many years later. Very simply put, at times it is opposition to another group that serves to forge identity.[38] As different as they may have been, the *Kubaner* and *Robinsoner* shared several common points: many of these children knew one another before their arrival, from Germany, as members of multi-generational social networks. Furthermore, both groups of children had come to France with their parents. In contrast, the *Eaubonner* children stood apart for multiple reasons. First, they were more religious than the others. Secondly, with the exception of those who arrived from the Frankfurt orphanage, the children did not know one another before arrival. Finally, they had come to France unaccompanied, leaving behind parents and often siblings. The mounting persecutions in Central Europe were of an even greater concern to these children.

Searching for news of their families in Central Europe helped reinforce their bonds. The case of two Frankfurt children in the home for orthodox children, Elfriede Meyer and Ernst Valfer, is significant in this respect. Elfriede had a cousin in Switzerland. After the outbreak of war, which ended postal service between Germany and France, Ernst was able to continue corresponding with his parents by sending his letters to Elfriede's cousin, who forwarded them on to Frankfurt.[39] According to Elfriede, her mother and grandparents, as well as Ernst Valfer's parents, after being forced out of their homes, were assigned residency in the same building.[40] So, while the two children had not known each other before their arrival in France, they, as well as their families in Central Europe, established relationships in the hope of gleaning precious news about their respective loved ones. A photo from Elfriede's personal collection, with the faint label "1940 Eaubonne," shows that the Frankfurt children remained a group in France. Without realizing it, the children were weaving a support network that in some lucky cases, such as Elfriede's and Ernst's, would accompany them into the winter of their lives.

As diverse as the refugee children may have been, they did share some common experiences. The first was the problem of staying connected to their parents and families in Central Europe. As the war advanced, postal service to Germany and Austria became more limited and eventually stopped. This rupture in communication forced the children to unequivocally acknowledge their separation from their parents. Indeed, as seen earlier, children's contemporaneous sources, with some exceptions, are relatively silent on the topic of parents.[41] This can perhaps be explained by the fact that Kindertransport initially felt similar to summer camp, but also due to the fact that parents remained present in children's lives, through their letters.[42]

As parent–child relationships took on an epistolary form, mail became extremely important. Alfred Brauner, from La Guette, explains: "The only concern that persisted for them was the postal delivery. The postman was eagerly awaited. He always had a good pile for the house. But out of one hundred and thirty children, such a 'pile' doesn't add up to much. Some children never received a letter. The disappointed ones went back to their chairs, their heads a little lower. [. . .] These letters were treasures for the children."[43] In the OSE homes, Ernst Papanek and his team of educators encouraged the practice of daily letter writing, so that the children would maintain their connection to home and transition slowly to their new life in France. Papanek recalled: "Mail call was always treated as a great event. As soon as the mail arrived from Paris, all activity came to a halt for twenty or thirty minutes. [. . .] Brothers and sisters, of whom we had our share, would automatically seek each other out to share their letters. As mixed as their feeling [sic] about their parents may have been, the ties of blood, the host of conscious and unconscious memories, held firm."[44] This vital connection between parent and child was threatened, if not ruptured, as a result of the war.[45]

Nonetheless, at the Château de la Guette, a group of resourceful children and a particularly generous woman (and prolific writer) in neutral Switzerland found a means of connecting the children to their parents after September 1939. Elisabeth Luz (1888) was living in Stäfa, Switzerland. She never married and appears to have had no children of her own. Somehow, in February 1940, a child at La Guette learned that she was willing to help separated Jewish families. Soon, several were exchanging letters with her, allowing these children to remain in contact with their families. Parents would send a letter addressed to "Tante Elisabeth," and she would recopy their letter, and respond to her "nephew" or "niece," the Kindertransport child in France or England. Not only was this time consuming for Elisabeth Luz, it was also expensive, especially since this *résistante de plume* also sent paper, envelopes, and international reply coupons, which could be exchanged throughout Europe for international postage. According to historians Deborah Dwork and Robert Jan Van Pelt, Tante Elisabeth exchanged more than 3,000 letters during the war.[46]

Over time, Tante Elisabeth, by pretending to be a family member in order to hold scattered families together, actually came to play a real role in children's lives and networks. Privy to the children's most intimate news, she became a confidante, friend, and informal tracing center. The familiarity one senses in the letters must be contextualized: she was writing, of course, with censors in mind. Nonetheless, Elisabeth Luz kept close track of the La Guette children during the occupation. Her voice, full of concern for her "*chères brebis*" (little sheep), as she referred to them, surely reminded them that they were not completely alone. After the round-ups in summer 1942, some of the La Guette teens were forced to flee to Switzerland. Tante Elisabeth provided concrete help, communicated directly with La Guette director Flore Loinger about the "little group," and even allowed one teen, Ursula Mazdorff, to stay with her, thus enabling her to leave the Münchwilen refugee camp.[47] Other children remained in contact with Tante Elisabeth even after the liberation of France.[48]

Tante Elisabeth was not magical, however, and not all were able to benefit from her help. Heinz Löw wrote on May 26, 1940: "Presently it's been eight months without word from home. I wrote four times with Mundi via Holland, but I believe the letters never arrived. Then I wrote innumerable times via the Red Cross in Switzerland and with Martin Axelrod [sic] via Italy where his parents lived."[49] His beloved grandmother, who appears only once in the first section of the diary, written between September and November 1939, is evoked almost each time he writes after May 1940.

The outbreak of war brought a second problem to all children: the added stress of bomb drills and, after the Nazi invasion of France on May 10, 1940, actual air raids and bombings. For Papanek and other child welfare specialists who were increasingly concerned about children's psychological well-being in times of war, such bombings were a subject of discussion.[50] Upon arrival in the United States, Papanek published several articles. In his attempt to reestablish himself professionally, his publications asserted his expertise as one of the only specialists who actually experienced the war's effect on children firsthand. Explaining how he and his staff coped with bombings, he detailed his therapeutic approach that encouraged children (and adults) to verbalize their fears and mobilize their agency, especially in groups:

> After the All Clear a few of the older girls came and declared that they were afraid of the next alert. Not that they were afraid of anything definite, not even of their own destruction. [. . .] "*It*" was so frightening. I was so lucky, they said, because I was so brave in spite of "*it*." In front of them all I declared that I also was frightened, but less of "*It*" than of the bombs. I could even picture quite concretely the devastation the bombs could bring but as a consequence, I simply did my best to determine what we could do to fight the danger. I told them I thought we must all pitch in and help, and then we wouldn't have any time to worry about "*It*."[51]

Papanek describes the use of music as a coping tool, stating that the children sang the "Marseillaise" (yet again!) in the bomb shelters to attenuate their collective anxiety. A hint of wistful nostalgia lingers in these publications, as one sees Papanek, yet again a refugee, concomitantly trying to convince the American social work establishment to adopt his child-centered pedagogy and harkening back to a moment in which such pleading was unnecessary.

Children's retrospective accounts, written from a safe distance, also reflect a great deal about their author's present needs. They downplay the anxiety provoked by the alerts, describing them as new occasions for play or, at worse, as an annoying interruption in a good night's sleep. Improvised bomb shelters were established in the wine cellar of the *Eaubonner*'s home, the Villa La Chesnaie. The children found that wine racks, when turned sideways, made a pretty comfortable bed. The long hours in the cellars also gave them time to carve their names into the walls.[52] Werner Dreifuss, one of the youngest children from the Frankfurt orphanage to be sent to the Eaubonne home, returned to France in 2001 on the occasion of his son's wedding. He made an impromptu visit to the Eaubonne home and discovered the names of his friends still carved in the wall. A few days later, seeing that the wedding venue also had a wine cellar, he brought his family and part of the wedding party downstairs so they could "transcend and possibly connect in some way to my childhood and time spent in the musty air raid shelter."[53]

Likewise, Hanna Papanek sent fellow *Robinsoner* Kurt Sonnenfeld a photo of himself during an air raid alert. According to Hanna, he wrote back: "What joy! What joy!" Hanna reflected on this to me and explained: "Now, I mean, what does it tell you? It tells you that the, the feelings that we had for the other children, or for many other children, and for being in a group . . . this was an extraordinary experience for all of us. There was so much friendship and love. I mean really, truly love. Some of it erotic, but just, I mean, a really, it was for so many of us, it was an extraordinary experience. And to be separated from that was terrible."[54]

The function of remembering makes it hard to grasp the utter terror the bombings must have incited among the children. On June 4, 1940, Heinz Löw wrote: "In the morning I was very nervous because I did not know what happened as a result of the alarm. After breakfast, the non-parishioners told us that Paris was bombed. There were 45 dead and 200 injured. I was very sorry to hear this, since most likely Klara [sister] and grandmother would read this in the German newspaper and they do not know that I'm outside of Paris."[55] Ever connected to his family in Vienna, this young teen voiced his emotion over the concern the bombings would provoke at home. The next day he corrected his diary, "I read in the newspaper that the actual count from the air raid was 200 dead and 906 wounded."[56] As this account suggests, the Nazi invasion of France put a brutal end to the enchanted parenthesis the children had experienced, and it would lead to a second uprooting for the Kindertransport children.

Far from being a distant event, the war led to profound changes for the refugee children and teens. The Château de la Guette transformed from a left-wing utopian experiment into a distinctly Jewish institution of Zionist orientation. Some of the children lost sight of their trusted educators or their closest friends, while others gained a new sense of purpose: *Eretz Israel*. The war also led to a conflictual yet stimulating encounter in the OSE homes among the *Robinsoner, Eaubonner*, and *Kubaner*, which in turn sharpened the children's sense of belonging to their respective groups.

As diverse as they were, children faced similar problems. Anxiety about the fate of their loved ones in Central Europe led some of them to devise intricate correspondence schemes with Tante Elisabeth, while others looked inward and recorded their lives in diaries. Drills and, later, air raids and bombings mark their memories of this moment, but such sources do not capture the sheer terror such events must have provoked, for the children and the organizations that had taken on their care.

France was now at war, as was most of Europe. The question remained: what would happen to the children and their caretakers when faced with the threat of a Nazi invasion?

CHAPTER 9

"The Real, Great Anxiety"

May–June 1940

If the children managed to cope with the air raids during the *Drôle de guerre*, they were not prepared for the upheaval provoked by the Nazi invasion of France on May 10, 1940. Suddenly, they realized, they too were in danger. As former educator Lida Jablonski later noted: "The real, great anxiety for the parents, for themselves, for the near future, only took hold of them in June 1940, [. . .] during the fierce German advance."[1] To flee the fighting and bombings, most (but not all) caretakers transferred the children from the Paris region to what would become, after the June 1940 armistice, the "free zone" (which I will refer to as the unoccupied zone, since it was anything but free). This led to a reconfiguration of the children's networks and their dispersal in new homes. Faced with the growing uncertainty, the children and teens strengthened their bonds with siblings and each other, while caretakers—also vulnerable to the growing persecution—scrambled to find solutions for the future.

In May 1940, several weeks before the Parisian population embarked upon the "exode," the La Guette children were evacuated by bus to a tiny spa town in Auvergne called La Bourboule, where the French banking industry was reestablishing itself. Most of the children were sent to live in the Hôtel des Anglais. It was run down and poorly heated, and many children recalled having to work, even if the Rothschild family still covered the costs of their care.[2] Germaine de Rothschild accompanied the children on the journey, staying at a local hotel that also lacked the comforts of home.[3] If this displacement was unsettling, the La Guette children soon lost all semblance of stability. Flore Loinger remained with the children, but the Baroness's personal secretary, Robert Jablonski, who had finally become French, was mobilized in the French army. Guy de Rothschild, the Baroness's son, was also mobilized. The mounting pressure on the Rothschild family led Germaine and Edouard de Rothschild to flee to New York in July 1940.[4] After their demobilization, Guy de Rothschild and Robert Jablonski took over the responsibility for the children.[5] They, too, realized that a more realistic solution was needed and began reaching out to the New York office of the JDC.[6]

The OSE children were also displaced from the Paris region. Their departure was in part facilitated by the French public health ministry, which had been evacuating children from the region since the declaration of war in September 1939. Indeed, while it left little trace in French collective memory, thousands of children were moved out of the Paris region before the May 1940 Nazi invasion.[7] Parisians with families outside the city were encouraged to send their children to the latter. Foreign families, however, did not have the rural connections of their fellow Parisians and could certainly not send their children back to Poland, for example. The OSE began helping foreign Jewish families in Paris find solutions for their children in fall 1939, registering over 1,000 children in need of evacuation.[8]

It may seem surprising that an organization exclusively run by foreigners could obtain help from the French Ministry of Public Health. Yet OSE came to France with a great deal of experience and a strong dose of political acumen. Soon after its arrival in Paris, in July 1933, it set up an honorary committee to protect its work, comprised of prominent Jewish and non-Jewish French personalities and presided by former Minister of Public Health and Senator Justin Godart.[9] The OSE also likely received help from Suzanne Schreiber-Crémieux, a board member of the CIE, who was also a member of Public Health Minister Marc Rucart's cabinet. Louise Weiss, the head of the CRC, had a personal relationship with Rucart.[10] Organizations advocating for Jewish refugee children therefore found an ally in Rucart, who assigned fellow freemason Félix Chevrier (1884–1962) the task of helping the OSE find new homes outside the Paris region.

To note that Chevrier had an atypical background is an understatement.[11] The son of a mason, he worked as a manual laborer and, through his activism in the labor movement, eventually became a journalist and composer. After the First World War, he turned to politics, as a republican-socialist. Marc Rucart's public health ministry relied upon Chevrier for five missions, including the task of finding homes for the OSE's evacuation work in 1939. In the same year, the OSE asked Chevrier, a non-Jew, to become its general secretary, a title he shared with its Lithuanian leader, Lazare Gurvic. Chevrier chose the Creuse region for the OSE homes and initially opened three. Eventually, the OSE became responsible for fourteen homes in the unoccupied zone.[12]

Chevrier loved music, children, and hunting for mushrooms.[13] This may explain why he accepted the directorship of the OSE's Chabannes home, in the village of Saint-Pierre-de-Fursac, which opened in November 1939. Along with several others, former La Guette educators Ernst and Lida Jablonski eventually joined Chevrier in Chabannes, bringing with them their progressive pedagogical methods.

While initially intended for foreign Jewish children from Paris, the homes began to receive even more children who had been brutally separated from their parents as a result of the increasing internment of foreign Jewish men and, as of May 1940, women. After October 1940, Vichy legislation made it possible to arrest and intern foreign Jews of all ages. One child, Ruth Avokat Keller, whose father was interned, recalled her tears, night after night, after arriving in the home.[14]

~

While chaotic, the situation of the OSE and La Guette children was far more stable than that of the Kindertransport children who were initially sent to Strasbourg, those sent to Quincy-sous-Sénart under the care of the Protestant Count Monbrison and his mistress, Princess Irène Paley, and the small group of girls from Vienna that was sent to the Rothschild orphanage in Paris.

The Strasbourg group, like the rest of the population in the region, had to be evacuated in September 1939 due to the city's proximity to the Maginot line. Strasbourg activist Andrée Salomon took charge of this with the help of her former house mother, Laure Weil. The women took the children to Bourbach-le-Haut, where an empty Jewish summer camp was made available. At this point, there were only thirty children under Salomon's care. "A semblance of family and strong fraternal ties,"[15] in Andrée Salomon's words, continued to unify the group long after the war years. It was clear that this improvised solution could not last, however, since the area was considered a war zone. Salomon sent as many children as possible to French boarding schools, as Flore Loinger continued to do with the La Guette children. This reduced the population under her charge to a certain extent. She took the remaining group of children to Clermont-Ferrand, where her husband's university had reestablished itself. The couple did not have enough room for the children, and so she rented a home for them. Eventually, the youngest children were sent to Dordogne, to be cared for in the reestablished Strasbourg and Haguenau orphanages. The older children were "placed individually," to avoid internment as enemy aliens.[16] In the process of moving and placing the children, Andrée Salomon transitioned out of her volunteer helper role to one of a paid employee for the OSE, which, as seen above, had begun to replace its foreign staff with French nationals. Her precious expertise dealing with the French administration and Jewish youth would continue to play a vital role, as we will later see.

The children in Quincy-sous-Sénart, south-east of Paris, did not fare as well. The forty boys, twenty-four of whom had lived together in the Auerbach orphanage in Berlin before their arrival in France,[17] initially benefited from a progressive pedagogical approach thanks to their first director, Heinz (later Henry) Jacoby, a German pacifist, Marxist, and disciple of Alfred Adler. Before the rise of Nazism, Jacoby joined, and quickly left, the German Communist party, yet he continued his political activism in Trotskyist circles. As a result, in 1934, Jacoby was sentenced to twenty-seven months in prison, after which he fled Berlin for Prague, and then Paris, where he arrived in 1937. In exile, Jacoby joined the Verband deutscher Lehreremigranten (Union of German Emigrant Teachers), founded to protect progressive educators in exile. He met Hubert de Monbrison thanks to fellow Berliner Hanna Eisfelder-Grunwald, who, as seen earlier, had started a medical clinic for refugee children in Paris. The Count recruited Jacoby to oversee the care of the German boys, and, in turn, Jacoby recruited a fellow member of the Union of German Emigrant Teachers, Zimmermann, who came with his sixteen-year-old son, as well as a kindergarten teacher, who may have been Alice Freistadt-Lederer, a Montessori-trained educator from Vienna.[18] They joined the staff of the boarding school for Russian and Spanish refugee girls. Jacoby recalled in his 1986 autobiography: "The kindergarten teacher soon had an affair with Zimmermann and became pregnant, which did not help our reputation and especially our relationship with the female director of the girls' home."[19]

Hubert de Monbrison and Irène Paley, general secretary and president of their school, did not spend a great deal of time at the château, and most likely were not concerned about the ideological rift between the staff of the girls' home and the progressive crew hired to care for the boys. One former child recalled in the 1990s: "I remember the Comte de Monbrison very well. He was a very handsome man who came to pick us up at the station and drove in his convertible in front of our bus, accompanied by a lady. When we arrived in Quincy, he broke bread with us as a sign of welcome and friendship. After that, we only saw him on rare occasions."[20] This anecdote about breaking bread is significant, in that it most likely confuses the Count with the home's director Heinz Jacoby. The latter recalled in his autobiography: "For their reception I had baked a narrow French white bread—a *flûte*—of table length. We made everyone break off a piece of it and explained to them, pledged to live in peace with the others. It was not only the length but also the whiteness of the bread that surprised them. The symbolism of breaking bread together was useful in the first difficult days."[21]

The confusion between the Count and Jacoby may also be due to the fact that in September 1939, just two months after the boys' arrival, both Jacoby and Zimmermann were interned as enemy nationals. At this moment, the boarding school was ordered to close. The Russian and Spanish refugee girls were sent elsewhere. This allowed for the boys to move out of their annex and into the main house, where they inherited the more austere staff of the girls' home, along with Alice Freistadt-Lederer.[22] The boys had a close relationship to one or two women caretakers, but their accounts indicate a great deal of self-sufficiency.[23]

In the 1990s, two of the former Quincy boys returned to France, alongside their wives. Armed with one of his childhood drawings of the château, Peter Gossels managed to convince the current occupants of the Château Leroy—a branch of the French police (*Compagnies républicaines de sécurité*)—to allow them in. One of the policemen's wives was particularly interested in the history of the château. She connected Peter to a former student of the Russian boarding school, who in turn introduced him to the Count's daughter. Peter reached out to her in a letter: "As a nine-year-old boy, I only have a dim memory of your father dressed in the uniform of a French officer bidding us 'au revoir' as he left the Chateau in June of 1940 (?) to join his unit."[24]

Peter's memory of the Count proved correct: Hubert de Monbrison had indeed come to say goodbye to the boys in June 1940. However, while most of the other Kindertransport children were removed from the Paris region before the Nazi invasion, the Count and the Princess did not evacuate their wards, leading to a wild—and extremely dangerous—adventure for them.

In late 1944 or early 1945—long before Peter wrote to the Count's daughter in the 1990s—seventeen-year-old Quincy child Hans Stern recorded his account of the June 1940 exodus in fictionalized form.[25] Both of Hans Stern's parents had committed suicide in August 1938. He was placed in the Auerbach orphanage and separated from his older sister Ursula, who remained in Germany. Hans was sent to France and then the United States, where he typed out his sixty-page manuscript in his newly acquired English. It is possible he saw in his account a means of emancipating himself from his difficult American foster care situation.[26] While Stern's account is fictionalized and the names of his main characters changed to protect their identity, cross-referencing it with other testimonies shows that it is anchored in fact.

According to Stern's account, Hubert de Monbrison came to the château on June 13, 1940:

His always smiling face, was now the image of sorrow and desolation. He knew how far Germany had gotten, and I think that he also knew what was still to come. There he stood in the uniform of a captain in the French army. [. . .] "Boys, the sad hour for

France has come. We can no longer keep the hordes of Barbarians away from our Capital, which will also means our little town here. I did not see any sense in calling the younger boys, as there would only be unnecessary noise. The only thing that I can tell you, is to try and reach a city in the middle of France, by the name of Clermont-Ferrand, where you will try to reassemble with several other committees."

The boys were not entirely alone —five staff members and the gardener accompanied them—but the Count essentially left the group with the task of travelling hundreds of kilometers on foot with a "two-wheeled push cart." According to Hans Stern, the count parted with the following words: " 'I don't know, whether I will ever see you again. So may God be with you.' There he went, head low on his shoulders, I think that he never expected to see us again."[27]

Armed with their push cart and some bicycles, the forty Quincy boys took off during the Battle of France, walking along the Seine. They witnessed considerable bombing and death before deciding to turn back to their château on June 16. When they returned, they found it occupied by French prisoners of war. Several days later, a unit of the Wehrmacht arrived. The boys, under the supervision of a handful of teachers, thus had to cohabitate with the German soldiers.

At this stage of the occupation, one could not foresee the genocidal path that Nazism would take in 1941, and the German army, comprised of both "ordinary men" and "real Nazis,"[28] were under strict orders to behave. Nonetheless, there was enough evidence against the Nazis to know that it was not safe to leave a group of Jewish children and teens in their vicinity; furthermore, the children themselves were keenly aware of the political situation and were concerned, if not terrified. As Hans Stern wrote, it didn't take long for the masks to fall. Hans described his assignment to assist the Captain in preparing his room:

Only after five full minutes did he turn back to me, ordering me in German to clean out the office desk that was standing in his room. I did not know, whether to keep playing the Frenchman, or to listen to his German. I had only a short time to make up my mind. I thought, that sooner or later he'd anyways find out that we were Jewish. So I went and opened all the droors [sic] on his desk. Only after I had finished, did the captain realize that he had talked German, and I had obeyed. "Ach, he said, so you understand German! How come?" I saw, that now I had to come out with it, whether I liked it or not. So after another short pause, I finally answered his question; "We, I said, are Jewish refugees from Germany." The captain looked at me thunderstruck. Then he simply said; "Jewish or not, we might just as well get along with each other while we live here." Der Fuehrer himself might have fainted, would he have heard one of his officers talk to a Jew like this.[29]

In this fictionalized account, Hans plays the role of a brave child who finds the courage to come out as Jewish. We must understand it not as reality but as a fantasy of power written at the end of the Holocaust, a moment when the teen was struggling with his own powerlessness. A later account of another Quincy boy confirms this period of cohabitation and states: "I wonder if it was possible they did not realize we were Jewish?"[30]

The question remains: how could responsible adults allow this to happen? I speculated earlier that the children may have been sent to the Protestant Count through Louise Weiss's and Georges Bonnet's CRC, since Louise Weiss and Renée de Monbrison had offices in the same building and were both members of Protestant-Jewish circles. If this was the case, the potentially dangerous cohabitation between the German soldiers and the Jewish German refugee children could be better explained. Two days before the French Armistice with Nazi Germany, Louise Weiss accepted a mission from the French Minister of the Interior to go to the United States to facilitate the sending of medicine to Vichy France. From August to December 1940, Weiss was making rounds in New York and Washington, DC.[31] While Weiss was in the United States, Hubert de Monbrison, as seen above, was mobilized in the French army, while Irène Paley seems to have retreated to her villa in Biarritz with her teenage son, Michel.[32] In the meantime, Renée de Monbrison was with her children at the family's vacation home on the Atlantic coast, where she remained, declaring herself

Jewish in the July 1941 census.[33] War had taken over the caretakers' lives, and their responsibility for the Quincy group seems to have taken a backseat to more pressing concerns.

After most likely three months of cohabitation, someone realized their potential danger. The boys' retrospective accounts show they were divided into groups in fall 1940: the older boys were placed in an apartment in Paris under the care of the Quakers and in the boarding school in Clamart; the younger boys were sent to the Rothschild orphanage in Paris and the Jewish orphanage in La Varenne, on the rue Saint Hilaire.[34]

Somehow, the group did make it over the demarcation line, which helped save many (but not all) of their lives.[35] One note, found by chance, points to a link between the German refugee of Jewish origin Hanna Eisfelder-Grunwald and the Count de Monbrison.[36] One will recall that it was Eisfelder-Grunwald, founder of Medical Assistance for Refugee Children, who recommended her friend Heinz Jacoby to the Count to direct the home. The Count most likely instructed the children to walk to Limoges, where Hanna (now using the less Jewish-sounding first name Jeanne) had reopened her clinic with the help of local Jewish socialists, creating a clinic for refugee children that would save many Jewish children's lives, la Pouponnière.[37] It was Hanna's employee Erna Magaziner who informed the director of Save the Children International about the need to evacuate the children to the unoccupied zone. It is quite possible, therefore, that it was the latter who reached out to the Red Cross, which organized their passage across the demarcation line in January 1941.[38]

The children also played a role in reuniting their group. Twelve-year-old Norbert Bikales, seen earlier in a photo with his parents, was particularly attached to an older Quincy boy, sixteen-year-old Bernd Warschauer. After their separation, the boys corresponded. Norbert recalled writing to Bernd from the Rothschild orphanage in Paris, asking: " 'Can't you do something so that I come to be with you?' He says: 'Let me see what I can do.' "[39] For Norbert, the passage over the demarcation line, most likely in April 1941, was an especially painful moment:

On the train to Chabannes in Vierzon, which was the demarcation line, the Germans came in and . . . with dogs . . . with real weapons, asking for papers and who knows what they wanted . . . and I got terrified having the German letters from my parents with me. So, in a panic, I took the letters from my parents that I had received in Quincy, there weren't many, because it takes time back and forth, but they were very precious to me, and I tore them all up and threw them out the window. And that hurts ever since.[40]

Norbert cried in our 2015 interview when he discussed losing his only trace of his parents. He was nonetheless temporarily reunited with Bernd Warschauer. From early 1941 through late August 1942, the date at which some of the older boys, including Norbert's surrogate brother Bernd, were arrested and deported, almost the entire group from Quincy was reunited at Félix Chevrier's Château de Chabannes in the Creuse.[41] The boys therefore officially became the wards of the OSE.

Only one group remained behind in Paris, now part of the occupied zone. One will recall the eight teenage girls sent from the Merores orphanage in Vienna to the Rothschild orphanage in the earliest phases of the Kindertransport to France. In the summer of 1939, the orphanage took its wards to Berck-sur-Mer, in northern France, where the Rothschild hospital operated a sanitorium and many Jewish organizations ran summer camps.[42] The children returned to the Paris region but then returned again to Berck during the Phoney war, staying for almost one year. They were in Berck during the terrible bombing campaigns that marked Nazi invasion. Like the Quincy boys, the Rothschild orphanage girls found themselves caught in the middle of the Battle of France. The group's only survivor recalled, "All on foot. All on foot. Hiked, hiked, hiked. On foot. And whenever the low-flying planes [came] [we all threw ourselves] on the ground. Spent the night in the open. [. . .] And then we went back to [Berck-sur-Mer] and there was nothing left to eat. And then came the real hunger."[43] The orphanage eventually returned to Paris and was incorporated into the Nazi-Vichy-imposed Union générale des Israélites de France (UGIF) in November 1941. The Viennese girls were often mistreated and, in turn, acted up. One former child recalls being slapped multiple times but that what "hurt me even more was that they cut off my hair, just like that, right across."[44]

～

As seen with the Quincy boys, the upheaval of May–June 1940 completely reconfigured the children's networks. Many of the children from OSE's Montmorency homes were sent to the OSE's new Château de Montintin, near Limoges, yet space was limited, and the children were split up in multiple homes. Likewise, the political situation led some of the parents of the *Kubaner* children to take back their children, perhaps with the hope of preventing their own internment as enemy aliens.[45] Eighteen of the original twenty-seven were still under the care of the OSE in February 1942, yet the group was now divided into four different homes.[46] The *Robinsoner* children also were starting to leave: some of their parents, as Austrian and German labor leaders, had been put on the emergency lists established by the United States President's Advisory Committee on Refugees with the help of the Jewish Labor Committee, which provided them with coveted visas to the United States. One by one, these lucky teens reunited with their parents and left for the United States. However, not everyone made the list. Their children stayed behind in the OSE homes, or returned to live with their parents, who were targeted. Hanna Kaiser's parents both made it onto the list; her best friend Dorli Loebl's parents did not.[47]

The orthodox *Eaubonner* group was also split up by the move south. Only fifteen spots were available at the Château des Morelles, in Broût-Vernet, which was run under strict orthodox auspices. Ernst Papanek turned to Ernst Valfer, the president of the Eaubonne home, for help. Who should be selected for the home? Young Ernst, only fifteen at the time, realized that this decision might have grave consequences in light of the Nazi advance. He told Ernst Papanek that he was unable to choose for the others; it was simply too much for him.[48] Ruth, encountered earlier, remembers this moment somewhat differently:

After about a year, after the Germans came, and you know, the other thing we all felt, I felt very protected, I was not ever . . . I don't remember being scared. I don't remember. Maybe I was. But I don't remember being scared. But we had a choice to make. [. . .] We had a decision to make. Fifteen of us could go to Broût-Vernet, which was a very orthodox home. And the rest of them would go to Montintin, which had not been established, but would probably not become as orthodox because they would have to be with the other kids. At least that's the way I understood it. And Miriam and I debated and debated what should we do. [We chose] the orthodox one. So we went to Broût-Vernet, fifteen of us. That was a big decision for kids to make. And we were so surprised that some of them who professed to be so orthodox and religious did not choose to go to Broût-Vernet.[49]

Indeed, with the occupation and the new circumstances it engendered, some of the children let go of the religious facade they had adopted as a survival strategy upon arrival in France. Others may have simply wanted to stay with their friends, at the expense of their religious practice. Yet, more importantly, displacement broke up the Eaubonne group and the children's friendship networks. Ruth explained: "So we went to Broût-Vernet, but there was one other reason that we didn't mind, because one of our favorite counselors, Martha Mann, was already at Broût-Vernet. So we knew she was there for us. They really tried very hard to make life, you know, humanize life there. I think we were, you know, after Eaubonne, after we had all been so close, then to be separated, and then just the fifteen of us. I think we just held on."[50]

Adding to their anxiety was the fact that activities at the Château de Morelles were conducted in French, not German. Until this point, most of the OSE Kindertransport children had not mastered French. Furthermore, the children were no longer under the progressive influence of Ernst Papanek but were in the care of more authoritarian orthodox educators.[51] Twelve-year-old Susi Hilsenrath's diary provides a cutting portrait of this home, describing in detail the physical and verbal abuse she witnessed among its educators and children. She reports being slapped by one of her educators: "The first time in one year that I was hit, or some similar thing."[52]

Displacement caused the children's friendship networks to transform, which in turn had effects on the relationships between siblings. Suddenly, they were invested with a new importance. Ruth and Miriam, we saw, were smuggled into France together yet were temporarily separated while under the care of their uncle. They were both placed in the

Eaubonne home, but it seems as if the sisters initially lived in separate worlds. At Eaubonne, there was a group called "the big seven," remembers Ruth. "My sister belonged to that. I did not, I was too young. And some of the kids used to meet each other at the stairwell in the back of the house. God only knows what was going on, but these were the teenagers."[53] The new home in Le Broût-Vernet reminded Ruth of her vulnerability, leading her to seek out her older sister for comfort:

We had all gone out on a picnic or something, a group of us, and then it started to really pour. I mean really bad. Thunder, lightning, pouring. Some of us ran home, and I got home before my sister did, and when my sister hadn't come yet, I was so scared. I really was. I was just petrified and started to cry. I was almost hysterical, or maybe I was hysterical. And yet my sister and I were not that close. She was not an older sister who protected her younger sister very much. But when push comes to shove, you know, when I thought that Miriam, I didn't know what happened to her, it was . . . So Miriam must have given me a sense of protection, of security. Not protection, but security, despite the fact that we weren't . . . There were some sisters who really looked after their younger sister, but that was never her style and it still isn't her style. So, it's kind of interesting. I do remember that it was just terrible. And finally she came home and everybody said: "It's okay, it's okay. Miriam is here." But it was really a bad, bad night. It was just terrible.[54]

As Ruth looks back on her past in France, she raises the question of protection and security. Siblings, especially when older, were expected to provide these things. Yet, like the distant relatives who provided a means out of Germany and little more, they often disappointed. Siblings simply could not replace parents. Benjamin Hirsh, who was separated from his older siblings upon arrival in France, was finally reunited with his sisters at the Château de Morelles in Broût Vernet. Years later, he wrote:

Immediately upon my arrival at Morelles, a rivalry began between my sisters to establish which one was going to be in charge of little

Bennie. If that was suppose[d] to make me feel good, it didn't work. Actually Flo [a sister], according to the charge from our parents before we left Germany, was supposed to be looking out for me. She was fifteen and a half years old and had already become interested in boys. She only started to focus on taking charge of me and my behavior when Sarah [another sister] tried to fill the void and challenge her authority.[55]

Ruth and Miriam quickly befriended a child from Bad Kreuznach, Susi Hilsenrath, seen above, who had a similar history to their own. Like the sisters, she had come to France illegally with her younger brother Josef in August 1939. The two children were put under the care of an older second cousin in Paris. While he was at work, the children spent their days roaming around the city and sneaking into the metro. After several weeks, the cousin placed them in a boarding home outside of Paris, in Orsay. Eventually, the children were placed under the care of the OSE.[56] On May 27, 1941, Susi celebrated her twelfth birthday in Broût Vernet. It was this event that sparked her decision to keep a diary, which would accompany her until she arrived in the United States, in September 1941. This contemporaneous source echoes what Ruth and Ben Hirsch describe: an anxiety-producing sense of responsibility and burden, in which siblings are expected to take the role of parents.

Susi's diary shows to what extent her connection to her parents remained intact. "When [sic] Edith and I talk about God knows what, but mainly about our dear parents, during the night."[57] On the same day, she wrote: "Today I finished *Jack* [a book], it is very nice, but not for children. What would the parents think if they knew that I read these [sic] kind of book."[58] Soon after being slapped, Susi noted that she had gained 20 pounds since leaving her parents. "If they would see me they would not recognize me."[59] She decided therefore to go on a "diet": "I have to get thinner. I hardly eat anything and I give everything away."[60] And finally she wrote of her decision to stop eating: "Today I stopped eating. Miss (?) had to open her mouth to tell Martha [a counselor]."[61]

Yet Susi was especially concerned with her brother Josef's upcoming birthday. She made him a bag for his toiletries, which she embroidered with his initials:

Now I am sitting in bed again and just want to embroider the monogram on Josef's bag. Josef is getting worse from day to day, and everyone complains about him. I do not know what I can do. What will the dear parents say when we arrive? We have changed quite a bit. Josef has always been a bad fellow, but now we can hardly stand him. I do not know what sort of presents I should give him. I will by [sic] comb for him and other things he needs for toiletries. This evening he will come to me and I will give him a toothbrush and a cup, etc. and I will have a good opportunity to make a cover for his prayer book, but I have nothing sweet.[62]

This twelve-year-old attempted to replace her parents, struggling to find appropriate presents and sweets in wartime France.

~

Displacement, followed by war and displacement, yet again, was occurring at a moment when many of the children were turning into teens, and romantic relationships suddenly took on great importance. This account of their lives would therefore not be complete without a love story. Former Eaubonne president Ernst Valfer was the most forthcoming of those I interviewed about how he felt at each stage of his life. After his arrival in the United States, he was cared for by his aunt and uncle. He initially earned a degree in engineering and later obtained a PhD in systems management. After his retirement, at the age of sixty-seven, he became a licensed psychologist, and he was still working part-time at a mental health clinic in 2015, at the age of ninety, when we began corresponding. A significant theme in our multiple interviews was his ability to engage with his emotions about his past. For decades, he had simply cut them off, leaving a great deal of regret over words unsaid.

Ernst discussed other teens' love stories, which I chose not to reveal for ethical reasons. He also shared his own. Ernst is now comfortable with his past and secure in his loving marriage. He has given me multiple encouragements to use his real name and to openly discuss his story. Ernst started the account of his love story by referring to another teen, who wanted to go out with him: "she wanted to be my girlfriend, but I was going with another woman. But we were very cautious. We would take long walks, talk about philosophy as we understood it, and every-thing, literature, but we never touched each other because it was forbidden."[63] I asked Ernst why. He explained:

> Well, my upbringing also was much more hesitant. I was not that at all confident about girls, I didn't know, I was very young, I didn't know what to do with them. I would have loved to kiss her, but there was a fear. And then later on, much later on, Heinz Schuster told me that whenever I went with her, some of the boys would follow us. We never knew. They would hide behind trees and follow us to make sure we didn't do anything. Or if we did to laugh at us or whatever it is. So no, we just took long walks in the forest, maybe sat on a meadow and talked and went back. I would have married her. She was a wonderful, wonderful woman.[64]

Ernst did not marry her. "I was not anywhere ready. She then went to Argentina to her parents and did get married. And she came back up here with her husband and two children." Ernst, too, eventually married and had children. They saw each other several times in their adult lives. At their last meeting, she "introduced me to her son and said: 'This is the man I loved.' And again I was too stupid and too thumpstruck [sic] to say anything but to smile. And I, *mea culpa*, had I been anywhere more mature I would have said: 'I loved you too. And I love you today. And I will love you tomorrow.' Because I did. I love her memory. She was just a lovely woman."[65]

It was to this young woman that Ernst gave "the biggest gift I ever gave to any person in my whole life." A friend of Ernst's had visited his parents and returned to Montintin with a "suitcase full of delicacies." The children had food at the home but, as Ernst recalled, "we saw no bread. We saw no potatoes. We saw no meat. We only saw *topinambour* [Jerusalem artichokes]." As a close friend of the boy, Ernst received a coveted slice of French bread with butter:

> That was a holy delicacy. And I was holding it, I would have prob-ably kept it until the mice ate it. It was gold! And I was walking back from Montintin to the *dépendance*, the little house called La

Chevrette, which was maybe 100 meters away. And on the way to Chevrette, I met [. . .] my girlfriend. And she looked at this [. . .], she said: "Where did you get that?" And I said: "Oh, here take it." She said: "I can't take your bread." I said: "Oh yeah, I had already lots of it." I gave her my bread. And that, without question—I've given my wife jewelry, clothing, a grand piano I bought for her, our wedding, rugs, clothing—nothing, nothing compared to that slice of bread . . . She didn't know.[66]

The declaration of war in September 1939, and displacement after the Nazi invasion of France, caused the children's lives—and networks—to be reconfigured yet again. When they were no longer able to send letters to Central Europe, we saw that children found helpers who could keep them in contact with family. These complex twists and turns forced the children to confront the separation from their parents, turning private emotions into public documents. Even if the children could not write to their parents (or surrogate parents), they wrote about them. As seen in Heinz Löw and Susi Hilsenrath's diaries, they were in children's daily thoughts. In this state of heightened anxiety, children increasingly turned to their siblings and one another for comfort. Yet even if they tried to substitute their parents, siblings could not replace them. A sense of disappointment, anger, and anxiety permeates several contemporaneous and retrospective siblings' accounts.

This social history on children's lives in France helps us probe deeper into what it meant for Jewish families to be scattered as a result of Nazi persecutions. Did the children create surrogate families in exile, as some of them later claimed? This question remains open to debate. The children certainly developed close relationships with others, including their educators and other children. But as seen in the discussion of parents and siblings, these relationships did not replace the families they had once had. Instead, the children gained a new set of individuals in their lives, "ship sisters and brothers,"[67] in other words, the relationships forged in extreme circumstances and "in-between" moments among individuals who shared complex migratory paths. Together, the children changed as they migrated. They refashioned their religious identities on multiple occasions. Contact with their left-wing or religious zionist educators left a lasting mark on their identities. They grew and discovered their sexuality. As twelve-year-old Susi wrote: "What will the dear parents say when we arrive? We have changed quite a bit."[68]

Displacement to the unoccupied zone was not a real solution for refuge for any of the children. Nazi and Vichy persecutions continually brought new children into the homes, including some of the 6,500 who had been expelled from the Baden, Palatinate, and Saar areas of Germany during the October 1940 Bürckel Aktion. Some of these children were evacuated from the Gurs internment camp into children's homes. Others were placed in the homes while their parents were interned or struggling for papers, a visa, and food. Still others witnessed their parents' arrests and landed in the homes after this brutal separation. The children's homes were therefore no longer exclusively for the German-speaking Kindertransport children; their mission had expanded to provide refuge for broader categories of Jewish child refugees, bringing together multiple languages and nationalities.

In this increasingly precarious setting, flight was one of the only ways to imagine a future. By July 1940, Germaine de Rothschild was safely resettled in New York and expressing her concern over the La Guette children. Ernst Papanek had been on the run since 1934. He knew he was in grave danger after the Nazi invasion of France. He fled to the United States in August 1940 with his wife and two children. It was in New York that he would turn to American childcare experts and Jewish organizations, with the hope of organizing an evacuation of the Jewish refugee children from occupied France. Reconstructing early Kindertransport experiences through the eyes of Ruth, Ernst Valfer, Benjamin Hirsch, and many others is only possible because they lived to talk about their past. As we will now see, many of the Kindertransport children owe their lives to the transports that would take them out of wartime France, to a second, permanent exile, in the United States.

CHAPTER 10

Peter and Werner

Two Brothers in Flight

Peter Gossels, a distinguished attorney, was still going to his office daily at the age of eighty-eight when we met in 2015. It was there that he shared the details of his childhood journey from his native Berlin to Boston, via France. Peter, born in 1930, did not leave home alone. He was accompanied by his younger brother Werner, born in 1933. Understanding how the Gossels brothers and other Kindertransport children managed to escape the sweeping violence of the Holocaust through flight, via France to the United States, requires multiple levels of analysis. Rapidly changing state policies dictated the framework in which humanitarian organizations could help individuals. In parallel, parents and even children tried to maximize their chances for inclusion in evacuation schemes by establishing their own strategies. The Gossels brothers' story shows how children and families sought help from organizations that in turn worked with states to facilitate migration and, at the same time, how individuals attempted to interact with states directly to find a way out of Nazi-occupied territories.

The rise of Nazism altered the brothers' lives indelibly, shattering their sense of security. Their father, a magistrate responsible for a section of Berlin and an occasional lecturer at the Administrative Seminary of Berlin, was forced out of his positions in 1933. He managed to find a high-level job working for the Jewish community.[1] The boys' parents divorced in 1936, which led Peter, Werner, and their mother to move in with their maternal grandmother. In 1939, the children were still living with their mother, who at this date listed her profession as masseuse and cosmetics distributer, reflecting her limited employment opportunities as a Jewish woman in the Third Reich.[2] In March 1939, the boys' father was warned by someone in the Gestapo that he should leave the country within three days. He fled to Antwerp, but when Belgium was invaded in May 1940, he was arrested as an enemy alien and deported by the Germans to France, where he was interned in a camp.[3]

Before fleeing Germany, the boys' father helped many individuals leave the Third Reich. Peter attributes his and his brother's rescue to their mother, Charlotte Lewy Gossels, who he recalls going to the French embassy regularly for a year with the hope of finding a Kindertransport for her sons.[4] This small family's decision to separate was part of its larger strategy to flee Germany. A letter from Charlotte in one of her son's American case files explains that she was trying to secure a visa to England but could only pursue this option after finding a Kindertransport for her children.[5] Charlotte managed to get her two children on the last Kindertransport for Paris, but she never did leave for England. Her elderly mother fell ill, and she remained behind to care for her.[6] Eight-year-old Peter and his five-year-old brother Werner arrived in France on July 4, 1939, just before their respective birthdays, and were sent to the Count Hubert de Monbrison's and Princess Irène Paley's Château in Quincy-sous-Sénart.

In Quincy, Peter, Werner, and the others had an extremely difficult time after the Nazi invasion of France. Unlike the La Guette or OSE children, who had been evacuated south in May 1940 as a precaution, their flight had not been organized in advance. Instead, as seen above, the children and a few of their educators set out on foot along the Seine during the peak moments of the Battle of France. After three days, they turned back, only to find their château occupied by French prisoners of war. Soon after, their château was requisitioned by a unit of the Wehrmacht. In fall 1940, after several months of tense cohabitation with German soldiers, the boys were dispatched to various institutions. Peter and Werner were sent to a Jewish orphanage in La Varenne. It was in this town that Peter recalls attending public school for the first time.[7]

Until this moment, Peter and Werner were in regular contact with their mother and family members in Berlin, who coped with their separation by engaging with it directly, marking birthdays and writing about feelings of longing and dreams about one another. The boys' uncle Fanti described a new birthday ritual in great detail: "Your Mutti put the big bouquet of flowers she would have otherwise given to you in person, next to your picture which is on the dresser that is now in the treatment room of your Mutti's, as well as the big green mirror and the children's table, where your Mutti keeps her chocolate and cigarettes. We had been meaning to go to the synagogue tonight in honor of your birthday but it is too hot for that."[8] After the outbreak of war in September 1939, the family continued to correspond, sending their letters via a relative in Amsterdam. "When I chat as I do now," wrote Charlotte, in February 1940, "I imagine that the three of us are sitting closely together talking to one another. Then I see you both in front of me with your shining eyes and hear your voices talking to me and I don't feel at all that we are so far apart from each other. Oh my beloved children, Mutti's thoughts are always with you and accompany you in all you do."[9] A few days later, she wrote that she often dreamt about her boys, "that we are together and chat and play, but, when I awaken in the morning, I realize that was only a dream."[10]

This vital connection between Charlotte Gossels and her children, however, was temporarily ruptured when the boys were evacuated from the château and sent to the Jewish orphanage in La Varenne, outside of Paris. For several months, she remained without news. Panicked, she arranged for their return to Berlin. When she finally found them in December 1940, she explained:

Now it is winter again and it's already been a year and a half since you have left. But now, my beloved boys, I want to tell you that we will see each other again <u>soon</u>. Have you heard yet that you are allowed to come back? I'm doing everything everything [sic] I possibly can so that you, my beloved children, can get back to me as soon as possible and I hope it won't be long now until we will see each other again. Then we will stay together and we will never ever part again.[11]

Charlotte was not the only parent to make this choice. An older Quincy teen, Egon Heysemann, born in 1925, was sent back to Berlin. He was deported in late March 1942, presumably with his parents, and was murdered.[12]

Fortunately, Peter and Werner did not go back to Berlin. Instead, and unbeknownst to their mother, they and many other of the Quincy boys were transferred to the OSE's Château de Chabannes in January 1941. At Chabannes, the boys discovered a world that was quite different from life in Quincy. Félix Chevrier, Chabannes's polyvalent director, led a joyful team of educators, including Lida and Ernst Jablonski, who sought to integrate the refugee children into the village. Chabannes was one of the rare OSE homes at which Jewish refugee children attended the local French public school. The children also were sent to help neighboring farmers during the harvest, leading to lasting ties between the villagers and the children.[13]

Peter and Werner, at this point almost eleven and eight years old, adapted quickly to their new life (Plate 14). Peter, with his serious manner and excellent grades, and Werner, with his impish grin, made a positive impression on the two sisters who ran the school, Renée et Irène Paillasou, and their caretakers.[14] In addition to their classes, the Chabannes children had access to workshops run by the Jewish vocational organization ORT, including leather-working and shoe repair. Finally, Chevrier and his staff kept the children busy with long walks in the forest to look for mushrooms, a house orchestra, musical theater productions, and the creation of a collective diary to mark the one-year anniversary of the home, in which some of the Quincy boys wrote about their experiences. As 1941 advanced, the children experienced homesickness and anxiety but maintained full lives with many opportunities to stimulate their emotional and intellectual development.

For the Quincy boys, who had been left with little supervision during the Battle of France, only to be separated in the Paris region, the reunion with their Kindertransport friends and first months at Chabannes must have felt enchanted. "Chabannes has a special place in my heart and mind,"[15] recalled Peter. It is most likely for this reason that his daughter Lisa, a filmmaker, dedicated years of her life to co-directing *The Children of Chabannes*, an Emmy-winning documentary.[16] In one of Peter's surviving letters to his parents, written in April 1941, he wrote: "The weather was good on April 17. Werner, a friend and I made a tent. It was so hot that we took off our shoes and socks. We ate in the garden all day. Now we have cut down a tree because we have run out of coal. It was very hot."[17] This sounds like a day at summer camp, if one ignores the fact that this German child was writing in French, which seems to have overtaken his native language.

~

Yet behind this idyllic environment grew a mounting and increasingly perceptible threat. New Jewish populations were arriving in France daily, through forced deportation and flight. By mid-May 1940, a French *circulaire* stipulated that all German refugees in France, male and female, between the ages of seventeen and fifty-six (and later sixty-five) were to be interned.[18] Furthermore, after the June 1940 armistice, German refugees who had fled to Belgium, as seen with Peter and Werner's father, as well as the Jewish populations of the Baden, Palatinate, and Saar areas of Germany, were rounded up and sent to French internment camps. On October 4, 1940, new Vichy legislation allowed for the internment of foreign Jews of all ages. As a result, the number of Jewish internees in the southern French internment camps, which was 5,000 of the 8,000 total camp population in spring 1940, had swelled to 28,000 of 40,000 six months later. By February 1941, Jews represented 40,000 of a total internee population of 47,000.[19]

As a result of the growing crisis in Vichy internment camps, humanitarian organizations began organizing aid in fall 1940 to compensate for their dismal sanitary conditions. These organizations later sought to evacuate children from the camps, sending the youngest to the Pouponnière in Limoges and older children to the OSE children's homes or those run by the AFSC or Schweizerische Arbeitsgemeinschaft für kriegsgeschädigte Kinder, known in France as Secours Suisse (Swiss Aid).

American humanitarian organizations, such as the AFSC and the JDC, but also the Unitarian Service Committee (USC) and the Young Men's Christian Association (YMCA), regularly sent reports to the United States on the degrading humanitarian conditions in Vichy France. They confirmed growing fears among American child experts who had been following the rise of Nazism and its spread throughout

Central, Eastern, and now Western Europe. While concern for Jewish children in Nazi Germany initially mobilized American Jews and their organizations, we will see that the 1938 November pogrom brought new helpers to the table. A group of progressive Jewish and non-Jewish individuals tried to reform American immigration laws to bring Jewish children to the United States by bypassing the restrictive quota system that had been in place since the early 1920s.

These pro-refugee activists proved incapable of reforming American immigration law, but they did manage to create a small possibility that allowed roughly 340 unaccompanied refugee children from France to enter the United States in 1941 and 1942. Peter and Werner were among the children selected for immigration to the United States.

In April 1941, their mother wrote from Berlin to a Dr. Lippmann: "I would be very grateful, dear Doctor, if you would let me know when the migration to the United States (I heard it would happen from Marseilles!) would take place. To know this is of the utmost significance to me because my own preferred emigration to the United States depends on it; my paperwork for it is already in place. The children were and are still for all of us here the center of our lives."[20] Instead of reuniting with her children in Berlin, as planned, this mother's hopes were now centered on the United States. As her letter suggests, behind one family's story were many individuals and organizations, all deeply engaged in rescue work. To understand how the brothers escaped France, we need to cross the Atlantic and explore the initiatives on behalf of European refugee children in the United States.

CHAPTER 11

American Networks to Evacuate Central European Jewish Children

A decidedly transnational perspective is needed to fully understand the dynamics that eventually brought Peter and Werner, but also Elfriede and Ruth and many other Jewish refugee children, from France to the United States, since United States immigration policy, as well as American organizations, proved fundamental to this rescue plan.

Evacuating Jewish children from France was not initially understood as a rescue from death. Few individuals, let alone organizations, anticipated that Vichy-Nazi persecutions against Jews would lead to the deportation and murder of children. The threat, while growing continuously throughout the 1940–1942 period, was not apparent to all. So why, then, did some American organizations engage in this complex and expensive mission in 1941? Who mobilized on behalf of Jewish children? We will return to the some of the themes explored earlier for France to question to what extent American Jews managed to build horizontal alliances with Christian and secular individuals and groups to rescue children.

Looking concretely at the work of humanitarian organizations, both on the ground in France and in the United States, points to the complexities of perception at a moment when *all* children were assumed to be deserving of protection. In the United States, the slow evolution of children's economic and social roles can be seen in nineteenth-century laws on compulsory education and the emergence of a juvenile court system at the turn of the twentieth century. One of the final steps in children's shift from being economically "useful" to "useless but emotionally priceless"[1] can be seen in the decades-long fight against child labor that led to its abolition in the Fair Labor Standards Act of 1938. Furthermore, in the aftermath of the First World War, protecting children's special status became an object of international concern, leading to the 1924 Geneva Declaration, which stipulated that in times of conflict, children should be the first to be rescued.[2] If children had become "priceless" in American and Western European societies, how did humanitarian organizations gauge and assess the situation of Jewish children during the Second World War, especially in light of the concomitant Spanish refugee crisis and its child refugees, and the more widespread problems of bombing and malnutrition? Were all children equally deserving of assistance, or should their situation be weighed and assessed according to a hierarchy of need? Studying the child evacuations from France raises these questions, showing the complexities of humanitarian aid and the varied nature of perception.

Approximately 340 children migrated alone to the United States from France in the 1941–1942 period, of whom roughly 280 were Jewish.[3] This dismal number helps explain why the successful evacuations to the United States have remained, with a few exceptions, in the footnotes.[4] In the past few years, however, historians have shown more interest in the evacuations. In general, their approaches reflect the segmented nature of archives themselves, which are scattered across two continents.[5] Likewise, historians have tended to focus either on the United States or France, but not both. This has led individuals to specialize in one organization, usually attributing it credit for the evacuations, which were in fact the result of a complex partnership that deserves its own analysis.[6]

The goal here is to understand how the political situation and preexisting networks in the United States shaped rescue in France. As we will see, American Jews managed to establish an infrastructure in which to receive Jewish refugee children as early as 1934, yet the political situation made actual visas scarce. After the November 1938 pogrom, non-Jews joined the cause, fighting to expand the number of visas by lobbying for new legislation in Congress in spring 1939. The failure to alter US immigration policy led nonetheless to the development of a new coalition. In this complex arrangement of actors and organizations, it makes sense to start our discussion in the American Jewish community, where the first initiatives to evacuate Jewish children from Germany emerged.

Voluntary organizations, as we have known since Alexis de Tocqueville, are an essential part of the American experience, lending flexibility to the social fabric.[7] A rich network of Jewish self-help organizations had long helped American Jews uphold what came to be called the "Stuyvesant Promise," the condition that they would care for their own to avoid becoming a burden on the seventeenth-century Dutch colony of New Amsterdam.[8] Jews continued to respect their promise long after the colonial period and began accepting public aid only when faced with the overwhelming poverty of the Great Depression.[9] Yet even after the Stuyvesant Promise had become obsolete, aid organizations remained a powerful force in American Jewish life. In the interwar period, a moment of rapid acculturation, they provided the diverse American Jewish population a means of asserting its various political and religious ideologies without actually setting foot in a synagogue.[10] It was here, at the "mezzo" level, tucked snuggly between the state and the individual, that American Jews responded to the Central European refugee crisis. Indeed, American Jewish organizations turned to states to influence policies, just as they helped potential and incoming refugees.

As Judith Tydor Baumel-Schwartz has analyzed, American Jewish organizations began discussing the need to evacuate children from Nazi Germany to the United States in the early months of Nazi rule. Three strikingly different American Jewish organizations established the Joint Council on German-Jewish persecution to assess the situation faced by Jews in Nazi Germany.[11] In fall 1933, this body established the Sub-committee to save German-Jewish Children coming to the United States. At the same time, a similar effort emerged through the National Conference of Jewish Social Workers.

While the precocious nature of these initiatives made the American Kindertransport somewhat different from the French one, in other respects it was quite similar. As had French Jews, American Jews centralized their efforts, creating one sole organization to oversee the children's care after arrival, the German Jewish Children's Aid (GJCA), created when the two above-mentioned initiatives merged in April 1934.[12] This structure would coordinate the reception and care of unaccompanied Jewish minors throughout the Second World War and its aftermath.

Another similarity with France was the important role played by Jewish women in coordinating the arrival and care of the refugee children. A Jewish American social worker named Cecilia Razovsky (1886–1968) became a crucial advocate. Born in St. Louis in 1886 to immigrant parents, she worked her way to the highest ranks of American Jewish welfare. A graduate of the Chicago School of Civics and Philanthropy, she served as an inspector in the child labor division of the United States Children's Bureau from 1917 to 1920.[13] It was in this governmental institution dedicated to children's rights, established in 1912, that women gained a foothold in American welfare.[14] Razovsky left the Children's Bureau to work in the Jewish community, yet remained integrated in the larger field of American social welfare.[15]

With the rise of Nazism, Razovsky became the general secretary and executive director of a new organization, the National Coordinating Committee (NCC), which became the National Refugee Service (NRS) in 1939. Despite their non-sectarian names, these organizations were in large part American Jewish responses to Nazi persecution, designed to coordinate aid for all refugees from Nazism in the United States but funded and run by Jewish groups and individuals.[16] If by the 1930s the majority of social workers in the United States were women, it was still rare for them to hold high-level positions. As one of the NCC's top leaders, Razovsky had therefore become an exceptional figure in American welfare circles.[17]

Razovsky helped establish the GJCA, of which she also became the executive director. In this capacity, she led the GJCA's negotiations with the United States Immigration and Naturalization Service, which determined that the children sponsored by the GJCA would enter the United States on permanent (as opposed to visitor) visas.[18] Importantly, the State Department granted the GJCA the ability to provide a "corporate affidavit," which thereby eliminated the need for financial affidavits from individuals in the United States. The Department of Labor, which handled certain aspects of immigration policy during this period, oversaw the placement standards for these children through its Children's Bureau.[19] American guidelines required that unaccompanied children be cared for according to their religion, which meant that Jewish children had to be turned over to a Jewish organization.[20] This provided the GJCA with greater legitimacy, since it was the sole Jewish organization in charge of caring for Jewish refugee children.

The GJCA eventually hired Lotte Marcuse, a German Jewish immigrant, to oversee the children's placements. As a mid-level worker in the American Jewish welfare bureaucracy, little is known about her other than the fact that she studied political history, philosophy, and economics at the Universities of Berlin and Heidelberg and obtained a certificate in social work from the Prussian Ministry of the Interior before coming to the United States in 1921. Upon arrival, she continued her career as a social worker, eventually working for the NCC under Razovsky's direction. Marcuse initially volunteered part-time for the GJCA. In 1937, she became its full-time placement director.[21] One contemporary praised Marcuse for her "knowledge of Germany, her knowledge of the child placement work, her capacity for understanding the psychology of children and for knowing what kind of a child belongs to what kind of a home."[22] Historians provide a more complex view: Stephanie Corazza notes that "Lotte Marcuse daily wore the hats of secretary, administrator, caseworker, logistical coordinator, immigration official and director of the agency. [. . .] One wonders whether Marcuse took on all the GJCA work because she only trusted herself to do it right."[23] As Judith Tydor Baumel noted diplomatically: "Despite her commendable devotion to duty, an argumentative and opinionated personality did not endear Marcuse to many of her colleagues."[24] Indeed, Marcuse left an important legacy for historians through her extensive correspondence with children, parents, and Jewish social welfare agencies on both sides of the Atlantic, in which one can ascertain an extremely dedicated yet rigid personality.

Like in France, the strong cultural association that bound women to children, as well as the emergence of new structures for child protection, gave women access to new positions of authority in the otherwise male-dominated field of Jewish social welfare.[25] If women were running the show at the GJCA, it should nonetheless be noted that Razovsky was one of only two women on its founding board, which gathered men from leading Jewish social welfare and communal institutions.[26] To complicate matters, it appears that Razovsky and Marcuse did not get along. Marcuse seemed continually frustrated with her behind-the-scenes role, writing to a colleague: "CR [Cecilia Razovsky] asked me to give her some material so she could make a speech; I would have preferred to use this material myself and in my own way: however, if she really gets money for tickets, I guess I can get over it."[27] Such comments and surely other conflicts led one male colleague to complain about "getting a little bit fed up about these female difficulties"[28] and suggest bypassing them altogether. Even if Razovsky and Marcuse were indeed carving out a space for women's authority in American Jewish welfare, it was not an obvious or easy process.

Unlike in France, where the Kindertransport children were cared for primarily in collective homes, the social work establishment in the United States showed a marked preference for foster care. Indeed, while orphanages had become widespread in the United States in the late nineteenth century, they were also subjected to criticism by advocates of family placement.[29] In 1909, the White House Conference on Children and Youth underscored the need to avoid to the extent possible family separation and, when necessary, to prefer family placements.[30] This policy was embraced by American social workers, who looked increasingly to Freudian theory in the 1930s and 1940s to justify their preference for foster care. As historians have highlighted, Freud spoke to American individualism. According to Tara Zahra, family placements symbolized "the children's psychological 'best interests' [. . .] and distinctly American values of individualism, self-reliance and family solidarity."[31]

In light of this context, it is hardly surprising that the state mandated foster care for the children under the care of the GJCA. This policy was further ensconced in 1941, when the Children's Bureau drew up standards for the care of refugee children in wartime, clearly stating in its guidelines that family placement was preferable, in keeping with the "generally recognized values inherent for growing children in home and family life."[32]

Eager to align their welfare practices with those of the larger American social work establishment, Jewish social work organizations did not oppose this policy. On the contrary: in the interwar period, Jewish orphanages continued to exist, yet family placement had gained widespread support. As one social worker noted as early as 1917: "While the results of the institutional treatment were satisfactory, still the general antagonistic attitude against congregate systems of child caring has also spread among the Jews. An institution necessarily lacks home atmosphere—the most important adjunct in child life—it neglects individuality and is detrimental to the free development of character."[33]

While the GJCA accepted foster placement without question, finding Jewish foster families represented a major challenge. Afraid of aggravating nativist sentiments, the GJCA tried to keep its efforts as quiet as possible, and limited mention of its work in the press. Once a family did offer hospitality, it needed to meet strict housing guidelines. This further limited placement possibilities, especially for orthodox children, since religious families tended to be larger and have less available space.[34]

Yet another constraint—this time imposed by Jewish organizations—was the desire to avoid creating a "refugee hub" in New York, which they feared would aggravate American antisemitism. "New York Is Big, America Is Bigger"[35] was the motto of the NCC, and the same resettlement policy applied to children. As a result, the GJCA sent its wards to Jewish social service agencies throughout the United States, which in turn supervised the children's foster care placements and served as the liaison with the GJCA office in New York.

Such constraints, as well as the political situation in Germany—not yet perceived by Jewish parents as life-threatening—kept the program small. In November 1934, the CJCA brought a first group of nine children to the United States. By March 1938, it was only caring for 351 children and was considering stopping the program.[36] The Nazi Annexation of Austria and the November pogrom in 1938 changed matters for Jewish families in Europe, as well as for those concerned about the rise of Nazism in the United States.

American refuge was held hostage by the quota system, which had emerged in the wake of the First World War. Nativists found support in Congress, which passed the Emergency Quota Act in May 1921 and renewed the legislation in 1922. This act set up quotas by nationality, allowing into the United States 3 percent of the number of each nationality present in the country at the time of the 1910 census. In 1924, Congress passed the Johnson Reed Act, which reinforced the quota system, basing the set number of visas for each nationality on 2 percent of those present at the moment of the 1890 census. By proceeding in this manner, the US government was able to avoid accusations of overt discrimination, all while privileging Northern European Protestant immigrants over the "New Immigrants"—primarily Jewish, Catholic, and Christian orthodox—who had come in increasing numbers after 1881 from Eastern and Southern Europe.[37]

In the 1920s, American Jewish organizations actively fought, but failed to change, the quota system.[38] The policy caused Jewish immigration to the United States to plummet: whereas in some years during the 1881–1920 period the immigration of Jewish individuals exceeded 125,000 individuals per year, after 1924 and until 1939 the number hovered around 20,000 persons per year.[39] While the quota system was keeping those fleeing Nazi persecutions out of the United States, it was not solely responsible for preventing refuge. American interwar immigration policy was also influenced by internal rivalries within the United States government. Until 1940, the Immigration and Naturalization service was under the auspices of the Department of Labor, headed by Frances Perkins, who took a pro-refugee stance.[40] However, the visa department fell under the control of the more conservative State Department.[41] United States consuls took their orders from the State Department but had the power to decide who received visas. For this reason, the number of visas granted to refugees fleeing Central European countries, already limited by the quota system, were under-issued. For example, in 1936, the German quota was 25,957, yet only 6,978 individuals were actually allowed to enter.[42] One of the reasons why this figure was so low was the concern that immigrants would become a public charge, which provided grounds to dismiss their application. Therefore, each visa application had to include a financial affidavit from a sponsor in the United States. Affidavits from

American Jews were usually disqualified, leading most visa applications to be rejected.

Things improved slightly in January 1937 when the State Department overtly stated that affidavits from American Jews were acceptable.[43] Furthermore, in response to the Nazi invasion of Austria in March 1938, President Roosevelt established the Presidential Advisory Committee on Political Refugees in April 1938, putting James MacDonald, a pro-refugee activist and former High Commissioner for Refugees, in charge. To address the particularly low Austrian quota number, the German and Austrian quotas were combined. Such policies increased the number of visas issued, leading to a slight improvement. For example, during the 1933–1936 period, only 18,000 Germans and Austrians entered the United States, whereas between 1937 and 1940, this number increased to 83,000.[44] While these policy changes provided some hope, pro-refugee advocates were lucid about their inability to influence public opinion on immigration. The November pogrom nonetheless incited some to try.

In December 1938, a group of about twenty-eight individuals began to meet in the home of Dr. Marion Kenworthy (1891–1980), the director of the Department of Mental Hygiene at the New York School of Social Work and a specialist in the emerging field of child psychiatry.[45] The goal of the meeting was to "gather together a group of people with experience and training in the field of child care and interested in the refugee problem"[46] in order to bring children out of Germany. Kenworthy seemed to know just whom to invite, casting a wide net into child welfare circles and the progressive philanthropic elite. She also included the less prestigious aid workers who knew the situation on the ground, such as GJCA representatives Cecilia Razovsky and Lotte Marcuse, in addition to other individuals from multiple religious and professional backgrounds.[47]

At first glance, it appears that the initiative stemmed exclusively from Dr. Kenworthy. However, Judge Justine Wise Polier (1903–1987) also played a central role and seems to have been at its origin. Before obtaining her law degree, Polier had worked in a settlement house and a textile mill. Later, as a law student at Yale, she supported a strike at the mill where she had worked. Initially focused on labor law, she eventually specialized in juvenile delinquency. In 1935, Polier became the highest-ranking female judge in the State of New York, and it was most likely in this capacity that she met Dr. Kenworthy, who was at the time working to introduce child psychiatry into the courts. Justine Polier's political activism reflected a family tradition, since both of her parents were well-known social reformers. Her mother, Louise Waterman Wise, worked on behalf of women and children throughout her life, having founded the Child Adoption Agency of the Free Synagogue in 1916. Her father was the reform Rabbi Stephen Wise, who was a founding member of the National Association for the Advancement of Colored People, the American Jewish Congress, and the World Jewish Congress. In the late 1930s, Wise proved to be one of the most outspoken rabbis in the United States on the persecution against Jews in Nazi Germany. He was also a friend of President Franklin Delano Roosevelt and a member of the newly formed Presidential Advisory Committee on Refugees. Justine Wise Polier was therefore a member of the progressive American Jewish elite and, we can assume, well-informed on the situation Jews faced in Nazi territories. Yet she was also marked politically by her family's activism on behalf of Jewish refugees and African Americans, a fact that did not serve the cause of building a broad coalition to bring unaccompanied Jewish children to the United States.[48]

This helps explain why she turned to her Protestant colleague Dr. Kenworthy for support in the aftermath of the November pogrom.[49] Together, they teamed up to enlist the support of Quaker Minister Clarence Pickett, the executive secretary of the AFSC. "The other evening I spent hours with Judge Polier talking about this need for working out some adequate assistance to the German refugee children, following her talk with you," wrote Kenworthy to Pickett. "As Judge Polier has indicated to you subsequently, we feel that you are the most significant person because of your wide experience, your rich knowledge and your fundamental interest in this whole field, and as she has told you, we wish to lean very heavily upon you for guidance in working out some sort of adequate program."[50] Kenworthy did not add that Pickett was also needed because he was a man, but she proved keenly aware of gender bias. Several months later, she would discuss the need to find an "adequate male" to replace some of the women in their group due to the "limitations of their femaleness."[51]

Pickett was indeed the perfect partner in this highly politicized combat, for he could hardly be accused of partisan politics. The son of an Illinois farmer, he had been raised in a Quaker colony in Kansas. He had attended Penn College and Hartford Seminary, before becoming professor of biblical literature at Earlham College. In 1929, Pickett had been appointed executive director of the AFSC, which had forged a unique reputation in humanitarian aid circles since its founding in 1917 by providing assistance to the German civilian population during and after the First World War, including feeding 1.2 million German children daily until 1924.[52] As a "neutral" Quaker leader, Pickett was especially crucial to Kenworthy's group for this reason, but also due to his access to President Roosevelt. According to Pickett, in fall 1938, Roosevelt asked him if he would be willing to replace the United States Ambassador to Germany. Pickett immediately dismissed the president's suggestion, but in spring 1940, his appointment was still being discussed.[53]

Pickett was thus a crucial asset to Kenworthy's group, which would continue to meet over the following months and years. The group's initial meeting set forth some of the key elements in their strategy to evacuate children from Nazi territories, whom they labelled, vaguely, "German children" or, curiously, "refugee children." These formulations reflect a certain level of ambiguity over the population they wanted to assist. In reality, the children they sought to bring were *not yet refugees*, at least for the most part, but Jewish and "non-Aryan" children targeted by the Nazi regime. The word "refugee" therefore seemed to serve as a handy euphemism, designed to smooth over the politically unpopular idea of bringing Jewish children to the United States.

Indeed, one of the group's main concerns was overcoming the American public's "anti-refugee" sentiments. The GJCA's director Cecilia Razovsky showed a pragmatic attitude at the group's first meeting when she pointed out that "special legislation would be necessary to bring in children under sixteen without their parents, and that it should not be proposed by the Jewish organizations."[54] Another participant, Dr. John Lovejoy Elliott, explained to the group that he was "very troubled by the prejudice in the minds of many Americans about receiving these refugee children."[55] Others stated that "it would be unwise and misleading to consider the problem other than as a

Jewish one"[56] and that the support of an "influential person such as John D. Rockefeller Jr. [. . .] would do much to sway public opinion."[57] The next day a smaller group met to work out the finer points of the group's strategy. It was here that "LW" (the progressive attorney Louis S. Weiss) made the point that "a very definite education program was needed to separate the child program from the adult problem in the general refugee picture."[58] Indeed, children's "useless but priceless"[59] status in American culture provided the group a small window in which they could argue that refugee youth would not threaten American jobs and, furthermore, deserved to be saved due to the simple fact that they were children.

In these initial meetings, one sees the contours of a debate that usually remained just under the surface: should (and would) non-Jewish organizations serve as "front" organizations in order to encourage the American public to accept the children? Should the Jewishness of the children (and some of their advocates) be downplayed? And who, exactly, was in need of evacuation?

By early 1939, the group had grown to thirty-five individuals, and their committee work had evolved into a proposal to challenge United States immigration law, framed as a call to help children of all faiths.[60] Building an ecumenical coalition was not only a strategy to broaden public support by downplaying the Jewishness of those involved, it reflected a reality that many on the committee embraced: what the Nazis had deemed as "non-Aryan" children included Catholic and Protestant children (and also many others with Jewish ancestors who did not fit nicely into categories). As the group's minutes note: "If the child welfare workers, Catholic, Jewish and Protestant, can prepare themselves to meet these children at the gates of America, place them in homes of their own faiths and care for them as long as necessary, the potentialities of good in such an enterprise seem limitless."[61]

One can see the American situation echoing the contours of the British Kindertransport, in which Lord Baldwin made his support conditional on establishing a " 'national' appeal on behalf of all the British religious denominations."[62] But what did this mean for the chil- dren themselves? In the Kenworthy group's February 1939 meeting, someone broached the question "as to whether there would not have to be a definite agreement as to how many of these children would be Jewish." Justine Wise Polier's response shows the attempt to downplay the number of Jewish children: "Justine felt that the question could be answered not by giving a guarantee which she thought would be inadvisable, but by quoting the experience that Holland and England are having in which the proportion of the children coming in is not much more than half Jewish."[63] In reality, the large majority of the children sent to Great Britain were Jewish. The notion that children were selected for the Kindertransport with respect to a Jewish and "non-Aryan" ratio—instead of according to need—nonetheless deserves further exploration.[64]

First Lady Eleanor Roosevelt wrote to Judge Polier on January 4, 1939:

> My husband says that you had better go to work at once and get two people of opposite parties in the House and in the Senate and have them jointly get agreement on the legislation which you want for bringing in children. The State Department is only afraid of what Congress will say to them, and therefore if you remove that fear the State Department will make no objection. He advises that you choose your people rather carefully and, if possible, get all the Catholic support you can.[65]

As this letter shows, Judge Polier's connections to the White House were real, as was Eleanor Roosevelt's support of new legislation that would bring "German refugee children" to the United States.

One month later, on February 9, 1939, Democratic New York Senator Roger F. Wagner and Republican Representative Edith Nourse Rogers of Massachusetts proposed joint legislation to allow for 10,000 visas to be issued in both 1939 and 1940 (for a total of 20,000, outside of the quota numbers) for German children aged fourteen or younger. Wagner, in addressing the Senate, echoed the Kenworthy group's strategy, framing the issue as a children's cause and downplaying the Jewishness of its beneficiaries: "Millions of innocent and defenseless men, women and children in Germany today, of every race and creed, are suffering from conditions which compel them to seek refuge in our lands. Our hearts go out to the children of tender years, who are the most pitiful and helpless sufferers."[66] Wagner was not incorrect to assess that individuals of every "race and creed" were suffering, but the meaning of his language depended on how one viewed the populations persecuted by the Nazis and, of course, how one defined race. To many Americans, including many Jews, in the late 1930s, Jews represented a separate race.[67] And as seen above, while the children were considered "Jewish" or "non-Aryan" in the eyes of the Nazis, some of them were indeed Christians, as descendants of converts to Christianity. Emphasizing the ecumenical nature of the refugee problem was therefore both a strategy to assuage antisemitic fears and a reflection of the complex realities in Nazi Germany. The question remained whether American Christians would extend their solidarity to the children labelled "non-Aryan Christians" by the Nazis, and whether this sentiment would carry over to the Jewish children who made up the large majority of "German refugee children."

In March 1939, one month after the legislation was introduced in Congress, Kenworthy's informal group became the Non-Sectarian Committee for German Refugee Children, with Clarence Pickett as its executive director and seventy prominent members, including Catholic and Protestant representatives such as the Cardinal Rudelein and Canon Anson Phelps Stokes. The committee lobbied for the Wagner-Rogers Bill and proposed a clear plan for the resettlement and care of the children.[68] The bill was supported by First Lady Eleanor Roosevelt, Secretary of Labor Frances Perkins, and Secretary of the Interior Harold Ikes, as well as popular figures such as the actress Helen Hayes. However, the opposition was powerful and came from diverse quarters.

While the idea of helping children abroad was a relatively novel concept, it is important to note that this was not the first time Americans, including the First Lady, had mobilized for children outside of the United States. In the aftermath of the Guernica bombing in April 1937, the American Board of Guardians for Basque Refugee Children was formed, with the First Lady as its honorary president. In June, the group presented a plan to bring 500 Basque children to the United States, petitioning the State Department for six-month visitor visas. When approximately 2,700 families offered hospitality to the children, the committee expanded its plan to include 2,000 children. However, the majority of Catholic Americans, especially Cardinal O'Connell of Boston, supported Franco in the conflict. Their campaign against the Basque children forced Eleanor Roosevelt to back down from the issue. By late June 1937, the State Department had denied the visas.[69]

The Wagner-Rogers Bill proved as divisive as the Basque initiative, even if it received positive coverage in the American Press.[70] Opponents had their choice of arguments. Overt antisemitism was one tactic. Democratic Senator Robert Reynolds of North Carolina voiced his protest to the bill by asking that an article from the English section of *Il Grido Della Stirpe* be included in the Congressional Record: "The people are being made refugee-minded through the usual high-pressure propaganda sponsored by the interested party—the Jew. They are systematically building a Jewish empire in this country, instead of in Palestine. The Palestine affair is just a make believe [sic], for the consumption of the 'good-natured people.' After all, how could they live in Palestine among themselves with no Gentiles to 'peel'?"[71] The president's own cousin and wife of Immigration and Naturalization Service director James L. Houghteling, Laura Delano Houghteling, only lightly masked her antisemitism when noting at a dinner party that "20,000 charming children would all too soon grow up into 20,000 ugly adults."[72] Just as the bill's supporters sought to frame the bill as a children's issue, its opponents pushed the children outside of their protected category, into the world of "ugly adults"—in other words, Jews. More subtle was the argument that the bill would lead to family separation, designed to garner antagonism from Catholic circles.[73]

As the debates raged, Congress amended the bill to a point where the 20,000 visas would be included within the pre-existing quota numbers, essentially rendering the legislation moot. The president, preparing for a larger confrontation in Congress over the Neutrality Acts, advised to "file, no action" when asked for a public statement on the legislation.[74] By the end of the first Congressional session in June 1939, it was clear that the legislation would never come to a vote.

The Non-Sectarian Committee for German Refugee Children regrouped but did not give up. In November 1939, it began reorganizing. By March 1940, the group that had been meeting in Marion

Kenworthy's living room since 1938 was ready for a feel-good moment. Attorney Louis S. Weiss was one of the first to take the floor. The tone of his speech captures his desire to continue their work, in spite of the failed Wagner-Rogers Bill: "It's much too easy to say that the Bill failed to pass. It did fail to pass. It was amended to a point where we were reluctant to have it passed. But in the holding of those hearings and in educating Congress in the kind of thing we meant, it's fair to say that many of us who were present at those hearings consider it as successful in a strange and subtle way. The bill didn't pass, but the idea gained."[75] At the end of the meeting, Adele Rosenwald Levy, one of the group's prominent Jewish members and the daughter of the well-known progressive philanthropist, Julius Rosenwald, spoke: "for all of us who have been occupied during these past months and years with this problem it gives us a great feeling of solace and a great feeling of new courage that we have the cooperation of this group, and so we say, 'Thank God for the Marion Kenworthys and for Marshall Field and Newbold Morris and Mr. Lovejoy,' so that we may carry this work shoulder to shoulder as United States citizens, not as Jews or non-Jews, but as people interested in children."[76] Using "we" to describe "those who have been occupied during these past months and years with this problem," Adele Rosenwald Levy seems to situate herself as a Jew here in order to express her gratitude to the non-Jews who decided to help. In the name of children, American Jews, especially Justine Wise Polier and Adele Rosenwald Levy, had managed to create a fragile, yet sincere, horizontal alliance.

One month later, in April 1940, the Non-Sectarian Foundation for Refugee Children Inc. was officially founded to care for and fundraise on behalf of unaccompanied child refugees, under the presidency of Clarence Pickett. The group dropped the "German" in its name, with the hope of helping children of other nationalities, in light of the Nazi expansion.[77] While the group had long embraced an ecumenical stance, there remained some ambiguity over who encompassed their targeted population. An internal suggestion, made in May 1940, to cut costs by turning over the resettlement work to the GJCA provoked the ire of the group's executive director, Owen R. Lovejoy:

Nothing seems to me more important in relation to a development of decent social standards than the bringing together on a factual, functional basis the various types of religious allegiance in this country. To turn this work over to the Jews and confess that Christians, whether Catholic or Protestant have no vital concern in the matter or in cooperating with the Jews in service to children of their race or other races, is a move I could not personally contemplate without shame.[78]

Lovejoy, a Methodist minister and child labor activist, expresses his solidarity here with Jews. His statement also shows that the committee served as a rare opportunity to move beyond the sectarian nature of American child welfare, which remained staunchly segregated by race and religion. This situation did not facilitate his goal of establishing common standards.[79] In the name of helping Jews, but also improving child welfare by working across denominational lines, the group continued its work. The foundation brought ten children to the United States before suspending its activities in July 1940, transferring its energy, and most of its actors, to a new group.[80]

Indeed, the Battle of Britain and the fall of France in June 1940 changed the terms of the debate: it was now clear that *all* European children, not just those in the Third Reich, were in danger. From the vantage point of the United States, it appeared that something could still be done, since immigration from Europe had not ceased as a result of the war. This situation caused many groups to emerge with the hope of bringing over refugee children from Europe. The US Committee for the Care of European Children (USCOM) was created to centralize their efforts in July 1940.[81] As she had for the initiative to bring Basque children, First Lady Eleanor Roosevelt, who had supported the Wagner-Rogers Bill, became its honorary president, while Marshall Field III, the department store magnate and philanthropist, served as its president.[82] With branches opening throughout the United States, the new organization was quickly developing into a grassroots movement, especially since it could withstand nativist criticisms: the USCOM was not established to help Jewish children escape Nazi Germany. Instead, the USCOM was harkening to the "Special Relationship"[83] that linked the

United Kingdom to the United States in a seemingly indelible cultural and political alliance. The children's perceived "Anglo-Saxon" background allowed the USCOM to achieve what the Wagner-Rogers Bill had failed to obtain: they secured 10,000 visitor's visas for the British children. This exception to United States immigration policy was made in July 1940, allowing the children to come without affidavits, outside the quota system.[84] The USCOM immediately began evacuating children from the United Kingdom, sending them to foster families throughout the country. Almost 900 had been transferred to the United States when, in fall 1940, a Mercy Ship was downed by a German torpedo, killing most of the 90 children onboard.[85] This tragedy caused the British government to end the evacuation program.

The USCOM was considering downsizing in October 1940.[86] It very well may have shut down if it hadn't been for the arrival in New York of a handful of refugees from France, determined to redirect the USCOM's mission. It is to their efforts that we will now turn.

CHAPTER 12

New York Negotiations

E rnst Papanek, former director of OSE's children's homes, recalled:

> I thought that once I reached the United States it would be only a
> matter of time before the children started coming over. Even the
> political climate seemed to be with us. [. . .] I was wrong. The US
> Committee had managed to obtain visas for English children, but
> they had little success, in the end, in cutting the red tape for Jewish
> children from the continent. But there was more to it than that.
> Political pressure was not applied because there was no sense of
> urgency among the leaders of the American Jewish organizations
> [. . .]. They would not, and could not, bring themselves to believe
> that the children were in mortal danger, because once they did it
> became incumbent upon them to move heaven on earth to rescue
> them. And in a time of increasing anti-Semitism in the United
> States they did not want to take the risk of fanning the flames by
> bringing Jewish children by the boatload.[1]

Papanek's observations, published posthumously in 1975, attribute
blame to American Jews for the fact that most Jewish children in France
did not find refuge in the United States. Yet the story is much more
complex, and our discussion will untangle the multiple actors—including
American Jews and Papanek himself, as well as Unitarians, Quakers, and
others—whose efforts led to a victory (albeit small), since about 280

Jewish children were brought to the United States in 1941 and 1942. Rescuing them from occupied France required convincing a cast of unrelated characters—individuals and organizations of very different backgrounds—to undergo an expensive and complicated transatlantic mission.

The collaboration among American Jewish, non-sectarian, and Christian organizations was not a straightforward process, even when goals overlapped. Indeed, it is often assumed that the non-Jewish and Jewish individuals and organizations that helped Jews during the Holocaust were fighting for the same cause and thus worked together seamlessly.[2] Instead of considering the need to help Jews as obvious, we need to take a step back in order to examine the path that led to what we now call rescue. Tensions and ambiguities existed, even when groups worked together in good faith.

As seen in the previous chapter, the establishment of the USCOM in July 1940 must be understood in light of the failure of the United States Congress to pass legislation on behalf of "German refugee children." Learning from this experience, and in response to the war itself, the leaders of the USCOM framed their cause more broadly, and set out to help civilian children at risk of Nazi bombs in the United Kingdom. We will see that American Jewish organizations—far from indifferent—and individual refugees felt a distinct strategy was needed to convince the USCOM to assist Jewish children in France. Indeed, the USCOM's decision to shift its focus to France was not an automatic next step for the non-sectarian committee.

The USCOM's decision was in large part influenced by an American Jewish organization, the JDC, which I will discuss soon, as well as a handful of European refugees who arrived from France in 1940 and 1941. Indeed, while immigration opportunities to the United States were dismal, some European refugees did manage to obtain visas for the United States. One such refugee was Ernst Papanek, who brought "his" OSE children to what became the non-occupied zone, and then tried—as seen in his quote above—to bring them to the United States. Another refugee was the founder of the CIE, Germaine de Rothschild, followed soon after by her cousin Yvonne de Gunzbourg, who oversaw the OSE's efforts to care for the Kindertransport children in France. They were not alone. With the threat of war, the OSE sought to develop its American presence by opening a New York office. Members of this organization's central committee from Poland and France also sought refuge in New York. The rescue networks that had been crucial for bringing Central European children to France were thus reconfigured in New York. As experts of the European situation, these individuals expected to find an easy foothold in American pro-refugee circles in order to continue the work they started in Europe. They were strongly mistaken.

~

The rise of Nazism led to a major reorganization of Jewish welfare, not only in Europe but also in the United States. As seen in the last chapter, new organizations emerged to help resettle the victims of Nazism, such as the NRS. In addition, American Jews managed to overcome their political divisions long enough to establish the United Jewish Appeal for Refugee and Overseas Needs in 1939.[3] This organization unified the fundraising campaigns of the American Jewish aid organizations working in Europe, Mandatory Palestine, and the United States, even if alliances proved tenuous. One of its main beneficiaries was the JDC, which received about 50 percent of its funds.[4]

Since its establishment during the First World War, the JDC had become American Jews' primary overseas philanthropic organization. With staff throughout Eastern Europe, a European headquarters based in Paris (and after 1940, in Lisbon), and a board of directors in New York, the JDC was a powerful player in Jewish welfare on two continents. Thanks to its widespread philanthropy, it had access to information from unlikely corners and a clear view of European Jews' needs during the rise of Nazism, which it addressed by funding a growing number of European Jewish self-help organizations.[5] The JDC also proved able to negotiate directly with states, as seen earlier with the SS *St. Louis* affair, in which the JDC, with crucial assistance from French feminist Louise Weiss, negotiated with the French, British, Dutch, and Belgian governments to help the refugees find shelter—at least temporarily—outside of Germany.[6]

The JDC's philanthropy led to longstanding collaborations with Jewish organizations in Europe. The OSE had been a beneficiary of the JDC since the First World War, when the organization still went by its original Russian name, OZE (*Obschestvo zdravookhraneniia evreev*). The JDC provided as much as 90 percent of the Russian organization's budget during and after the First World War for its programs throughout Eastern Europe and between 15 and 20 percent of its budget in the 1930s. It increased its contribution dramatically in the years leading up to the Second World War.[7] In 1939 alone, the JDC provided the OSE with $25,000 for its work in Europe.[8] In France, the JDC subsidized OSE's Kindertransport initiative, providing for a quarter of the costs of its children's homes in Montmorency, and progressively more after their displacement in May and June 1940.[9]

One of the underlying assumptions of the JDC's philanthropy was that its beneficiary organizations would remain in Europe. While the OSE was active exclusively in Eastern and Western Europe, it nonetheless attempted to expand its activities in the United States as early as 1925.[10] In 1929, it set up an American committee, composed of a small circle of American Jewish doctors, who had served on the JDC's medical delegation to Ukraine and Poland after the First World War. Because these individuals had worked closely with the Polish branch of OSE, TOZ, they were naturally inclined to help OSE in the United States.[11] At its beginnings in 1929, the American OSE committee cultivated the hope of setting up a nationwide membership association.[12] This goal began to take shape in 1937, when Lithuanian-born gynecologist Dr. A.J. Rongy took over as chairman.[13] Dr. Rongy's most ambitious plan was to collaborate with Phi Delta Epsilon, a Jewish medical fraternity with a nationwide membership, in order to garner support for OSE among American Jewish physicians.[14] By the late 1930s, the American OSE Committee was thus on its way to becoming an American Jewish organization, integrated into American Jewish medical circles.

By 1938, however, it became clear that the OSE's expansion in the United States would be problematic for its main benefactor, the JDC, who felt this would "upset the apple cart,"[15] or, in other words, threaten the fragile order of American Jewish philanthropy. The concern was that OSE would start fundraising on its own behalf. Indeed, as a JDC beneficiary organization, the OSE was allowed to raise funds in the United States, but only for the JDC (and after 1939, for the United Jewish Appeal).[16]

In Europe, OSE leaders were especially interested in avoiding conflict with JDC due to their organization's growing financial dependency on the American organization. Nonetheless, from OSE's perspective, an American presence was essential to protecting its work. The OSE sent a representative to New York to negotiate with the JDC in January and June 1939, arguing that, in case of war, OSE would need an office in a neutral country.[17]

JDC representatives in New York as well as in Paris nonetheless maintained that the OSE's expansion in the United States would endanger the JDC's work. "In this country," wrote one JDC representative in New York, "whether it be in the field of medical service or in the large economic activities or welfare work or refugee assistance, the communities here look to the JDC as the centralized medium through which the problems in Eastern and Central Europe and among the refugees can best be presented and interpreted."[18] The JDC thus explained that a strong OSE presence in the United States would "set an undesirable precedent" and "confuse the American Jewish community."[19]

Faced with the JDC's opposition, OSE leaders had limited room to maneuver but carried on their campaign, emphasizing the emergency created by the outbreak of war in September 1939. Their insistence intensified after the arrival *in extremis* of Dr. Leon Wulman, the general secretary of Union OSE's Polish branch, TOZ, just weeks after the Nazis invaded Poland.[20] Detained at Ellis Island, then living in a hotel and unemployed, Dr. Wulman made it his mission to open a New York branch for the OSE, a cause that was certainly influenced by his own precarious situation. Writing to the JDC in February 1940, Wulman affirmed the OSE's desire to establish an executive committee in the United States.[21]

Wulman was not the only OSE leader now in the United States. One by one, its central committee members sought refuge in New York, leading to the reconstitution of the Union OSE's central committee there in October 1940. This act was congratulated by OSE leaders in France, who felt it was "only natural that the presence in America of so many members of our central organization resulted in an effort to build up there a body which in the present conditions will certainly be of great value to our common cause."[22] Yet without the JDC's approval and funding, the OSE was still unable to open an actual office.

The situation finally evolved in favor of the OSE in late November 1940, when the JDC's general secretary Moses Leavitt wrote a letter of recommendation for the OSE to rent property in New York City.[23] The American Committee of OSE, known as Amerose, was officially formed on December 18, 1940, with Dr. Leon Wulman at its head.[24] Now based at Princeton, the physicist Albert Einstein presided its honorary committee. On December 25, 1940, the creation of Amerose was announced in the Jewish press.[25] It was only in April 1941, four months after its establishment, that the JDC approved a monthly grant to cover the latter's operating costs.[26] Annoyed yet resigned to the situation, JDC's Executive Vice-Chairman Joseph Hyman demanded that several conditions be met to obtain the JDC's assistance, notably that Amerose "should not be permitted to do anything except engage in necessary letter writing, etc. [. . .] it should not appear as an American organization engaged in any activity on the American scene. Obviously, that would mean too, that the OSE could have nothing to do with attempting in any way to bring children over from France, or with the conduct of any operative or functional activity."[27]

Indeed, one of the main reasons why the OSE had sought to open an office in New York was to garner support for the children under its care in France. In light of its limited ability to maneuver in the United States, would the OSE be able to help these children? Would the JDC really block the OSE's efforts to maintain its own dominance? A critical approach to rescue requires asking to what extent these intra-communal tensions influenced their initiatives to save children.

While OSE leaders were busy making sense of the dynamics in New York, former director of the OSE's children's homes Ernst Papanek managed to escape France with his wife Helene and their two children. As an Austrian socialist, Papanek had obtained a coveted emergency visa to the United States thanks to his political activism.[28] He made a promise to the children under his care in August 1940, before he left France:

No one wanted to say "What is going to happen to us now?" But that was the question behind everything that was being said. For while the children knew I might well be killed if I stayed, they could not help but wonder whether they weren't going to be killed because I wasn't staying. [. . .] I said "As soon as I'm in the United States I will begin to work to get you over." They said "Sure, we'll meet you in America." And all the while I could feel the barrier rising between us in the night air. For the first time, I felt they distrusted me.[29]

Papanek's arrival in New York in September 1940 coincided with the American OSE Committee's transition from a refugee aid committee, headquartered in Leon Wulman's hotel room, to an official organization with an office in midtown Manhattan. But his arrival also corresponded with the German torpedo sinking of the SS *City of Benares*, which killed so many British child evacuees and caused the British government to terminate the evacuation scheme to the United States. As seen in the previous chapter, the attack left the USCOM at a crossroads: it could either stop its work or redirect its energy to helping children in France. The second option seemed especially daunting, and the USCOM had keen knowledge of its difficulty.[30]

Papanek acted quickly to fulfill the promise he had made to the OSE children. His first objective was to obtain the support of JDC. The latter was well aware of the urgent situation for children in France, having funded the Kindertransport initiatives from Central Europe to France since 1938. Before leaving Lisbon, Papanek met with the JDC's acting head of European operations, Joseph Schwartz.[31] Around the same time, Schwartz received a letter from Guy de Rothschild, who had been demobilized from the French army in late August 1940 and now found himself responsible for his mother's La Guette children. Rothschild spoke about the children's degrading conditions in La Bourboule and affirmed that the latter needed to be rapidly evacuated from France: "It would be a great pity if these children were to suffer as a result of a generous initiative that has been taken on their behalf."[32] Working independently, both Papanek and Rothschild seem to have convinced Schwartz that the children needed to emigrate from France. On September 9, 1940, Schwartz wrote to his superior in New York, Morris

Troper, suggesting that the JDC contact Clarence Pickett's Non-Sectarian Foundation, which by fall 1940 had become the USCOM.[33] Troper was not at all surprised by Schwartz's request, stating that the emigration idea had been "under consideration for quite some time."[34]

Papanek was not the only refugee from France in contact with the JDC: the Baroness Germaine de Rothschild made news in New York by arriving with $1 million's worth of jewelry in July 1940.[35] The JDC immediately reached out to the Baroness at her daughter Jacqueline's home in upstate New York. She responded, asking if something could be done for the children in France, perhaps through the Red Cross: "It seems dreadful for these unhappy children!"[36] she wrote, in her distinctive handwriting.

Troper could not easily ignore the requests for help from members of the Rothschild family. Not only did the JDC need its financial support, it also sought out Germaine de Rothschild to speak publicly on its behalf.[37] Yet the Baroness, overwhelmed with homesickness, seemed too disoriented to organize a campaign on behalf of the La Guette children. Instead, she tried to overcome her sense of uprootedness by exploring the city's buses, subways, and streets.[38] Letters she wrote to her friend and confidant Dorothy de Rothschild (née Pinto), the wife of her husband's cousin James (Jimmy) de Rothschild, shed light on her state of mind: "Two letters from you in the morning and seven from France! It's been a good day! Yes, correspondence is a precious help and I'm going to write to you every week. Too happy, my Dollie, to be closer to you too, whom I miss terribly—and some days in spite of everything we might still have a few of our 'good laughs.'"

Rothschild distracted herself by accepting a daunting task: speaking at fundraisers for American Jewish organizations. Such events helped her fill the hours in this strange new environment:

> Can you believe I've been asked to give speeches, and I've already done two! One for the Joint [JDC] by heart in English in front of a thousand people—the other in front of the Union of Orthodox Women! (This time I read) where I had to explain how religion and proper study had sustained Jewish morale in recent times. It all worked out quite well—they're kind and forgiving here. And they

seem to like my ramblings! [. . .] I'm going to keep myself busy at the National Refugee Service, children's section. We don't do any socializing; we live in a small, very restricted circle of old friends and relatives, and there's quite a few—no desire to spend money, no outings.[39]

Keeping busy seemed to provide the Baroness with a means of coping. Nonetheless, France remained home: "My Dollie, I'm so homesick! It's just awful. One has to make plans . . . organize the summer! When only a sense of the temporary can help one endure this exile!"[40]

Working on behalf of refugee children in the United States enabled the Baroness to continue what she had begun in France. It also mirrored the activities of Dorothy de Rothschild, who had evacuated a group of thirty Jewish children from Frankfurt to the Rothschild's Waddesdon Manor, an hour north of London.[41] The women, though separated by the war, shared the common experience of helping refugee children, a fact that seems to have brought some comfort to Germaine de Rothschild. "The National Refugee Service is opening a new section for the summer placement of refugee children," she wrote, "and I've been asked to head it up. I'll probably accept. I'll learn something new. I'm glad to be able to be of some use, even in a very modest way. If my work might bring me closer to you, it would fulfill everything I desire most!"[42] The Baroness accepted the NRS's request and organized summer camps for refugee children in 1941, heading a five-woman committee.[43]

Over the course of her exile in the United States, Germaine de Rothschild's position in Jewish life evolved from discreet philanthropist to public speaker. Indeed, in France she had filled an important role by funding welfare initiatives but had not made speeches to thousands of individuals, let alone in English. By March 1941, this new role led her to meet Eleanor Roosevelt. This was no small event for Rothschild, who seemed somewhat intimidated by the First Lady, yet perhaps even more surprised at her own capabilities: "Sometimes, like last week, I'm very busy. Other weeks are slower. Yes, last week I spoke 3 times and at one of the receptions was the Mrs. Roosevelt-*mère* [Eleanor Roosevelt]— it was for Youth Aliyah. I chatted for 10 minutes! No accidents. Tomorrow I have another one of those functions that now seem incorporated into my life. [. . .] Everyone charming and indulgent in a way I might not find in Europe. Let's make the most of it!"[44]

The "charm and indulgence" that she found in exile led Germaine de Rothschild to take on an exciting new role, allowing her to cultivate a relationship with Eleanor Roosevelt. Thanks to the Baroness, the First Lady certainly heard a first-hand account of the La Guette children, for if the Baroness's letters to "Dolly" suggest she threw herself into more general Jewish causes, we will soon see that she had not forgotten them.

Ernst Papanek's first moments in the country stood in stark contrast with those of Germaine de Rothschild, at least from a material point of view. His wife Lene, a doctor, was working as a night nurse. He tried to become a janitor in order to have time to read yet only found work as a dishwasher.[45] Still, Papanek had been on the run since 1934. New York was yet another step in a long journey, and the archives he left behind for historians suggest he was too busy to get mired down by yet another exile.

When he wasn't working, Papanek dedicated his time to advocating for the OSE children in the United States. His 1940 agenda as well as a report he authored for Amerose in December 1940 may not reveal the intimate emotions expressed in the Baroness's letters, yet they do provide the names of each person he met after his arrival on September 12, 1940 through the end of December 1940, underscoring his active role in alerting American organizations to the plight of the Jewish children in France.[46] Just days after his arrival in New York, Papanek turned to the JDC, including Harold Troper, JDC's European chairman, who directed him to the USCOM.[47] Unable to reach Troper's USCOM contact person, Adele Rosenwald Levy, a member of the Kenworthy group from its earliest phases, Papanek met instead with Elsa Castendyck on October 14, 1940. The latter was director of the USCOM's childcare department, all while serving as director of the Child Guidance division at the Children's Bureau.[48] As former United States delegate to the Advisory Committee on Social Questions of the League of Nations, Castendyck had visited the OSE homes in Montmorency in 1939. She was thus familiar with Papanek's work in France and had even published an article mentioning the OSE homes in December 1939.[49] Clearly supportive, Castendyck opened her address book to Papanek and connected him to the American network working on behalf of European children. Through her, Papanek met with GJCA leaders Cecilia Razovsky and Lotte Marcuse. Castendyck also introduced Papanek to the inner circle of the USCOM. He met several times with Marshall Field and Eric Biddle, its president and executive director, respectively, as well as with Judge Justine Wise Polier, who, as seen above, was at the origin of the initiative to bring German children to the United States. Wise Polier would soon become even closer to Eleanor Roosevelt, taking a leave of absence from her judgeship in 1941 to serve as special counsel for the office of civil defense under the First Lady.[50] On November 2, 1940, Castendyck arranged a meeting between Papanek and Clarence Pickett, executive director of the AFSC and USCOM board member.[51] This meeting proved decisive: two days later, Pickett sent a telegram to the AFSC director in France, Howard Kershner, asking him to assess the feasibility of evacuating about 300 children under the care of the OSE.[52]

As the above suggests, these conversations certainly influenced the USCOM's decision to evacuate the children from France, yet the organization's archives have been scattered, leaving incomplete holdings in multiple collections throughout the United States.[53] The extensive archives of the JDC, whose leadership was not represented on the USCOM board, nonetheless provide a window onto the relations between the USCOM and Jewish organizations, casting new light on the USCOM's decision to evacuate children from France.

Even if the JDC was irritated by the OSE's arrival on the American scene, it was nonetheless working actively behind the scenes to facilitate the emigration of Jewish children from France to the United States.

The archives reveal the care JDC leaders took in dealing with the USCOM. Their strategy to convince the latter to help, while never clearly articulated, involved several steps. First, they cultivated relationships with the USCOM's Jewish board members, including the attorney Louis S. Weiss, the head of the NRS William Haber, and, most importantly, the philanthropist Adele Rosenwald Levy (1892–1960).[54] Adele Levy's second husband was Dr. David Levy, a child psychologist, which most likely explains the couple's presence at Dr. Kenworthy's initial meeting in

December 1938.[55] Adele Levy was still active in the Kenworthy group—now the USCOM—in fall 1940. The importance the JDC attributed to Levy can be seen in its decision to introduce her to Joseph Schwartz, its acting chairman in Europe, during one of his rare trips back to the United States.[56]

The JDC also sought to shape the opinion of USCOM leaders by providing them with detailed reports from its representatives in France and, better yet, directly from the children's former caretakers. As seen above, Papanek's many meetings with USCOM representatives were facilitated by JDC's Morris Troper, who introduced him to the network.[57] By October 1940, the JDC had also organized an encounter between Germaine de Rothschild and the USCOM board to present the case of the 130 La Guette children.[58] The JDC thus played a crucial role in connecting United States decision-makers to those from the field, making the former aware of the European realities. By late November 1940, the JDC in New York was able to write to its Lisbon office: "Certain members of the Board of the US COMM have sought to keep this matter before that organization in such a way as to assure concrete results. I am glad to let you know that in principle the Board of the United States Committee has agreed to make itself responsible for the maintenance and upkeep of non-English children, as may be brought into this country. This is a very decided step forward."[59]

If the USCOM accepted the principle of caring and, very importantly, paying for non-English children, it still had not decided whether an evacuation scheme from France would be feasible. The USCOM had no infrastructure in Europe and would need a partner organization to carry out its work there. This is where Clarence Pickett and the AFSC enter the picture.

As seen earlier, Pickett was among the first advocates for bringing German children to the United States, as an initial member of the Kenworthy group and now as a member of the USCOM's board of directors.[60] As the executive director of the AFSC, Pickett was able to strengthen a collaboration with the JDC that had originated in Germany in the aftermath of the First World War.[61] In 1934, Pickett met with newly arrived JDC representatives in Paris who had just transferred their European headquarters from Berlin. According to Pickett, "these Paris conversations were really the beginning of a much closer relationship in America"[62]—and also in Europe, one may add, since the AFSC remained active in places where American Jewish organizations could no longer easily operate. Pickett's autobiography shows he was especially willing to capitalize on the AFSC's positive reputation in Germany to help Jews. Historian Haim Genizi makes a more tempered assessment, stating that the AFSC's response to the JDC's request for assistance in 1933 was "cautious and conditional," since the AFSC demanded funding from the JDC in exchange for its assistance, but eventually led to a "productive and trustworthy collaboration."[63] In the aftermath of the November 1938 pogrom, the JDC asked Pickett if he might be willing to open feeding centers for Jews in Germany. Pickett obliged, and the AFSC quietly sent three representatives to Germany.[64] Pickett also offered the State Department additional staff for the United States consular offices in Europe to help them process visa applications more quickly.[65] In August 1939, the AFSC sent three women to Central Europe to help find Jewish children to evacuate to the United States. While one of the women was an employee of the GJCA, she traveled "as the officially accredited representative of the American Friends Service Committee, so that in Central Europe she will seem to have no relationship to the Jewish organizations of America."[66]

Pickett was clearly willing to let AFSC serve as a front for Jewish rescue operations, not only in Europe but also in the United States. Pickett notes he spoke out to the American public about the situation for Jews under Nazism with the awareness that, as the leader of a non-Jewish organization, he would not be accused of exaggerating the facts.[67] The same logic led the AFSC to approve the April 1939 publication of a pamphlet under its own name, but written and financed by the American Jewish Committee, entitled "The Truth About the Refugees." When the AFSC sent the pamphlet to the Jewish Anti-Defamation Council of Minnesota for distribution, the latter asked the AFSC if it would take care of sending it to American labor leaders, since it "would have a great deal more effect than being mailed from a Jewish source here in the Twin cities [. . .] there is so much propaganda spread through the country at this time both anti and favorable that these labor leaders would be suspicious of this material if the same originated from a Jewish source."[68] Following established patterns, the Jewish organizations covered all of the costs, including postage, and the AFSC lent its name.

This kind of help showed a solidarity toward Jews and their organizations that was quite rare at this moment in the United States.[69] But nonetheless, it was one thing to lend one's name and quite another to orchestrate a complex rescue mission to evacuate Jewish children from France. Such a mission would require convincing the AFSC to mobilize its staff and limited resources. Papanek seems to have succeeded in persuading Pickett to try. As we saw, after meeting Papanek, Pickett sent a telegram to the AFSC director in France, Howard Kershner, who replied several weeks later that exit and transit visas for the children would probably be available.[70]

At this delicate stage in the negotiations, the JDC decided to centralize all contact between Jewish organizations and the USCOM through a trusted liaison, William Haber, one of the few Jewish USCOM board members.[71] The JDC knew quite well that American Jewish organizations did not speak in one voice and thus sought to minimize any cacophony that might discredit their cause. At the same time, JDC leaders maintained contact with the USCOM directly, taking pains in November 1940 to forward a letter from Guy de Rothschild with a list of 120 La Guette children in need of emigration, thus providing the USCOM with a concrete example of the problem.[72] While the efforts of the JDC and Papanek were surely significant, it is quite possible the situation was also influenced by the arrival of a new organization on the scene.

In May 1940, the Unitarian Church, based in Boston, took inspiration from the Quakers' AFSC and established a new American aid committee, the USC.[73] Unlike the politically neutral Quakers, however, the USC was decidedly anti-fascist. It sent a small team to Europe in June 1940 with the goal of assisting refugee intellectuals, including Martha Sharp, née Dickie (1905–1999), the American-born daughter of an English steel worker, and her husband Reverend Waitstill Sharp (1902–1983), who hailed from an old New England family. This was actually a return trip to Europe for the Sharps, who had spent six months in Prague in early 1939 assisting refugees. While in Prague, Martha Sharp had orchestrated the evacuation of fifty-two Unitarian children to the United Kingdom. This may be why the USCOM asked her to represent its work during her second trip to Europe.[74] She arrived in France in the summer of 1940 and distributed milk to the French population, working closely with the Protestant representatives of the YMCA, Donald and Helen Lowrie, and eventually with Varian Fry. In September 1940, the USCOM obtained authorization from the State Department to reserve fifty visas for children from France. By October 1940, Martha wrote that she had identified fifty children for evacuation from the "most distinguished families of France."[75]

Sharp's evacuation scheme was not intended to rescue Jewish children from Vichy-Nazi persecution but was instead framed as an expression of American solidarity with the French, and even Protestant French, population. As she wrote in a September 5 telegram: "Already found intelligent children middle class Protestant parents desirous to send America duration."[76] Vichy officials viewed the American woman and her evacuation scheme with suspicion. Their internal surveillance reported that her program targeted young Protestants: "Jews, however, will not be admitted."[77] While this may have reassured Vichy officials, it was not entirely accurate. Transport lists do not provide the children's religious affiliation, but various other sources show that the group Sharp assembled was diverse, comprised of different religions and nationalities.[78] However, removing children of French nationality from Vichy France proved almost impossible. Sharp was forced to seek out children with American relatives. With great difficulty and delay, the group of twenty-seven children and five adult escorts arrived in Lisbon in late November 1940, and in New York in December 1940.[79]

Sharp's efforts nonetheless showed American child refugee advocates that children could indeed be evacuated from France. However, the USC felt the program led them astray from their mission of helping refugee intellectuals. This evolution paved the entry for the AFSC, which was surely motivated by the Unitarian's success.[80]

~

On December 10, 1940, good news from France reached the JDC in New York: its representative in Marseille announced that AFSC leader Clarence Pickett had wired its representative in France, Howard Kershner, indicating that the USCOM was interested in bringing the OSE children to the United States. The cable advised that the OSE in France was busy preparing "full dossiers including Rothschild group."[81] The OSE staff worked quickly, and by late January 1941, the JDC was able to inform Clarence Pickett that OSE had submitted full emigration dossiers for 284 children. But at this point the JDC was out of the loop. Confused by the multiple emigration initiatives, it asked the AFSC if they were working independently from the USCOM.[82] A few days later, the AFSC informed the JDC that it was indeed looking into an emigration project, at the request of the USCOM.[83]

As 1940 turned into 1941, however, the USCOM was still debating what to do. Its executive director Eric Biddle submitted a report in January, setting a pessimistic tone:

> There is a scattered interest in bringing children in from the Continent, particularly among persons who are interested in various nationality groups of children now refugees in various parts of the Continent. However, the Committee's recent experience in bringing over the 16 [sic] children from unoccupied France indicated how slowly these individual projects move, how very expensive the transportation over land and ocean is, and the many obstacles which result in reduction of numbers of children for whom evacuation plans can be achieved.[84]

He continued: "On the continent, there are relatively few children not with their families. The exception to this would be groups of refugees who are the normal concern of such organizations as the JDC, AFSC and the American Red Cross."[85] Biddle did not seem to think it was a good idea to pursue an ambitious evacuation program and was against the USCOM's creating a new branch on the European continent. If the USCOM would act, he suggested it do so through the AFSC.

In early February 1941, the USCOM's president Marshall Field wrote to the AFSC's director Clarence Pickett, clarifying the terms of their potential collaboration: the USCOM would "work through representatives of the AFSC in investigating possibilities for the evacuation of children from the continent and in the actual evacuation of any groups of children that the Committee accepts as a responsibility."[86] His letter included a memorandum, detailing what kind of children the USCOM would like to select, noting the committee was "undetermined as to whether it will or will not continue to receive or assist in bringing more children to the United States."[87] The USCOM turned to the AFSC's European director Howard Kershner to explore this possibility, with a list of eighteen questions on the children in France. Field not only wanted more information on those who desired to leave the country, the proportion of the children who were Jewish and Gentile, and their nationalities and ages, but also on Vichy's attitudes toward the children's emigration:

> We are aware of the great need of Jewish children and the US Committee wishes to make every effort to rescue these children. There is a risk, however, that the plight of this group may obscure the need of other children. In the circumstances, it would seem best, in the interest of fairness and in order to work out with the various groups who have cooperated with us, to work out mixed national groups on any given sailing. If, however, the effort to work out mixed groups results in delay, or appears otherwise impracticable, we would gladly receive sailings of all Jewish, French, Swiss, Dutch, Czech, Polish, Russian or other children. The US Committee has fixed no racial or national proportions.[88]

This statement provides a window into the USCOM's perceptions in early 1941: rare were those who considered Jewish children to be in acute danger, in spite of Vichy and Nazi anti-Jewish measures that were already affecting thousands of children. Viewed from New York, the USCOM's perspective on Jewish children in Vichy France was that they were certainly in need of help, but might "obscure the need of other children."[89] Concerned with "fairness," the USCOM sought to make the evacuations about saving children, not Jews. They reiterated this message to the top leaders of the JDC in a February meeting, at which USCOM secretary pointed out "that if they [USCOM] were in a position to include non-Jewish children with the Jewish group, there would be a better chance of something being done, both on the part of the State Department, as well as so far as the US Committee is concerned."[90] This statement suggests an internal debate was occurring within the USCOM on the desirability of organizing a rescue mission for Jewish children, specifically. In this framework, non-Jewish children became coveted elements, as they had the potential to make the USCOM appear less controversial in the eyes of the American public and, in its own words, "fair[er]."

A final report, issued by a USCOM sub-committee led by Pickett, Weiss and Alfred Whitman in late February 1941, addressed these tensions, providing the final push in favor of pursuing evacuations from France:

> It is readily admitted that the emotional drive which brought about the organization of the Committee was primarily the desperate plight of the English child, and that the possibility of assistance to English children has been curtailed by the present policy of the British government. [. . .] With respect to Continental children, the need is so acute that any group refusing to consider aid bears a heavy responsibly. One cannot read of the "Continental Situation" in the Administrative Report [. . .] without a profound realization of the extent of the suffering among children now in Southern France, Portugal and other parts of Europe. Bearing this in mind and bearing in mind that the State Department has recently, in part through the efforts of the Committee, unblocked the quotas, and further bearing in mind that the Committee was established not alone to aid English children but for the care of European children, and has consistently maintained as one of its objectives its desire to assist all children from Europe without regard to nationality or race, it is the sub-committee's view that to such extent as may be possible efforts should be made to rescue at least some further children from the Continent.[91]

The USCOM board finally accepted to fund and oversee the evacuation of children from France on February 26, 1941.[92] The GJCA executive director Cecilia Razovsky announced the decision to her staff on March

13, the date on which AFSC in France learned that the USCOM had obtained a blanket affidavit from the State Department—in other words, the ability to provide the necessary financial guarantee for the children.[93] The JDC agreed to advance the costs for passage to the United States. After six months of debate and hesitation, the selection of children in France could begin in earnest.

As originally conceived in New York, the plan to evacuate refugee children in France was a response to a larger humanitarian goal, not a mission to rescue Jewish children from Nazi persecution. Refugees from France played a key role in this process. One retrospective account, by the former USCOM migration director, attributed the project entirely to Papanek's intervention: "In 1941, Dr. Ernst Papanek came to the Committee to plead for the unaccompanied children then living in unoccupied France who were orphans who had been in concentration camps and who were now being cared for by the American Friends Service Committee."[94] This chapter confirms the significant role of Ernst Papanek but also highlights the role of the JDC as a key intermediary, fostering communication among the multiple parties. The JDC found a sincere ally in the AFSC's Clarence Pickett, who, along with several other USCOM board members, encouraged their organization to accept a very complicated mission.

What can be made of Papanek's remarks against American Jewish leaders, seen at the beginning of the chapter? Their timing is important, since they were written in the early phases of the debate on the American response to the Holocaust. In the context of the Vietnam war, Americans began to demand why more had not been done to save the Jews of Europe during the Holocaust, attributing blame to their government and the "American Jewish community."[95] Papanek had known and loved the children who were not selected for the USCOM transports. His anger and his grief, emotions he carried until the end of his life, are understandable when we consider that some of his wards were deported from France and murdered in Nazi extermination camps.[96]

Contrary to what Papanek implied, however, American Jewish individuals and organizations were not passive or indifferent. Their organizations had been actively trying to evacuate children from the Third Reich since 1933. When anti-Jewish violence intensified in 1938, non-

Jewish child experts joined their cause. The failure of the coalition to pass the Wagner-Rogers Bill was not due to indifference or a lack of urgency but to widespread populist sentiment and antisemitism. It wasn't that American Jews didn't *want* to "bring Jewish children over by the boatload,"[97] as Papanek claimed; the historical record suggests that they *could* not.

Still, American Jews were not only victims. They were also actors. Their organizations disputed territory and defended their turf, as seen in the JDC's negative reaction to the OSE's arrival in New York. It seems surprising—and even petty—that such a large, established organization would feel threatened by the arrival of a European beneficiary organization. However, the JDC was facing multiple pressures. On the one hand, it was struggling to maintain the fragile balance that had allowed for the creation of the United Jewish Appeal in 1939. On the other, the JDC was working actively to respond to the rapidly degrading situation in Europe. Building new coalitions with Jewish and non-Jewish organizations was crucial. A refugee organization such as OSE didn't know the "American way" of doing things and could have caused delicate negotiations to sour. The JDC's cold reception did not prevent it from welcoming OSE caretakers, now refugees themselves, into its orbit and eventually providing funds for Amerose's New York Office. The JDC encouraged the participation of Germaine de Rothschild and Ernst Papanek in American discussions, knowing they lent credibility and urgency to the cause of Jewish children in France.

What is more difficult to explain is why Papanek focused the blame on American Jewish organizations exclusively. Writing on the USCOM, he simply stated that "The US Committee had managed to obtain visas for English children, but they had little success, in the end, in cutting the red tape for Jewish children from the continent."[98] According to Papanek, the Quakers were "anxious to do everything possible to help."[99] This positive assessment of the Quakers makes sense, since Papanek's main interlocutor was Clarence Pickett, who was deeply concerned with Jewish causes. Nonetheless, it took the USCOM six months to decide whether it would evacuate children from France. A closer look at its decision-making process suggests that real tensions existed within the organization over which children should actually be helped.

The situation on the ground in France would prove even more complicated, as multiple groups of children were in dire need of help. In the words of one AFSC delegate, writing from Marseille in September 1940: "It is heart-breaking to be charged with the responsibilities of deciding who shall eat and who shall go hungry, who shall have clothing and who shall have none. Dispensing charity in France today means exercising the power of life or death over one's fellows. How does one do it and retain his sanity?"[100] As 1941 turned into 1942, being selected for a USCOM transport had indeed become a matter of life and death.

CHAPTER 13

Perceiving Jewish Persecution in Wartime France

Fifteen years after the war, Andrée Salomon, the Kindertransport organizer from Strasbourg, shared her frustration over the plan that had emerged in the United States to evacuate the children. "From a welfare point of view, it was absurd," she observed, "because from a welfare point of view, we strive for children to be reunited with their parents because of war."[1]

As imperfect as it was, the USCOM's program to evacuate refugee children from France represented an opportunity and hope as conditions for Jews in France worsened. As seen earlier, Salomon took her group of Kindertransport children to Clermont-Ferrand to join her husband Tobie, where the University of Strasbourg had reestablished itself shortly after the outbreak of the Second World War. It is from there that she experienced the first phases of the Nazi occupation and the demise of France's Third Republic.

After the Nazi invasion and the armistice, signed on June 22, 1940, the French parliament granted Marshal Pétain full powers. France's decision to collaborate with Nazi Germany led to the division of the country into several zones. Furthermore, the Nazis quickly incorporated Alsace-Lorraine into the German Reich and expelled its Jewish populations into areas that remained part of France.[2] The new geographic divisions led to very different wartime experiences for the French population in general and for Jews in particular. The newly minted "French State," based in the so-called "free zone," which I refer to as the unoccupied zone, generated antisemitic legislation and asserted its right to apply it to the entire French territory. The Nazis also established their own administrative framework for persecuting Jews, which applied exclusively to the occupied zone.[3]

Initially, Vichy legislation was not overtly antisemitic, even if its anti-Jewish intentions were easy to ascertain. One of the first steps it took in July 1940 was to exclude those in the civil service whose fathers were not born French. A few days later a new measure authorized the Ministry of Justice to revoke the French nationality of those naturalized after 1927 on a case-by-case basis. A Vichy commission examined the cases over the following years, discriminating against Jews, leaving this population disproportionately affected and vulnerable to new measures targeting foreign and stateless Jews.[4] On August 27, 1940, the French State repealed the Marchandeau Law, which had banned hate speech in the press, opening the flood gates for antisemitic propaganda.

In late September 1940, Nazi ordinances set up discriminatory measures against Jews in the occupied zone, including the requirement for Jews to register with the police and identify their businesses. The French State quickly followed suit by publishing the first Jewish Statute on October 3, 1940, which applied to both the occupied and unoccupied zones, forcing Jewish citizens and foreigners out of a vast number of professions, excluding journalists, teachers, and other civil servants, among many others, from their livelihoods.[5] Furthermore, the Vichy law of October 4, 1940 permitted the internment of foreign members of the "Jewish race," which led to arrests and internments, especially in the unoccupied zone.[6] Vichy published a second Jewish Statute in June 1941, which expanded restrictions on Jews' employment and education, and called for a census of the Jewish population on the entire French territory, including in the unoccupied zone.[7] It is important to keep in mind that the term "Jew" after 1940 did not reflect an individual's personal attachment to Judaism: the term now embodied an administrative and legal category, designed to enable the discriminatory treatment of those it identified.[8] The violence of transforming this complex and multifaceted identity—a vibrant tradition and culture that could be beloved or contested by those with Jewish backgrounds—cannot be underestimated.

Vichy despoiled, degraded, and singled out its Jewish populations—both French and foreign—using the legal infrastructure of a modern, industrialized society. It did so transparently, publishing its acts for all to see in the *Journal officiel*. Today we understand this legislation as the first steps of the Holocaust in France, yet at the time, few grasped the implications of the discriminatory measures against Jews. We must bear in mind that it was not until late 1941 or early 1942 that the Nazis decided to systematically annihilate Jews, and it was not until August 1942 that the first news on Jews' systematic murder began to circulate.[9]

Nonetheless, the effects of the anti-Jewish legislation were real, and not just for Jewish adults. Children were affected not only by the destabilization of their parents' lives, but also as individuals, through forced displacement, arrests, and even internment, as early as 1940. It is therefore important to question how humanitarian workers in wartime France perceived the persecution of Jews in the 1940–1942 period, since they would be in charge of selecting the children for the USCOM evacuations. Did they consider Jewish children to be in a special category of risk?

It is also necessary to consider whether Jews themselves felt a sense of danger, since most of the Kindertransport organizers and caretakers were considered "Jews" by the Vichy and Nazi legislation, whether they embraced this identity or not. Jews in France were, and remain, a diverse group, and not a unified "community." Each faction, shaped by its distinct ideology, debated the anti-Jewish legislation and its implications. As 1940 turned into 1941, many came to the conclusion that it was time to leave France.[10] Rare, however, were those who had a choice in the matter, since visas were scarce. Among the lucky few were Andrée and Tobie Salomon, who were eligible for emergency visas for the United States. Yet, unlike most in this category, the couple made a conscious decision to stay in France. Salomon recalled: "We had already decided that we weren't going to go off on our own and leave behind our families and threatened children, and we didn't set our emigration in motion."[11]

As seen above, not all of the Kindertransport organizers and caretakers were in a position to take this risk, and some made the difficult decision to flee. Others remained in France but, due to their mobilization in the French army (and later in the Resistance), found themselves unable to care for the children. Such is the case of the Count Hubert de Monbrison, whose young wards remained in their Château in Quincy-sous-Sénart with a unit of the Wehrmacht in summer 1940, then were split into groups in the Paris region, and finally were transferred to OSE homes in the unoccupied zone in early 1941. The Œuvre de la Guette continued to function in la Bourboule in the absence of Germaine de Rothschild, who fled to New York, thanks to her son Guy, her secretary, Robert Jablonski, and La Guette's director, Flore Loinger. Nonetheless, La Guette officially turned over the care of its wards to the OSE in December 1941.[12] Salomon, too, became an OSE employee, along with many other Jews from Strasbourg's Zionist and Jewish scouting circles. The targeting of Jewish children in particular made Salomon and the OSE key players in the children's evacuations, alongside the delegates of the AFSC in France, whom the USCOM had mandated to lead the initiative.

The policy to evacuate the children may have been made in the United States, but its outcomes were determined on the ground in France by the humanitarian workers who selected the lucky few. We therefore need to head back to France to make sense of who was helping and how these individuals perceived the situation facing Jewish and other children as they attempted to address the growing humanitarian crisis in French internment camps in the unoccupied zone. A portrait of two very different humanitarian organizations, acting on very different perceptions, emerges from the array of archival and secondary sources on the OSE and the AFSC.[13]

Humanitarian organizations in the hexagon were struggling to deal with the overwhelming needs in the unoccupied zone of France, where displaced French populations added to an already tense refugee crisis. The French government spent the year of 1939 opening internment camps for the 400,000–500,000 Spanish refugees who had fled over the border in early 1939 at the end of the Spanish Civil War. By March 1939, 226,000 Spanish and Basque refugees were interned in these camps, located primarily in southern France. Repatriation programs facilitated the return to Spain of about 200,000 of the refugees, even if some remained in French camps.[14] After the outbreak of the Second World War, the same camps were used to intern enemy nationals, a population comprised in large part of foreign Jews. In May and October

1940, new internment laws targeting foreigners and Jews were passed, forcing even more into the camps.[15]

The French internment camps also became a dumping ground for the Nazis, who transported unwanted populations from Belgium and Germany to France. In May 1940, Central European refugees in Belgium were arrested and sent to French internment camps.[16] Likewise, the Wagner-Bürckel Aktion on October 22, 1940 expelled 6,504 Jews from the Palatinate, Baden, and Saar areas of Germany. This group, which included very young as well as elderly individuals, was sent to Gurs, where they lived (and for some, died) in deplorable conditions. In total, 5,000 Jewish children were interned in the camps in November 1940.[17] In February 1941, 47,000 individuals were interned in camps in the unoccupied zone alone, of whom 40,000 were Jews.[18]

New groups of Jewish children also arrived in France through flight, in response to the Nazi invasion of Belgium. In May 1940, a group of almost a hundred Central European refugee children who had been sent to Belgium in a Kindertransport initiative was forced to evacuate to France. They found refuge in a barn in Seyre, a village south of Toulouse. Like the La Guette children, who had lost their patroness, the Baroness de Rothschild, the "children of La Hille," as they came to be known, were handed over to new caretakers, since those who had been responsible for bringing them to Belgium were now in New York and Switzerland. Still, before leaving, these individuals managed to convince the head of the Secours Suisse to take over the care of the children. Secours Suisse leader Maurice Dubois repeated a familiar motif when he suggested that it would be "desirable to add non-Jewish French and Spanish children to the colony."[19] Avoiding large groups of Jewish children may have been a strategy for remaining under Vichy's radar, implying that Secours Suisse leaders were aware of the different treatment Jewish children might receive in late 1940. Or it may have simply reflected a desire among the Secours Suisse leadership to offer aid to all children, not just Jewish ones. The children struggled through the cold winter of 1940–1941 and moved into the slightly more comfortable Château de la Hille (Ariège) in February 1941. The château operated as a children's home throughout the war, although many of its young Jewish inhabitants would be forced into hiding after August 1942.[20]

The case of Aron Pruszinowski, today the renowned psychologist Henri Parens, illustrates the new population of children that entered France, and consequently the OSE homes, in 1940. Born in Lodz in 1928, he and his mother settled in Brussels in the 1930s after his parents' divorce. When Belgium was invaded in May 1940, he and his mother fled to France. They spent summer 1940 in a village, but in the fall, they were arrested, transported to Toulouse, and interned in the Récébédou internment camp.[21] At the end of 1940, they were transferred to the Rivesaltes camp. After several months, his mother, along with the parents of another boy, Savic, decided to orchestrate their sons' escape. They chose the date of May 1, assuming correctly that there would be fewer guards on the national workers' holiday. At the last minute, Savic's parents changed their mind. Twelve-year-old Aron thus walked out of the camp alone and into Perpignan, where his mother told him to buy a train ticket to Marseille. Once in Marseille, he was to go to the OSE office. From there, the OSE placed him in a children's home in Boulouris.

Aron's escape attests to the circulation of information within the camps, in large part due to the presence of OSE resident social workers who were living in Rivesaltes since early 1941: his foreign mother understood the importance of May 1; she knew the price of a ticket from Perpignan to Marseille and was able to provide this modest sum to her son. Finally, she obtained the address of the OSE office and, most importantly, trusted this organization enough to hand over her child.[22] If Aron's route to OSE is somewhat exceptional, many other children were released through legal channels in 1941 and early 1942. In this manner, the OSE saw its numbers swell: it was caring for 792 children by the end of 1941.[23] The AFSC was initially opposed to removing children from the camps but opened as many as twenty-three colonies for Spanish children, which eventually accepted Jewish children.[24] Secours Suisse, as seen above, was also running a network of children's homes and accepted Jewish children from the internment camps,[25] while the youngest were sent to the Pouponnière in Limoges. These structures helped reduce the number of children in the camps, which would become crucial to saving lives.

The refugee crisis, coupled with the dire sanitary conditions in the overcrowded internment camps, called for new collaborations among the humanitarian organizations that had come to France to help. The AFSC had been active in Spain during the civil war and followed the Spanish refugees into France. By February 1939, the Quaker organization had developed an extensive food distribution program in towns throughout southern France, in addition to providing aid for Spanish and Basque refugees.[26] The JDC had been present in France since 1933. Instead of providing direct aid to refugee populations, it gave funds to Jewish and non-Jewish organizations to assist Jewish refugees, as well as some aid to the general population.[27] While the JDC and the AFSC were certainly among the largest American aid programs in France, as seen above, the USC also sent two representatives to Europe in summer 1940, Unitarian Minister Waitstill Sharp and his wife, Martha, who organized a small children's evacuation from France in December 1940. The Sharps worked closely with the American YMCA representatives in France, Donald and Helen Lowrie, who had been running the Fondation des États-Unis in the Cité Universitaire in Paris before the war.[28] In addition to these groups, Secours Suisse, as well as the American, Belgian, and Polish Red Cross committees, worked alongside French aid organizations such as the Service social d'aide aux émigrants and the newly created Protestant group, the Comité inter-mouvements auprès des évacués (Cimade), to name only a few. Finally, French and international Jewish organizations were also active, drawing on the network that had been assisting German refugees since 1933: the CAR, the Fédération des sociétés juives de France, the OSE, and ORT, as well as the migration agency HICEM. Now reimplanted in the unoccupied zone, each of these organizations worked with refugees and internees, who were struggling to meet basic needs and, for the most part, escape France.[29]

In fall 1940, the idea of coordinating aid work in the internment camps emerged. Herbert Katzki, a young American representative of JDC in France, recalled in an oral history interview:

There were a number of organizations, as I say, Jewish and non-Jewish in Marseilles and in the Marseilles area. [. . .] At the time, in order to avoid duplication of services, we decided to have a united front as there could be some value in organizing some kind of coordinating arrangement among all the groups. My recollection of that particular time was that I went around to talk to Donald Lowrie, who among other agencies represented the YMCA.[30] He spoke a very good French, was a very personable person. I talked with him and I suggested that perhaps this was something which the YMCA in the person of Donald Lowrie could undertake, to try to do something to bring all the agencies together in order to sit down and have some kind of coordinating process. It turned out that he had been thinking along the same lines.[31]

Lowrie, in his 1963 memoir *The Hunted Children*, states that the committee was indeed his idea, which he promptly presented to the French Minister of the Interior, who approved it enthusiastically. Lowrie was a natural choice for chairman. He was in his early fifties and seems to have been one of the rare American humanitarian workers who mastered French. In addition to his extensive experience working abroad was the fact that he was representing a Christian (albeit Protestant) organization. This was no small detail in Vichy France, where the National Revolution encouraged a return to a "moral order." As Lowrie wrote in his memoirs: "One of the outstanding achievements of the Nimes Committee was the complete and sympathetic collaboration of Christians and Jews. [. . .] And in frequent cases where it seemed diplomatic for a Jewish organization not to appear in the picture, some special project would be turned over for execution to the French Protestant CIMADE or to the Quakers, the Jews simply providing the necessary funds."[32] Echoing the JDC–AFSC partnership discussed earlier, certain Christian organizations willingly provided a front for Jewish aid work, even if it was expected that Jews pay for their own. Meeting regularly in Nîmes from November 1940 onward, the members of the "Nîmes Committee" discussed the conditions in the camps and developed partnerships, as seen in the joint efforts of the USC and the OSE to provide medical care.

The JDC was one of the major American aid organizations, leading Katzki to conclude that "We [JDC] were more or less regarded, I suppose, as one of the senior members of the group."[33] Still, Katzki himself was only thirty-three years old in 1940, most likely did not speak French well, and was trained in accounting and economics, not in social work.[34] Lowrie seems to be describing him when he spoke of the "young American, baffled and frightened by his first experience in a strange country and still more by the anti-Semitic atmosphere in which he had to work, yet with no idea of retiring, as he might have, to safer and more normal Lisbon."[35] As the head of JDC's Marseille office, Katzki coordinated aid to French Jewish organizations in the occupied and unoccupied zone until he was forced to leave for Lisbon, at which point the JDC program was run by French Jewish representatives Jules (Dika) Jefroykin and Maurice Brener.[36] At the center of these multiple initiatives, Katzki acted as a crucial communications hub for the children's evacuation project, sharing information with JDC in New York via Lisbon, as well as with the OSE and the AFSC. Nonetheless, it is the AFSC, as the USCOM's official partner in France, that proved determinant to the children's evacuations.

In Spain, the AFSC had operated throughout the civil war under its philosophy of political neutrality.[37] In France, the AFSC specialized in Spanish refugees. In 1940, AFSC's European director Howard Kershner told Clarence Pickett: "Do not let anyone forget that the problem of the Spanish refugees, especially the children and the mutilated, is an obligation which we cannot shirk. [. . .] We are now the only organization interested in or working for these people."[38]

Kershner's dedication to those who had fled to France from Spain during the *Retirada* should not, however, be interpreted as an affiliation with the Republican cause. Kershner became director of the AFSC program at the end of 1938 or in early 1939 as the conflict was winding down, perhaps with the hope that he would facilitate the AFSC's relations with the Franco regime. Kershner's leadership in Spain provoked criticism when an AFSC relief worker denounced the misappropriation of Quaker aid by the Franco regime in *The New York Times*.[39] Contrary to contemporary preconceptions about humanitarian aid workers, this American businessman was no liberal. Raised as a Quaker in Kansas, he denounced the New Deal in his 1936 book *The Menace of Roosevelt and His Policies*.[40] His wartime diary provides a window into his political ideology, suggesting that his position on the Nationalist victory in Spain was pragmatic, if not pro-Franco. Describing a return trip to

Spain in fall 1939, he refers to Franco as "the *Generalísimo*" and observes that the retaliatory executions were a result of "red plotting" and "red scheming."[41] On November 5, 1939, Kershner noted a conversation he had with an Englishman who had lived in Spain for the past seventeen years: "His observations confirm my own conclusions that the guilt and the virtue are about equally divided between the two sides in Spain. The people are not ready for self-government. There are fine, conscientious men and great devotion on both sides and there is much intolerance and will to suppress opposition on both sides. Spain must learn tolerance and forgiveness."[42]

Kershner's focus remained on Spain long after his arrival in France. Touring the Argelès internment camp in February 1941, he praised the Spanish children, who "sang in Spanish, French and English. Having just inspected the living quarters of these children, which were about like [sic] ordinary dog kennels, one could scarcely believe that they could appear so happy, healthy and sing so beautifully. It is one of the miracles of the Spanish race. I was overwhelmed with the thought of human wastage that is taking place in this Camp. Much excellent material for fine sturdy citizens of the next generation is about to be lost."[43] Protecting the next generation meant feeding children, a mission that impassioned Kershner. Yet food was scarce in Vichy France due to German economic exploitation and the British blockade. Obtaining it required tricky negotiations, dependent upon the authorities' perception of the Quakers. Under Kershner's direction, the AFSC received considerable funds from Vichy's national welfare organization, Secours National, and in turn was able to use its own budget to purchase food, milk, meat, and cheese in Switzerland to be distributed in France.[44]

Kershner's commitment to maintaining the AFSC's neutrality may have kept the Quakers from initially partaking in the Nîmes Committee. Herbert Katzki of JDC recalled:

In those early days there was one group, as I remember it, that did not want to associate itself with this Nimes crowd, and it was the Quakers in Marseille. The director at the time was a man by the name of Howard Kirschner [sic]. The Quakers were the only organization that had a food program going on. They were getting food from the outside which they were using for feeding programs and for distribution purposes. Kirschner [sic] seemed to feel that he preferred keeping complete freedom of action and independence for the Quakers and the programs which they were undertaking. He perhaps thought the Quakers['] renown would be impinged upon if it became identified with all the other organizations that were around [. . .]. Subsequently, though, the Quakers did come in and of [sic] the time they were represented at these meetings in Nîmes by their delegate in Toulouse, Princess Leven [sic], I think that was her name.[45]

Nîmes Committee chairman Donald Lowrie downplays any conflict in his memoirs, and states: "Someone remarked to me at the time: 'If you can coordinate the Quakers you will accomplish something no one has ever done yet,' but I have to record that no other organization collaborated more wholeheartedly with the Committee throughout the whole of its existence."[46] If the Quakers initially had a negative response, their absence was not felt for long. At least three of its representatives were present at the December 1940 meeting, just one month after its establishment.[47] The Nîmes Committee archives show that the Quakers indeed played an active role in the group, especially since its non-American delegates were able to remain active in France after the rupture of diplomatic ties between Vichy and Washington, DC, in November 1942.[48]

Still, in early 1941, Howard Kershner's priority was protecting the AFSC's feeding programs, not evacuating children. Even though he initially endorsed the USCOM evacuation scheme,[49] he soon expressed his reservations to his US-based colleagues. Kershner stated in late February 1941:

we have made no definite commitments with reference to the USCOMM children. We are well aware of the tragic situation of the children on the lists which I have submitted to you [. . .]. We are not in a position to interest Jewish committees in the United States with reference to the maintenance of these children, so we must leave that to you. For the cost of taking one child to America and back we could take care of twenty or more children here. I am therefore opposed to sending over children who expect to return here. The lists which we have sent and will send apply only to the children who are going as permanent emigrants. [. . .] I definitely do not believe it is practical to go on with these schemes, except as stated above for children who are going to America for permanent residence.[50]

While Kershner was not entirely opposed to evacuating children, his was not an enthusiastic endorsement of the project. Still, the AFSC agreed to the USCOM partnership, leaving Kershner little choice but to proceed. JDC representative Herbert Katzki maintained his crucial role as the eyes and ears of the JDC in France, sending the JDC Lisbon office an update from France in late March 1941. "The Quakers want to run the whole show," he wrote:

I do not know whether they have the experience to do it, but they have given the OSE to understand that, insofar as the question of the inclusion of Jewish children in the group is concerned they wished to deal with the OSE and with the OSE alone. This means that they do not desire to have the HICEM do anything in connection with the matter. I have my own views as to Howard's attitude and this opinion I am sure you have likewise. I hope the matter goes smoothly.[51]

In reporting Kershner's resistance to working with HICEM, Katzki seemed to imply that Kershner was not cooperating. There seemed to be consensus at the JDC as to the reasons behind Kershner's attitude, and Katzki's veiled reference suggests a sensitive topic.

Perhaps Katzki was referring to the fact that Kershner was cultivating a relationship with Marshal Pétain. Kershner met the Marshal for the first time in January 1941. On this occasion, although the USCOM evacuation had not yet been approved by its board, Kershner's notes show he planned on discussing "the desire of USCOM to bring about 800 children to the US. What would be the policy of France with reference to permitting non-Jewish French children to go and with reference to permitting non-Jewish children of other nationalities to go?"[52] Strangely, Kershner did not ask Pétain his attitudes on Jewish children, an issue of central importance.

Kershner's "diary"—which is actually a patchwork of multiple sources—suggests that he was seduced by the attention of Pétain, who took pains to walk through "three doors" to escort Kershner out of his office. Pétain invited Kershner to accompany him on a tour of Savoy in September 1941. Kershner accepted, stating he "felt it to be my duty to express friendship and goodwill towards the Chief of the State and to the Members of his Government, as well as to the hungry people for whom we have so long been working in France."[53] His three-page description of this tour, entitled "Two Days with Maréchal Pétain," provides an overwhelmingly positive image of the leader of the French State:

> He [Pétain] advocates hard work, self denial, temperance and thrift. [. . .] He was received with a most enthusiastic acclaim everywhere. The chant of the crowd was usually "Vive Pétain" or "Vive le Maréchal" often varied with "Vive la France." There is no doubt that the Maréchal has a remarkable hold upon the affection of the people of France and there is likewise no doubt that he is devoted to their welfare and shows the greatest interest in and concern for them. It is quite evident that he is the leader of the people. [. . .] His affection for the people and interest in them is unbounded.[54]

One senses Kershner was writing for a broader audience, perhaps with the hope of publication, especially when he concluded: "That the Vichy Government is beset with insurmountable obstacles is well known. The efforts that the Government is making on behalf of the people of France and the great devotion shown by the Maréchal and his associates are not so well known."[55] Indeed, the piece, like the rest of the diary, was typed. Some parts of the diary were reports, which definitely circulated within the AFSC.[56] In October 1941, Kershner read one paragraph of his account on Pétain to his staff during a delegates' meeting.[57] In June 1942, he published an article in *The New York Times*, framing the French people and the Vichy government as victims: "There are 16,000 [sic] political or racial refugees still living in the internment camps of unoccupied France. They are a pathetic lot, rapidly dying from undernourishment. France did not invite them and does not want them but generously attempts to provide for them."[58]

While Kershner needed to adopt a diplomatic tone in the press, his language suggests an admiration of the French efforts to care for the internees. One might imagine a more critical stance in his diary, especially after Vichy's first and second Jewish Statutes, established in October 1940 and June 1941, respectively, and in light of his first-hand knowledge of the conditions in the French internment camps. Yet Kershner showed no concern over Vichy's treatment of Jews in his diary. In fact, the diary mentions Jews only once, in October 1942, to complain about the AFSC collaboration with Jewish organizations.[59] It is possible that Kershner avoided the topic out of concern that his diary might fall into the wrong hands. He also does not mention AFSC's aid to Jewish refugees in a 1942 promotional film, in which he discusses AFSC aid to three groups: the Spanish, the French, and foreign refugees.[60] In the context of American antisemitism during the Second World War and the AFSC's fundraising goals, this omission is not surprising. Furthermore, it is possible the film was funded and produced with the help of Vichy.[61] Avoiding explicit references to Jews was not uncommon among American humanitarian workers in Second World War France,[62] and Kershner does mention the "racial refugees" in the camps in his June 1942 article in *The New York Times*. Nonetheless, by the time Kershner's memoirs were published in 1950, there was no longer a reason to hide the Quaker aid to Jewish populations. Yet Kershner's postwar assessment of the AFSC contribution in wartime France gives the impression that Jews were basically absent.[63] Kershner provides a puzzling lesson in perspective: his silences, especially in his postwar memoirs, are curious.

Like his writings, Kershner's actions were also ambiguous. He did not support accepting funds from the JDC for feeding programs in camps, a point of contention with AFSC delegate Helga Holbek in May 1941. He wrote to her: "To accept Jewish money and buy food for this purpose when it is a known fact that many French people outside the camps do not eat as well as a foreigner in the camps would probably make it impossible for us to secure the unblocking of foodstuffs."[64] While in the United States over the summer of 1941, Kershner met with the leader of Selfhelp of Emigres from Central Europe, an organization created in the United States in 1936 by recent German refugees, some of whom had known the French camps first hand. Selfhelp raised funds among refugees to support feeding programs in the camps and to help remove children.[65] Back in France, Kershner shared with his staff what he explained to Selfhelp's representative, that there "might be objections to feeding adults in the camps when many French children are not being fed."[66]

Kershner's views seem to have incited some internal criticism. The AFSC headquarters in Philadelphia showed empathy for Selfhelp, composed of "refugees in this country, who only have very little and want to make this generous recognition to their former neighbors and friends of the Baden and Palatinate areas"[67] and suggested that "the program be continued at least until there has been an opportunity to evaluate the value of the work."[68] In Marseille, a staff member also disagreed with Kershner, noting that it couldn't be argued that the food given to camp internees was being taken away from the French, and the AFSC staff decided collectively to continue the program. In light of this decision, however, Kershner suggested that the AFSC reduce its budget from $1,000 monthly for Rivesaltes to fit into the $500 monthly grant provided by Selfhelp.[69]

What appears to be a simple reallocation of funds takes on a different meaning with closer knowledge of the conditions in the southern internment camps in 1941. By this date, many Jewish internees had been transferred to Rivesaltes, which had become a "family camp." In April 1941, its Jewish residents were transferred into a Jewish section, Îlot B, on the pretense that they would be able to celebrate Passover together. However, food in Îlot B was even more lacking than in the rest of the camp, leading historian Anne Grynberg to qualify this as a "discriminatory regime against Jews."[70] More generally, sanitary conditions in the French southern internment camps in early 1941 were so grave that the AFSC in Philadelphia released a report on Gurs sent by its delegates, excerpted in a *New York Times* article entitled "Misery and Death in French Camps."[71] By winter 1941–1942, the lack of food in all of the southern camps had grown so alarming that the Nîmes Committee decided to undertake a systematic study of starvation. They concluded that hunger had caused several hundred deaths.[72] Likewise, there were 140 infants at Rivesaltes in early summer 1941, but 60 were dead by September.[73] Perhaps the best way to comprehend the conditions in the camps is to visit the vast cemetery in Gurs and contemplate the very young and advanced ages of those who died while interned there.[74]

Kershner's suggestion to cut the AFSC budget for Rivesaltes in fall 1941 suggests he was either grossly out of touch with the reality in the camps or unmoved by the situation. Nonetheless, the vast AFSC archives suggest a complex personality. One scholar suggests that Kershner supported helping Jewish refugees on a basis of need but was "not always consistent in this message nor did he seem aware of the increasing needs of Jews in contrast to non-Jews."[75]

Fortunately, Kershner's views did not characterize the entire AFSC's operation in France. In addition to the French Quaker aid operations in the occupied zone,[76] there were a hundred AFSC staff members working throughout the unoccupied zone, roughly fifty in the Marseille office and fifty in the other branches, with a total of fifteen to twenty-five American aid workers until November 1942.[77] While Kershner was developing a personal relationship with Pétain, others took a more critical stance of Vichy and in turn of Kershner, who incited criticism from at least two delegates, Helga Holbek and Ross McClelland.[78] According to Norwegian AFSC worker Alice Resch, Kershner:

> was a wise and friendly man, who unfortunately lacked Helga Holbek's flexibility and ability to do the right thing at the right time. We had worked independently all summer, so it took some adjusting suddenly to have to ask permission for everything. When and if permission was granted, it was often too late. Helga insisted on having a Quaker delegate in permanent residence at Camp de Gurs [sic]. That finally went through a year later.[79]

Indeed, two women had run AFSC operations during one of Kershner's absences, and tensions were rampant when Kershner sought to reassert his authority after his return. According to Resch, in the aftermath of Pearl Harbor, "Helga Holbek and Ima Lieven immediately went to the district office to assess the Americans' situation in light of recent events.

[. . .] They found Howard Kershner playing the harmonica, while Henry and Gilbert demonstrated American folk dancing! *They* certainly weren't worried."[80] Kershner was thus a controversial figure, within and outside the AFSC. Tensions between the Marseille headquarters and the other delegations, especially the Toulouse office, were palpable. Nonetheless, it was Kershner, as AFSC's European director, who was ultimately responsible for overseeing the children's evacuations. His staff, while well intentioned, came primarily from the United States and Northern Europe.[81] Even if Quakers had experienced religious persecution in the seventeenth century, most AFSC delegates had grown up as members of the Christian majority in stable democracies, with little reason to be suspicious of states.

When the evacuation project was approved by the USCOM in New York in the last days of February 1941, the AFSC and the OSE were already well acquainted. As we saw, both organizations were active on the Nîmes Committee and providing aid in the French internment camps. Furthermore, Dr. Joseph Weill, a doctor from Strasbourg and longtime acquaintance of Andrée Salomon, had become active with the OSE by 1940 and had also been working closely with AFSC's Toulouse delegation to assist the several thousand French Jews who had been expelled from Alsace-Lorraine.[82] Yet if the OSE and the AFSC were collaborating together, it is clear that their representatives did not share the same perceptions of the situation in wartime France.

Andrée Salomon and her husband may have decided to remain in France after 1940, yet this was not out of optimism or naïveté. The couple shared a long-term political engagement with the Zionist cause, as well as a profound belief in Jewish peoplehood. Salomon, who had been working on the front lines of the refugee crisis since 1933, witnessed the breakdown of the situation for Jewish refugees. Even if she was French and from a Francophile Alsatian family, factors that encouraged trust in the state, she had lived under German rule for a considerable part of her childhood. Furthermore, she was married to a Polish Jew whose family had fled Galicia.

Salomon, while not strictly orthodox, seems to have interpreted the Jews' situation under Vichy through the prism of Jewish memory, in

1. In the aftermath of the November 9–10, 1938 pogrom, the Jewish orphanage of Frankfurt am Main became home to a growing number of Jewish children. Its director, Isidor Marx (third row toward the left, holding a child), reached out to his contacts outside of Germany to find new homes for his wards.

2. Andrée Salomon, seen here with a group of refugee children, worked from her native Alsace to evacuate Jewish children from Nazi territories and, once France was occupied, to transport them to the United States. After deportations of children began in 1942, she ran a clandestine network, hiding children in France and smuggling them into Switzerland and Spain.

3. Baroness Germaine de Rothschild (center) created the Comité israélite pour les enfants venant d'Allemagne et d'Europe centrale to bring Jewish children to France from Central Europe. She is seen on the steps of a children's home run by the Jewish organization OSE with Dr. Helene Papanek, the home's doctor, on her right.

4. Baron and Baroness Pierre and Yvonne de Gunzbourg provided the funding for many of OSE's children's homes. In late 1938, Yvonne de Gunzbourg headed an OSE committee to organize the care of the refugee children. After fleeing to the United States in 1941, she continued her work with OSE.

5. Ernst Papanek (seen here c.1939) was a well-known educator and socialist from Vienna who became the beloved director of OSE's children's homes. Targeted by the Nazis, he fled with his family to the United States in August 1940, where he played a crucial role in the efforts to bring the children to the United States.

6. Progressive educators Ernst and Lida Jablonski (seen here c.1947) cared for children and teens at the Château de la Guette and later at OSE's Chabannes children's home in the southern zone. They remained close to many of the children after the Holocaust, in the absence of their parents.

7. Norbert Bikales, age ten, sits with his parents for a photo in Berlin in May 1939. Soon after, his parents were expelled to Poland. Norbert left for France on a Kindertransport in July 1939.

8. Norbert Bikales (second row, second from the right) at OSE's Chabannes home in August 1941, following the Nazi invasion and the evacuation of refugee children to the unoccupied zone.

9. Upon arrival in France, the older refugee children were sent to the Rothschilds' Château de la Guette. Their progressive educators' pedagogy included sports and gardening.

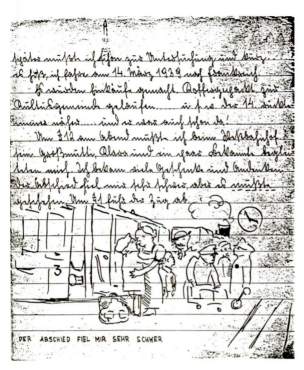

DER ABSCHIED FIEL MIR SEHR SCHWER

10. Thirteen-year-old Heinz Löw began his diary on the day Germany invaded Poland, September 1, 1939, six months after his arrival in France. "The Farewell was very hard on me," he concluded, looking back at his separation from his loved ones. His friend Paul Peter Porges illustrated parts of the diary.

11. La Guette's educators such as Alfred Brauner encouraged the children to draw their lives. "I promise," wrote this child, in two languages, incorporating the French flag and gardening in her art. Note the month "July" is written in the corner, an indication that Brauner was studying the children's art for his doctoral research.

12. The United States Committee for the Care of European Children was created in New York in July 1940 by a small group of activists. Its first mission was to bring British children to the United States. Convincing the organization to orchestrate the evacuation of Jewish refugee children from France was no small task.

13. Andrée Salomon (far right) and the Joint Distribution Committee's representative Herbert Katzki (center) in Marseille with the children before the first departure for the United States in June 1941.

14. Brothers Werner and Claus Peter Gossels, from Berlin, were cared for in Quincy-sous-Sénart before being transferred to OSE's Chabannes home in early 1941. The two brothers were selected for a USCOM transport for the United States in September 1941.

15. Children and caretakers relaxed at the OSE's Chabannes home, just before the August 26, 1942 round-up, organized by Vichy authorities throughout the unoccupied zone. Children and teens in OSE's children's homes were targeted. Those arrested were transported to Drancy and then to Nazi camps, including Auschwitz.

16. Refugee children on the SS *Mouzinho*, sailing to New York from Lisbon in June 1941. One can see Heinz Schuster (left) as well as Werner Dreifuss (top left), Eric Gruenbaum, Evelyne Fuchs, and Gertrude Pfferling. The photo was most likely taken by fellow teen Elfriede Meyer.

17. Elfriede Meyer Schloss (here in 2016) was one of the children from the Frankfurt orphanage. She left for France in early 1939 with photos of her family and carried them with her to the United States in 1941. The photos have accompanied her over the decades and represent a rare trace of her past.

which persecution is an ever-present theme.[83] An example of this can be seen in the advice she gave to Isidor Marx, the head of the Frankfurt Jewish orphanage, with whom she organized the reception of German Kindertransport children. During one of his trips to France, Marx asked Salomon for help on a moral dilemma: should he return to Germany, where he thought he would be shot by the Nazis, or should he flee? Andrée Salomon advised him to flee. Marx wrote to Salomon after the war after discovering—with great surprise—that she had survived, to thank her:

> I never shall forget what <u>you have done for me</u>—in those dark days of disaster—when I was "out off" from "at home" [sic]—with the intention to go back to my beloved wife—but with the fear to be shot by the Nazis—you remember the story about the Omer Tabelle?—and you told me: You never more must go back to Nazi Germany—and in my despair—my loneliness—beeing [sic] separated from my beloved wife—you in your charming way supported me—you acted as a "pillar" for this "fading" plant called Mr. Isidor Marx![84]

Marx's reference to the Omer, the forty-nine-day period of the Jewish calendar between Passover and the holiday of Shavuot—often counted on a table (*Tabelle*) or calendar—requires some exploration. For traditional Jews, the Omer period is a time of mourning to commemorate the death of the students of Rabbi Akiva, killed in the year 137. One could argue it also marks the liminal state between slavery and freedom. In 1939, Salomon may have used the metaphor of the Omer—a moment of mourning with a clear endpoint—to help Marx realize his bleak situation was not permanent. Marx listened to Salomon and fled to England. Neither Salomon nor Marx could have predicted that Rosa Marx and the remaining children in Frankfurt would be arrested and murdered by the Nazis.

Andrée Salomon's pragmatic pessimism led her, along with the Jewish scouting movement's founder Robert Gamzon and several others, to meet in her apartment in July 1940 to determine an "action plan" for the difficult years to come.[85] Dr. Joseph Weill, with whom Salomon had established the Merkaz HaNoar Jewish youth center in Strasbourg in 1938, had, as seen above, started working with the OSE.[86] The Russian-Polish OSE leadership also had reason to be suspicious, having experienced the 1905 revolution, the First World War, the Russian Revolution and the violent pogroms that followed, OSE's expulsion from the Soviet Union, and flight from Nazi Germany. They knew first hand that states could be fickle and even deadly.[87]

This explains why the OSE was a precocious advocate of its children's emigration to the United States. Its leaders dated the beginning of their efforts to evacuate children to September 1940, which corresponds to Ernst Papanek's arrival in New York.[88] Historian Sabine Zeitoun traces the initiative to Andrée Salomon, who, in November 1940, turned to the OSE for emigration solutions for "her" children.[89] Salomon became the OSE's first resident social worker in Rivesaltes and Gurs in 1941. In this capacity, she recruited several other young Jewish women to work with the OSE, while becoming one of the most vocal advocates for the children's evacuations.

Decades after the Holocaust, we have the conceptual framework to understand that a genocide was unfolding during the larger conflict of the Second World War. We can apprehend these two phenomena—genocide and war—and contemplate their fundamentally different nature. In 1941, however, there was not yet a concept of genocide, nor an indication that Jewish children's lives were in particular danger. And yet, as seen above, the humanitarian workers did not perceive the persecution of Jews in the same manner: each individual was shaped by their particular experiences—personal and political—as well as their organization's larger missions. The members of the OSE, as well as those from Strasbourg, shared a common awareness that Jews were being targeted as Jews. They sensed an urgent need to remove their wards from harm. They had a very different profile from the AFSC's delegates, whose work depended on a respectful attitude toward authority. The AFSC's philosophy of neutrality allowed it access to hard-to-reach populations in need, which also led the organization into close relationships with problematic states and regimes. There is evidence, however, that its leader in France, Howard Kershner, shared affinities with Vichy, and he certainly admired Pétain. He did not seem particularly concerned by its persecution of Jews.

The children's evacuations thus brought together two very different organizations, one that had access to scores of children who wanted to leave France, and another mandated to select children for "mixed sailings" to the United States. For the next year, from spring 1941 through July 1942, these two groups would confront their differences as they set out to evacuate children.

CHAPTER 14

Evacuating Children, Not Jews

From Berlin, Peter and Werner's mother Charlotte Gossels remained intent on getting her children out of harm's way, even as her own situation deteriorated. Armed with a pen, she continued her epistolary campaign and, through her acquaintances, managed to find the address of a German Jewish woman living in St. Louis, Missouri. Charlotte wrote to her in February 1941, providing a brief synopsis of her family's recent history:

> After seven years of married life I divorced my husband. Our two children Claus [Peter] 10 years old and Werner, 7 year [sic] stayed with me in Germany until conditions forced me to send them to France. While I myself intended to go to England and find a livelihood as a domestic I never would have gotten my permit with my children.
>
> Therefore their emigration to France where they found a home in the Rothschild [sic] Children's home was the best solution for all of us, hard as it was for me to be separated from my children. My trip to England never materialized, the war broke out and I am still in Germany. The Rothschild [sic] home was dissolved in 1940 and my boys sent to private homes and later orphan homes gave them a shelter. For some time the rumor went around that the children would be send [sic] back to their parents but the final outcome—they shipped the children to unoccupied France. [. . .] My latest

informations [sic] speak of a children's transport to America through an American committee via Marseille.

Charlotte then explained the reason for her letter:

> I do not have any possibility of communication with my children or any official authority and therefore, I am asking you to help me to secure those much wanted informations [sic] for me. Could you find out if American committees are working to bring those children over, if those stranded child-refugees frm [sic] France will find a place and family in America when they come and if anything is known about time and transportation of the little ones. Hoping that you'll try everything possible to secure these informations [sic] for me I remain, in deep gratitude, Charlotte Gossels"[1]

Charlotte Gossels was correct: by the time her letter arrived in the United States and was forwarded to a Jewish aid agency in February 1941, the USCOM evacuations from France were becoming a reality. Technically, the AFSC was mandated to select the children, but it did not have many candidates among its own, primarily Spanish, wards. The OSE, however, had access to many Jewish children who wanted to leave Europe, as did the Rothschild's Œuvre de la Guette and Secours Suisse, which was caring for the Kindertransport children who had initially fled to Belgium. From the perspective of the USCOM, there were, in addition to the above organizations, other sources of children for the transports: the Unitarians claimed to have access to 1,000 children, both French and refugee, in need of evacuation. Ottilie Moore, an American heiress who was renting rooms to refugees in her villa outside of Nice, was also asking for help for a small group of children. And finally, the International Assistance for Catholic Refugees, run by the Duke of Württemberg Dom Odo, was seeking help for Jewish and "non-Aryan" children in French internment camps.[2] With so many individuals and organizations vying for the limited places on the evacuations for "their" wards, how did selection play out on the ground and according to what criteria? To what extent did children and their families manage to influence this process? I am not the first to ask some of these questions, and I build on previous scholarship to show in greater detail, and with different archival sources, the twists and turns of the evacuations.[3]

Even before the USCOM evacuation project was official, OSE leaders wrote to their American committee in New York in January 1941, stating they had already selected a group of children from four different categories of need: refugees with parents in Central Europe; refugees with parents or relatives in the United States; refugees with parents in internment camps; and orphans. "It is of utmost importance to us to get these children out of this country as soon as possible,"[4] they told their American collaborators. Their multiple letters to the United States, which reported on the situation in France throughout the war, repeated this injunction regularly.[5] Sending children to the United States not only moved those perceived as most vulnerable into a safer environment. It also liberated coveted space in OSE homes, allowing the organization to remove more children from the French internment camps.

The instructions from the USCOM set forth their own selection criteria, different from those of the OSE. First and foremost, due to visa requirements, the children had to be under sixteen. Other factors to be taken into account included the "physical condition of the children, adequacy of existing care, availability of other means of evacuation, and general possibilities of adjustment in this country [the United States]."[6]

AFSC representatives in France received the USCOM's instructions from the AFSC's USCOM liaison person in Philadelphia, Margaret Frawley, a Catholic American journalist. Frawley had spent time in France in 1940 to generate publicity on the AFSC children's colonies.[7] As a public relations specialist, Frawley emphasized to Howard Kershner the preference for "mixed sailings" in May 1941: "The question which has been raised from time to time about sending a mixed group is one which the [US] committee is not inclined to press since they assume you have reached the conclusion that Jewish children are most needy." She explained:

> There is one point which may have been emphasized before but which I re-state again in order to give you as clear a concept as possible of the thinking here and that is that at no time has the

insistence on a mixed group had any relation to prejudice but that if you could possibly have sent a mixed group it would have been possible for the U.S. Committee to get wider public support and enlist more general interest in the plight of European children. May I state it another way the value of the program is not merely in rescuing a few children from the misery of present-day Europe but in centering public attention on the needs of children—and that means all nationalities and races.[8]

Frawley suggested that framing the program in the broadest way possible would better serve larger humanitarian (and fundraising) goals. Yet her letter is unclear: she states the USCOM was "not inclined to press the issue" but then discusses the "insistence on a mixed group." It suggests that there may have been a difference in the USCOM mission and how certain AFSC representatives conceived of the program.

While the AFSC had basic—albeit subjective—instructions, trans-atlantic transportation was limited, and ship availability dictated the outcomes of the project. From its Lisbon office, the JDC played a key role in booking passage for the children, securing 100 places on the SS *Mouzinho*, scheduled to leave Lisbon in early June 1941. The children would therefore have to travel through Spain and Portugal to leave Europe. While the AFSC initially offered the OSE 70 places out of 100, technical constraints caused them to raise this number, since the final list had to be provided by mid-May and the AFSC did not have other candidates ready.[9] Nonetheless, the OSE was not free to dictate the selection criteria: its representatives preferred older children who were at risk of internment at age seventeen and fought the age require-ments to avoid separating siblings, arguing that foreign children were considered adults in the eyes of the French administration at age fifteen, and that there was "a hierarchy in grief."[10] In addition to selecting the children, the OSE was able to suggest two of the five escorts for the trip, Dr. Isaac and Masha Chomski. The latter had worked for the OSE and knew some of the children well.[11]

The USCOM transport also enabled the OSE and the Œuvre de la Guette to include eleven additional children with individual visas to the United States, who would be sent to family members. In total, the first transport drew from three different Kindertransport groups in France: seventy-two came from the OSE homes, twenty-five were La Guette children, and fourteen were Kindertransport children initially sent to Belgium, now under the care of Secours Suisse.[12] All of the children were Jewish, with the exception of one "non-Aryan" Catholic and two Protestant girls.[13] Many of the children discussed in this book thus far made it onto this first transport, including Heinz-Henri Schuster, Elfriede Meyer, Ernst Valfer, and Ruth and Miriam. Peter and Werner Gossels, however, were rejected at this stage, and we will soon discover why.

Most of the selected children were listed as "stranded in France" without their parents (in other words, Kindertransport children).[14] However, some of their parents had been expelled to France by the Nazis after the departure of their children, from Belgium in May 1940 and from the Baden, Palatinate and Saar in October 1940. Trapped in French internment camps, especially Gurs, they had not seen their children in years. Andrée Salomon recruited several resident social workers for the OSE, most of whom from Strasbourg, to work in the internment camps. When the children's departure appeared imminent, one young social worker, Ruth Lambert, attempted to facilitate a reunion between the parents and their children for a final farewell.[15] There are multiple accounts of this moment—produced during the events and from later recollections. They merit our attention because they illustrate not only what the children experienced, but also the different perceptions of caretakers and how the latter instrumentalized the children's suffering. Lambert described the encounter in her retrospective account:

> A group of children was leaving for the United States, via Spain, very legally. The parents in Gurs wanted to see them again, which seemed perfectly legitimate to us. I obtained permission to bring the parents down to Pau [sic: Oloron-Sainte-Marie] (under gendarmerie surveillance!). [. . .] When the meeting took place, it was very painful: the children no longer recognized their parents, had forgotten German, their mother tongue, and spoke only French . . . Where was the fault? Who was to blame? Whose fault was it?

Everyone was crying, and I saw gendarmes wiping their eyes. The experiment was not repeated, and with good reason . . . firstly because it was too hard, and secondly because what happened next was perfectly . . . illegal![16]

Accounts from the period show different perceptions of the same event. An AFSC representative mentioned the farewell to his colleagues, and, in contrast to Lambert's negative recollection of the French authorities ("under gendarmerie surveillance!"), his account shows his positive perception of them: "There was a touching moment at Oloron, where the coaches stopped and where some of the children were able to see, possibly for the last time, their parents who were still interned in Camp Gurs. The commandant of the camp kindly placed at their disposition a camion to take them to the station to see their children off."[17] In the United States, Margaret Frawley echoed this assessment of the French authorities: "It was one of the most moving stories any of us had ever heard, the arrangement for it was characteristically French but from the standpoint of the children it is not good."[18] Everyone agreed that this emotional experience should not be repeated.

In September 1941, a few months after the children's arrival, JDC leader Morris Troper used this anecdote in a speech he gave at a USCOM fundraiser at the Waldorf Astoria in New York. Taking pains to avoid labelling the children as Jewish, he sought to move the audience with stories of their suffering. "The memories these children had!" He explained:

They had been permitted to say farewell to their families—those still having relatives. The train on which they traveled from Marseille stopped at the station of Oloron, and fathers and mothers interned at the Gurs camp were brought to the train under police escort and given a last three minutes with their children. Most of the children had foregone their breakfasts on the train that morning, and had wrapped up bread and rolls and bits of sugar to hand to their parents when they met. One little girl of seven had been separated from her mother for over two years. When they met at Oloron they were unable to converse, for the child had forgotten her native German in

229

the effort to learn French and English. They had no common language except tears.[19]

His was not the only account. Isaac Chomski, one of the children's escorts and a journalist, published a seven-page account of the departure in October 1941 in the *Contemporary Jewish Record*. He, too, focuses on the role reversal, in which children sought to feed their parents bread. According to Chomski, the parents' eyes told "a tale of hunger. But they refuse to take the bread. [. . .] The children are persistent. Again and again they cry, 'Please take . . . please take.' One little girl attempts to force a slice between her mother's teeth. It is evident that the mother can hardly control her hunger. But she dares not eat the bread."[20] Chomski concludes with a plea: "They [the evacuated children] are free from the terror of persecution and starvation. [. . .] But for the millions of children left behind there is no hope. Only a handful can be rescued—how many depends upon the help American men and women will give."[21]

One cannot remain indifferent to such accounts, designed to incite empathy and open purses. They encourage us to step back and acknowledge not only the children's suffering, but also the uses of their pain. Taking these accounts at face value, as some historians have done, prevents us from recognizing the actions Jews took to raise awareness about the situation in Europe.[22] Troper's remarks on the children's suffering—not only at this moment in Oloron but in France in general— were quickly republished in the form of a letter to Eleanor Roosevelt and used as fundraising material.[23] Ernst Papanek later criticized Troper's letter, claiming it gave Laval a reason to deny children exit visas at the moment when they were most needed, in fall 1942, once the deportations of children had started. According to Papanek, Laval explained why he denied the crucial exit visas in an interview in *Aufbau*: "You want to parade these children down Fifth Avenue and show everybody what the terrible French people have done to them."[24] But alas, Papanek, too, in making this observation, was using Troper's remarks to settle his own score with American Jews, on whom he focused his anger, instead of directing it at Laval, who not only blocked the exits visas, but suggested the Nazis deport Jewish children from France.

As adults plied children's experiences to suit their own needs, the children themselves were experiencing profound loss—of their parents, of security, of their maternal languages—just as they played and fought and loved.

La Guette teen Heinz Löw, from Vienna, wrote in his journal that he learned of his departure on May 17 and had to leave La Bourboule on May 18 for Marseille to go to the American consulate. "And I just hoped I would see the ocean. Marseille is the largest port in the Mediterranean Ocean [sic]. As told so it happened."[25] From Marseille, the group traveled to Madrid, where they spent the night in a convent, then went by train to Lisbon, where they spent a fabulous six days at a vacation colony run by the *O Seculo* newspaper, playing in the sun. As another La Guette teen Heinz Lonnerstädter notes in his diary, they also spent time at the movies: "After eating we took a bus and went to the movie. The observant religious kids walked. We watched the movie. After dinner another movie. We went to bed a [sic] 1 o'clock in the morning."[26] Elfriede also documented their journey, thanks to a camera given to her by her relatives in Switzerland.[27] Her photos of fellow children show their bonds, formed years before in children's homes across Germany and France (Plate 16). The group arrived in New York on June 21, 1941, beginning a new chapter of their lives.

They faced their second exile separated, in foster homes throughout the country. Indeed, both Ernst Papanek and the OSE expected care for "their" children in the United States.[28] "We consider that our duty towards the children does not end with putting them safely on board the steamer," wrote OSE leaders in France. "Forty children from our homes will arrive in the United States without any connections whatever [sic], and our duty will be to take care of them."[29]

However, opposition to OSE's project was paramount. At the end of 1940, Papanek was invited to speak at the New York School of Social Work. He took advantage of the moment to present his plan to open an OSE home in the United States. To his great surprise, Papanek recalled being "attacked savagely": "One of the difficulties was language. I wasn't aware that the word *institution* had such an unfortunate connotation in this country—probably because it brought to mind the word *institutionalized*, a word which had no counterpart in Europe. 'This is not the American way!' they shouted at me."[30]

Papanek's project to establish a home for the OSE children not only challenged American social work policy, which strongly endorsed family placement over institutional care. It also questioned the hard-earned authority of the GJCA, as well as the American Jewish practice of dispersing refugees upon arrival to avoid provoking American antisemitism.[31] The issue thus became a both symbolic and very real fight between newcomers and the establishment. While Papanek expected the full support of Amerose, its leader Dr. Wulman fired Papanek on May 22, 1941, several weeks before the arrival of the first transport of OSE children.[32]

Even though the first transport required a great deal of preparation and led to the dispersal of the children throughout the United States, the OSE was heartened by its outcome and especially pleased by its collaboration with the AFSC. "We greatly value our cooperation with the Quakers and wish to continue along the same lines,"[33] they wrote to Amerose in New York. In fact, in the course of their collaboration, only one disagreement took place, when the OSE insisted on including a French child, the son of Rabbi S.[34] As seen in Chapter 5, this family, only two years before, had been helping refugees: Rabbi S. had been instrumental in establishing OSE's Eaubonne home for religious children, while Madame S. used the family passport to smuggle their nieces Ruth and Miriam into France. Now it too was dependent upon the whims of bureaucracy and the goodwill of organizations. This case did not spoil the OSE–AFSC relationship, however. The OSE sent the AFSC a letter after the transport, thanking them profusely for their work, taking care of this precious relationship.[35]

The AFSC, however, walked away from the first transport with an altogether different impression of the project. AFSC delegate in Marseille Allen Bonnell wrote a cutting letter to Philadelphia headquarters just after the arrival of the first transport, providing a critical assessment of the emigration scheme from its earliest phases. Confusion had stemmed from a major misunderstanding: in March 1941, the AFSC in France had been informed that the children would be evacuated on a blanket affidavit, that is, a corporate affidavit, allowing the

USCOM to be held financially responsible for the group of children. However, according to Bonnell, a cable from the United States spoke of a blanket *visa*. It was not until May 16, two weeks before departure, that they learned the children actually needed quota numbers to obtain visas! The USCOM's close relationship with the State Department allowed the children to miraculously receive American visas by the end of the month, but on the day of their scheduled departure, May 30, they still needed Spanish and Portuguese visas, as well as exit visas from Vichy.

After great panic ("no stapling apparatus was to be found"!) and bribes of chocolate bars, the children were finally loaded onto two coaches: "Our feelings towards the children were much more kindly and sympathetic as they pulled out of the station at 6 o'clock than they had been for the previous eight days,"[36] wrote the disgruntled delegate. The letter concluded with the following assessment: "Expenses for the emigration of these children were extremely high and there is considerable question in our minds whether or not the expenses were warranted, in view of other uses for which equivalent funds could have been placed."[37] In this case, the AFSC did not seem willing to act as a front for a Jewish operation, as it had done in many other instances.

Those at the AFSC's Philadelphia headquarters also saw reason to question the viability of the program. Four of the children were detained at Ellis Island because they required medical care, including one case of possible mental retardation and cases of scabies and impetigo.[38] In addition, one child was sixteen and thus over the age limit.[39] The AFSC soon realized that the "child detained for supposed mental incapacity was in our opinion suffering from shock. [. . .] We finally learned that this child celebrated his birthday the morning that his parents were permitted to come from Gurs to see him, that it was the first meeting in three years, and was obviously much more upsetting that any one [sic] could have anticipated."[40] Nonetheless, such cases undermined the OSE's credibility, even if a joint committee, comprised of OSE and AFSC representatives, had made the final selection. At the moment of the first departure, Andrée Salomon had been present in Marseille and had tried to keep siblings together, even if it meant overlooking minor health issues and age limits (Plate 13).[41]

Concerned that the future of the evacuations was under debate, OSE leaders in France wrote to their American Committee with instructions:

> Get in touch with the Quakers in Philadelphia. Howard E. Kershner is now in America. You should approach him, express your thanks for his help in the matter of the first transport of children, and secure his cooperation for the future. He is an ambitious man and likes honours. Besides, they really were very helpful and greatly helped us with the utmost energy and true philanthropic spirit, which we underlined in all our communiqués. Let them assume the direction of the formalities, as it is not a matter of prestige, but of results.[42]

They did not have to ask: Amerose leaders in New York had already requested an appointment with Kershner, but the latter remained elusive and did not grant a meeting.[43] Amerose also had its honorary president Albert Einstein write an appeal directly to the head of the USCOM, Marshall Field. "I appeal to you that you help us put an end to this torturing of innocent children, this maiming of their souls and spirit, and aid us to find for them a safer haven and a possibility to grow up as useful members of a decent society."[44] If any doubt remained on the future of the evacuations, it was allayed by a $25,000 grant from Jewish USCOM board member Adele Rosenwald Levy's Rosenwald Family Foundation, made just after the arrival of the first transport.[45] This funding encouraged the USCOM to organize a second evacuation for another hundred children.

Over the summer of 1941, Howard Kershner, who was back in the United States, and Margaret Frawley at the AFSC headquarters sought to refine the selection criteria. A meeting on this subject, held in late June between the AFSC and the USCOM, prompted AFSC director Clarence Pickett to write to his subordinate, Kershner:

> At the meeting of the US COM today your question [. . .] was raised as to whether in the selection of further children it was necessary to have a mixture or whether it was more satisfactory from their point of view to have an all Jewish group. It was quite clearly decided

that there should be no racial discrimination of any kind. From the point of view of public opinion on this side, it would be well if there could be some non-Jewish children but the guiding principle was to get at the children who needed most to get out. It would be secondary as to their national or religious affiliation.[46]

Pickett's letter provided a very clear answer to Kershner's inquiry: "no racial discrimination of any kind." However, this message was blurred when Margaret Frawley wrote to AFSC staff in Marseille one month later, continuing to push for "mixed sailings" in her instructions:

In stating the basis for its selection the United States Committee has emphasized its non-sectarian character and has expressed itself as wishing to care for the neediest children. If this happens to be a predominantly Jewish group, the US COMM will assume that responsibility. In talks with Howard Kershner we tried to arrive at some ratio on this racial question since our feeling here was that in giving instructions for the first project the American committee [USCOM] had directed your attention primarily to groups caring for Jewish children. The presence of some non-Jewish children strengthens the United States Committee position as a non-sectarian group and will enable it to make its financial appeals to a larger group. If you send only Jewish children, it is more than likely that the appeals for funds will meet response only from individuals who will thereby be compelled to reduce their contributions to Jewish refugee agencies. The United States Committee is anxious to avoid this latter situation if possible.[47]

By bringing up yet again the "racial question," Frawley presented the idea of establishing a "ratio," which implied lowering the number of Jewish children on the transports. She framed this as a pro-Jewish strategy, designed to enable a broad funding base for the evacuations. According to her logic, the American public would not fund exclusively Jewish evacuations, which would cause Jewish donors to divert their donations away from other Jewish causes. While this argument shows a keen—if cynical—assessment of American public opinion, it also displays a staunch disregard for the situation Jewish children faced in France. Frawley seems to have been taking liberties with the USCOM's instructions by returning to an issue that had been settled at the previous meeting. The AFSC instructions to its Marseille delegates followed her logic, as seen in a July 15, 1941 cable: "recommend selection children non sectarian basis with representation gentile and Jewish with consideration need also child's intelligence and capacity adjustment American life."[48]

The latter criterion, on adjusting to American life, meant giving priority to younger children, and this put the AFSC directly at odds with the OSE, which sought to evacuate those most at risk of internment. Assessing a child's capacity to adjust was difficult, Frawley admitted in an explanatory letter, but "a child who is extremely nervous and difficult in France is likely to be the same here."[49] This criterion, she noted, should encourage the AFSC to select younger children. Noting the high percentage of teenagers on the first transport, she wrote: "we realize that this age group is likely to be most seriously jeopardized with possibility of internment. With some reluctance the US COM feels that it must ask that as much as possible the group be kept to the younger age categories. Younger children have a better opportunity to identify themselves with life here and in the minds of the public the program is identified with the younger children."[50] Frawley (and in her interpretation, the USCOM) were thus fully aware that refugee teens faced internment in France but asked for children under the age of twelve, with the exception of sibling groups, even though the visa requirements, imposed by the State Department, remained the same: under sixteen.[51]

In addition to these goals, the AFSC suggested that the evacuations should bring children directly from the camps. A final note of advice from the AFSC, having discovered that one of the children from the first transport had epilepsy, was not to fully trust the partner organizations in France: "This instance as well as some of the other problems [. . .] lead us to the conclusion that some of the cooperating committees: OSE, the Rothschild group and others have not been completely frank with you in presenting the children for emigration." The OSE "quite obviously failed to give you additional information about relatives as well as experiences of the children which were extremely relevant." Frawley advised the AFSC in Marseille, "your own scrutiny of the children will need to be more careful."[52] A few days later, another cable followed, backtracking on previous AFSC instructions for mixed sailings: "USCOM nonsectarian policy emphasizes need not race and predominantly Jewish group acceptable if you convinced most needy stop."[53]

In spite of the greater involvement of AFSC staff in the selection process, the OSE yet again selected most of the children for the next hundred visas, which were divided into two separate groups, leaving France in August and September 1941. Only six of the children in the second and third transports were selected by the AFSC, and, yet again, the large majority was Jewish.[54] The OSE reported to its American Committee that it had not been successful in bringing children directly out of the camps for the first group, even if many of the children selected from their homes had in fact previously been in the camps. Promising to do better for the second group, it still felt that the collaboration had gone well: "Complete harmony in the joined action of the Quakers and the OSE with efficient and continual support from the Joint [JDC]."[55]

Yet again, AFSC representatives in France did not share the OSE's opinion. AFSC delegates explained why the OSE selected the children at an August 1941 meeting: "In reality it is very difficult to find any Christians to include under this plan, and on short notice we can get only Jewish children. French children are not allowed to leave their country, and Spanish children can not [sic] get a visa de sortie except for repatriation."[56] AFSC workers also tried to recruit children from camps and managed to select a group of thirty-five children. However, they could not be prepared in time for the departure.[57] AFSC delegate Ross McClelland wrote to console his colleague Mary Elmes, who had selected the children who did not leave, noting Howard Kershner's concern that the project might become an exclusively Jewish one:

We hope they [the selected children] will be able to leave [on a future transport], although I understand that Mr. Kershner's reaction to the group which just left while we were in Nimes was not favorable. He did not feel that we were doing the States a great service by sending over these children. He felt that if it was to turn into a 100% Jewish affair that it should be handled by the Jewish organizations rather than ourselves. This seems reasonable, but still you have gone to all your trouble already. Now I suppose if it is turned over to the Jews they will have hundreds of their own children available, and won't be interested in the ones you have assembled. Well, let's hope for the best. Nothing is definite yet.[58]

To introduce more diversity in the transports, AFSC decided to open a registry for potential (assumedly Christian) children in August 1941.[59] Yet the USCOM and AFSC guidelines did not seem to withstand the reality on the ground in France, where only Jewish parents were desperate enough to part with their children. Instead of explaining this to AFSC headquarters, Kershner argued the project was too expensive and inefficient. He was still in the United States during the selection process but returned to France in late August suggesting that they should write to Philadelphia to "question the whole UsCom scheme as a very expensive and not particularly satisfactory solution to the problems of these children. A great deal of money is spent to help a relatively small number of children, and it is a matter of debate whether it is desirable to separate them such a distance from their parents. The US Comm. is now in the process of raising a half million dollars to bring over another 500 children. We shall suggest that they should send their own representative to take charge of this."[60] A few days later, the AFSC in France "registered a protest with Philadelphia."[61]

As seen above, in his letter to fellow AFSC delegate Mary Elmes, Ross McClelland suggests a different reason for Kershner's opposition, stating that the latter didn't feel the AFSC was "doing the States a great service by sending over these children."[62] In light of the fact that the first three transports were comprised almost exclusively of Jewish children, McClelland seems to have been suggesting that Kershner had antisemitic sentiments. Kershner shared his negative opinion of the children during his travels, including with Dr. Robert Dexter of the USC in Lisbon. USCOM executive director Robert Lang learned of Kershner's comments indirectly and wrote to Frawley in alarm in December 1941. According to Lang, Kershner "discussed with Dexter the inadvisability of the American Friends Service Committee's participating in this work because of the general undesirability of the children.

If Howard Kershner is discussing his opinions, even with responsible people such as Dr. Dexter, I would be a little concerned because these people carry real weight in terms of opinion, etc., in this country."[63] Kershner may have also influenced his colleague in Lisbon, Phil Conrad, who wrote:

> We would raise again the question as to whether for the next group there could not be found a number of Christian children. Marseille answered our inquiry saying that it was not possible on short notice, and when he was here, Howard Kershner explained the difficulties. But the Lowries [YMCA representatives] who passed their vacation here recently told Dr. Dexter [USC] that they knew of about 2,000 Protestant children who could be available for evacuation. They are not in colonies and it would require more time to enlist them. It is much more easy to go to the Jewish colonies which have thousand [sic] of children and choose, but we are confident that the impression made on all who come into contact with the project (particularly here in Lisbon) would be happier if we were "giving a chance in life" to others as well as to these who are getting through. Dr. Swartz [sic, Joseph Schwartz, head of the JDC in Europe] says that such a result would be ideal from the point of view of Joint, but that he has the same report from Marseille that Christian children cannot be found for evacuation. Of course, these remarks do not imply any reflection on the attractiveness of these little folks whom we are helping.[64]

Jewish children are considered here as an easy solution. Conrad adopts a similar rhetorical technique as Frawley in the United States by stating that the JDC supported decreasing the number of Jewish children to allow for more Christian children. In reality, Jewish organizations were not in a position to argue. Conrad's remarks demonstrate the fact that for some AFSC delegates, Jewish children were not in an urgent category of need, and that they were, on the contrary, perceived to be benefitting disproportionately from a program that was designed to "give a chance in life." The notion of *rescuing* Jewish and "non-Aryan" children from Nazi and Vichy persecution is resoundingly absent.

After the arrival of the second and third transports in fall 1941, the OSE sensed that something was awry and sent a confidential memo to Amerose, noting that relations were good in France but that the Philadelphia AFSC was not happy, wondering: "Maybe this dissatisfaction is due to the fact that the over-enthusiastic praise directed toward us affects their fundraising campaign."[65] The OSE was equally concerned over the lack of news on future transports: "We are greatly worried over the dilatoriness of this work. A month has already elapsed since the last departure for the States. It is imperative that the next transport should leave in November. We repeat again and again that this [sic] our work has a tremendous importance for us. We have to think of the future of our children who are no longer small and whose living we cannot guarantee. They must leave this country."[66] If the sense of urgency is clear here, the English is not. By stating that they cannot guarantee the children's "living," OSE leaders were most likely referring to their upkeep, and not their actual lives. They could not predict what was to come, even if they sensed decisive action was needed.

Amerose was set up exactly for this reason: to apply pressure from New York. It demonstrated its knowledge of centralization-minded American Jewish welfare by turning to the New York JDC for help, to which Herbert Katzki had just returned from France.[67] Katzki managed to speak with the USCOM leadership and obtained a meeting for Amerose leaders in early December. The latter had a new weapon. The OSE's French patroness, Baroness Yvonne de Gunzbourg, had arrived in New York in spring 1941 and proved more than willing to continue her work on its behalf. Even better, she had relatives and friends in the American Jewish establishment.[68] The Baroness brought a needed sense of respectability to the refugee committee and accompanied Amerose's Leon Wulman to see the director of the USCOM. They learned the USCOM was going to send a new representative to France to select children but would not commit to a time frame. Not even the presence of the Baroness made a difference: "We did all we could to have them expedite the matter but neither Mr. Troper, nor Mr. Katzki [JDC representatives], nor the efforts of our committee could prompt them to more rapid action."[69]

Indeed, it appears that the AFSC in France had thrown in the towel, forcing the USCOM to start looking for its own representative to send to

France. This prospect alarmed USCOM leaders, who perceived the urgency of the situation and wrote to the AFSC: "I wish to express the opinion of the Board of directors of the US COM that it is their feeling that the element of time is a vital factor at this moment and that we should not delay in bringing children out as fast as we are financially able."[70]

A few days later, on December 7, 1941, Japan bombed Pearl Harbor. The United States entered the Second World War but maintained its diplomatic ties with Vichy until November 1942. On the ground in France, the dangers for Jews increased tremendously. Deportations to Auschwitz began in March 1942 in the occupied zone. In late May 1942, a new German ordinance declared that all Jewish individuals over the age of six in the occupied zone were required to wear a yellow star. By this time, the OSE had been forced to join the Union générale des Israélites de France, the Vichy-Nazi-imposed Jewish council established in each zone in November 1941 that centralized Jewish welfare organizations into two separate branches. The creation of this structure had profound implications but did not change the fact that the OSE had become the main Jewish childcare organization in Vichy France. The well-being of increasing numbers of children was entirely dependent upon its ability to function. By April 1942, there were still 158 children in the internment camps and 1,350 children in OSE homes. Throughout spring 1942, OSE representatives worked closely with parents in the camps to encourage them to separate from their children. "We hope we can convince them of their parental duty,"[71] they wrote in May 1942. This statement shows the OSE's mindset several months before deportations in the unoccupied zone began. Asking parents to consider their children's well-being over their own emotions suggests the OSE sensed the children were in danger. OSE resident social worker Ruth Lambert recalled: "I don't want to imply we had a 'vision' of events to come. We didn't know. But what we did know was that life at Gurs for the children was horrible, abnormal to say the least."[72]

After a pause due to the "shipping situation,"[73] a new opportunity to evacuate more children to the United States arose in January 1942. The USCOM did not sent a representative to Europe. This time, the AFSC staff was determined to direct the selection process. Their enthusiasm was bolstered by the possibility of including Spanish children in the transports, which became possible due to the fact that there were ships to the United States leaving from Marseille via Casablanca, which allowed them to bypass Spain altogether.[74] AFSC delegate Marjorie McClelland was put in charge of selecting the children, altering her instructions to choose children directly from the camps. Trained in child psychology, McClelland felt that the shock of going from camp life to the United States would be too intense; she thus privileged children from the OSE and Quaker homes.[75] She toured the OSE homes with the criterion of selecting children who were all alone in France. However, the same rule did not apply to the non-Jewish children: the Spanish children selected were, with only a few exceptions, not alone. All of them were children of Republican refugees in extremely precarious situations. Many had fled Spain in catastrophic circumstances, usually with only one parent and siblings. Only four out of the forty cases show the children to be completely alone in France, without a parent. All of the children were selected from AFSC children's colonies. In some cases, the parents proved quite difficult to convince.[76] As Corazza notes: "They [AFSC] selected the 'best' children in their colonies, with above average intelligence according to their tests, who would make good citizens if they remained in the US after the war. The workers knew the children and their families well, and the families trusted the advice and information from the AFSC workers."[77]

Paradoxically, as dangers objectively increased for Jewish children in France, their percentage on the transports dropped: fifty-four children were included in the first group, which left Marseille in May 1942; another forty-two children left France early July 1942. Of the total of ninety-six, forty were Spanish. Before their departure, a goodbye was organized with their parents, who were interned in French camps. Writing in May 1942, Majorie McClelland echoed the earlier accounts of her colleagues: "The French authorities not only gave them [the parents] the leave from the camp, but paid their train fare to Marseille and back—a very generous gesture, and the nice kind of thing that the French will do."[78] McClelland may not have heard about the deportations of Jews already underway in the occupied zone, yet one might have expected a more critical view of the French State that interned the parents on the grounds that they were foreigners and Jews, separating them from their children for up to three years. One senses, nonetheless, her sincere concern for the children, regardless of their background:

> I have become very much attached to the children, and almost wish I were going back to America now so that I could go with them. Heaven knows they probably won't look like much when they arrive. [. . .] You will notice that the Spanish children, from our colonies, are a good deal better dressed that the children from the OSE colonies, as we have had more clothing at our disposal for the number of children we care for than the OSE has had. I would like to see the children dressed decently, really cleaned up and properly groomed. I think on the whole they would be an attractive looking bunch—or maybe that's just because I'm fond of them. I will be eager to hear of any comments and reports from you after their arrival.[79]

The forty Spanish children on these transports proved to the American public that USCOM was indeed running a non-sectarian operation, even if they created a placement challenge for the USCOM, since the GJCA was only authorized to care for Jewish children.[80] There was also tension with American Catholics when it was discovered that a considerable number of the Spanish parents preferred their children to have a non-sectarian or a Protestant upbringing. This prompted the AFSC to turn to Kershner's wife, Gertrude, who was in charge of the AFSC colonies, to inquire how the Spanish republicans had become Protestants. She denied any proselytization: "I have made a great effort (in the selection of personnel for each colony) to choose persons who are Christians and have an unselfish outlook on life, and great devotion to the children . . . No effort has been made to coerce the children to religious training."[81] In spite of these problems, USCOM president Marshall Field was elated, writing to a collaborator: "The best information we could get indicated that the children faced certain death if they remained in Europe. As you know, there isn't enough food in unoccupied France and apparently no possibility of getting enough food. Theoretically the children should get 1,000 calories of food a day, but actually this is impossible."[82]

Marshall Field wrote this letter on July 14, 1942. Two days later, almost 13,000 Jewish men, women, and children were arrested by the French police in Paris and its surroundings during the Vélodrome d'Hiver round-up. The danger facing most of the children from the transport was not only malnutrition, as Field had written, but arrest, internment, deportation, and murder. Reports on Vichy's persecutions against Jews had circulated in the American press since 1940, alarming Vichy's diplomatic corps in the United States.[83] Yet the specific dangers Jews faced did not become evident until they had become lethal. Perception was not just a matter of distance from the war zone. AFSC delegates in France also misread the Nazi and Vichy regimes, perhaps influenced by Kershner's pro-Pétain attitudes.

In total, the 5 USCOM transports from June 1941 to July 1942 allowed for 309 children to gain entry from France to the United States under the USCOM's corporate affidavit.[84] Approximately thirty children with independent visas were also able to join the transports. The transports not only benefited Central European children who had been granted refuge in France and Belgium through Kindertransport initiatives in 1938–1939 but also included new populations of Jewish children that had entered France through flight and expulsion in 1940. The large majority of USCOM children from France—at least 253 of them—had been cared for in OSE homes.[85] Once exit from France proved impossible, several transports were organized directly from Lisbon, bringing an additional 100 children to North America over the course of the war.

We have thus far focused on humanitarian workers and their organizations, who negotiated complex and changing state policies. Yet in wartime France and elsewhere, children refused to be passive wards; their families, even when far away, tried to help them.

Individuals took matters into their own hands, and not all Jewish refugees turned to organizations for help. Ottilie Moore was a wealthy German-American heiress, daughter of the "Sausage King of Brooklyn," who lived *la belle vie* in France until the Great Depression forced her home. She traveled back to the United States in steerage with her five-year-old daughter and maid, while apparently placing her dog Pansy in first class with a valet.[86] By 1940, this quirky American was back in France. Her villa, L'Ermitage, near Nice, had become a haven for Central European Jewish refugees, to whom she rented rooms. According to Moore's nephew, over 300 refugee children lived in the villa during the course of the war.[87] One young German refugee had studied at the prestigious State Art Academy in Berlin and became the object of Moore's attention. Twenty-four-year-old Charlotte Salomon created *Life? Or Theatre?*, a moving testimony comprised of almost eight hundred paintings and several hundred captions, so that the story of her German Jewish family could be sung as an operetta. Salomon dedicated her opus to Moore, the "somewhat unbalanced rich American [who] wanted to awaken joy."[88]

Looking for solutions for the refugee children in her villa, Moore learned of the USCOM transports to the United States. In August 1941, she reached out to the AFSC with the hope of placing five of them on the transports.[89] Moore then took matters into her own hands. According to her nephew's account, she took off in her station wagon with her daughter and nephew, "nine children, two goats and a pig"[90] in October 1941, driving from France through Spain to Lisbon, where the group managed to find passage to New York. Little trace of this private evacuation remains, except in the scholarship dedicated to the artist Charlotte Salomon, who was deported from France to Auschwitz in October 1943.[91] It is quite likely that other informal evacuations of Jewish children occurred in this manner yet remain undocumented.

The OSE children, too, proved to be ardent advocates for their own migration. In 1941, the organization attempted to set up a more equitable system of selecting children for emigration by establishing a registry. By October 1941, it had received 1,049 requests for emigration from children living in homes, in camps, and with their parents, and determined that 34 percent of the children in the OSE homes wanted to emigrate. According to the same report:

In some homes, we've even observed a veritable obsession with departure, to which the children have fallen prey; they pester the staff with requests, only resting when they're assured that their names are on the list of candidates. This shows the importance of the place that emigration projects have taken in the lives of the poor little ones; it also proves, once again, that we must look at these cases with great care, doing everything we can to ensure that the most unfortunate and deserving see a new life open up before them.[92]

As children clamored for a place on the transports, some received help from family members in the United States. One of the Viennese La Guette children, the artist Paul Peter Porges, was assisted by his older brother Kurt, who had been sent to the United States. While a young and recent refugee himself, Kurt harassed the NRS, as well as his relatives in the United States, to find affidavits for his parents in Vienna, and for his brother in France.[93] His request made it to the desk of Lotte Marcuse, the placement director of the GJCA. Marcuse intervened, but Paul Peter Porges never received a place on a USCOM transport. Instead, he had to be smuggled to Switzerland, and he immigrated to the United States only after the war.

Quincy teen Stephan Lewy received precious help from his father and stepmother, who had left Berlin for the United States after his Kindertransport departed for France. Once in the United States, the couple—now working as servants—began an arduous process to reunite with their son. They eventually managed to hire a lawyer, but the State Department rejected his visa. In September 1941, upon the advice of fellow refugees, both parents wrote letters to the President himself. His stepmother promised President Roosevelt that their sixteen-year-old son would make "the very best soldier in the American Army."[94] The family never received a response from the President, but Stephan received a visa. The family assumed it was due to Roosevelt's intervention, but it is perhaps more realistic that Amerose helped. In January 1942, Stephan's parents had turned to its New York office: "Couldn't you help us in any way to bring the boy over? He is our only child, 16 years old, and we have been separated now for nearly three years. We have lost everything over there what was dear to us; he is our very hope and pride, help us to save him."[95] Stephan Lewy was ineligible for the USCOM transports due to his age, but he was able to travel with an individual visa on the fourth transport, and he arrived in New York in June 1942.

These cases of family advocacy attest to the ardent desire of families to remain together yet only sometimes yielded positive results. What is missing from such accounts, however, is the complexity of family dynamics that also shaped flight. Jewish families, like all families, can be fragile entities. The Holocaust violently ruptured this most intimate space.[96] Returning to the story of Peter and Werner Gossels' departure reminds us that family choices during the Holocaust, while often the result of persecution, were also shaped by the intricate nature of family relations.

As seen above, the Gossels brothers' parents were divorced. The boys were sent by their mother on a Kindertransport to France after their father had fled to Belgium. Their father was arrested in Belgium in May 1940 and sent to a French internment camp. By spring 1941, however, he was living in the Allier region of France with a new wife, Melanie. His sons were now living in the OSE's Château de Chabannes, not far from their father.

Peter and Werner were among the children selected by the OSE to leave on the first USCOM transport to the United States, that is, until their father visited them at the château and reappeared to say goodbye to them in Marseille in June 1941. This is how Peter recalled events in our oral history interview, but the boys' OSE case file indicates a somewhat different version.[97] It shows that the father made his presence in France known to the OSE by coming to visit his boys at the Château de Chabannes in March 1941, where he learned that his children had been selected for the transport. Unaware of the strict selection criteria, he wrote to thank them for selecting the boys, and stated in this letter that he and his new wife were also hoping to immigrate to the United States.[98] The sudden appearance of the boys' father and his new wife cast doubt on the Gossels children's need for a group immigration scheme, especially since their father was planning on emigrating. This caused the OSE to write to the father to explain they were not on the list of eligible children.[99]

The boys' father, however, had not planned on emigrating with his children, and did not have an affidavit for them. He thus set out on a letter-writing campaign to the OSE, reminding them—in French—of his past services to the Union OSE in Berlin. In this letter, he sought to justify why he wasn't pursuing immigration plans with his children: "You are certainly right to want to especially help orphans but if for once a father cannot care for his own children because he was working above all towards his duty to help Jews, neglecting the fate of his own family, until the last moment, don't you think one should make an exception?"[100] His new wife also tried to intervene, and later claimed she had been responsible for reversing the decision.[101]

The boys were indeed selected for the September 1941 USCOM transport. The reasons for this most likely had little to do with the boys' father and his wife. First and foremost, the children made themselves extremely likable, an important factor in their selection. An OSE social worker described Peter as a "very bright child [*très éveillé*], gifted and very developed" and Werner "like brother."[102]

Perhaps most significantly, the boys' mother, Charlotte, continued to advocate for her children from Berlin, actively seeking a means for them to leave France for the United States. While she had worked selling cosmetics in the late 1930s, by 1941, the family had been forced to sell its home.[103] Through acquaintances, she managed to reach out to Mrs. Gruenfeld, as seen above. The latter took the time to translate Charlotte Gossels' letter from German into English and sent it to a local aid committee for emigrants, which forwarded the letter to the NRS, where it landed on the desk of the placement director for the GJCA, Lotte Marcuse.

The strict centralization of American Jewish welfare, as well as Charlotte Gossels' tenacity and Mrs. Gruenfeld's solidarity, made an important difference. Marcuse wrote to the committee in St. Louis, asking if Mrs. Gruenfeld might be willing to help the boys. Mrs. Gruenfeld, however, was busy trying to get her own relatives out of Germany. The case was referred to the local Jewish child welfare agency, which contacted Lotte Marcuse in July 1941 on behalf of Mrs. Gruenfeld, inquiring whether the boys had been included on the June 1941 USCOM transport. In the meantime, Mrs. Gruenfeld had learned that Charlotte Gossels was "a friend of the grandparents of a French child whom the Gruenfelds have in their home." This provided enough of a connection for Mrs. Gruenfeld to suggest that the boys be placed in St. Louis. Mrs. Gruenfeld could not financially support the children, but "would take a personal interest in them which she feels would be very comforting to their mother."[104]

At this point, Lotte Marcuse promised to include the boys on a list that would be presented to the representatives of the USCOM or

Quakers, who were responsible for deciding who would be selected for the second and third transports, leaving in August and September 1941.[105] On September 11, 1941, Marcuse wrote to her colleague in St. Louis: "I know that you will be happy to hear that these two boys will be in the group of 51 we expect in next two weeks. Do you accept them for placement in St. Louis?"[106]

From Berlin, this mother orchestrated the rescue of her two boys through a transatlantic letter-writing campaign that succeeded in transforming two unknown German refugee boys into a personal concern for American organizations. This most likely caused the OSE to overlook the presence of their father in France. Peter and Werner arrived in New York on September 22, 1941. Their father and stepmother managed to find visas for Venezuela. Their mother remained in Berlin and soon became a slave worker in a railroad communications factory.

Eleven-year-old Peter's stoicism continued to impress his caretakers. He had slipped on the ship and broken his leg, causing him to be detained at Ellis Island and later transferred to a hospital. When Lotte Marcuse visited him, Peter instructed her not to tell his mother about his leg. Marcuse reported their conversation: "'Be sure not to let her know; after all it's nothing and she would only worry. I shall be out so soon, and then she can find out.' His brother [Werner] said he 'ought to have an ever sharp pencil and stamps and he would like to send him a parcel, but he had no money!' 'Nonsense, I need nothing,' was Claus's [Peter's] comment."[107] This child later asked his caseworker "whether television might develop quickly enough so that he might 'see' his mother some time soon."[108]

Charlotte Gossels' last letter to her sons is dated November 1941, just after the boys' arrival to the United States: "Work hard in school and make your foster parents happy. As I heard, you will be placed with a family and not into a home, but I don't know anything exact about it, and I am waiting for your exact answer concerning this. In either case, whatever it may be, whether a home or a family, always be obedient and work hard! And always care for each other because you both always belong together."[109] Her wish that they remain together, at least in its literal sense, was not respected. Like many other siblings on the transports, the brothers were sent to the same city but cared for in separate foster care homes.[110]

Like many other Kindertransport parents who remained behind in Central Europe, Charlotte Gossels was deported to Auschwitz, on February 2 or 3, 1943, where she was murdered.

Let us take a step back to note the evolution of the initiative to evacuate children from Germany that began in Marion Kenworthy's home after the November 1938 pogrom. From the first meetings in December 1938, those who gathered were doing so because they were moved by Nazi persecution. By fall 1940, these persecutions had spread throughout Europe. But paradoxically, at least for some on the ground in Europe, the notion of *rescuing* Jewish and "non-Aryan" children faded as the persecutions intensified.

Rescue plans conceived in the United States took on their own life in France, leading to new outcomes. When forty Spanish children were selected for the USCOM transports in the summer of 1942, that meant that forty Jewish children remained in France, threatened by deportations. Yet Jewish children were not the only ones affected by the USCOM and the AFSC's attachment to "mixed sailings." Many decades later, with the help of the internet, the Spanish children began reaching out to one another, trying to make sense of their displacement to the United States and separation from their families. In 2006, they self-published a collective volume entitled *We Came Alone*. One former child used this occasion to question the wisdom of his evacuation:

> A reunion with strangers who long ago shared a life. Two decades of separation forcing awkward affected familial love. A room filled with people a little boy once knew so well—a teary-eyed mother, a father head bowed, and a brother and sister happy to see *el ameri-cano*. And the little boy now a man, wishing to quell a mother's guilt; to quiet a father's anger, to give comfort to these now strangers, kind people who were forced into making painful but correct decisions, decisions now questioned.[111]

Spanish families made the decision to send their children to the United States during their postwar period. In this fragile moment of taking stock, they counted their dead, plagued with grief and uncertainty but also, perhaps, holding a certain hope for the future. Not all of the Spanish children viewed their migration in negative terms, yet many would experience challenges similar to those experienced by Jewish refugee children in the United States: siblings rarely remained together under one roof; foster care placements proved unstable. Girls and boys ended their placements with early marriages and enlistment in the army, respectively. For all unaccompanied children, foster care was part of an assimilatory goal that implied a clean break with the past.

While one might be tempted to engage in backshadowing, to use Michael André Bernstein's term,[112] to condemn an action that could have saved forty Jewish children from deportation and murder, I instead argue here that evacuating children from occupied France cannot be understood without a firm understanding of the perceptions of the humanitarian aid organizations that were helping Jewish children in occupied France. They did not perceive danger in the same manner, nor did they prioritize children's needs in the same fashion. Nonetheless, it appears that anti-Jewish attitudes were not entirely absent from the decision-making process that shaped the evacuations.

The Jewish children left in France in summer 1942 faced a life-threatening situation. We will now turn to the final attempt to evacuate them to the United States.

CHAPTER 15

Those Left Behind

A Rescue Attempt

In fall 1942, Ernst Papanek received "the most terrible letter [he had] ever received" from an OSE educator at the Montintin home, referring to the St. Bartholomew massacre of 1572, in which thousands of French Protestants were murdered:

> Last week we lived through a kind of a St. Bartholomew Night. At five o'clock in the morning we had guests who arrived with trucks. They took a lot of people away with them. Then it was said that the boys under eighteen would be released again, but in the meantime they were already sent further on. Allegedly to Poland but we don't really know anything definite. Among those taken were Emil Geisler, Beeno Singer, Hans Martin. Guenther and Horst, who were on vacation [at Gurs] with their parents, were also taken; also girls from the other houses. In the days that followed there was a hunt for those who had escaped, but the forests are large. [. . .] Yesterday the little ones were taken from our houses, allegedly to be sent to their parents in the concentration camps. They took even two-year-olds from the nursery and let them sleep at the railway station. What they intend to do with them we don't know.[1]

Thousands of Jewish children remained in France after the five USCOM transports. Their lives changed dramatically after July 1942. Just days after the last transport's departure, the French police, acting on German orders, arrested 12,884 mostly foreign Jews in Paris and its suburbs. They targeted men, women, and children, and detained them in the Vélodrome d'Hiver round-up, including 4,051 children under sixteen, most of whom of French nationality.[2] Almost 5,000 individuals were sent directly to the Drancy transit camp, where deportation trains carried them to Auschwitz in a steady stream after July 19. Families with children under sixteen, more than 8,000 in number, were taken to the Vélodrome d'Hiver in Paris. Most of these families were then taken to the Pithiviers and Beaune-La-Rolande internment camps in the Loiret. French Prime Minister Pierre Laval made it clear in his dealings with the Germans that he "did not care about the children arrested in the Occupied zone."[3] However, permission to deport young children from France had to be formally granted from Berlin.

Even before Vichy received permission from Berlin, which arrived on August 13, its officials included children on the transports to Auschwitz. On July 31, Vichy officials decided to deport parents and children over fourteen years of age, but at least fifteen children between the ages of twelve and fourteen were on that transport. On August 3, mothers were deported, leaving the 3,500 youngest children on their own in the Loiret camps, with very little assistance.[4] On August 5, children were deported with their parents from Beaune-la-Rolande, while another 290 children, aged between eleven and fifteen, were deported on August 7. On August 15, the remaining children under thirteen were transferred from the Loiret camps to Drancy. From August 17 through 31, Vichy and Nazi officials deported the children, now separated from their parents, on convoys 20–26.[5] Laval took credit for convincing the Nazis to take the children, in the name of "humanitarian intentions."[6] These first deportations of children, among the cruelest chapters of the Holocaust in France, occurred in the occupied zone, where French internment camps functioned with limited humanitarian aid. There were few witnesses to these atrocities.

While most of the Kindertransport children were evacuated to the unoccupied zone between May 1940 and January 1941 as a safety precaution, one group of Kindertransport children remained behind in the occupied zone: the eight teenage girls who had come from the Merores orphanage in Vienna, now under the care of the Rothschild orphanage in Paris. The girls became targets in July 1942. With one exception, all were arrested and deported to Nazi camps, where they were murdered.[7] The reason we know what happened is that one child survived to bear witness. As historian Michaela Raggam-Blesch has uncovered, fourteen-year-old Berta Romana Seidenstein, alarmed to see her older friends arrested, managed to alert her mother, in Vienna, via an aunt in Romania. Her mother, who had converted to Judaism, moved mountains to get her child classified as a "*Mischling*" ("half-breed"), a Nazi category that was not used in France. With the help of a Jewish acquittance and her non-Jewish Dutch husband in Paris, Berta's mother managed to get her on a transport back to Vienna in April 1943. Berta worked as a slave laborer until the end of the war but was not deported.[8] Ironically, going back to the German Reich saved this teen's life.

The first details on the Nazi plan to systematically exterminate Jews arrived in the United States in early August 1942, although it took several months for this information to be made available to the American public.[9] The round-ups and deportations of Jews in France, however, were reported in the American press.[10] Humanitarian workers in southern France were also privy to direct information on these events as they unfolded, since the unoccupied zone was not spared. This fact sets the Vichy government's actions apart from those of others during the Holocaust: no other unoccupied area in Western Europe turned over its Jewish population so willingly.[11]

On August 13, 1942, Lazare Gurvic of the OSE wrote a four-page description of the first deportations from the unoccupied zone, reporting on the convoys that left from the southern internment camps: "the internees were loaded into completely empty freight cars with no straw, no benches, containing only water jugs and a policeman. Offers from social workers from the American Quakers and the OSE to accompany the convoys to the demarcation line, and to set up supply posts there, were rudely refused—they don't want witnesses."[12] Gurvic then describes how the situation affected the OSE, which was asked by the Ministry of the Interior to accept 1,200 new children into its homes on the spot. The OSE acquiesced yet found itself overwhelmed: more and more children were arriving daily in deplorable physical and psychological condition. The OSE received offers from other organizations to help care for them, but it had no illusions: "even when all the children have been temporarily taken in, they do not seem to be effectively protected against the dangers of deportation for long. We must therefore do all we can to rescue these unfortunate children by trying to obtain as many emigration licenses as possible."[13] OSE's representative in Switzerland, Boris Tschenloff, transmitted this document to JDC's European chairman Joseph Schwartz in Lisbon, along with a clear message: "There is a possibility to save a few thousand children from unoccupied, and possibly also from occupied France. If we do not undertake anything, they will certainly be deported, and perish sooner or later. They can only be saved by emigrating as soon as possible. Principally one must think in this connection of North America. One has to secure visas for several thousand children for the United States."[14] JDC's Joseph Schwartz sent the materials directly to New York on August 26, lending his full support to the project. He wrote to his superiors:

> You must realize that literally thousands of fathers and mothers are leaving their children behind in unoccupied France rather than take them along on their journey eastwards which can have but one conclusion. As a result the institutions are being filled with father-less and motherless children, who can look only to the existing agencies for their support. Unless a good many of these children can be emigrated, there will soon be many others for whom no facilities of any kind will be available.[15]

These sources show that OSE representatives, as well as JDC's Joseph Schwartz, equated deportation with death as early as August 1942. OSE officials proved even more lucid than the JDC, arguing that children would not be exempt from deportation. As seen above, the OSE was correct.

Word traveled quickly. On September 3, 1942, the USCOM's president Marshall Field sent a cable to Clarence Pickett to invite him to an emergency meeting with the very clear words: "Children also subject to deportation."[16]

On September 18, another cable arrived in New York from Nîmes Committee president Donald Lowrie to the USCOM: "Returned from France yesterday stop Latest deportations contained four hundred children stop All foreign Jews including children whatever date entry France now ordered arrested for deportation or permanent internment living constant terror stop Vichy adamant about adults but apparently might exempt children if America accepts thus quick permission entry US only hope sufficiently speedy action to save five thousand children under sixteen."[17]

This information, provided to the USCOM and the AFSC, transformed the orientation of the evacuation initiative, eliminating the ambiguities that had shaped the project from its initial stages. The notion of rescue takes on its fullest meaning here, as the USCOM and AFSC officials, as well as the JDC, set out intentionally to save the lives of Jewish children.

A similar realization occurred on the ground in France, where emigration had come to be understood as the only antidote to the children's deportation. This heretofore unimaginable fact provided a new sense of unity and urgency among humanitarian workers. By late summer 1942, the AFSC seems to have entirely revised its negative opinion of the USCOM children's evacuations. This probably had little to do with Kershner's return to the United States in May or early June 1942, even though this certainly allowed his staff greater freedom of action.[18] It was the deportations that caused the AFSC to grasp the urgency of the situation. On August 13, Helga Holbek wrote: "Like you, I believe, we've spent the most appalling days of our lives, watching the people we've cared for for a year and a half go off to new suffering. It was confirmed to me this morning that they are all being sent to work in the Silesian salt mines. So you see, we have to keep protesting, protesting, protesting!"[19] Holbek did not, unlike the OSE and JDC representatives, associate deportation with death—at least at this date—but she understood the gravity of the situation and called for protest.

Under the leadership of YMCA representative Donald Lowrie, a new group formed in Geneva on August 14 to work toward the emigration of children to the United States in order to "impress upon the authorities and the public the urgent necessity of saving the lives of thousands of children."[20] On August 17, the AFSC informed the JDC in New York of a plan to bring 7,000 children from France to the United States.[21] Members of the Nîmes Committee, as well as JDC's Joseph Schwartz, who arrived in France from Lisbon, coordinated their efforts and targeted the authorities with whom they had cultivated relationships. Jewish organizations were asked to stay out of the negotiations with Vichy officials, although OSE's Joseph Weill initially disregarded these instructions.[22] JDC's Joseph Schwartz thus met with US chargé d'affaires S. Pinkney Tuck,[23] whereas negotiations with Vichy officials were conducted from late September through early November by YMCA's Donald Lowrie and AFSC's Lindsley Noble and Herbert Lagler. The goal of these extensive negotiations was to secure exit visas for the children.[24]

In the meantime, in New York, the JDC was working behind the scenes to help the USCOM obtain emergency visas to the United States for Jewish children.[25] JDC leaders made it clear to the USCOM that it would find the funds to support the children once in the United States and pledged $400,000 to cover part of the transport costs, estimated at $900,000.[26] Following a well-established pattern, the JDC intentionally let the USCOM take the lead in negotiations with the US government and instead met privately with Jewish USCOM board members to help them persuade the USCOM to support a massive evacuation project.[27] By September, the USCOM had turned to its honorary president Eleanor Roosevelt for support and sent its board member George L. Warren, secretary of the President's Advisory Commission on Refugees, to negotiate with the State Department.[28] By late September, the USCOM had received the news that the State Department would grant 1,000 emergency visas. However, Vichy officials remained vague on the number and categories of children they would release, eventually floating the much lower number of 500.[29] The USCOM returned to the State Department to request 5,000 visas, which were granted in early October 1942.[30]

Over the months of September and October, a team of OSE–AFSC workers worked around the clock to select eligible children.[31] They grappled with Vichy officials' ever-changing requirements, which eventually specified that only orphans would be allowed out of the country. However, Vichy officials refused to consider children with deported parents to be orphans.[32] The organizers of the evacuation continued to plan. They expected the children to leave France via Spain and Portugal in small groups during the month of November, sailing to the United States from Lisbon in December on the SS *Nyassa*, which had left the Port of Baltimore with twenty-eight escorts on November 7.[33] By early November, the children were gathering in Marseille, yet Vichy still had not provided exit visas. On November 9, a final appeal was made to Laval for the exit visas. By this time, the Allies had invaded North Africa, which led to the rupture in diplomatic ties between France and the United States. Laval refused the exit visas. According to Marrus and Paxton, Vichy's changing attitudes on Jewish emigration can be explained by mounting pressure on Vichy to turn over Jews in order to meet Nazi deportation quotas.[34] The Nazis occupied the southern zone on November 11. In spite of the continued intervention of humanitarian workers, the evacuation was cancelled and thousands of Jewish children remained trapped in France.

A photograph taken at OSE's Chabannes home captures a moment of relaxation on a hot day: teachers and children are lightly dressed, and a group posed for the camera, arms enlaced. The children were not yet aware they were targets of Vichy-Nazi deportation measures and continued to play.

According to one of their educators, Lida Jablonski, the photo was taken on August 26, 1942, the day of a sports tournament. The children must have been tired after a long day of physical activity and sun. At 10:30 that night, they were awakened by French policemen (*gendarmes*) who had come to arrest the foreign children and adults over the age of sixteen.[35] Their list had seventeen names on it. Nine children escaped. Eight children, as well as two adults, including Ernst Jablonski, the beloved educator from La Guette, were arrested. Just after his arrest, before leaving Chabannes, Gerhard Rosenzweig, just a few days short of his sixteenth birthday, leaned out of the window of the police bus to give his friend the key to his bicycle.[36] This simple gesture, in a moment of extreme distress, suggests the importance of this bike to this teen, as well as his understanding of the gravity of his situation. Children may not have had structural agency—the power to shape the outcome of their situation—but they did have tactical agency—the ability to act and to make choices.[37] Let us not underestimate the importance of the bike key.

The group was first taken to a detention center in Boussac, where one of the teens was released. Seven children were then sent to the Nexon internment camp, where two more were eventually released. The educators also accompanied the teens to Nexon but were then liberated.[38] The remainder, a group of five or six teens from the Chabannes home, were immediately put on trains to Drancy.[39] The group was made up primarily of Quincy boys, who had arrived legally in France from Berlin on July 4, 1939. They were deported from France on August 31, 1942, on Convoy 26 to Auschwitz. Their refuge in France had lasted just over three years.

Convoy 26 made several stops before arriving at its final destination.[40] Several of the Chabannes–Quincy boys were taken off the convoy before its arrival at Auschwitz, in Cosel, and entered the Nazi camp system as slave laborers. Only two of the teens survived deportation: Gert Rosenzweig and Wolfgang Blumenreich. It is from them that the group would learn that one of the boys was killed when he jumped from the train.[41] They also described how two others, Arno Kaczynski and Bernd Warschauer, died from typhus after three months in the labor camp.[42]

As seen from the letter Ernst Papanek received, the round-up at Chabannes was not an isolated event. Other OSE homes, now caring for the Kindertransport children and many others, were targeted over the same period. The children at the Château Montintin, which had been directed by Ernst Papanek, were victims of a raid on the same day as those in Chabannes, August 26, 1942, and possibly another in the following week. These raids led to the deportation of at least eleven children.[43] The OSE's Château Le Couret, north of Limoges, was also raided in August 1942. Dorli Leibl, the last *Robinsoner* girl in the OSE homes and Hanna Kaiser Papanek's best friend, had been transferred to this religious home but was arrested, perhaps with her mother, in the town of Saint-Antonin.[44] Along with the other girls arrested at Le Coret, Dorli was deported on Convoy 30 to Auschwitz, which left France on September 9, 1942. Fewer than 500 Kindertransport children came to France in 1938–1939, of whom I have identified 292 with certainty, based on archival evidence. Of the 292 children, at least 36 were deported to Nazi camps.[45]

The group experience, so central to the children's experiences in exile, continued during their deportation. Some of the Kindertransport children who had been separated over the course of the war were reunited at Drancy. Luz Scheucher, from La Guette, survived deportation on Convoy 26 and forced labor in twenty-three camps. He remembers arriving at Drancy and seeing his former La Guette comrade Ellen Rosen, who had been arrested at the OSE home in Le Couret. Ellen had been considered for the summer 1942 USCOM transports but was deemed ineligible because she was over twelve.[46] When Luz saw her in Drancy, Ellen was crying. Her hair had been shaved, and she had tied a cloth around her head to hide her shame.[47] She did not survive Auschwitz.

After the summer of 1942, the idea of refuge for the children was shattered, despite the efforts of the humanitarian organizations and their representatives. One will recall eleven-year-old Norbert Bikales from Berlin, who arrived at Chabannes thanks to his older friend, Bernd Warschauer, who was rounded up on August 26, 1942. After this, Norbert recalls his mounting sense of fear at Chabannes, where he had to remain until April 1943. In September of that year, he and several others managed to flee to Switzerland with the help of OSE social workers.[48]

Indeed, from summer 1942 until the liberation of France in 1944 and 1945, the care and rescue of Jewish children took a very different direction. The homes—structures initially designed to protect children—had become targets. They had to be dismantled, and the children dispersed. Andrée Salomon continued her work on behalf of Jewish children, having refused a visa for the United States. Under the auspices of OSE, her "network" worked in parallel with other clandestine networks to hide Jewish children throughout France under new identities, in Christian families and institutions.[49] Others, especially with the help of Georges Loinger, whose wife Flore had served as the director of La Guette, escorted hundreds of children to safety in Switzerland. The Loingers never forgot La Guette, however. The château, requisitioned by Secours National, a

Vichy-sponsored welfare organization, became the perfect hiding spot for about fifteen Jewish children.[50] Still other children, especially after 1944, crossed the Pyrenees into Spain with the hope of later reaching mandatory Palestine.[51]

As these children fought for their lives, about 300 others faced an entirely different challenge, far away from the round-ups and deportations. Confronted yet again with a new language and culture, these children and teens had assumed that they would remain a group in the United States. As seen above, Ernst Papanek and the OSE expected that they would open a home for them in New York, but they underestimated the attachment of American social workers to foster care.[52] The children were dispersed in foster homes throughout the United States.

One of the children from Vienna, Oswald Kernberg, who had been cared for in the OSE homes while in France, now found himself in New York. In October 1941, soon after his arrival in the United States, Oswald turned the symbolic age of thirteen. On the occasion of his bar mitzvah, his father sent the traditional parental blessing in his letter from the Opole ghetto in Poland, where the family had been resettled in spring 1941. They were later deported to Sobibor, where they were murdered.

My dearest love,

Today on your birthday as well as your day of Bar-Mitzvah, we all, that is dearest Mother, your brother Fritz and I, are sitting in a tiny, tiny room, and are constantly both thinking and talking about you. Our total longing and thoughts are only addressed at you and you alone, and our deepest wish is to be able to be together with you again in peace and in joy. How we inwardly, my dearest child, are longing to hear any news from you or about you, I can not express in words, but your child's heart alone must somehow reflect our total longing for you. Before anything else we long to know where you are, if in an orphanage or by your Uncle Sigmund or Aunt Erna, furthermore if you are healthy, how you look and how you feel in your new surrounding [sic]. Please do not let us wait long for any news from you, but write us as often as you can, and the more often we hear from you, the greater will be our joy. And now my golden youngest son, I give you my innermost congratulations and blessings on this your most important and solemn day. May your luck shine and be bright as the stars in heaven and may it be written in our future to be able to hold you into our arms and make life again nicer for you as we have always strived to do. You alone are our total longing and hope, and therefore you must remain healthy, big and strong. In my thoughts I lift my hands over your head and bless you with the blessing from the bible, "May God bless, shelter and protect you and always hold his right hand over you—Amen!!" We are healthy and well. Again with the most urgent wishes to see you again in peace and joy. I embrace and kiss you many thousand times, your always loving and faithful Papa.[53]

Let us quietly contemplate the love, the longing, and the tremendous sense of loss in this letter. Somehow Oswald Kernberg, who became Art Kern in the United States, found the strength to translate it from German and share it with an archive many decades later. Let us consider the time between his reception of the letter and his act of sharing it, for the distance between these two decisive events represents an entire chapter of the history of the children's lives, one that remains to be told.

Conclusion

I am a refugee girl and a Jew, this is my pride
however turbulent it may be, we are tough!
Sailing the raging waves of life's tempest
we dodged the cliffs, now dawn is near, so clear.
We are on Swiss soil, it fills us with joy
We feel the breath of freedom, "onwards" it goes instead of
   "backwards"

Ursula Matzdorff, November 18, 1942[1]

This poem, written by an eighteen-year-old from Berlin who had
been cared for at the Château de la Guette, suggests that by 1942, the
Kindertransport children who had fled to France had come to think of
themselves as refugees. Ursula affirms her identity as a Jewish refugee girl
from a place of relative security, having crossed successfully into Switzerland
after a failed first attempt. This teen's experiences in France after August
1942 proved that France was no longer a place of refuge. She decided to set
out alone, with the hope of connecting with Tante Elisabeth, the Swiss
woman whose letter-writing campaign on behalf of Jewish refugees had
kept Ursula in contact with her father in Germany.[2] Her poem, especially
her use of "we," invites reflection on the experiences of Jewish children in
France during the Holocaust and the collective contexts of their exile.

At the center of this book is the question of networks. First and
foremost, I sought to document the networks that developed to rescue

children from Nazi persecution, in other words, the horizontal alliances Jews wove with fellow citizens in order to evacuate Jewish and "non-Aryan" children from Nazi territories. But, of equal importance, this book offers a new perspective on children's experiences during the Holocaust by exploring them in groups and probing the networks they brought to France and created in exile. What happened to children's relational worlds when they went into exile alone? How did their groups form and evolve, over place and time? These questions led me to address not only the evacuation of Jewish children from France to the United States—my initial research question—but also their arrival in France on the eve of the war. Indeed, to understand the genesis of their relationships, one must start in Central Europe and consider how Jewish families faced Nazi persecution, as well as the ties children formed in Austrian and German Jewish orphanages. Some of the Kindertransport children brought these relationships to France, where they created new bonds with caregivers and fellow refugee children. Following the trail of networks caused me to stumble upon the French Kindertransport initiatives, a subject that until now appeared only in footnotes. Its significance lies not in the number of children saved, but in the fact that the land of refuge quickly became a trap. This makes the French story quite different from the one that unfolded in Great Britain.

This book also explores a curious incident of serial exile: Kindertransport initiatives sought to protect Jewish children from Nazi persecution by sending them to France. When the Nazi occupation made this country unsafe, a new evacuation scheme emerged to bring them across the Atlantic. I have attempted to write a child-centered social history in dialogue with both childhood and Holocaust studies by probing children's feelings and actions as I explore the strategies of caretakers, humanitarian workers, and their organizations. This book thus tells a complex story, one of children and families on the run and the adults and the organizations that helped them.

Focusing on a case study through microhistory challenges us to rethink the very concept of Holocaust rescue. Rescue initiatives did indeed exist, as did rescuers, who at times risked their own lives to save others.[3] Yet in our contemporary search for heroes, we tend to retroactively attribute prescience and intention to rescuers, qualities that only rarely withstand historical inquiry. Furthermore, as Claire Andrieu has underscored, the model of the individual rescuer is often oversimplified: most survivors benefited from "small anonymous acts"[4] that, when successful, formed a protective net. Finally, as we saw in the final chapter, rescue doesn't always work: well-intended individuals and organizations can do little when faced with the crushing nature of state-sponsored genocide. In spite of the complexity of rescue, there is great public demand for feel-good stories of the Holocaust. Reframing the Holocaust as a narrative of heroism allows for commemoration without raising uncomfortable subjects such as collaboration, deportation, and murder. And in contemporary Europe and elsewhere, such narratives serve a real political function by masking state and civilian complicity in genocide.[5]

By analyzing rescue as it unfolded, in historical perspective, this book intentionally embraces a messier narrative. Exploring the early phases of the Holocaust in France shows the varying perceptions of danger in a moment of intensifying persecution. No one could have predicted in 1941 or early 1942 that Jewish children would be deported from France and murdered in Nazi camps. And yet some individuals sensed danger and sought to remove Jewish children from harm, while others wanted to help children (in general) escape wartime France. The awareness of what was at stake in the selection process for the evacuations can only be grasped retrospectively, after the Holocaust. Lives were saved: not 5,000—as attempted in fall 1942—nor 1,000, but about 280. The children sent from France to the United States during the war represent about 28 per cent of the unaccompanied Jewish children accepted into the United States during the Second World War.[6] They are often the sole survivors of entire families.

Placing children at the center of this history leads to new observations on Jewish experiences during the Holocaust, showing the active role Jews played in their own rescue, not only as leaders of rescue initiatives but as *rescuees*. Children became refugees not only through the efforts of organizations that negotiated on their behalf, but also by taking matters into their own hands. They coped with separation by maintaining and creating relationships with family, caretakers, and fellow children. They developed group strategies, such as lying about their level of religiosity, to maximize control over their lives as they struggled to make sense of their changing surroundings. They lobbied to be included in the evacuations to the United States. They actively documented their lives. The children were not only victims of Nazi-Vichy persecution, they were historical actors in their own right. Not only does their example refute claims of Jewish passivity, it also suggests the need to rethink the way we study Holocaust rescue. I argue here for the need to focus not only on the actions of rescuers but also on those being rescued, for it was the encounter of these two groups that shaped this process. It would be ahistorical and dangerous to overestimate Jewish children's ability to act during the Holocaust, but they nonetheless exercised tactical (as opposed to strategic) agency when they could.[7]

To help children, adults worked within the framework of organizations and sometimes acted alone. In both France and the United States, committees first emerged within Jewish communities to negotiate with states on behalf of Jewish children in Nazi Germany. As early as 1933, American Jews established Kindertransport programs that began functioning in 1934. In France, where some 25,000 German refugees fled in 1933, followed by consequent waves in 1935 and 1938, the French Jewish population was overwhelmed by the task of helping those already on French soil and did not try to bring more refugees.

The November 9–10, 1938 pogrom proved to be a turning point for individuals in Central Europe, France, and the United States. The pogrom made it clear that women and children would not be spared from Nazi violence. Central European Jewish parents, especially mothers, increasingly turned to Jewish emigration organizations and sought private solutions to send their children abroad. While Nazi policies forced migrations, the decision to flee was ultimately made by Jewish families. A myriad of factors—out of the control of these individuals—eventually determined whether these decisions would materialize into actual migrations. Nonetheless, family separation and flight were not passive responses to Nazi persecution: they were survival strategies that families enacted with the hope of reunification. In France, the November pogrom led a small number of individuals, primarily within Jewish organizations, to begin planning a large-scale evacuation to rescue Jewish children from Nazi violence. In the United States, the unprecedented violence sparked the indignation of non-Jewish individuals and created a new coalition to reform American immigration law with the Wagner-Rogers Bill. Their efforts failed, but their network, comprised primarily of child welfare experts of all religious backgrounds, remained active.

Indeed, helping Jewish children escape Nazi Germany and occupied Europe was never just a Jewish project. In France, a lack of archives prevents a detailed exploration of the ecumenical efforts that may have existed, making it difficult to assess to what extent Jews managed to build horizontal alliances. Nonetheless, there is evidence that the Comité français de secours aux enfants and, especially, the CRC, run by Louise Weiss, played a significant role in the French Kindertransport. In the United States, abundant archival holdings show that Jews were indeed successful in building horizontal alliances in the name of saving children. Jewish and especially non-Jewish child welfare specialists, as well as other influential figures, eventually formed the USCOM. Finally, in both occupied France and the United States, humanitarian work led to the encounter of Jewish, Quaker, Protestant, Catholic, and secular actors of multiple nationalities. Tracing the evacuations of Jewish children from Central Europe to France, and from occupied France to the United States therefore takes the historian far beyond the borders of Jewish communities and engages with David Hollinger's provocative call for a shift from "communalist" to "dispersionist" approaches to Jewish history.[8] Questioning how Jews interacted with others and participated in their larger societies to achieve shared goals, in this case, a movement to save Jewish and "non-Aryan" children in Nazi-occupied Europe, probes American and French societal responses to war and humanitarian crises as much as it interrogates Jewish and Holocaust history.

It is often assumed that the non-Jewish organizations that helped Jews during the Holocaust were fighting for the same cause and worked seamlessly with Jewish organizations. Yet in the context of American antisemitism, the partnership between American Jewish organizations and non-Jewish organizations was not a given. Even if most of the members of the USCOM were New Deal liberals, they saw children's needs through a broad lens. Making Christian and non-sectarian organizations aware of the specific situation faced by Jewish children in

Europe was essentially advocating that Jewish children's needs were more pressing that those of other children. This was no small task for Jewish organizations. They adopted multiple strategies to make the needs of Jewish and "non-Aryan" children a non-sectarian priority.

American political considerations also shaped rescue. All actors had embraced non-sectarian language, yet there was a great deal of ambiguity about who was really behind the "children of all creeds and races" that required help. I demonstrate here that non-sectarian discourse was sometimes a political strategy to help Jewish children while appeasing nativists and, other times, a sincere dedication to saving all children, without prioritizing certain groups. Some pro-refugee advocates felt that efforts to rescue Jewish children required the presence of non-Jewish children to avoid sparking outrage in the American public. Yet others truly believed that Jewish children would "obscure the needs of other children."[9]

Mobilizing on behalf of children not only brought about the evacuation efforts, it also led to concrete changes in Jewish communities. On both sides of the Atlantic, Jews responded to Nazi persecutions by expanding their self-help networks and importing organizations from Europe to the United States, as seen in the OSE's successful attempt to open a branch in New York. In both places, social welfare took on a new importance in organized Jewish life, making room for new forms of collective identity.

Perhaps more significantly, the Kindertransport movement both reflected and challenged gender hierarchies in Jewish life. Deep-seated cultural associations helped women take on public roles as child advocates. The presence of women in child-centered initiatives seemed natural and non-threatening but ultimately led to new leadership positions for them. In a 1960 interview, Andrée Salomon reflected upon the influence of the Second World War on her own evolution:

I'd almost have to start with a joke, by saying that, in truth, this war enabled me to do all the things I'd always wanted to do, and hadn't been able to do . . . it sounds a bit baroque, I'm not actually a social worker, but assistance in all its forms was a kind of hobby carried over from my life as a married woman after a long life of professional work close to the social sphere, and an intense activity at the center of an active community of young people in Strasbourg. Most of it was devoted to Zionism. During the war, I was really able to free myself from some of the handicaps and impediments of bourgeois [*mondaine*] life, of everyday life, of the grip of material life, which completely disappeared with the war and our retreat south [*repliement*]. After all of the displacements, it may sound like a joke, but [. . .] it's a kind of red thread that runs through all years of the war: [. . .] we were able to make certain activities happen because conformism disappeared, and no longer weighed on us; along with this severe conformism, certain external obstacles disappeared that had "eaten up" a large part of our lives.[10]

Andrée Salomon suggests that the war years altered the status of Jewish women in France, freeing them from the "severe conformism" and the "grip of material life." While she remains an exceptional figure in the history of the Holocaust due to the number of lives she saved, our two baronesses also experienced an evolution in their roles, from behind-the-scenes philanthropists to public leaders. In New York, Germaine de Rothschild became a sought-after public speaker at Jewish fundraisers, while Yvonne de Gunzbourg lent needed clout to the male-dominated OSE. Jewish women in the United States, while more numerous in Jewish welfare in the 1940s than in France, were nonetheless rarely in positions of authority. Efforts for children changed this. It is no coincidence that Cecilia Razovsky made a reputation for herself at the Children's Bureau, before becoming executive director of the NCC and the German Jewish Children's Aid. Lotte Marcuse almost single-handedly ran the American side of Kindertransport, frustrated by her behind-the-scenes role but unflagging in her authority. This context helps explain why Ernst Papanek and the OSE failed to open a children's home in the United States: they threatened not only the established childcare standards but also the "female dominion"[11] that had emerged to care for Jewish refugee children.

By analyzing the connections that linked families and organizations in Central Europe, France, and the United States, this book argues for the need to consider the Holocaust in a transnational perspective, which means understanding the larger spaces in which people and information circulated, as well as the political conditions on both sides of the Atlantic. Holocaust historians have not neglected transnational approaches entirely, and tend, when looking across borders, to focus on intra-European dynamics.[12] Yet rescue, while at times a local affair, also originated outside of Nazi-occupied territories.

Mounting persecutions forced Central European families to mobilize the extremities of their networks in far-off places, growing increasingly dependent upon distant cousins and relatives through marriage. These "weak ties"[13] proved extremely valuable, providing information, affidavits, and at times even illegal use of a passport, but often fell short when it came to actually caring for unaccompanied children. Nonetheless, some Jewish families managed to cultivate transnational webs. Their bonds, both weak and strong, sometimes provided real rescue solutions.

Organizations within and outside of occupied Europe also helped. Here we turned the gaze westward, toward the United States. Understanding the American dynamics not only broadens our understanding of the Holocaust in France, but also confronts the debate, now entering its sixth decade, on the American response to the genocide. For more than fifty years, "moralizer" and "contextualist" historians have sought to accuse or defend the Roosevelt administration, civil society, and American Jewish organizations.[14] Here, I have taken a different path, in the footsteps of Moshe Gottlieb or, more recently, Catherine Collomp, by conducting a case study to explore the American response through a concrete example.[15] Approaching the question on a small scale and from the bottom up allows us to discern its complexity and ambiguities. The agency of the actors, including Jewish children, adults, and their organizations, become visible. The 280 Jewish children evacuated from France in 1941–1942 were not "saved" from Nazi persecution as Jews; they benefited from a larger non-sectarian project to evacuate children from occupied France. Humanitarian workers did not perceive the situation for Jews in Nazi-occupied France in the same manner: OSE representatives insisted on getting "their" children on transports, motivated by a great sense of urgency. The AFSC delegates, for the most part, did not perceive Jewish children to be in greater danger than others, and some even had a negative opinion of this group.

Nonetheless, perceptions rapidly realigned after the deportations began in the unoccupied zone in August 1942. The American-based leadership of the USCOM and the JDC united their efforts to orchestrate a massive evacuation, eventually obtaining 5,000 American visas for Jewish children. On the ground in France, representatives from the AFSC, OSE, JDC, and YMCA set out on a furious mission to select Jewish children before their deportation and to negotiate with Vichy officials to obtain exit visas. This rescue mission has been glossed over by historians because it never came to fruition, yet it remains a powerful example of an American rescue attempt of Jews on European soil, long before the Roosevelt administration established the War Refugee Board in January 1944. Originating in non-governmental organizations with the approval of the Roosevelt administration, this rescue attempt shows how an ambiguous partnership to evacuate children quickly transformed itself into a mission to save Jews (albeit an unsuccessful one). It also provides the missing backstory to the better-known efforts to hide Jewish children in France in the 1942–1944 period.

Understanding child evacuations in transnational perspective also sheds new light on the French historiography of the Holocaust. The "Paxtonian revolution" has led to a decades-long debate on the role of the French State and population in the Nazi "Final Solution" that is far from over. Scholars have mobilized microhistorical and regional approaches to explore these questions empirically, just as they have deepened analyses of Jewish experiences and self-help as explanatory models for France's survival rates. They have also documented international humanitarian aid in the French camps. Yet, with little exception, their analyses have remained staunchly fixed on metropolitan France and Nazi Germany. Decisions made in New York and Philadelphia, however, clearly affected the lives of Jewish children in France.

Making room for the transnational actors who influenced Jewish rescue in France helps to deepen our understandings of the occupation. So does thinking critically about Holocaust representation. Historians of the Holocaust, in their attempt to document this crime, have broadened their source base, progressively incorporating the voices of the victims, initially thought to be lacking in objectivity. We have also progressively taken into account retrospective sources, produced long after the events. Nonetheless, the latter can leave historians with a skewed vision, for the simple reason that they reflect the experiences of those who survived. The dead cannot provide testimony or share their stories. Their absent voices must be recognized. Following Alexandra Garbarini's suggestion, I have sought here to create a tension between the sources produced as events unfolded, and those created long after the genocide. While equally authentic, they provide the historian with "near-sighted" and "far-sighted" vision of the events.[16]

Indeed, all sources are mediated, and studying children's evacuations from the bottom up creates an epistemological puzzle. Even the most ardent detective work digs up uneven coverage of historical events, due to the fact that archives have their own history.[17] I have sought to use as many child-produced sources as possible, yet, as other historians of children and childhood have underscored, these sources often bear the imprint of adults and must be read as palimpsests.[18] Oral history, a methodology that I embrace fully, cannot fill every silence: this study comes several decades too late and captures only some of the views of the former children, now in the winter of their lives. Oral history tells us less about the events themselves than about the meaning ascribed to the events by those who lived them. Finally, not everything can be put into words. As former OSE resident social worker Ruth Lambert concisely stated at the end of her 1984 testimony, "I keep deep inside the indelible memories that can't be written down or told."[19]

Between silence and cacophony, contemporaneous and retrospective perspectives, and the inherent difficulty of finding children's voices, my sources have created a unique set of challenges. Few traces remain of the children's evacuations from Central Europe to France, documented in the first chapters of the book, most likely due to the looting and dispersion of French and German archives during and after the Second World War. Documenting children's experiences in France as young refugees led to a different problem: how does one weigh the variegated contemporaneous sources with retrospective sources, produced years after the events? The final chapters on the evacuations from France to the United States revealed an entirely different problem: a multitude of contemporaneous documents on the events exist, dispersed throughout the United States and Europe, dooming any retelling to be incomplete. This book attests to the fact that total historical reconstruction is an unattainable goal, yet by raising these questions, and accepting doubt, I hope to contribute to further integrating Jewish and Holocaust studies into the larger theoretical debates on historical writing.[20]

In light of these challenges, what can be said about Jewish children's experiences in France from 1938 to 1942? One thing is certain: Jewish refugee children in France experienced the first years of the Holocaust in collective contexts. Far from the individual experiences in hiding portrayed in most works on the 1942–1944 period and in contemporary cultural representations, many Jewish refugee children spent a considerable part of the war in children's homes and families.[21] Children's sources, both contemporaneous and retrospective, demonstrate the importance of their friendship groups and affective ties in transit. Their networks changed in France, expanding and taking on new weight, in the absence of parents. Their writings, drawings, and photos provide a detailed and multifaceted portrait of life in French Jewish children's homes.

"Ship sisters and brothers"[22] had, for some, become family, although experiences should not be generalized. Former children emphasized their surrogate family bonds in the context of the rise of Holocaust memory and the development of "child survivor" associations in the 1990s and 2000s.[23] Nostalgia for one's youth seems to grow as we age. It is quite possible that children were not as bound to one another as they later suggested. Nonetheless, their lives were enmeshed with those of others, in collective contexts. Even negative accounts attest to this fact. As a child, the historian Saul Friedländer was placed in a children's home in Montmorency for six months. This experience was intolerable expressly because of the other children:

> It is difficult for me to say today whether all the children there were pious, but many of them were, among them Jacob—to my misfortune. He noticed immediately that his prayers were as foreign to me as his Yiddish, his yarmulka, and his earlocks, and alerted the others.

I was a non-Jew, a *goy*. And so the little Jews of Montmorency were to avenge themselves for all the things that the *goyim* had made them suffer—whether they had directly experienced them or not— them, their families, the entire Jewish people; I was on my way to becoming doubly Jewish.

I was tied to a tree and beaten. So many nightmares rush in and gather around this instant! I can still see the tree and, if you can believe me, I can still remember the bark and feel its greenish rough- ness, and see, farther away, the spacious building where we were lodged, surrounded by a long terrace. A sunny day, flower beds, mown lawns. Beaten by Jewish children because they thought I was different from them. So I belonged nowhere. At that moment the only thing I knew was that my parents were far away and that the children terrified me. I screamed in terror and knocked my head against the tree trunk.[24]

Contemplating collective experiences sheds new light on the depth of children's wartime trauma. Former children and psychologists have documented the severe anxiety provoked by hiding under an assumed identity or in camps.[25] Yet the life in collective homes, as seen above, could also be traumatic. Likewise, the brutal rupture of the children's friendship networks, through migration and hiding, has yet to be acknowledged.

For the Central European Jewish children who had become refugees together in France (and at times in orphanages before leaving Central Europe), American foster care policies meant not only turning the page, but also scattering their networks. Children lost sight of their "siblings."[26] These children would face the silence of the war years and the uncer- tainty of the postwar period primarily on their own, as they struggled to grasp the catastrophe that befell their young lives and those of their loved ones, all while adopting a new language and, for some, a new name. Aron Pruszinowski, who escaped Rivesaltes and was selected for a USCOM transport, writes on this period as an adult, under the name Henri Parens:

No, we did not pick up living our life; it was not that. Before the war I was in a world with my mother, my uncles, aunts, cousins, friends, my school, Bruxelles [sic], speaking French and Yiddish. My father and my brother were in Lodz, apart but accessible, in my world. Of course this life, as of May 1942, was not the life I was living before the war. My life was taking a turn very different than I had ever imagined. I did not realize then that it really was the start of my new life; my old life had been violated, fragmented; and it is taking me the rest of this life in America to bring some closure to what happened to my life of origin. It was not until a decade after I came to America that I knew my original life was over. That it had been shattered. But as it did even in Riversaltes [sic], life went on, and from the fragments, with the help of many on the way, it evolved into this very different, new and eventually very good life.[27]

Historians have cast the postwar years in a somber hue for Jewish child survivors who found refuge in the United States,[28] and Henri Parens' statement indeed suggests an individual mourning process. Yet this is not the full story.

One will recall the child Heinz Schuster from the introduction, who traveled from Frankfurt to Paris to Shreveport, Louisiana, where he became Henry. By the late 1970s, he had linked up with a group of other OSE children in California that had been meeting regularly since the mid-1950s. Indeed, fellow Eaubonne child Oswald Kernberg, who, as seen earlier, changed his name to Art Kern, made it his personal mission to find the former OSE children in the United States. He literally went knocking on doors looking for the now adult children. He and his wife organized a book club in the mid-1950s and eventually began hosting an annual garden party.[29] In 1979, Kern organized a reunion to celebrate the forty-year anniversary of their arrival in France.[30] In 1989, Kern, Schuster, and a few others organized the fifty-year OSE reunion in Los Angeles. Five years later, in 1994, a group on the East Coast incorporated the OSE-USA, a Holocaust survivor organization. In these examples of contemporary memory work, former Eaubonne and Chabannes children played a key role, suggesting that the connections they had established in France remained salient.

Their actions spark a new question: What really happened to children's networks after they migrated to the United States? Did they remain connected after the war, or did their groups dissolve and later reignite? If so, why? Children's networks provide a clue to understanding the rise of Holocaust memory and the emergence of contemporary Holocaust survivor identities. The next task at hand is to explore them, from the bottom up.

Researching *Who Will Rescue Us?*

Methodological Considerations

*W*ho Will Rescue Us? mobilizes oral history and archival research, as well as multiple national, transnational, and group contexts, each with its own historiography. This essay offers a discussion on the historiographical, methodological, and theoretical considerations that shaped this book.

I approach the story of the children's rescue through several levels of analysis in this study. First, I consider the interconnections between France and the United States, bringing a much-needed transnational perspective to the question of Holocaust rescue, which has remained entrenched within national borders.[1] Scholars of wartime France have tended to favor regional perspectives, since the geographical divisions within occupied France greatly influenced the execution of Vichy-Nazi persecution policies.[2] Such studies provide important nuance to our understanding of the Holocaust, yet they neglect the key role of individuals and organizations working from abroad to rescue Jews. Transnational "poles" developed during the Second World War to assist Jews in France, specifically in the United States and Switzerland, linking these countries in a triangle in which each "apex" influenced the other.[3] Policies made in New York, Boston, and Philadelphia affected Jewish children's lives in occupied France, especially those interned in French camps.[4] Furthermore, the immigration policies of foreign governments had a strong influence on the lives of refugees in France.

Secondly, as a social history of two child evacuation schemes, this book intentionally lingers on the mezzo level,[5] focusing on the organizations that negotiated between states and individuals, moving children to safety and overseeing their migrations. Humanitarian organizations not only proved determinant in the flight of these young children, they also influenced the conditions of their exile. For child refugees, questions of care and family were intrinsically linked to social policies set forth by organizations and states. This led to new interactions involving organizations in different countries, across denominational lines and within, between individuals and organizations, and, of course, individuals and the larger host society.

Finally, as an intimate portrait of several groups of children and their caretakers, this study draws upon the *microstoria* method, in that it seeks to create and maintain a tension between the specific case study explored here and the larger historical trends that shaped children's experiences during the Holocaust. As Saul Friedländer noted, it is at the micro level that one can discern the interaction of the Holocaust's protagonists: its perpetrators, victims, and bystanders.[6] If migration turned the children into refugees, the children themselves participated in this process by advocating for their inclusion in evacuations and attempting to control the conditions of their care. Micro-level interactions require paying attention to power, not only to discern how Nazi-collaborator persecutions unfolded, but also to understand the criteria that shaped interactions and influenced the actions of individuals.

The question of power raises the important, yet often neglected, question of gender. I seek in this book to integrate the variable of gender throughout my analyses.[7] First of all, women emerged as the main advocates for the evacuation of Jewish children from Central Europe to France and, later, from occupied France to the United States. Their central role in these initiatives reflects the gender dynamics within Jewish communities in France and the United States, as well as in larger American and French societies. Conversely, the children's evacuations led to shifts in gender relations, allowing women access to new leadership positions. Second, the experiences of the children and teens as they became refugees cannot be understood without paying attention to gender. In their attempt to find a place in collective children's homes, boys and especially girls faced highly politicized gender performance choices. Religious identities (in their multiple forms or absence), age, class, and geographical origins also shaped this process.

Exploring the emergence of networks that allowed for the evacuation of children from Central Europe to France and from France to the United States, as well as the networks the children brought to and created in France, raises important epistemological questions. While researching the children's evacuations from Central Europe to France, I quickly understood why this topic had not been discussed in the historiography: the archives of the French organizations involved in Kindertransport have been plundered, destroyed, or lost. French state archives provide some fragmentary documentation, but many were also destroyed. Nazi and Soviet pillaging furthered the losses and dispersal.[8] When tracing the evacuations of children from France to the United States, I encountered the opposite problem: the vast body of sources is scattered in private archives throughout the United States. This has led to historians specializing in one organization or location, instead of looking at the evacuations from a transnational and multi-organizational point of view. I hope to have corrected this segmented vision by "crossing" French and American archival sources and taking into account the multiple contexts in both places that shaped the migrations of children.

While organizational records also provide key details on children's lives, I have preferred whenever possible the contemporaneous sources the children created themselves, albeit under the influence of their caretakers and peers. While in exile in France, Jewish refugee children kept diaries and autograph books and sometimes corresponded with family. They produced collective newspapers and documented their lives through photography and drawings. Their yearning to maintain contact with their parents can be seen through their disciplined decisions to write diary entries in German even after French had become second nature. Some children participated in complex letter-forwarding schemes, via Switzerland, to remain in contact with their families after the outbreak of war. Ties to parents, siblings, other children, and caretakers are richly documented in these child-produced sources. The comparatively higher Jewish survival rate in France, coupled with the fact that many of the individuals in this study left France before the deportations of children began, preserved certain wartime sources. Some of them were donated to archives; others have remained in private hands, and others have been lost. As Alexandra Zapruder has noted, these sources should be considered as fragments: "extant records stranded in a sea of missing material—evoking but surely not representing the vast, uncountable, incalculable loss."[9] They cannot be considered to be representative, but they do provide us with a rare view into children's inner worlds.

The networks children built and maintained over time collectively shaped their memory of the past and, inherently, my writing of their story. In the aftermath of the Holocaust, the children's group dynamics informed their testimonial practices, commemoration work, archival initiatives, and willingness to share their past. Germany, and to perhaps an even larger extent France, created a heavy pull that they could not initially explore, due to their young age. Yet even later in life, they were not on equal footing when it came to engaging with their past. Financial resources and educational levels proved determinant, helping some return to Europe and record their impressions.

Gender dynamics also affected their ability to explore the past.[10] Many of the young men enlisted in the United States Army at age eighteen, either by choice or through the draft. Some returned to Europe as GIs in the aftermath of the Second World War. As veterans, these young men were able to benefit from the 1944 GI Bill, which paid for all or most of their university studies. The spectacular educational and professional attainment of the refugee children, analyzed by sociologists Sonnert and Holton, cannot be generalized for both men and women. If women attained an equally high social standing, it was often not due to their own careers, but through marriage. Indeed, for refugee girls, the only immediate way out of foster care was marriage, although some did live independently, having obtained professional training, usually as secretaries and nurses. While more highly educated on average than American women, Central European women immigrants were less able to access university study than their male counterparts, and they generally required a merit-based scholarship.[11] For women, returning to Europe usually came later in life and required diverting family resources. Social class, educational levels, and gender thus greatly influenced the former children's ability to seek out their places of origin and sites of memory.

All of these factors have determined their inclusion in the historical narrative. The fact that many former children maintained their networks made my investigation of their past easier, allowing me to conduct over fifty interviews. However, because many belong to the same networks, these interviews cannot be considered representative of all children's experiences.[12] Furthermore, my sources overwhelmingly reflect the perspectives of those who survived the Holocaust. I have only scant written traces and second-hand accounts of those who did not. This fact must be recognized, for it warps our perception of the Holocaust: experiences of survival were in fact the exception and not the rule.[13]

More generally, all sources are mediated, with the contemporaneous and the retrospective offering different, though equally authentic, visions of the past. For historian Alexandra Garbarini, analyzing diaries and other contemporaneous sources provides a "near-sighted vision"[14] of the Holocaust and is part of a theoretical commitment to understanding Jews' agency: "Examining what people invested with meaning and what they imagined expands historians' notion of Jewish agency beyond simply understanding decisions Jews made that helped them survive or perish. Limiting historical importance to actions that had life-or-death consequences reduces people's experiences to a binary outcome. We need to consider the depth and breadth of Jews' experiences so that their lives do not become 'epiphenomena' of the catastrophe."[15]

As they grew into adulthood, and later in life, the children in this book wrote letters and memoirs that grappled with the past and provided insightful testimony. These retrospective sources, qualified by Garbarini as "far-sighted,"[16] tell us a great deal about the meaning individuals impart on their past experiences. Distance from the event does not make these materials less authentic than sources from the period, but it does provide an additional narrative of distanced reflection that requires analysis in and of itself.[17]

This is especially true for oral history. The usage of the latter in Holocaust history, initially subject to debate, has given way to a rich body of scholarship.[18] "What makes oral history different"[19] is how the interviewees, now in the winter of their lives, ascribe meaning to their pasts and connect disparate events into a narrative. In this respect, oral history interviews are not fundamentally different from memoirs or letters written after the events. Yet, while they are similar to retrospective accounts in some ways, oral history interviews led me to a direct encounter with my subjects and their emotions, allowing for surprises that caused me to rethink my project's scope, as well as its fundamentals. For example, I did not impose an individual format on my interviews; I just assumed this would be the case. On several occasions, however, in order to "help me," or because they thought it would be "good for them," those I interviewed invited siblings or fellow "children" to participate in our interview. These moments proved determinant to my research, as they underscored the importance of friendship and family networks. Furthermore, while I initially planned on beginning my research on the Kindertransport with the children's arrival in France, I realized that I needed to understand the networks they brought with them, which required originating my study in Germany and Austria.

Studying the lives of those who experienced the Holocaust raises important ethical issues. I have actively sought to gain consent from those I have interviewed. Almost all of the individuals I interviewed granted me written permission to use their real names, and some even insisted upon it. As others have noted, survivors show a strong desire to document the crimes of the Holocaust.[20] However, using real names can create further ethical problems, especially when using children's case files. It can also lead to self-censorship on the part of the historian for fear of over-revealing the spontaneous and deeply personal thoughts expressed in interviews. For these reasons, I considered using false names in this study. However, anonymity leads to other problems: how would I cite works published by the former children?[21] I have sought, when in doubt, to show individuals the sections of this book that pertain to them and have offered to provide a pseudonym. At times, I simply use a first name and last initial or discuss events without naming those involved. When authorized, I use real names. This is the imperfect solution I have found to conduct this research in the most ethical manner possible.

I hope that taking these precautions will help attenuate any pain this book may cause to those who opened their homes and lives to me. Yet I also know that—like the events in this study—the findings presented in this book may take on different meanings for different individuals. This was gently revealed to me when I showed Ernst Valfer, a child from this study, the section of the manuscript that pertained to him. Ernst had followed his mother's advice to pass as orthodox in France, even though the family was liberal, which caused him to be placed in the OSE home for orthodox children run under the auspices of a particularly beloved educator, Ernst Papanek.[22] "I shivered to read that had my mother not impressed on me to stay with the orthodox group from Frankfurt, I probably would have ended up in La Guette, would have never met Ernst P[ananek] and probably would not have ended up on the transport from France to the USA in May 1941."[23] To my great surprise, Ernst found a renewed sense of his mother's protection in the pages of this book, attributing to her the discovery of a father figure, Papanek, and a new life in the United States. Indeed, one cannot predict the meanings individuals will attribute to the events that shape their lives. It is perhaps this fact that renews my conviction that to comprehend the Holocaust to the extent possible, we must approach its history not only with archives but with those who experienced it.

Appendices

Table 1. Transports from Central Europe to France, 1938–1939

Date of Departure/ Arrival	Sending Institution and/or City	Number of Children	Organizing Institution in Central Europe/France	Receiving Institution in France
December 6, 1938 (b)	Frankfurt Jewish Orphanage	52*	Frankfurt Orphanage/ Central Fund for the East	Family placements in Paris and Strasbourg; Strasbourg and Haguenau Jewish Orphanages, Le Nid
December 26–27, 1938 / February 1939 (a)	Merores Girls' Orphanage, Vienna, several arrivals from Germany	12	Israelitische Kultusgemeinde Wein/ Nathalie Lourié, Rothschild Orphanage, Paris	Rothschild Orphanage, Paris
March 8, 1939 (c)	Frankfurt	10	Frankfurt Jewish Orphanage and Reichsvertretung der Juden in Deutschland/CIE	Œuvre de la Guette, OSE
March 8, 1939 (c)	Mannheim and Palatinate Region	40	Mannheim Orphanage and Reichsvertretung der Juden in Deutschland/CIE	Œuvre de la Guette, OSE
March 13–14, 1939 (a)	Vienna	49	Israelitische Kultusgemeinde/CIE	Œuvre de la Guette, OSE
March 21, 1939 (c) (f)	Berlin and surrounding area	50	Reichsvertretung der Juden in Deutschland/CIE	Œuvre de la Guette, OSE

March 21–22, 1939 (a)	Vienna	53	Israelitische Kultusgemeinde Wein/ CIE	Œuvre de la Guerre, OSE
July 3–4, 1939 (d)	Berlin, Auerbach Jewish Orphanage	40	Reichsvertretung der Juden in Deutschland/CIE	Comité de secours aux enfants réfugiés, Quincy-sous-Sénart
n/a	Independent arrivals and sponsored children (c) from Germany and Austria	55–150*** (c, e)	CIE and Central Fund for the East	Placement in families/colonie de vacances de Schirmeck
Approximate Total		**361–456 children**		

Sources: (a) USHMM, RG 17.017, Archive of the Jewish Community of Vienna-Jerusalem Component Collection, A/W 1985; (b) Hirsh, *Home Is Where You Find It*; Andrée Salomon et al., *Une femme de lumière*; (c) USHMM, RG 17.017, Trude Frankl Report, April 1939; Presse: *Samedi*, March 18, 1939, no. 11; (d) OSE Headquarters Archives, Listes de Quincy; (e) Interview with Andrée Salomon by Mme. Benitt, Israel, 1965; (f) *La Tribune Juive*, March 31, 1939, no. 13/14.

* Hammel states 52 children; Hammel, *Souviens-toi d'Amalek*, 10. However, Ernest Stock, a child at the time, states 80 in his memoirs; Stock, *Tricontinental Jew*, 27.

** Andrée Salomon states in her 1965 interview (e) that a total of 100 children came to the Strasbourg area, and later 50 independent children, for a total of 150. A contemporaneous source, an article in *La Tribune Juive*, July 28, 1939, no. 30, states that the Central Fund for the East was caring for 90 children total as of July 28, 1939.

Table 2. US COMM Transports from Europe to the United States, 1941–1943

Transport Number	Departure Date, Europe	Arrival Date, United States	Number	Name of Ship
1.	June 10, 1941 (from Lisbon, left May 31 from France)	June 21, 1941	119 (a) (100 USCOM, 8 GJCA, 11 individual visas)	*Mouzinho*
2.	August 20, 1941 (from Lisbon)	September 2, 1941*	53 (b) (46 USCOM, 7 GJCA)	*Mouzinho*
3.	September 9, 1941 (from Lisbon)	September 24, 1941	51 (b)	*Serpa Pinto*
4.	May 14, 1942 (from Marseille to Casablanca)	June 25, 1942 (in New York)	50 USCOM (c) (27 Jewish children, 23 Spanish refugee children)	*Serpa Pinto* (via Casablanca)
5.	1st week of July 1942 (Marseille to Oran, Algeria, then by train to Casablanca)	July 30, 1942 (in Baltimore)	32–5 USCOM (d, f) (15–18 Jewish children, 17 Spanish refugee children)	*Nyassa*
6.	December 1942 from Lisbon**	January 1943	31 (e)	
7.	Lisbon, departure date unknown	March 13, 1943	21 (d)	*Serpa Pinto*
8.	Lisbon, departure date unknown	April 30, 1943	35 (d, e)	
9.	Lisbon, departure date unknown	June 22, 1943 (in Philadelphia)	21 (d)	
	Approximate Total		**414–16***	

Sources: (a) YIVO, GJCA, RG 249, File 290; (b) YIVO, GJCA, RG 249, File 481; (c) YIVO, GJCA, RG 249, File 483; (d) YIVO, OTC, RG 1941, Folder 119; (e) Ostrovsky, "We Are Standing By," 244; (f) Fernandez and Llerandi, *We Came Alone*, 222.

* Arrival photographed by Roman Vishniac.

** Left the United States on November 7, 1942, with the expectation of evacuating hundreds of children, who were denied exit visas.

*** This figure includes only *some* of the children who were included in USCOM transports, but who had an individual visa.

Notes

Introduction

1. Jacques Fein papers, OSE 50th Reunion Video, 1989. The reunion took place in Los Angeles on March 25–26, 1989.
2. Deborah Dwork, *Children with a Star: Jewish Youth in Nazi Europe* (New Haven, CT and London: Yale University Press, 1991), xxxiii. Dwork bases this figure on a 1946 report of the Union OSE, which estimated there were 1.6 million children under 16 in Europe before the war and 175,000 present in its aftermath, including 30,000 children repatriated from the Soviet Union to Poland and Romania. For a critical discussion of these figures, see Rebecca Clifford, *Survivors: Children's Lives after the Holocaust* (New Haven, CT and London: Yale University Press, 2020), 5–7. In this book, I use the term "Holocaust" in accordance with the most common practices in English language histories of this period. However, I am fully aware of its problematic etymology.
3. Henry D. Schuster, "Kinder Transport," in Phillip K. Jason and Iris Posner (eds.), *Don't Wave Goodbye: The Children's Flight from Nazi Persecution to American Freedom* (Westport, CT: Praeger, 2004), 20–3; Henry D. Schuster and Caroline A. Orzes, *Abraham's Son: The Making of an American* (Baltimore, MD: Publish America, 2010).
4. On OSE in France during the Holocaust, see Hillel J. Kieval, "Legality and Resistance in Vichy France: The Rescue of Jewish Children," *Proceedings of the American Philosophical Society*, 124, no. 5 (1980), 339–66; Sabine Zeitoun, *L'Œuvre de secours aux enfants (OSE) sous l'Occupation en France* (Paris: L'Harmattan, 1990); Martine Lemalet (ed.), *Au secours des enfants du siècle* (Paris: Seuil, 1993); Katy Hazan and Serge Klarsfeld, *Le sauvetage des enfants juifs pendant l'Occupation, dans les maisons de l'OSE, 1938–1945* (Paris: OSE/Somogy éditions d'art, 2008); Sabine Zeitoun, *Histoire de l'OSE: De la Russie tsariste à l'Occupation en France, 1912–1944: L'Œuvre de secours aux enfants, du légalisme à la résistance* (Paris: L'Harmattan, 2012). On its global history, see Laura Hobson Faure, Mathias Gardet, Katy Hazan, and Catherine Nicault (eds.), *L'Œuvre de secours aux enfants et les populations juives au XXe siècle: Prévenir et guérir dans un siècle de violences* (Paris: Armand Colin, 2014).

5. My numbers, based on my database, differ somewhat from Kathryn Close, *Transplanted Children: A History* (New York: USCOM, 1953), 27. The transports continued after 1942 from Portugal.

6. YIVO Institute for Jewish Research (YIVO), One Thousand Children (OTC) Collection, RG 194, Folder 3, Unpublished Memoirs by H. Schuster, 30. YIVO, OTC, RG 1941, Folder 3, Unsigned Letter from K. Schuster to Annelise Thieman, AFSC, February 10, 1941.

7. A Google Books Ngram analysis shows the term "Holocaust hero" emerging in 1977, with an exponential rise in since 2010. Even a cursory look at titles on Holocaust rescue shows the tendency to frame it in heroic terms: Samuel P. Oliner, "The Unsung Heroes in Nazi Occupied Europe: The Antidote for Evil," *Nationalities Papers*, XII, 1 (Spring 1984), 129–36; Martin Gilbert, *The Righteous: The Unsung Heroes of the Holocaust* (London: Doubleday, 2002); Mordecai Paldiel, *Diplomat Heroes of the Holocaust* (Jersey City, NJ: Ktav, 2007). On the emergence of the "Righteous rescue narrative," see Yu Wang, "The Witness-Scholars of the Holocaust and their Righteous Rescue Narratives (late 1970s–early 1990s)" (PhD Dissertation, University of Toronto, 2022). For a critical analysis of the emergence of the Righteous Among the Nations category, see Sarah Gensburger, *Les Justes de France: Politiques publiques de la mémoire* (Paris: Presses de Sciences Po, 2010).

8. In its praise of courageous individuals, rescue provides contemporary European societies a way to talk about the Holocaust without confronting state and societal complicity in genocide, shifting the focus to a more positive, feel-good narrative. In France, from where I write, one often hears (and not without pride) that "75 per cent" of Jews survived the Holocaust, ignoring the fact that 25 per cent were murdered and, more significantly, that historians really do not know how many Jews were living in occupied France when the deportations began in 1942, which prevents us from determining an accurate percentage. On the current debates, Robert Paxton, "Jews: How Vichy Made It Worse," *The New York Review of Books*, March 6, 2014; Robert Gildea, "Jacques Sémelin and the French Recovery of Righteousness," *Shofar: An Interdisciplinary Journal of Jewish Studies*, 39, no. 2 (2021), 246–56. For observations on the UK, see Tony Kushner, *Remembering Refugees Then and Now* (Manchester: Manchester University Press, 2006), 141–80. More generally, see Natalia Aleksiun, Raphael Utz, and Zofia Woycicka (eds.), *The Rescue Turn and the Politics of Holocaust Memory* (Detroit, MI: Wayne State University Press, 2023), especially Sarah Gensburger's contribution, "Bringing the State Back into Memory Studies: Commemorating the Righteous in France, 2007–20," in Aleksiun et al. (eds.), *The Rescue Turn*, 143–65.

9. As Mark Roseman writes, "As a subject of scholarship, rescue has until recently been the preserve of psychologists, ethicists and to a smaller extent, social scientists." Mark Roseman, *Lives Reclaimed: A Story of Rescue and Resistance in Nazi Germany* (New York: Metropolitan Books, 2019), 7. For an overview of the historiography, see Roy Koepp, "Holocaust Rescuers in Historical and Academic Scholarship," in Gerald Steinacher and Ari Kohen (eds.), *Unlikely Heroes: The Place of Holocaust Rescuers in Research and Teaching* (Omaha, NE: University of Nebraska Press, 2019), 15–36; Bob Moore, *Survivors: Jewish Self-Help and Rescue in Nazi-Occupied Europe* (Oxford and New York: Oxford University Press, 2010), 5–8. For an example of the individual approach to rescuers, see Samuel and Pearl

Oliner, *The Altruistic Personality: Rescuers of Jews in Nazi Germany* (New York: The Free Press, 1988). An excellent example of a historical approach to rescue: Laura Brade and Rose Holmes, "Troublesome Sainthood: Nicholas Winton and the Contested History of Child Rescue in Prague, 1938–1940," *History & Memory*, 29, no. 1 (2017), 3–40.

10. Hannah Arendt states, "Of all European peoples, the Jews had been the only one without a state of their own and had been, precisely for this reason, so eager and so suitable for alliances with governments and states as such, no matter what these governments and states might represent. On the other hand, the Jews had no political tradition or experience, and were as little aware of the tension between society and state as they were of the obvious risks and power possibilities of their new role." Hannah Arendt, *Antisemitism: Part One of The Origins of Totalitarianism* (New York: Harcourt, Brace and World, [1951] 1968), 23.

11. Yerushalmi builds on Salo Baron's work on the royal alliance. Yosef Hayim Yerushalmi, *Serviteurs du roi et non serviteurs des serviteurs* (Paris: Allia, 2011).

12. Claire Andrieu, "Sauvetages dans l'Europe allemande," in Alya Aglan and Robert Frank (eds.), *1937–1947: La Guerre-Monde. Tome II* (Paris: Gallimard, 2015), 1821–67; *Tombés du ciel: Le sort des pilotes abattus en Europe, 1939–1945* (Paris: Tallandier, 2021).

13. Lucien Lazare, *La Résistance juive en France* (Paris: Stock, 1987). More recently, Moore, *Survivors*; Mordecai Paldiel, *Saving One's Own: Jewish Rescuers during the Holocaust* (Lincoln, NE: University of Nebraska Press, 2017).

14. For the sake of linguistic simplicity, I include both groups when I use the term "Jewish children." However, I seek in my analysis to explore how the children viewed themselves.

15. I am attentive to children's and parents' expressed emotions in my sources. However, while informed by the scholarship on this topic, I do not claim to be writing a history of their emotions. See Daniella Doron, "Feeling Familial Separation: Emotions, Agency, and Holocaust Refugee Youths," *Jewish Social Studies*, 28, no. 3 (2023), 1–30; Marion Kaplan, *Hitler's Jewish Refugees: Hope and Anxiety in Portugal* (New Haven, CT and London: Yale University Press, 2020); Lindsay Dodd, "Le prix de la résistance: Rupture et absence parentale dans les souvenirs de l'enfance de la Seconde Guerre mondiale," in Laura Hobson Faure, Manon Pignot, and Antoine Rivière (eds.), *Enfants en guerre: "Sans famille" dans les conflits du XXème siècle* (Paris: CNRS Éditions, 2023), 349–70.

16. Claudia Curio, "Were Unaccompanied Children a Privileged Class of Refugees in the Liberal States of Europe?," in Frank Caestecker and Bob Moore (eds.), *Refugees from Nazi Germany and the Liberal European States* (Brooklyn: Berghahn Books, 2010), 183–4; Kushner, *Remembering Refugees*, 148–9; more generally, Louise London, *Whitehall and the Jews, 1933–1948: British Immigration Policy, Jewish Refugees and the Holocaust* (Cambridge: Cambridge University Press, 2000).

17. Thank you to Alexandra Garbarini for her thought-provoking comments on this topic. On the attitudes in Great Britain on child separation, see Laura Lee Downs, "Enfance en guerre: Les évacuations d'enfants en France et en Grande-Bretagne (1939–1940)," *Annales: Histoire, Sciences Sociales*, 2 (2011), 413–48.

18. Susanne Heim, "Immigration Policy and Forced Emigration from Germany: The Situation of Jewish Children (1933–1945)," in Paul Shapiro (ed.), *Children and the Holocaust Symposium Presentations* (Washington, DC: Center for Advanced

Holocaust Studies, United States Holocaust Memorial Museum, 2004), 11. On Kindertransport to Belgium, see Walter Reed, *The Children of La Hille: Eluding Nazi Capture during World War II* (Syracuse, NY: Syracuse University Press, 2011). On the Netherlands, see Miriam Keesing's commemorative website, https://www.dokin.nl, consulted March 11, 2022.

19. Eric Jennings makes a similar point in his study on escaping Vichy in 1940–1941: Eric Jennings, *Escape from Vichy: The Refugee Exodus to the French Caribbean* (Cambridge, MA: Harvard University Press, 2018), 81. As Claire Andrieu points out, conditions throughout Nazi-occupied Europe were vastly different, as was the repression of rescuers: in Poland, rescuers of Jews were threatened with execution. In France, it appears that neither the Nazi nor Vichy authorities targeted those helping Jews. Andrieu, "Sauvetages dans l'Europe allemande," 1843–44; Patrick Cabanel, *Histoire des justes en France* (Paris: Dunod, 2024), 126–34. On the concept of rescue, see Claire Andrieu, "Conclusion: Rescue, a Notion Revised," in Jacques Sémelin, Claire Andrieu, and Sarah Gensburger (eds.), *Resisting Genocide: The Multiple Forms of Rescue* (London: Hurst, 2011), 495–506.

20. On the role in the evacuations played by the OSE, see Katy Hazan, "Le sauvetage des enfants Juifs de France vers les Amériques, 1933–1947," in Hélène Harter and André Kaspi (eds.), *Terres promises: Mélanges offerts à André Kaspi* (Paris: Publications de La Sorbonne, 2008), 481–93 and Zeitoun, *Histoire de l'OSE*, 346–62. On the USCOM, see Michal Ostrovsky, "'We Are Standing By:' Rescue Operations of the United States Committee for the Care of European Children," *Holocaust and Genocide Studies*, 29, no. 2 (Fall 2015), 230–50. On the Quakers AFSC, see Stephanie Corazza, "The Routine of Rescue: Child Welfare Workers and the Holocaust in France" (PhD Dissertation, University of Toronto, 2017), 38–103 and Shannon Fogg, "The American Friends Service Committee and Wartime Aid to Families," in Lindsey Dodd and David Lees (eds.), *Vichy France and Everyday Life: Confronting the Challenges of Wartime, 1939–1945* (London: Bloomsbury, 2018), 107–22 and forthcoming work. The most extensive work on the Kindertransport to the United States remains Judith Baumel-Schwartz, *Unfulfilled Promise: Rescue and Resettlement of Jewish Children in the United States, 1934–1945* (Juneau, AK: Denali Press,1990).

21. An exception: Deborah Dwork and Jan. Van Pelt, *Flight from the Reich: Refugee Jews, 1933–1946* (New York: W.W. Norton & Co., 2012), 163–84, 236–63.

22. The historiography on Jews in France during the Holocaust is too vast to enumerate here. Significant works include Jacques Adler, *The Jews of Paris and the Final Solution: Communal Response and Internal Conflicts, 1940–1944* (New York and Oxford: Oxford University Press, 1987); Asher Cohen, *Persécutions et sauvetages: Juifs et Français sous l'Occupation et sous Vichy* (Paris: Éditions du Cerf, 1993); Susan Zuccotti, *The Holocaust, the French, and the Jews* (New York: Basic Books, 1993); Renée Poznanski, *Les Juifs en France pendant la Seconde Guerre mondiale* (Paris: Hachette Littératures, [1994] 1997), among others. Historical works on children include André Rosenberg, *Les enfants dans la Shoah: La déportation des enfants juifs et tsiganes de France* (Paris: Les Éditions de Paris, 2013); Katy Hazan, *Rire le jour, pleurer la nuit: Les enfants juifs cachés dans la Creuse pendant la guerre, 1939–1944* (Paris: Calmann-Lévy, 2014); Daniel Lee, *Pétain's Jewish Children: French Jewish Youth and the Vichy Regime, 1940–1942* (Oxford: Oxford University Press, 2014). There are many journalistic works on children, including Raphael Delpard, *Les enfants cachés* (Paris: J.-C. Lattès, 1993); Delphine Deroo, *Les enfants de la Martellière* (Paris: Grasset, 1999); Jean-Marc Parisis, *Les inoubliables* (Paris: Flammarion, 2014).

23. Among the first and most well-known, Elie Wiesel, *La nuit* (Paris: Éditions de Minuit, [1958] 2007); Saul Friedländer, *Quand vient le souvenir . . .* (Paris: Seuil, [1978] 2008); Nechama Tec, *Dry Tears: The Story of a Lost Childhood* (Westport, CT: Wildcat Pub. Co., 1982); Ruth Klüger, *Refus de témoigner: Une jeunesse* (Paris: V. Hamy, [1992] 2005); Sarah Kofman, *Rue Ordener, Rue Labat* (Lincoln, NE: University of Nebraska Press, [1994] 1996). Friedländer and Kofman discuss their experiences in France.

24. Dwork, *Children with a Star*, 59. The Izieu children's home, for example, was still open in April 1944 when a raid occurred, leading to the deportation of its children and most of its educators.

25. Dwork, *Children with a Star*, 68. On France, see 55–65, 81–109.

26. Henry Greenspan, *On Listening to Holocaust Survivors: Recounting and Life History* (Westport, CT: Praeger, 1998); Sharon Kangisser Cohen, "A Child's View: Children's Depositions of the Central Jewish Historical Commission (Poland)," in Sharon Kangisser Cohen, Eva Fogelman, and Dalia Ofer (eds.), *Children in the Holocaust and Its Aftermath: Historical and Psychological Studies of the Kerstenberg Archive* (New York: Berghahn Books, 2017), 43–61.

27. "The 'new paradigm' in childhood studies of the 1990s . . . involved far more than a call to see childhood as a social construction. A key point was the insistence that children be seen as active in determining their own lives and the lives of those around them." Colin Heywood, *A History of Childhood: Children and Childhood in the West from Medieval to Modern Times* (Cambridge: Polity Press, 2009), 359.

28. Notably, historian Philip Friedman sought to set a research agenda on the breadth of Jewish experiences during the Holocaust that was not limited to Jews' victimization. Laura Jockusch, *Collect and Record!: Jewish Holocaust Documentation in Early Postwar Europe* (New York: Oxford University Press, 2012), 169–73; Roni Stauber, *Laying the Foundations for Holocaust Research: The Impact of the Historian Philip Friedman* (Jerusalem: Yad Vashem, 2009), 37; Natalia Aleksiun, "An Invisible Web: Philip Friedman and the Network of Holocaust Research," in Regina Fritz, Éva Kovács, and Béla Rásky (eds.), *Before the Holocaust had its Name: Early Confrontations of the Nazi Mass Murder of the Jews* (Vienna: New Academic Press, 2016) 149–65.

29. "The 'History of the Holocaust' cannot be limited only to a recounting of German policies, decisions, and measures that led to this most systematic and sustained of genocides; it must include the reactions (and at times the initiatives) of the surrounding world and the attitudes of the victims, for the fundamental reason that the events we call the Holocaust represent a totality defined by this very convergence of distinct elements." Saul Friedländer, *The Years of Extermination: Nazi Germany and the Jews, 1939–1945* (New York: HarperCollins, 2007), xi; Saul Friedländer, *Nazi Germany and the Jews, Volume One: Years of Persecution (1933–1939)* (New York: HarperCollins, 1997). See also Yehuda Bauer, *Rethinking the Holocaust* (New Haven, CT and London: Yale University Press, 2001), 112–18. One should note that both Marion Kaplan and Renée Poznanski wrote significant works based on perpetrator and survivor sources before this publication: Marion Kaplan, *Between Dignity and Despair: Jewish Life in Nazi Germany* (New York: Oxford University Press, 1998); Poznanski, *Les Juifs en France*.

30. See also Joanna Michlic's important contributions, including "Mixed Lessons from the Holocaust: Avoiding Complexities and Darker Aspects of Jewish Child Survivors' Life Experiences," *Journal of the History of Children and Youth*, 17, no. 2 (2024), 272–86 and " 'The War Began for Me After the War': Jewish Children

in Poland, 1945–1949," in Jonathan C. Friedman (ed.), *The Routledge History of the Holocaust* (New York: Routledge, 2012), 484–99.

31. On Jewish children in the postwar period in France, see Katy Hazan, *Les orphelins de la Shoah: Les maisons de l'espoir, 1944–1960* (Paris: Belles Lettres, 2000); Daniella Doron, *Jewish Youth and Identity in Postwar France: Rebuilding Family and Nation* (Bloomington and Indianapolis, IN: Indiana University Press, 2015); more generally, see Ivan Jablonka, *L'Enfant-Shoah* (Paris: Presses Universitaires de France, 2014) and Clifford, *Survivors*.

32. He does not state where this practice began. It may date from Frankfurt, where the directors referred to themselves as mother or father, or auntie. Schuster, *Abraham's Son*, 198.

33. International Institute of Social History (IISG), Ernst Papanek Collection, File F-22, Letter from Renée Eisenberg (née Spindel) to Ernst Papanek, July 11, 1956.

34. Elfriede Schloss papers, "We are Growing," c.1979. IISG, Ernst Papanek Collection, File F-22, Letter from Henry Schuster to Dr. Lene Papanek, July 25, 1978. This letter shows he was in contact with three other children that accompanied him from Frankfurt to France.

35. IISG, Ernst Papanek papers, File H-2, Reunion Photo Album, Gabriella Kaplan, "Children of Special Blessing: 200 Youngsters were taken from Nazi Europe and Reunited Here 50 years Later," *The Jewish Journal* (May 12–18, 1989).

36. William Sewell, *Logics of History: Social Theory and Social Transformation* (Chicago, IL: University of Chicago Press, 2009), 175–81.

37. Greenspan, *On Listening to Holocaust Survivors*.

38. Laura Hobson Faure, *A "Jewish Marshall Plan": The American Jewish Presence in Post-Holocaust France* (Bloomington, IN: Indiana University Press, 2022).

39. On this essential issue, see Carlo Ginzburg, "Just One Witness," in Saul Friedländer (ed.), *Probing the Limits of Representation: Nazism and the Final Solution* (Cambridge, MA: Harvard University Press, 1992), 82–96.

40. Hanna Papanek, "Exile or Emigration: What Shall We Tell the Children?," in Viktoria Hertling (ed.), *Mit Den Augen Eines Kindes: Children in the Holocaust. Children in Exile. Children under Fascism* (Amsterdam and Atlanta: Rodopi, 1998), 220–36; Hanna Papanek, "Quatre enfants à Montintin: Mémoire et histoire, 1940–42," in Pascal Plas and Michel Kiener (eds.), *Enfances juives: Limousin-Dordogne-Berry, terres de refuge, 1939–1945* (Saint-Paul: Souny, 2006), 386–402; Inge Hansen-Schaberg, Hanna Papanek, and Gabriele Rühl-Nawabi, *Ernst Papanek. Pädagogische und therapeutische Arbeit: Kinder mit Verfolgungs-, Flucht- und Exilerfahrungen während der NS-Zeit* (Wien: Böhlau Verlag, 2015).

41. Papanek wrote this important work in English, yet it remains unpublished in this language. Instead, she had it translated and published in her native German in 2006; Hanna Papanek, *Elly und Alexander: Revolution, Rotes Berlin, Flucht, Exil— eine sozialistische Familiengeschichte* (Berlin: Vorwärts-Buch Verl.-Ges, 2006). Papanek shared the unpublished English manuscript with me in December 2014. All page numbers provided correspond to the unpublished English version.

42. Papanek, *Elly und Alexander*, 12.

Chapter 1

1. The Israelitisches Waisenhaus Frankfurt was established in 1874. Helga Krohn, *Vor Den Nazis gerettet – Eine Hilfsaktion für Frankfurter Kinder 1939/1940:*

Schriftenreihe des Jüdischen Museums Frankfurt am Main Band 3 (Stuttgart: Jüdisches Museum Jan. Thorbecke Verlag, 1995).

2. Oral history interview (hereafter interview) with Elfriede Meyer Schloss, San Diego, California, December 17, 2016. Henry Schuster echoes this idea in his memoirs: "A kind and loving person, we loved Rosa Marks as much as we loved Isador [sic]. She was our surrogate mother, our mom away from home for those of us who had a living mother, and a real live mom for those of us whose mothers were deceased." Schuster, *Abraham's Son*, 71.

3. Chris Webb and Terry Nichols, "Frankfurt am Main: The City and the Holocaust," Holocaust Education & Archive Research Team, http://www.holocaustresearch-project.org/nazioccupation/frankfurt.html, consulted December 11, 2017.

4. This movement developed in Germany in the 1850s. Hirsch advocated for "Torah im Deretz Eretz" (Torah with the way of the world), a strict adherence to Jewish law and belief in the divine origin of the texts, yet at the same time, participation in surrounding society; Michael Brenner, *A Short History of the Jews* (Princeton, NJ: Princeton University Press, 2010), 202–3.

5. On Shabbat at the orphanage, Schuster, *Abraham's Son*, 70–1.

6. YIVO, GJCA Collection (RG 249), Casefile: Elfriede Meyer.

7. YIVO, GJCA Collection (RG 249), Casefile: Elfriede Meyer. Letter from the Welfare Office of the Representation of Jews in Germany to GJCA, NY, October 25, 1938.

8. Renée Poznanski suggests that class privilege was not a determining factor in resistance or flight. On the contrary, Eastern European Jews in France had a more suspicious view of the state, favoring early resistance. Renée Poznanski, "A Methodological Approach to the Study of Jewish Resistance in France," *Yad Vashem Studies*, XVIII (1987), 1–39.

9. Kaplan, *Between Dignity and Despair*, 116. In the United States, for example, three different initiatives to evacuate children emerged in 1933. They merged in 1934, creating the German Jewish Children's Aid, which will be explored fully in Chapter 11. See also Baumel-Schwartz, *Unfulfilled Promise*.

10. Reichsgesetzblatt N.43, April 26, 1933, Paragraph 4, limited the presence of "non-Aryan" Germans in schools, colleges and universities to 1.5 per cent of the number of "Aryan" students. American Jewish Committee, *The Jews in Nazi Germany: A Factual Record of their Persecution by the National Socialists* (New York, 1933), 6; Kaplan, *Between Dignity and Despair*, 94–103. On the Youth Aliyah program to evacuate Jewish youth from Nazi Germany, see Erica Simmons, *Hadassah and the Zionist Project* (Lanham: Rowman & Littlefield, 2006), 115–51.

11. Downs, "Enfance en guerre," 413–48.

12. Kaplan, *Between Dignity and Despair*, 119–44; Andrea Hammel, "The Future of Kindertransport Research: Archives, Diaries, Databases, Fiction," in Andrea Hammel and Bea Lewkowicz (eds.), *The Kindertransport to Britain 1938/39: New Perspectives* (Leiden: Brill, 2012), 142–3.

13. Hammel, "The Future of Kindertransport Research," 142–3. Hammel and others emphasize that Kindertransport was seen by many families as a means of family unification, involving a temporary separation. Marion Kaplan emphasizes that mothers often made this decision when their spouses were interned or abroad. Kaplan, *Between Dignity and Despair*, 116–18; Claudia Curio, "'Unsichtbare' Kinder. Emigration und Akkulturation von Kindern und Jugendlichen. Das

Beispiel Kindertransporte 1938/39" (PhD Dissertation, Technische Universität Berlin, 2005), 40–4. Many of the children in this study emphasize the role of their mothers in this decision. See, for example, Benjamin Hirsch, *Home Is Where You Find It* (Self-published, 2006), 76–85. More generally, on maternity and German Jews, see Marion Kaplan, *The Making of the Jewish Middle Class: Women, Family and Identity in Imperial Germany* (Oxford: Oxford University Press, 1991), 41–63.

14. The historiography on the November pogrom is too vast to cite here, highlighting the extreme violence unfurled against Jews in Nazi territories, including Germany, Austria, and the Czech Sudetenland. The pogrom occurred several days after the assassination of Germany's First Secretary Ernst Vom Rath in Paris by a Jewish teen, Herschel Grynszpan, whose parents had just been expulsed to Poland. Using Vom Rath's death as a justification, Nazi officials encouraged multiple forms of violence against Jewish individuals, property, and places of worship. In Germany alone, at least 91 Jews were murdered, and 30,000 Jewish men were arrested and sent to concentration camps. Figures from the USHMM Kristallnacht Bibliography, https://www.ushmm.org/collections/bibliography/kristallnacht, consulted January 4, 2023; Kaplan, *Between Dignity and Despair*, 119–44.

15. Kaplan, *Between Dignity and Despair*, 129.

16. Hirsch, *Home Is Where You Find It*, 84.

17. Stephan Lewy's memoirs were written by Lillian Herzberg, *The Past Is Always Present* (Bloomington, IN: Archway Publishing, 2015), 79–81. The Baruch Auerbach orphanage was opened in 1833 in Berlin. Its papers have been largely destroyed. Its director, Jonas Plout, escaped to England in 1939 and wrote a history of the orphanage, c.1940. Leo Baeck Institute (LBI), ME 503, Geschichte der Baruch-Auerbachschen Waisen Erziehungs-Anstalten fuer juedische Knaben und Maedchen in Berlin: anlaesslich ihres hundertjaehrigen Bestehens, c.1940.

18. Jewish Museum Berlin, Marianne Hirsch diary 2019/211/18, Gift of Marianne Philipps née Hirsch. This passage was written in August 1939.

19. Schuster, *Abraham's Son*, 82–3.

20. Schuster, *Abraham's Son*, 82–3.

21. Isidor Marx report, 1959, reproduced in Krohn, *Vor Den Nazis gerettet*, 24–5.

22. USHMM, RG 17.017, Archive of the Jewish Community of Vienna-Jerusalem Component Collection, A/W 1985 (hereafter RG 17.017), Letter from Robert Jablonski to Israelitische Kultusgemeinde, February 13, 1939.

23. Interview with Elfriede Meyer Schloss, San Diego, California, December 17, 2016.

24. On the significance Kindertransport children assigned to their belongings, see Mona Körte, "Bracelet, Hand Towel, Pocket Watch: Objects of the Last Moment in Memory and Narration," *Shofar*, 23, no. 1 (2004), 109–20.

25. Orthodox Jews do not write out the word God. Elfriede Schloss papers, memory book, c.1938–194, September 21, 1939, Maison Eaubonne, France, trans. from German.

26. Elfriede Schloss papers, memory book, c.1938–1941. From Lia Apfel, on September 21, 1939.

27. Clifford, *Survivors*, 4.

28. Werner Dreifuss papers, photo album, undated, trans. from German.

Chapter 2

1. Frédéric Chimon Hammel, *Souviens-toi d'Amalek: Témoignage sur la lutte des Juifs en France (1938–1944)* (Paris: CLKH, 1982), 10.
2. Hammel, *Souviens-toi d'Amalek*, 3–6. Ernest Stock, one of the children on the transport, states that 80 children were on the transport. Ernest Stock, *Tri-Continental Jew: A 20th Century Journey* (s.l.: Mendele Electronic Books, 2015), 27.
3. In the course of the 1920s, France also received 135,000 Russian and Armenian stateless refugees, which was a higher number than any other nation. Mary D. Lewis, *Boundaries of the Republic: Migrant Rights and the Limits of Univeralism in France, 1918–1940* (Palo Alto, CA: Stanford University Press, 2007), 158; Marie-Claude Blanc-Chaleard, *Histoire de l'immigration* (Paris: La Découverte, 2001), 22–46.
4. Lewis, *Boundaries*, 173–4; Vicki Caron, *Uneasy Asylum* (Palo Alto, CA: Stanford University Press, 1999), 13–42; Julie Fette, *Exclusions: Practicing Prejudice in French Law and Medicine, 1920–1945* (Ithaca, NY: Cornell University Press, 2012), 38–68, 108–32.
5. Roughly 40 per cent of those who fled sought refuge in France. Catherine Nicault, "L'accueil des juifs d'Europe centrale par la communauté juive française," in Karel A. Bartosek, Réné Gallissot, and Denis Peschanski (eds.), *De l'exil à la résistance: Réfugiés et immigrés d'Europe centrale en France, 1933–1945* (St Denis Paris: Presses Universitaires de Vincennes Arcantère, 1989), 54. Between 37,000 and 45,000 Jews left Germany in 1933, as well as 10,000 non-Jews. Dwork and Van Pelt, *Flight from the Reich*, 18.
6. The repression of Jews and communists in interwar Poland brought many to France, with or without papers. Didier Epelbaum, *Les enfants de papier: les Juifs de Pologne immigrés en France jusqu'en 1940* (Paris: Grasset, 2002). Ivan Jablonka provides a microhistory of the emigration from Poland to France of his own grandparents, who fled as Communists in 1937–1938. Ivan Jablonka, *Histoire des grands-parents que je n'ai pas eus: Une enquête* (Paris: Seuil, 2012), 95–126. On the cultural lives of these immigrants, see Nick Underwood, *Yiddish Paris: Staging Nation and Community in Interwar France* (Bloomington, IN: Indiana University Press, 2022).
7. Lewis, *Boundaries*, 118–54. Historians have often approached the 1930s refugee crises in a segmented fashion, treating the Jewish and Spanish crises in France separately. Integrated approaches include: Gérard Noiriel, *Réfugiés et sans-papiers: La république et le droit d'asile, XIX–XXe siècle* (Paris: Hachette, 1998); Denis Peschanski, *La France des camps: L'internement de 1938 à 1946* (Paris: Gallimard, 2002); Frank Caestecker, "Children in Twentieth Century Europe Affected by War: Historical Experiences in Giving them Refuge," in Ilse Derluyn (ed.), *Re-member: Rehabilitation, Reintegration and Reconciliation of War-affected Children* (Cambridge: Intersentia, 2012), 267–88.
8. Karen Akoka, *L'asile et l'exile: Une histoire de la distinction réfugiés-migrants* (Paris: La Découverte, 2020), 7–35; Lewis, *Boundaries*, 180–4.
9. In 1931, the French census counted 2.7 million foreigners in France (out of a general population of 41.5 million), with Italians and Poles making up the largest immigrant groups. By the time of the 1936 census, there were just under 2.2 million foreigners in France. Claire Zalc, "Les pouvoirs publics et les émigrés du

IIIe Reich en France de 1933 à 1939: Problèmes d'identité" (Master's Thesis, Université de Paris-VII, 1993), 26.

10. The 60,000 figure is based on data from organizations who assisted refugees and is problematic because not all refugees sought assistance, while others did from multiple organizations. Ruth Fabian and Corinna Coulas, *Die deutsche Emigration in Frankeich nach 1933* (Munich: KG Saur, 1978), cited by Zalc, "Les pouvoirs publics et les émigrés du IIIe Reich," 27. Vicki Caron includes Eastern Europeans in the 60,000. Caron, *Uneasy Asylum*, 305.

11. Célia Keren constituted a database indicating that at least 10,000 Spanish children, aged 5–15, were sent to France. Célia Keren, "L'évacuation et l'accueil des enfants espagnols en France: Cartographie d'une mobilisation transnationale (1936–1940)" (PhD Dissertation, École des hautes études en sciences sociales, 2014). Keren's later work uses the figure 10–15,000. Célia Keren, "Les raisons que le cœur ignore: Envoyer son enfant en France pendant la Guerre d'Espagne, 1936–1939," in Hobson Faure, Pignot, and Rivière, *Enfants en guerre*, 31–46.

12. Ralph Schor, *L'antisémitisme en France pendant les années 1930* (Brussels: Éditions Complexe, 1992), 71–81; Caron, *Uneasy Asylum*, 13–93, 268–301. On the French government's stigmatization of Jewish refugees, see Claire Zalc, "Des réfugiés aux indésirables: Les pouvoirs publics français face aux émigrés du IIIe Reich entre 1933–1939," in Éric Guichard and Gérard Noiriel (eds.), *Construction des nationalités et immigration dans la France contemporaine* (Paris: Presses de l'École Normale Supérieure, 1997), 259–73. For a new analysis of Jews' attitudes towards Nazism, see Jérémy Guedj, *Les Juifs de France et le nazisme, 1933–1939: L'histoire renversée* (Paris: Presses Universitaires de France, 2024).

13. An exception: Meredith Scott Weaver, "Republicanism on the Borders: Jewish Activism and the Refugee Crisis in Strasbourg and Nice," *Urban History* (2015), 599–617.

14. Georges Weill, "Introduction," in Andrée Salomon, Katy Hazan, Georges Weill, and Jean Salomon (eds.), *Andrée Salomon, une femme de lumière* (Paris: Fondation pour la mémoire de la Shoah/Le Manuscrit, 2011), 41–2.

15. Scott Weaver, "Republicanism on the Borders," 5; Julian Fuchs, *Toujours Prêts!: Scoutismes et mouvements de jeunesse en Alsace, 1918–1970* (Strasbourg: La Nuée Bleue, 2007), 158. Freddy Raphaël notes 30,000 Jews in Alsace and Lorraine in the early 1930s. Freddy Raphaël, *Les Juifs d'Alsace et de Lorraine de 1870 à nos jours* (Paris: Albin Michel, 2018), 110.

16. Cited in Pierre Birnbaum, *Un mythe politique: La "République juive"* (Paris: Fayard, 1988), 253–4, 356–8. More generally, see Raphaël, *Les Juifs d'Alsace et de Lorraine*, 111–19. The 1905 separation of Church and state did not apply to this region due to the Concordat.

17. Jeanne Vincler, *Communautés juives en péril: Alsace Lorraine, 1933–39* (Metz: Serpenoise, 2010), 205–13; Guedj, *Les Juifs de France et le nazisme*, 223–35 and Valeria Galimi's forthcoming book on antisemitism in 1930s France.

18. Hammel, *Souviens toi d'Amalek*, 8, trans. from French.

19. In the 1960s, she was interviewed for several Israeli oral history projects. Her deep attachment to OSE led her to donate some of her private papers to this organization, which began collecting its archives in the early 1980s, when the French branch of the organization celebrated its 50-year anniversary. This occasion prompted her to write a short account of her work. These oral and written sources became the basis of a book on Salomon. Salomon et al., *Andrée Salomon*.

20. This expression was first used by Edoardo Grendi, in 1977. Edoardo Grendi, "Micro-analisi e storia sociale," *Quaderni Storici*, no. 35 (1977), 506–20.

21. Weill, "Introduction," in Salomon et al., *Andrée Salomon*, 48. More generally, see Paula Hyman, *The Emancipation of the Jews of Alsace* (New Haven, CT and London: Yale University Press, 1991); Vicki Caron, *Between France and Germany: The Jews of Alsace-Lorraine, 1871–1918* (Stanford, CA: Stanford University Press, 1988).

22. Women such as Gaby Wolff Cohen, Ruth Lambert, and Simone Weil Lipman knew Andrée Salomon from Alsace, where she recruited them for the Jewish resistance. Laura Hobson Faure, "Un 'plan Marshall juif:' La présence juive américaine en France après la Shoah, 1944–54" (PhD Dissertation, École des hautes études en sciences sociales, 2009), 306–10. See also Renée Poznanski, "Women in the French-Jewish Underground: Shield-Bearers of the Resistance?," in Dalia Ofer and Lenore J. Weitzman (eds.), *Women in the Holocaust* (New Haven, CT and London: Yale University Press, 1998), 234–52.

23. Her nephew Georges Weill provides an exceptional account of his aunt. Weill, "Introduction," 33–73. See also Georges Weill, "Andrée Salomon et le sauvetage des enfants juifs (1933–1947)," *French Politics, Culture & Society*, 30, no. 2 (2012), 89–112.

24. Avram Harmon Oral History Division (OHD), Hebrew University of Jerusalem, (27)28, Interview with A.S. by Ms. R. Bannit, 1965, 14.

25. OHD, (27)28, Interview with A.S. by Ms. R. Bannit, 1965. The recording is available at https://www.youtube.com/watch?v=U_8iQRLC230, consulted February 19, 2018; Two other dates, 1924 and 1923, are provided by Weill, "Introduction," 12, 44.

26. Several examples include André Spire, *Quelques juifs et demi-juifs* (Paris: Grasset, 1928); Edmond Fleg, *Pourquoi je suis Juif* (Paris: Les Éditions de France, 1928); Catherine Fhima, "Au cœur de la 'renaissance juive' des années 1920: Littérature et judéité," *Archives Juives: Revue d'histoire des Juifs de France*, 39, no. 1 (2006), 29–45; Nadia Malinovich, *French and Jewish: Culture and the Politics of Identity in Early Twentieth-Century France* (Liverpool: Littman Library of Jewish Civilization, 2007); and Sally Charnow, *Edmond Fleg and Jewish Minority Culture in Twentieth-Century France* (Milton Park: Routledge, 2021).

27. Maurice Barrès included Jews in his book, *Les diverses familles spirituelles de France* (Paris: Émile Paul Frères, 1917).

28. A great deal has been written on Jewish youth movements in France. See Paula Hyman, *From Dreyfus to Vichy: The Remaking of French Jewry, 1906–1939* (New York: Columbia University Press, 1979), 179–98; Malinovich, *French and Jewish*, 116–38; Lee, *Pétain's Jewish Children*, 34–43. On the role of Edmond Fleg in theorizing new forms of Jewish identity, see Charnow, *Edmond Fleg*, 85–117.

29. The national organization Éclaireurs Israélites de France was established by Robert Gamzon in Paris in 1923. The Strasbourg branch, after some resistance, affiliated with the national structure in Paris. On Jewish youth movements in interwar Strasbourg, see Erin Corber, "The Kids on Oberlin Street: Place, Space and Jewish Community in Late Interwar Strasbourg," *Urban History*, 43, no. 4 (2016), 581–98; Fuchs, *Toujours Prêts!*, 57–8.

30. Weill, "Introduction," 46.

31. The multiplicity of actions initiated in France on behalf of German Jewish youth from 1933 to 1939 requires far greater attention. Scholarship has focused on

efforts to bring German youth to France in preparation for emigration to Palestine. Organized by the Hehaloutz movement, agricultural training centers, or *hachsharot*, were a means of providing temporary visas to German youth; such programs began in 1933 and continued throughout the war. Nicault shows there were 4 *hachsharot* in France from June 1933 to 1935, after which date there were 7. Approximately 624 German Jews were sent to Palestine via France from them, in the period between 1933 and 1939. Archives Nationals (AN), F7/16079, Réfugiés israélites, Rapport, Directeur des renseignements généraux à Monsieur le Préfet de Police, May 11, 1934. The many lists available in these files show the youth were in their late teens and early twenties. On France, Catherine Nicault, "L'émigration de France vers la Palestine, 1880–1940," *Archives Juives: Revue d'histoire des Juifs de France*, 41, no. 2 (2008), 19, 10–33; Anne Grynberg, "Un Kibboutz en Corrèze," *Les cahiers du Judaïsme*, 30 (2011), 89–103; Vincler, *Communautés juives*, 117–204. More generally, see Simmons, *Hadassah and the Zionist Project*, 115–51.

32. OHD, (27)28, Interview with A.S. by Ms. R. Bannit, 1965.

33. Born in 1875, she established the Jewish Girls' Home in 1908, where Andrée Salomon lived between 1923 and 1931. Weil and Fanny Schwab (born in 1898) remained active in Jewish life during the occupation, helping the Jewish populations evacuated from Alsace in 1939 through their Œuvres d'aide sociale israélite aux populations évacuées d'Alsace et de Lorraine and rescuing children. Joseph Weill, "Laure Weil (1875–1952)," consulted December 20, 2017, http://judaisme.sdv.fr/today/laurew/biog.htm; Jean Daltroff, "Fanny Schwab (1989–1991): Une vie au service des autres," http://judaisme.sdv.fr/today/laurew/fanny.htm, consulted December 20, 2017. See also Fanny Schwab, *Laure Weil: Sa vie, son œuvre* (Strasbourg: Home Laure Weil, 1969).

34. AN, F7/16079, Correspondance avec les Services d'Alsace-Lorraine, Lettre du préfet du département du Bas-Rhin au Ministre de l'Intérieur, December 1, 1933; Lettre du Ministre des Affaires étrangères au Ministre de l'Intérieur, January 16, 1934. It is unclear what happened to the young women after this decision. See also Meredith Scott Weaver, "Lobbyists and Humanitarians: French Jewish Activism in Interwar Strasbourg, Nice, and Paris, 1919–1939" (PhD Dissertation, University of Delaware, 2012), 232–5.

35. Scott Weaver, "Lobbyists and Humanitarians," 232 and "Republicanism on the Borders," 13.

36. Salomon dates the creation of this committee to the arrival of the first refugees in 1933; however, the Central Fund for the East was established in early 1937, according to *La Tribune Juive*, January 20, 1939 and June 2, 1939. It was considered a branch of the CAR and received a generous budget from JDC; OHD, (27)28, Interview with A.S. by Ms. R. Bannit, 1965, 16.

37. Mémorial de la Shoah, Oppenheimer collection (1650), Letter from Marc Haguenau to Rabbi René Hirschler, March 21, 1938, trans. from French.

38. According to Erin Corber, this moment of crisis had the paradoxical effect of helping Jewish life flourish. Corber, "The Kids on Oberlin Street," 592–8. Other towns, including Paris (1936) and Mulhouse, created similar structures in the same period. See Lee, *Pétain's Jewish Children*, 34–43; Alain Hirschler, *Grand Rabbin résistant: René Hirschler, 1905–1945, mon père* (Paris: Éditions Caractères, 2016).

39. See forthcoming work by Renée Poznanski, *Repenser la résistance des Juifs en France*, and Lazare, *La Résistance juive en France*.

40. At this moment, Rabbi Hirschler was rabbi of Mulhouse. Soon after, in June 1939, he was promoted to *Grand Rabbin* of Strasbourg and the Lower Rhin. Both he and his wife perished in deportation. "René Hirschler, 1905–1945," http://judaisme.sdv.fr/histoire/rabbins/hirschl/hirschl.htm, consulted December 20, 2017. There are several collections of his correspondence, including the René Hirschler collection at YIVO, which covers the period spanning from March to December 1943 when he worked as head of the General chaplaincy (RG221).

41. OHD, (27)28, Interview with A.S. by Ms. R. Bannit, 1965, 18.

42. OHD, (27)28, Interview with A.S. by Ms. R. Bannit, 1965, 18.

43. AN, F7/16080, Letter from le Préfet du département du Bas-Rhin à (illegible), Direction Générale des Services d'Alsace et de Lorraine, February 8, 1939. This letter states that 53 children were granted visas and entered on December 6, 1938. A second request was made to allow another 40 children entry, which was pending in February 1939.

44. Mémorial de la Shoah, Oppenheimer Collection, 1650.

45. I searched in multiple collections at the Archives Nationales and in the Departmental archives of the Lower Rhin (98AL Fonds Valot, 1925–40), but was unable to find a trace of the decision of the Lower Rhin Prefecture to grant visas to 52 Jewish children. I also did research at the Archives diplomatiques in La Courneuve, which did not yield results, as well as in Nantes, where the consular records, containing visa requests from Germany and Austria, were being treated and closed to the public.

46. A.S., "Un groupe d'enfants de la région de Francfort est venu en France," *La Tribune Juive*, December 9, 1939.

47. Future research should explore the place(s) accorded to women in the French Jewish press. Articles in *La Tribune Juive* are rarely signed with full names, making it hard to determine whether Salomon was a rare female writer or not.

48. Hammel, *Souviens-toi d'Amalek*, 10. OHD, (27)28, Interview with A.S. by Ms. R. Bannit, 1965, 19–20.

49. *La Tribune Juive*, May 5, 1939.

50. On the placement policies for the children, see *La Tribune Juive*, May 5, 1939.

51. Cohn, originally from Strasbourg, was running the École Maïmonide in Paris and was in contact with Andrée Salomon. Salomon et al., *Andrée Salomon*, 88. On the École Maïmonide, see Joseph Voignac, *Juive et républicaine: l'École Maïmonide* (Paris: Éditions l'Antilope, 2022).

52. Hirsch, *Home Is Where You Find It*, 32–3.

53. On Ernest Stock, see Hammel, *Souviens-toi d'Amalek*, 3–6; Georges Weill, "Introduction," 55–6; OHD, (27)28, Interview with A.S. by Ms. R. Bannit, 1965. See also his own account, Stock, *Tri-Continental Jew*, 42–59.

54. AN, F7/16080, Letter from le Préfet du département du Bas-Rhin à (illegible), Direction Générale des Services d'Alsace et de Lorraine, February 8, 1939. OHD, (27)28, Interview with A.S. by Ms. R. Bannit, 1965, 23.

55. Salomon's passport shows stamps on the dates January 12, April 26, July 7 and 17, 1939. Salomon et al., *Andrée Salomon*, 52. OHD (27)28, Interview with A.S. by Ms. R. Bannit, 1965, 26. USHMM, RG 17.017, Letter from Robert Jablonski to Israelitische Kultusgemeinde, February 13, 1939. The family link between Isidor and Sigmund Marx is confirmed in Eric Green (aka Erich Grünebaum, aka Elizar Bar Yona), "The Loneliest Boy," 2000, https://archive.org/details/loneliestboy/page/n1/mode/2up, consulted February 9, 2024.

56. *La Tribune Juive*, November 25, 1938, no. 47; December 2, 1939, no. 48; December 16, 1938, no. 50; January 6, 1939, n.1.
57. *La Tribune Juive*, May 5, 1939, no. 18.

Chapter 3

1. Yerushalmi, *Serviteurs du roi*.
2. David Weinberg, *A Community on Trial* (Chicago, IL and London: University of Chicago Press, 1977), 103–47, 112–13.
3. Hyman, *From Dreyfus to Vichy*, 220–9; Nicault, "L'accueil des juifs d'Europe centrale," 53–9.
4. Hyman, *From Dreyfus to Vichy*, 221. Helbronner was deported to Auschwitz in 1943.
5. Caron, *Uneasy Asylum*, 96–7. Philippe Sands sheds light on aid provided by Christian churches to Jewish refugees, a topic that needs further research. Philippe Sands, *East West Street: On the Origins of "Genocide" and "Crimes against Humanity"* (New York: Penguin Random House, 2017), 129–30.
6. Caron, *Uneasy Asylum*, 98–101; Lewis, *Boundaries*, 123–6.
7. Vicki Caron, "Loyalties in Conflict: French Jewry and the Refugee Crisis, 1933–1935," *Leo Baeck Institute Yearbook*, 36 (1991), 305–38; Caron, *Uneasy Asylum*, 95, 103–4.
8. It is important to note that there was never a moment when the National Committee's hardline policies went uncontested. Caron, *Uneasy Asylum*, 107–8.
9. Hobson Faure, *A "Jewish Marshall Plan,"* 15–39.
10. Yehuda Bauer, *My Brother's Keeper: A History of the American Jewish Joint Distribution Committee, 1929–1939* (Philadelphia, PA: The Jewish Publication Society, 1974), 21–2, 251.
11. Between 1933 and 1936, French Jews raised almost 15 million francs (roughly $800,000). Nicault, "L'accueil des juifs d'Europe centrale," 55. During this same period, JDC contributed approximately $567,000 to French Jewish welfare. American Jewish Joint Distribution, *Catalogue*, n.d., France 1939–1944. In 1933 alone, the budget of the National Committee reached $477,000. More than one-fifth of this budget was provided by JDC, and one-third was given by Baron Robert de Rothschild: Bauer, *My Brother's Keeper*, 141; Caron, *Uneasy Asylum*, 98. The JDC Primer estimates JDC participation at 44 per cent "shortly after 1933": JDC-NY, Uncatalogued, *JDC Primer*, France-4.
12. It raised a total of £203,823, of which £10,479 (roughly $50,000) were allocated to French refugee committees: Bauer, *My Brother's Keeper*, 140.
13. For an analysis of the Popular Front refugee policy, see Caron, *Uneasy Asylum*, 117–70; Lewis, *Boundaries*, 155–87.
14. Raymond-Raoul Lambert, who had led the internal opposition, was the only member of the National Committee to serve on the new one. He was head of the Nazi-imposed Union Générale des Israélites de France (UGIF) in the southern zone until his arrest and deportation to Auschwitz. Raymond-Raoul Lambert, *Carnet d'un témoin, 1940–1943: Présenté et annoté par Richard Cohen* (Paris: Librairie Arthème Fayard, 1985).
15. Caron, *Uneasy Asylum*, 303. The leadership of the CAR included Albert Lévy and William Oualid, among others. Jefroykin was the president of the immigrant landsmanshaftn organization, Fédération des Sociétés Juives de France.

16. As also shows Robyn Muncy, who looks at American women and their work on behalf of children. Robyn Muncy, *Creating a Female Dominion in American Reform, 1890–1935* (Oxford: Oxford University Press, 1994).

17. Vincent Vilmain, "Les femmes juives françaises face à l'émancipation," *Archives Juives: Revue d'histoire des Juifs de France*, 48, no. 2 (2015), 4–10.

18. Paula Hyman, *Gender and Assimilation in Modern Jewish History: The Roles and Representation of Women* (Seattle, WA: University of Washington Press, 1995), 10–49; more generally, Kaplan, *The Making of the Jewish Middle Class*.

19. Derek J. Penslar, *Shylock's Children: Economics and Jewish Identity in Modern Europe* (Berkeley, CA: University of California Press, 2001), 190; Beth S. Wenger, "Jewish Women and Volunteerism: Beyond the Myth of Enablers," *American Jewish History*, 79, no. 1 (1989), 16–36. Other historians have criticized the notion of the third sphere, arguing that women were indeed engaging in the public sphere all along. Linda Kerber, "Separate Sphere, Female Worlds, Woman's Place: The Rhetoric of Women's History," *Journal of American History*, LXXV (1989), 9–39; Amanda Vickery, "Golden Age to Separate Spheres?: A Review of the Categories and Chronology of English Women's History," *The Historical Journal*, 36, no. 2 (1993), 383–414.

20. There were also several prominent female Jewish writers and actresses, such as the writers Eugenie Foa and later Dick May (Jeanne Weill), as well as the actress Rachel and later Sarah Bernhardt. Maurice Samuels, *The Right to Difference: French Universalism and the Jews* (Chicago, IL: University of Chicago Press, 2016), esp. 50–72.

21. A common feature in Western European synagogues were the ladies' benevolent societies, which later became known as sisterhoods, allowing women an opportunity, albeit clearly delimited, for participation in the running of synagogues. However, France remains almost absent from the historiography. Hyman, *Gender and Assimilation*, 41–4; Hyman, *The Emancipation of the Jews of Alsace*, 60–3; Penslar, *Shylock's Children*, 190–2.

22. Among the founders of the Jewish reform movement in France, one sees a strong presence of women, including Clarisse Eugène Simon and Marguerite Brandon-Salvador. Catherine Poujol, "Les débuts de l'Union Libérale Israélite (1895–1939): Le pari de moderniser le judaïsme français," *Archives Juives: Revue d'histoire des Juifs de France*, 40, no. 2 (2007), 65–81. Jewish women, as well as other feminists, embraced a political role during the Dreyfus Affair. Michelle Perrot, "Féminisme," and Florence Rochefort, "Dreyfusisme et femmes nouvelles," in V. Duclert and P. Simon-Nahum (eds.), *Les événements fondateurs: L'affaire Dreyfus* (Paris: Armand Colin, 2009), 132–9, 174–84; Juliette Marin, "'Et je crois qu'il faudra encore beaucoup d'années pour arriver à l'égalité': L'engagement des femmes d'origine juive dans la bienfaisance féministe en France (1895–1939)" (Master's Thesis, Université Paris 1 Panthéon-Sorbonne, 2024).

23. Cécile Formaglio, "Cécile Brunschvicg, femme, féministe, juive, face aux défis de l'intégration et de la neutralité religieuse," *Archives du féminisme*, no. 9 (December 2005), 29–42, http://www.archivesdufeminisme.fr/ressources-en-ligne/articles-et-comptes-rendus/articles-historiques/cecile-brunschvicg-femme-feministe-juive-face-aux-defis-lintegration-neutralite-religieuse/, consulted November 24, 2017; Cécile Formaglio, *"Féministe d'abord": Cécile Brunschvicg, 1877–1946* (Rennes: Presses Universitaires de Rennes, 2014), 185–97; Yolande Cohen, "Protestant and Jewish Philanthropies in France: The Conseil National des

Femmes Françaises (1901–1939)," *French Politics, Culture and Society*, 24, no. 1 (2006), 74–92; Yolande Cohen, "Le Conseil national des femmes françaises (1901–1939): Ses fondatrices et animatrices juives," *Archives Juives: Revue d'histoire des Juifs de France*, 44, no. 1 (2011), 83–105.

24. Formaglio, "Cécile Brunschvicg, femme," 29–42.
25. Formaglio, "Cécile Brunschvicg, femme," 29–42.
26. Weiss provides a cutting portrait of Brunschvicg in her postwar book, *Ce que femme veut: Souvenirs de la IIIè République* (Paris: Gallimard, 1946), 12–15.
27. I refer to Weiss as being of a Jewish background, without assuming that she embraced a Jewish identity. During the war she obtained a certificate of non-belonging to the Jewish race. More indicative of her identity, her funeral was conducted in a Protestant temple. Vicki Caron, "Louise Weiss," *Jewish Women: A Comprehensive Historical Encyclopedia*, March 1, 2009, https://jwa.org/encyclopedia/article/weiss-louise, consulted January 18, 2018.
28. Louise Weiss, *Souvenirs d'une enfance républicaine* (Paris: Denoël, 1937), 11.
29. Bibliothèque Nationale de France (BNF), Louise Weiss collection, NAF 17794, 281.
30. Robert Jablon, Laure Quennouëlle-Corre, and André Straus, *Politique et finance à travers l'Europe du XXe siècle* (Brussels: P. Lang, 2009), 60–1.
31. The date of their affair is not given, nor the author's source. Weiss's divorce was finalized in November 1938. Célia Bertin, *Louise Weiss* (Paris: Albin Michel, 2015), 321. According to Jacques Puyaubert, Weiss maintained a correspondence with Georges Bonnet throughout the 1920s. Jacques Puyaubert, *Georges Bonnet: Les combats d'un pacifiste* (Rennes: Presses Universitaires de Rennes, 2007), 100.
32. Louise Weiss, *Mémoires d'une européenne, Tome III (1934–1939)* (Paris: Payot, 1970), 233.
33. BNF, NAF 17794, 276.
34. Décret-loi November 12, 1938, article 25. On these policies and Bonnet's role in them, see Caron, *Uneasy Asylum,* 187–205.
35. Bonnet voted to give full powers to Pétain in July 1940 and, at the end of the war, fled France for Switzerland due to his collaboration. Inculpated by an honor court, he was excluded from the Radical party. However, Bonnet was granted a "non-lieu" and was thus able to return to France in 1950, where he renewed his political career. Puyaubert, *Georges Bonnet.* Georges Bonnet takes his own defense in *De Munich à la Guerre: Défense de la paix* (Paris: Plon, 1967) and *Dans la Tourmente, 1938–48* (Paris: Fayard, 1971).
36. See Chapter 4 for more details.
37. BNF, NAF 17794, 276.
38. Weiss, *Mémoires d'une européenne*, 248.
39. Weiss, *Mémoires d'une européenne*, 249.
40. A slightly different version of this account can be found in her notes for her memoirs. BNF, NAF 17794, 278.
41. Nathalie Lourié wrote over 25 handwritten letters in German that are extremely difficult to decipher. Her first letter indicates that she was taking over the project from Dr. Vita Stein. USHMM, RG 17.017, Letter from Nathalie Lourié to Herr Dr. (name not specified), July 15, 1938; Lilly Maier, "das Schicksal Des Arthur Kern: Eine biographische Studie zu den französischen Kindertransporten" (Master's Thesis, University of Munich, 2017), 20–3.

42. USHMM, RG 17.017, Letter from Visa Stein to Herr Dr. (not specified), July 13, 1938.

43. See a problematic yet useful source on Lourié on a genealogy website: "Natalie Lourié," Geni, https://www.geni.com/people/Natalie-Lourié/600000001905378 2305, consulted December 27, 2017. Lourié's three children were born around the turn of the century: Email correspondence with Dieter Hecht, October 4, 2017. See also Sophie Lillie, *Was einmal war: Handbuch der enteigneten Kunstsammlungen Wiens* (Vienna: Czernin Verlag, 2003), 707–8.

44. *Neue Freie Presse*, January 17, 1915, March 28, 1915, April 18, 1915; This publication lists her address as 4. Bezirk, Hegelgasse 6, Vienna.

45. She is referred to in correspondence as Frau Dr, but this may be due to her husband's status as a doctor, following Austrian epistolary traditions. I made an inquiry to the University of Vienna and they did not have any records on her. The full name of the orphanage was the Waisenhaus fuer israelitische Maedchen Charlotte Merores Itzeles, Bauernfeldgasse 40, Vienna, founded in 1904.

46. "Natalie Lourié," Geni.

47. USHMM, RG 17.017, Letter from Nathalie Lourié to Herr Dr. (name not specified), July 15, 1938.

48. USHMM, RG 17.017, Letter from Rothschild Orphanage Director M. Georges Salomon to Mme. Lourié, July 16, 1938.

49. USHMM, RG 17.017, Letter from M. Berril (illegible) to Mme. Lourié, July 26, 1938. USHMM, RG 17.017, Letter from (illegible) to Mme. Lowen, September 6, 1938, file 3 of 13.

50. USHMM, RG 17.017, Letter from Georges Salomon, head of Rothschild Orphanage Paris, to Dr. Lowenfeld, Director of the Merores Orphanage, August 12, 1938.

51. Six other girls came in December, January and February 1939, suggesting that the Baroness was able to use the 20 visas allotted to her. Elizabeth Hernandez, *La Fondation Rothschild sous l'Occupation, 1939–44* (Paris: Fondation de Rothschild, 2010), 35. For a list of the eight children, see USHMM, RG 17.017, Letter to the Consul General de France à Vienne, November 28, 1938, File 4 of 13; USHMM, RG 17.017, Letter from (no signature) to the Director of the Rothschild Orphanage, Paris, December 20, 1938. Lizzie Landau was scheduled to leave for the United States after this transport. Two of the children on the list came later, in February 1939: USHMM, RG 17.017, File 5. Letter from (no signature) to the Director of the Rothschild Orphanage, Paris, February 3, 1939. According to one of the children from the December transport, there seven children on the transport (including her), and one came later. Interview with Berta Romana Seidenstein conducted by Michaela Raggam-Blesch, Vienna, December 2, 2015.

52. Interview with Berta Romana Seidenstein conducted by Michaela Raggam-Blesch, Vienna, December 2, 2015.

53. On the lives of the French Jewish elite in the early twentieth century, see James McAuley, *The House of Fragile Things* (New Haven, CT and London: Yale University Press, 2021); Cyril Grange, *Une élite parisienne: Les familles de la grande bourgeoisie juive (1870–1939)* (Paris: CNRS Éditions, 2016); Céline Leglaive-Perani, "Donner aux féminin: Juives philanthropes en France (1830–1930)," *Archives Juives: Revue d'histoire des Juifs de France*, 48, no. 2 (2015), 11–24 and forthcoming PhD dissertation. On Jewish philanthropy in France, see Nancy L. Green, "To Give and to Receive: Philanthropy and Collective Responsibility

Among Jews in Paris, 1880–1914," in Peter Mandler (ed.), *The Uses of Charity* (Philadelphia, PA: University of Pennsylvania Press, 1990), 197–226; Hyman, *From Dreyfus to Vichy*, 115–52.

54. James de Rothschild and his descendants not only supported the Comité de bienfaisance israélite de Paris, but also developed a parallel network of philanthropy, which included the Rothschild hospital-hospice-orphanage foundation, which opened in 1852. Klaus Weber, "La philanthropie des Rothschild et la communauté juive de Paris au XIXè siècle," *Archives Juives: Revue d'histoire des Juifs de France*, 44, no. 1 (2011), 17–36; Céline Leglaive-Perani, "Le judaïsme parisien et le Comité de Bienfaisance Israélite (1830–1930)," *Archives Juives: Revue d'histoire des Juifs de France*, 44, no. 1 (2011), 41.

55. Grange, *Une élite parisienne*, 428–33. Émile Halphen, Germaine de Rothschild's father, was the brother of Louise Thérèse Deutsch de la Meurthe (née Halphen), Yvonne de Gunzbourg's mother.

56. The Halphen family, originally from Metz, settled in Paris at the end of the eighteenth century. Salomon Halphen was a jeweler and member of the Paris and Central Consistory. Grange, *Une élite Parisienne*, 23. I build here on my discussion of Germaine de Rothschild in Laura Hobson Faure, "Baroness Germaine de Rothschild," in *Shalvi/Hyman Encyclopedia of Jewish Women* (Jewish Women's Archive, February 14, 2022), https://jwa.org/encyclopedia/article/rothschild-baroness-germaine-de.

57. Jacqueline Piatigorsky, *Jump in the Waves: A Memoir* (New York: St. Martin's Press, 1988), 11.

58. Céline Leglaive shows that Jewish women had similar intentions to Jewish male philanthropists: their philanthropy was designed to assert their membership in larger society. Leglaive-Perani, "Donner au féminin."

59. Jacqueline Piatigorsky makes the point that women who married into the Rothschild family obtained more power than the female children born in the Rothschild family: "Many Rothschild girls married cousins or even uncles because the wife of a Rothschild enjoyed the importance of being a Rothschild more than did a woman with the family genes, who married an outsider." Piatigorsky, *Jump in the Waves*, 149–50.

60. Grange, *Une élite parisienne*, 429.

61. Mémoires de Louise Halphen Fould, cited in Grange, *Une élite parisienne*, 429.

62. This idea requires further exploration, since Louise Halphen may have also been giving to Jewish organizations, just as her daughter may have given to non-Jewish causes.

63. She authored two books, on Bernard Palissy and Luigi Boccherini; Germaine de Rothschild, *Bernard Palissy et son école* (Paris: Au Pont des Arts, 1952) and *Luigi Boccherini, sa vie, son œuvre* (Paris: Plon, 1962).

64. Piatigorsky, *Jump in the Waves*, 6.

65. Guy de Rothschild, *Whims of Fortune: The Memoirs of Guy de Rothschild* (New York: Random House, 1985), 44.

66. Mémorial de la Shoah, Werner Matzdorff Collection (1528), Box 1, Interview with Robert Jablon, 1991; OHD (27)28, Interview with A.S. by Ms. R. Bannit, 1965, 24.

67. Jablon, Quennouëlle-Corre, and Straus, *Politique et finance*, 65.

68. USHMM, RG 17.017, Letter from M. Berril (illegible) to Mme. Lourié, July 26, 1938; OHD (27)28, Interview with A.S. by Ms. R. Bannit, 1965, 24.

69. Étienne Pénard, "Le 'peuple du livre' à l'épreuve du 'judaïsme du muscle': Les communautés juives de France et le sport (fin XIXe–1948)" (PhD Dissertation, Université Rennes 2, 2020), 200–5.

70. USHMM, RG 17.017, Letter from Nathalie Lourié to Herr Dr. (no name), July 15, 1938. I have found no trace of this migration in my research, which may be due to the lack of archives.

71. AIU, Central Committee Minutes, Central Committee, December 21, 1938. It appears that this was requested of the Minister of the Interior, Sarraut.

72. The archives do not contain 1938, but the following years show their correspondence on their respective wards. Rothschild Archive Waddesdon Manor, Correspondence Germaine de Rothschild and Dorothy (née Pinto) de Rothschild, 1939–40, JDR2/15/13. The refugee children at Waddesdon were not from the same Frankfurt orphanage as the those in Chapter 2 who went to Strasbourg. The "Cedar Boys," as they came to be called, were students of the Philantropin who boarded at an boy's home run by Lili and Hugo Steinhardt. Jon Nordheimer, "15 Who Fled the Nazis as Boys Hold a Reunion," *The New York Times*, July 28, 1983.

73. Her grandson, Peter Hablan, was unaware of his grandmother's philanthropic work on behalf of Jewish children. The letters Yvonne exchanged with her family during the Second World War have not been made available to me. Telephone interview with Peter Halban, April 18, 2017; Interview, London, June 24, 2022.

74. The Deutsch de la Meurthe family came to Paris from Alsace in 1843. Grange, *Une élite parisienne*, 92–5. The Gunzburgs added an O to their last name in France, becoming the Gunzbourg family. Grange, *Une élite parisienne*, 37–40. The four children were Philippe, Béatrice, Cyrille, and Aline de Gunzbourg. On this family, see Lorraine de Meaux, *Une grande famille russe, les Gunzburg: Paris–Saint-Pétersbourg, XIXe–XXe siècle* (Paris: Perrin, 2018).

75. The idea behind this organization was that by reforming Jewish society from within and changing Jews' economic position, there could be a solution to modern antisemitism. Penslar, *Shylock's Children*, 205–16, 225–32. ORT functioned exclusively in the Russian Empire until 1919, when it expanded its work to Latvia, Poland, Romania, and Lithuania. In August 1921, the World ORT Union was established in Berlin to manage its various branches. JDC-NY, AR 33–44, Folder #323, Untitled report on ORT, n.d. Item ID 434309.

76. JDC-NY, AR 33–44, Folder #323, Untitled report on ORT, n.d. Item ID 434309.

77. OSE used several names at this time in France. Zeitoun, *Histoire de l'OSE*, 109. For the sake of simplicity, I will use the name OSE in this book, since the leadership for the French section and the Union OSE was the same in the late 1930s. It was only after the Second World War that the name "Œuvre de secours aux enfants" was adopted to fit the OSE acronym. Samuel Boussion, "A la croisée des réseaux transtationaux de protection de l'enfance: L'OSE et les communautés d'enfants de l'après-guerre," in Hobson Faure et al. (eds.), *L'Œuvre de secours aux enfants et les populations juives*, 188. Rakefet Zalashik, "De l'est vers l'ouest: Déménagements, expansion, évolutions structurelles de l'OZE-OSE (1912–1933)," in Hobson Faure et al. (eds.), *L'Œuvre de secours aux enfants et les populations juives*, 118–21. On the early days of the French branch of OSE, see Martine Lemalet, "Les comités d'accueil aux réfugiés et l'Œuvre aux Secours aux Enfants (1933–1939)," in Annette Wieviorka and Jean-Jacques Becker (eds.), *Justin Godart: Un homme dans son siècle (1871–1956)* (Paris: CNRS Éditions, 2004), 87–104.

78. On the role of the Gunzbourgs, see Zeitoun, *Histoire de l'OSE*, 108–9.

79. Virginie Michel, "L'action médico-sociale de l'OSE à Paris dans les années trente," *Archives Juives: Revue d'histoire des Juifs de France*, 39, no. 1 (2006), 110–24; Zeitoun, *Histoire de l'OSE*, 138.
80. Zeitoun, *Histoire de l'OSE*, 138.
81. One woman, Dr. Valentine Kremer, was on its central committee. Zeitoun, *Histoire de l'OSE*, 109.
82. JDC-NY, AR 1933–1945, France, file 610, OSE, December 19, 1938. Members included: Maître Raoul Aghion, M. Naoum Aronson, Professor A. Besredka, M. Charles Breyner, Mme. Dr. A. Bass, Mme. Dr. V. Crémer, Mme. D'Esmond, Baroness Philippe Gunzbourg, Baroness Robert Gunzbourg, Baron Robert Gunzbourg, M. I. Gourevitsch, Professor Weill-Hallé, Mme. H. Hertz, M. Sam Mayer, Mme. M. Michelson, Dr. E Minkowsky, M. Joseph Millner, Mme. G. Netter, Mme. S. Perquel, M. B. Prégel, Mme. Strauss, and Dr. et Mme. L. Zadoc-Kahn. At the time, Dr. Benjamin Weill-Hallé was director of the École de Puériculture de Paris: "Benjamin Weill-Hallé (1875–1958)," http://www.histrecmed.fr/index.php?option=com_content&view=article&id=254:weill-halle-benjamin&catid=9, consulted January 31, 2018.
83. Ernst Papanek with Edward Linn, *Out of the Fire* (New York: Morrow, 1975), 44.
84. Papanek, *Out of the Fire*, 44–5.
85. The archives of the French chapter are not accessible to historians, which prevents further exploration of this question. Myriam Gattegno, "Aux pays de la croix gammée: Enfants à louer," *L'Univers Israélite*, April 14, 1939, no. 30. On the child sponsorship programs of this organization, see Yves Denechère, "Les parrainages des enfants étrangers au 20ème siècle: Une histoire des relations interpersonnelles transnationales," *Vingtième Siècle: Revue d'histoire*, 126 (2015), 147–61.
86. State Archives, Geneva, Union Internationale de Secours aux Enfants (UISE), see 92.1.10 and especially 91.18.4, Letter from Union OSE to Mlle. Morsier, February 6, 1939. OSE cancelled this request for help the next day, having found a solution.
87. State Archives, Geneva, UISE, Letter from Union OSE to UISE, February 21, 1940.
88. State Archives, Geneva, UISE. Their response was negative. Letter from UISE to Union OSE, February 29, 1940.

Chapter 4

1. Keren, "Les raisons que le cœur ignore," 31–46.
2. On the affair and its role in creating the Alliance, see David Kertzer, *The Kidnapping of Edgardo Mortara* (New York: Knopf, 1997), 250–2.
3. The historiography on the Alliance is vast. Two general histories include André Chouraqui, *L'Alliance israélite universelle et la Renaissance juive contemporaine (1860–1960): Préface de René Cassin* (Paris: Presses Universitaires de France, 1965) and, more recently, André Kaspi (ed.), *Histoire de l'Alliance israélite universelle de 1860 à nos jours* (Paris: Armand Colin, 2010). On its role in nineteenth-century French politics, see Lisa Moses Leff, *Sacred Bonds of Solidarity: The Rise of Jewish Internationalism in Nineteenth-Century France* (Palo Alto, CA: Stanford University Press, 2006). On the AIU schools, see Aron Rodrigue, *French Jews, Turkish Jews: The Alliance Israélite Universelle and the Politics of Jewish Schooling in Turkey, 1860–1925* (Bloomington and Indianapolis, IN: Indiana University Press, 1990). On its alumna networks, see Nadia Malinovich, "From the Muslim World to France and North America: A Transnational History of the Students and Teachers of the Alliance Israelite Universelle after 1945" (Habilitation à diriger des recherches, Université de Paris, 2021).

4. Frances Malino, "L'émancipation des femmes," in Kaspi, *Histoire de l'Alliance israélite*, 263–93; Elizabeth Antebi, "Changer la femme pour changer l'homme: Le modèle des institutrices de l'Alliance israélite universelle," in Sonia Sarah Lipsyc (ed.), *Femmes et judaïsme aujourd'hui: Colloque Femmes et judaïsme dans la société contemporaine* (Paris: Éditions In Press, 2008), 257–68; Frances Malino, "Prophets in Their Own Land?: Mothers and Daughters of the Alliance Israélite Universelle," *Nashim*, 3 (2000), 56–73.

5. From 1932 to 1962, Madame Fernand (Alice) Halphen was a member of the AIU's Central Committee: Grange, *Une élite Parisienne*, 408. She seems to have not attended meetings in the 1937–1939 period.

6. In 1934 and 1935, its secretary general, Jacques Bigart, and its president, Sylvain Lévi, died. The latter was replaced by Arnold Netter, who also died in 1936. Catherine Nicault, "Dans la tourmente de la Seconde Guerre mondiale, 1939–1944," in Kaspi, *Histoire de l'Alliance israélite*, 295–6 and, more generally, 295–330. This remains the most complete analysis of the AIU during this period. See also Simon Epstein, "Les institutions israélites françaises de 1929–1939: Solidarité juive et lutte contre l'antisémitisme" (PhD Dissertation, Université de la Sorbonne, 1990), 136–7 and, more generally, Chapters 4 and 5. The neutral stance of the AIU during the refugee crisis can be seen in the Archives du Ministère des Affaires étrangères, Série C. Administrative, Culte, 27CPCOM/520, Extrait du PV de la réunion commune du bureau [. . .] du comité pour la défense des droits des israélites en Europe centrale et orientale, avec le Bureau et la commission des affaires extérieures de l'Alliance israélite universelle, le mardi 24 mars, 1936; Letter from Justin Godart to Georges Leven, April 7, 1941.

7. Pierre Dreyfus (1891–1946) was actively involved in the refugee crisis through the committee he established with Maurice Vanikoff, the Comité de défence des Juifs persécutés en Allemagne, which organized a boycott of German products and offered assistance to refugees from 1933 to 1936: Epstein, "Les institutions israélites françaises," 78. Dreyfus fled to New York in 1942 and remained active in French Jewish circles. He was killed in a plane crash in 1946, returning from an inspection of Jewish orphanages in France. "Pierre Dreyfus, Prof. Alexander Pekelis Killed in Airplane Crash En Route to U.S.," *Jewish Telegraphic Agency* (JTA), December 30, 1946.

8. AIU, Central Committee Minutes, Central Committee, November 16, 1938. This quote and all others from this source trans. from French.

9. AIU, Central Committee Minutes, November 16, 1938. As Derek Penslar points out, in times of heightened antisemitism, Jews focused their philanthropic energies on vocational and agricultural training, with the hope that by changing their economic position, they would alleviate antisemitism: Penslar, *Shylock's Children*, 205–16. On the discourses on regeneration in French Jewish life, see Jay Berkovitz, *The Shaping of Jewish Identity in Nineteenth-Century France* (Detroit, MI: Wayne University Press, 1989).

10. AIU, Central Committee Minutes, December 7, 1938. Vicki Caron states that they received authorization for 1,000 children; this did not come to fruition: Caron, *Uneasy Asylum*, 308.

11. Including the Free Mason and Minister of Public Health, Marc Rucart, who was closely linked to Jewish organizations such as For Our Children and the Union OSE.

12. The minutes do not specify that the children should be placed in Jewish institutions but give only Jewish organizations as examples. This was most likely

assumed. For Our Children was established in 1930. By the late 1930s, its leadership included Jean Zay and Marc Rucart. Its secretary general was M. Midlarski. *Univers Israélite*, June 9 and June 23, 1939; more generally, Erin Corber, "L'Esprit du Corps: Bodies, Communities, and the Reconstruction of Jewish Life in France, 1914–1940" (PhD Dissertation, Indiana University, 2013), 144–94.

13. AIU, Central Committee Minutes, December 7, 1938. Committee members from Belgium, Holland, and Switzerland shared their experiences in late December. AIU, PV, Exceptional Annual Meeting, December 21, 1938.

14. *La Tribune Juive*, December 30, no. 52; USHMM, RG 17.017, Press Clipping, "Ein Aufnahmebuero Fuer Juedische Kinder," no date, File 4 of 13. The *Univers Israélite* also reported on the Bureau on December 30, 1938, noting its creation on November 16, 1938, cited in Epstein, "Les institutions israélites françaises," 119. The Alliance used several names for this structure, including "Bureau central d'accueil aux enfants" and "Comité d'accueil aux enfants."

15. *Journal officiel*, December 30, 1938, 14806. See Chapter 3 for its leadership.

16. The wording of the minutes leaves some ambiguity as to which body should be considered outside of the AIU auspices, yet most likely refers to the Ladies' Committee: "A Ladies' Committee will be formed to assist the Reception Bureau. It should, moreover, constitute an independent Committee to which the Alliance will grant its patronage, without being confused with it." AIU, Central Committee Minutes, December 7, 1938. Historian Catherine Nicault agrees with my interpretation of this sentence: Email correspondence with Catherine Nicault, February 1, 2023.

17. AIU, Central Committee Minutes, January 4, 1939.

18. AIU, Central Committee Minutes, January 4, 1939.

19. The minutes state she attended the beginning of the meeting only. AIU, Central Committee Minutes, January 4, 1939.

20. AIU, Central Committee Minutes, January 4, 1939.

21. OHD 1(20), Interview with A. Salomon in German, cited in Salomon et al., *Andrée Salomon*, 210–11.

22. *Le Matin*, November 19, 1938; Salomon et al., *Andrée Salomon*, 211–15.

23. AIU, Central Committee Minutes. I verified the minutes for the 1937–1939 period.

24. AIU, Central Committee Minutes, December 21, 1938.

25. AIU, Central Committee Minutes, January 4, 1939. This contradicts the claim Bonnet later made in his autobiography: "This influx of refugees posed serious financial questions for us. But we never opposed them to prevent their entry in France." Georges Bonnet, *Dans la tourmente: 1938–1948* (Paris: Fayard, 1971), 82.

26. JDC-NY, AR 1933–1944, France, File 610, Letter from Troper to Hyman, January 27, 1939.

27. AIU, Central Committee Minutes, December 21, 1939.

28. AIU, Central Committee Minutes, January 4, 1939.

29. AIU, Central Committee Minutes, January 4, 1939.

30. Bonnet, *Dans la tourmente*, 81–3. See Caron for a detailed portrait of Helbronner and his position on Jewish refugees in *Uneasy Asylum*, 94–116.

31. Its existence was already published in the *Journal officiel* at this point, but it had not yet conducted its first meeting, which took place on January 14, 1939. AIU, Central Committee Minutes, January 4, 1939; Caron, *Uneasy Asylum*, 494.

32. AIU, Central Committee Minutes, January 4, 1939.
33. Caron, *Uneasy Asylum*, 493–4. Correspondence with the CIE letterhead begins in February 1939 but may have existed before this date. USHMM, RG 17.017, File 7 of 13.
34. *L'Univers Israélite*, April 21, 1939, no. 31, 545. Robert Jablon states he was secretary general: Jablon, Quennouëlle-Corre, and Straus, *Politique et finance*, 60.
35. *La Tribune Juive*, January 27, 1939.
36. JDC-NY, AR 1933–1944, File 189, Report on the Situation of German and Austrian Refugees in France in January 1939. A report by Trude Frankl, a Viennese Aid worker, noted that all of OSE and CRC's efforts were centralized by the CIE. USHMM, RG 17.017, Trude Frankl Report, April 1939.
37. JDC-NY, France, 1933–44, France, File 610, Letter from Troper to Hyman, January 27, 1939.
38. Marquis de Mores et ses amis, *Rothschild, Ravachol et Cie* (Paris: 1892), http://gallica.bnf.fr/ark:/12148/bpt6k5400848j. The Rothschild Archive in London was unable to state when they acquired this property, consulted January 19, 2017.
39. Staff included Roland Assathiany and Henriette Dasse.
40. Robert Jablonski changed his name to Jablon after the Second World War. The family was in Switzerland when the First World War broke out, causing them to return to Germany, where Jablonski studied law in Fribourg and Berlin. He was a member of the Social Democratic Party (SPD) yet joined the extreme left in 1932 and, later, Neu Beginnen. He lost his job as a lawyer (*referendar*) in 1933. Jablon, Quennouëlle-Corre, and Straus, *Politique et finance*, 15–16, 59–60.
41. According to Laure Quennouëlle-Corre, who did extensive interviews with Jablon late in his life for the above-mentioned book, Jablon's syntax in French showed a strong German influence. We can thus assume he was not perceived as a native French speaker in 1939. Email correspondence with Laure Quennouëlle-Corre, January 30, 2023.
42. Jablon, Quennouëlle-Corre, and Straus, *Politique et finance*, 61. Rucart, as seen above, was already involved in Jewish organizations in the 1930s and, furthermore, seems to have been on close terms with Louise Weiss, according to Bertin, *Louise Weiss*, 241, 320–5.
43. The CRC was located at 102 rue de l'Université. The same building housed Renée de Monbrison's committee for Spanish refugees, whose papers were also looted by the Germans, captured by the Russians and returned to France. The archives of the CRC have not been located and are not in the Weiss collection at the Bibliothèque Nationale de France nor at the Louise Weiss museum in Saverne. In addition to brief mentions in the press, I found only one brochure in the Louise Weiss collection at the BNF 228438 (47) and the Felix Chevrier collection at the Mémorial de la Shoah.
44. The CRC also sought to evacuate elderly populations from Germany. Efforts to bring Jews in retirement homes, requested by Jews in Strasbourg and Bayonne, failed as well. AN, F7/16080, Letter from Amédée Bussière to the Vice-Président du Conseil, March 30, 1939. The author justified the refusal by citing security reasons.
45. USHMM, RG 17.017, Letter from Robert Jablonski to Israelitische Kultusgemeinde, February 13, 1939.
46. Jablon, Quennouëlle-Corre, and Straus, *Politique et finance*, 61–2.

47. BNF, Louise Weiss, NAF17794, 271. This quote and all others from this source trans. from French.
48. Béranger, a senator of Guadeloupe, served as France's principal delegate at the Evian conference and worked closely on refugee policy. BNF, Louise Weiss, NAF17794, 271.
49. BNF, Louise Weiss, NAF17794, 271.
50. JDC-NY, AR 1933–44, File 189, Report on the Situation of German and Austrian Refugees in France in January 1939.
51. BNF, Louise Weiss, NAF17794, 274. Undated note.
52. USHMM, RG 17.017, Letter from Robert Jablonski to Israelitische Kultusgemeinde, February 13, 1939 states the 200 visas were to be distributed by the French consulates in Vienna (100), Berlin (50), Frankfurt (10), and Mainz (40). Trude Frankl's report, in my opinion less accurate, states that there would be 100 children from Vienna, 50 from Frankfurt, and 50 from Saarpfalz. Trude Frankl Report, April 1939.
53. In Vienna, for example, the IKG registered 10,000 applications after it reopened following the annexation of Austria; in June 1939, there were still 8,000 children waiting, most of whom were murdered in the Holocaust. Claudia Curio, " 'Invisible' Children: The Selection and Integration Strategies of Relief Organizations," *Shofar*, 23, no. 1 (2004), 43. See also Kaplan, *Between Dignity and Despair*, 116–18; Curio, " 'Unsichtbare' Kinder," 20–7.
54. USHMM, RG 17.017, Trude Frankl Report, April 1939.
55. These observations are based on Curio's research on the Kindertransport from Vienna to England. Selection for France may have been somewhat different. Curio notes that selection became stricter after March 1939, involving an interview with the children to match them to potential foster families. Curio, " 'Invisible' Children," 41–56. On transports from Vienna to France, it is clear that children with disabilities were screened out. Such was the case for Oswald Kernberg and his brother, who was not accepted due to his epilepsy. Maier, "Das Schicksal des Arthur Kern," 20–3.
56. USHMM, RG 17.017, File 10 of 13, trans. from the German.
57. Information on independent arrivals is especially difficult to evaluate, since Andrée Salomon and Trude Frankl provide different figures and may be referring to the same children. The Vienna Jewish communal archives lists do not state whether the children actually left for France. USHMM, RG 17.017, File 10 of 13.
58. Mémorial de la Shoah, Fonds Enfants CMLXVIII (1) 6, Weitzmann, Walter. State Archives (Geneva), UISE collection, folder AP 92.18.3 (3). As adults, one group of former children reconstituted their transport list. OSE Headquarters, Lists Château de Quincy. Thanks to the help of OSE's team of volunteers, a significant part of the OSE children's files have also been studied to see if they hold documentation from the CIE. I have also looked for lists, without success, in the Archives Nationales, Archives du Ministère des Affaires étrangères, and the OSE archives, among others. In May–June 1940, the Foreign Affairs ministry burned a great deal of their files in anticipation of the war. Sophie Cœuré, *La mémoire spoliée: Les archives des Français, butin de guerre nazi puis soviétique (de 1940 à nos jours)* (Paris: Payot, 2007). French consular records, available in Nantes, may have individual files from the children and could provide more information; however, a considerable part of the archives was unavailable when I

visited in 2020. Through these multiple sources, I have created a database of the Kindertransport children, which currently has about 292 names out of an estimated 500 children.

59. Mémorial de la Shoah, Félix Chevrier Collection, CCCLXXIII-6a, "Le Comité des Réfugiés et son œuvre, janvier-septembre 1939." This most likely represents the total number of visas received for Kindertransport children in France who arrived in 1939 and probably does not include the 52 children who arrived in Strasbourg in December 1938, and certainly does not include all of the children who smuggled themselves (or were smuggled) over the border, or who were sent directly to family members in France.

60. I reach this figure independently. However, Claudia Curio provides the figure 700. Curio, "'Unsichtbare' Kinder," 32, citing Salomon Adler-Rudel, *Jüdische Selbsthilfe unter dem Naziregime, 1933–1939* (Tübingen: Mohr, 1974), 217. This higher figure most likely includes youth between the ages of 18 and 24 ["*Kindern und Jugenlichen*"].

61. USHMM, RG 17.017, Trude Frankl Report, April 1939. According to Claudia Curio, in June 1939 the French government was still blocking immigration of children, with the exception of exceptional individual cases. Curio, "'Unsichtbare' Kinder," 110.

62. Again, I refrain from giving an exact number here due to the fact that I am not sure which children actually arrived in France. USHMM, RG 17.017, File 7 of 13, Liste d'enfants venant d'Allemagne prévus pour la Colonie de Vacances de Schirmeck, April 3, 1939.

63. Weill, "Introduction," 52.

64. *La Tribune Juive*, May 19, 1939.

65. *La Tribune Juive*, July 28, 1939. This figure is lower than the one Andrée Salomon provided in her 1965 interview. She stated that a total of 100 children came to the Strasbourg area, and later 50 independent children, for a total of 150. OHD, (27) 28, Interview with A.S. by Ms. R. Bannit, 1965, 23.

66. OHD, (27)28, Interview with A.S. by Ms. R. Bannit, 1965, 16.

67. *La Tribune Juive*, March 31, 1939.

68. *La Tribune Juive*, April 21, 1939.

69. See editorial in *La Tribune Juive*, April 28, 1939.

70. It is unclear at what date the school took on this name. Its archives have not been located. The exact name of the organization can be seen on its 1939 letter-head. AN, 72AJ, file 2935, "Liste des enfants basques et espagnoles évacuées le dimanche 10 septembre de l'internat de Quincy-sous-Sénart au Foster Parents Committee."

71. On this family and its experiences during the Second World War, see McAuley, *The House of Fragile Things*.

72. Keren, "L'évacuation et l'accueil des enfants Espagnols en France," 152–6; Interview with Christian de Monbrison, Paris, September 15, 2016.

73. By chance, I discovered the connection between Monbrison and Eisfelder while consulting the Save the Children International papers (UISE) at the State archive in Geneva.

74. AN, 20010221/1, Letter to Renée de Monbrison from the Minister of the Interior, February 9, 1940. Renée de Monbrision was active in several organizations, including the Secours international aux femmes et aux enfants des républicains espagnols.

75. Patrick Cabanel, *Juifs et protestants en France: Les affinités électives, XVIe–XXIe siècle* (Paris: Fayard, 2004).

76. *L'Univers Israélite*, May 2, 1939, 584. On the work of this group, see Caron, *Uneasy Asylum*.

77. Archives départementales de la Creuse, René Castille and Alfred Bourdet Collection, 147J/95, Gaston Kahn, Mémoires. Interview with Christian de Monbrison, November 4, 2017. The boys were the offspring of the Count's first marriage to Léonino, who converted to Protestantism. The boys feared being considered Jewish by Vichy legislation. Before leaving France, the boys turned over their French francs to the JDC, for reimbursement after the war.

78. Henry Jacoby, *Davongekommen, 10 Jahre Exil 1936–1946, Prag-Paris-Montauban-New York-Washington: Erlebnisse und Begegnungen* (Frankfurt am Main: Sendler Verlag, 1982), 63–4.

79. Georges Grunwald Papers, Reinhard Otto, *Wie haste det jemacht?: Lebenslauf von Hanna Grunwald-Eisfelder* (Soltau: Schultze Hermann, 1992). I was able to use the unpublished translation by Barbara Guggemos.

80. The film is now held by the US Holocaust Memorial Museum; USHMM, 2011.350.1; RG-60.1340. It can be viewed at https://collections.ushmm.org/search/catalog/irn1004610, consulted February 20, 2018.

81. The Parisian Jewish press makes no mention of the boys' arrival.

82. Keren, "L'évacuation et l'accueil des enfants espagnols en France," 13–41.

83. OHD, (27)28, Interview with A.S. by Ms. R. Bannit, 1965, trans. from French.

Chapter 5

1. After reading the sections of the book that pertained to her, "Ruth" asked me to change her name, as well as those of her family members and her city of origin, for fear of appearing ungrateful.

2. Kaplan, *Between Dignity and Despair*, 120–1.

3. Interview with Ruth, California, December 11, 2016.

4. She used the term "modern orthodox" to describe her family, but this term was most likely not used in the 1930s.

5. Interview with Ruth, California, December 11, 2016.

6. Interview with Ruth, California, December 11, 2016.

7. Interview with Ruth, California, December 11, 2016.

8. IISG, Ernst Papanek Collection, E19, Letter from Ernst Papanek to Wolfgang Neugebauer, April 5, 1968, 32. He estimates that "hundreds" of children came in this manner. Philippe Sands' mother was brought to France from Vienna by an unmarried woman missionary, providing another example; Sands, *East West Street*, 121–30.

9. Interview with Ruth, California, December 11, 2016.

10. Jonathan Boyarin, *Jewish Families* (New Brunswick, NJ: Rutgers University Press, 2013), 58.

11. Mark Granovetter, "The Strength of Weak Ties: A Network Theory Revisited," *Sociological Theory*, 1 (1983), 201–33.

12. Hirsch, *Home Is Where You Find It*, 32–46.

13. Dwork and Van Pelt, *Flight from the Reich*, 245–63.

14. Stock, *Tri-Continental Jew*, 67.

15. Alexandra Garbarini has argued for a broader historical contextualization of diaries written by Jews during the Holocaust. Alexandra Garbarini, *Numbered Days, Diaries and the Holocaust* (New Haven, CT and London: Yale University Press, 2006), 11–12. See also Kaplan, *The Making of the Jewish Middle Class*, 47 and Martha Arendt's book *Unser Kind*, published in Hannah Arendt, *À travers le mur, suivi de Notre fille de Martha Arendt* (Paris: Payot, 2017).

16. Ernest Stock, Julie Stock, and Edward Timms, *Jugend auf der Flucht: Die Tagebuecher von Ernest und Julie Stock* (Berlin: Metropol Verlag, 2004).

17. Nicholas Stargardt, "Children," in Peter Hayes and John K. Roth (eds.), *The Oxford Handbook of Holocaust Studies* (Oxford: Oxford University Press, 2010), 218–31. Dwork, *Children with a Star*, xxiii.

18. Boaz Cohen and Rita Horváth, "Young Witnesses in the DP Camps: Children's Holocaust Testimony in Context," *Journal of Modern Jewish Studies*, 11, no. 1 (March 2012), 103.

19. USHMM, Susi Hilsenrath Collection, RG 2000.127, Diary, July 22, 1941, trans. from German.

20. Mémorial de la Shoah, Werner Marzdorff Collection MDXXVIII, Box 2, Ursula Matzdorff journal, c.1942–1943, trans. from German.

21. Alexandra Garbarini, "Diaries, Testimonies and Jewish Histories of the Holocaust," in Norman J.W. Goda (ed.), *Jewish Histories of the Holocaust: New Transnational Approaches* (New York: Berghahn Books, 2014), 91–104.

22. The six diaries include those from Minnie Engel, Ursula Matzdorff, Heinz Lonnerstädter, Heinz Löw, Peter (Pierre) Feigl, and Susi Hilsenrath Warsinger.

23. At least ten La Guette children were deported, and only one survived the Nazi camps. W.M., "Les enfants de la Guette, 1988," in Centre de Documentation Juive Contemporaine (CDJC) (ed.), *Les enfants de La Guette: Souvenirs et documents (1938–1945)* (Paris: CDJC, 1999), 13–24, 82–7.

24. The first American reunion took place in the home of one of the children in New York in 1983. Hilda Mann Private Papers, Tammy Karol, "Reunion Held for Recipients of Rothschild Aid," *The Canadian Jewish News,* August 11, 1983. Matzdorff wrote to the former children with a questionnaire in 1986. Mémorial de la Shoah, Matzdorff Collection MDXXVIII, Box 1, Letter from Werner Matzdorff to "Friend," March 19, 1986.

25. CDJC, *Les enfants de La Guette*. The collection also includes the papers saved by former educators Alfred and Françoise Brauner, as well as responses to a questionnaire Matzdorff sent to fellow La Guette children.

26. Papanek, *Out of the Fire*, 107.

27. Interview Susi K., New York, July 13, 2015.

28. IISG, Bruno Kurzweil Papers. See also Christian Ehetreiber, Heimo Halbrainer, and Bettina Ramp, *Der Koffer der Adele Kurzweil: Auf den Spuren einer Grazer jüdischen Familie in der Emigration* (Graz: CLIO-Verein f. Geschichts- u. Bildungsarbeit, 2001).

29. This diary was recently reproduced in Hazan, *Rire le jour, pleurer la nuit*, 103–74.

30. This includes Gustav Papanek's autobiographical paper, "On Friendship," most likely written in 1940–1941, Hans Stern's "Children Under Nazi Invasion Boots," written most likely in 1944–1945, and Ruth Safrin's "Recalled to Life," written in 1946.

31. As noted in the methodology essay, I used the OSE-USA newsletter to recruit interviewees, as well as the snowball method, which kept me primarily within the

OSE networks. These networks also included some who had been in the Château de la Guette. However, the original OSE children are heavily represented in my sample: I interviewed only one child from La Guette. Likewise, I have only found one or two memoirs from La Guette children and many more from OSE children.

32. Exceptions include: Mia Amalia Kanner and Eve Rosenzweig Kugler, *Shattered Crystals* (Lakewood, NJ: CIS Publishers, 1997); Papanek, *Elly und Alexander;* Edith Mayer Cord, *Becoming Edith: The Education of a Hidden Child* (New Mildford, NJ: Wordsmithy, 2008).

33. Interview with Ruth, California, December 11, 2016; *La Tribune Juive*, November 25, 1938, no. 47.

34. Interview with Ruth, California, December 11, 2016.

35. Interview with Ruth, California, December 11, 2016.

36. Interview with Ruth, California, December 11, 2016.

37. *L'Univers Israélite*, June 9, 1939, no. 38. The sisters were initially placed in a less traditional OSE home.

Chapter 6

1. Erving Goffman, *Asylums: Essays on the Social Situation of Mental Patients and Other Inmates* (New York: Random House, 1968). On the usage of this concept of children's homes, see Chloé Maurel, "Yvonne Hagnauer et la Maison de Sèvres (1941–1970)," *La revue de l'enfance irrégulière*, no. 10 (2008), 161–79.

2. Some of the older children in the OSE homes attended French public schools, even if Ernst Papanek sought to provide schooling within the homes. Papanek, *Out of the Fire*, 115–19.

3. This discussion builds on my article, Laura Hobson Faure, "Jewish Child Refugees from Central Europe in France and the United States: The Challenges Related to their Care, 1938–1945," *European Holocaust Studies*, 5 (April 2024), 131–49.

4. In England, orthodox Rabbi Solomon Schonfeld fought the Refugee Children's Movement policy of placing Jewish children in non-Jewish households. Barbara Barnett, *The Hide and Seek Children* (Glasgow: Mansion Field, 2012), 51–69; Mary Fraser Kirsh, "La politique de placement des enfants en Grande-Bretagne et en Palestine," in Jablonka, *L'Enfant-Shoah*, 51–66; Jennifer Craig-Norton, *The Kindertransport: Contesting Memory* (Bloomington, IN: Indiana University Press, 2019), 33–91; Judith Tydor Baumel-Schwartz, *Never Look Back: The Jewish Refugee Children in Great Britain* (Purdue: Purdue University Press, 2012), 112–22.

5. Forty of the Irish Catholic orphans were kidnapped by "Anglo" vigilantes who were outraged that white children would be assigned to Mexican families. The case went to the Supreme Court in 1905, which ruled in favor of the vigilantes. Linda Gordon, *The Great Arizona Orphan Abduction* (Cambridge, MA: Harvard University Press, 1999), 275–306. In the United States in the 1940s, it was not uncommon for Jews to refer to themselves, or for others to refer to Jews, as a race. Eric Goldstein, "Contesting the Categories: Jews and Government Racial Classification in the United States," *Jewish History*, 19, no. 1 (2005), 94–5.

6. Robert Bremner, "Other People's Children," *Journal of Social History*, 16, no. 3 (1983), 88.

7. This was the federal policy for caring for unaccompanied minors during the Second World War in the United States. Ron Coleman Papers, "Care of Children coming to the United States for Safety under Attorney General's Order of July 13, 1940. Standard's Prescribed by the Children's Bureau, Washington, 1941," 2; Tara Zahra, *The Lost Children: Reconstructing Europe's Families after World War II* (Cambridge: Harvard University Press, 2011), 70–8.

8. *La Tribune Juive*, May 12, 1939, no. 19, trans. from German.

9. *La Tribune Juive*, May 12, 1939, no. 19, trans. from French.

10. Corber, "The Kids on Oberlin Street," 588–93.

11. To my knowledge, there has been no research on this region's Jewish child placement activities in the interwar period. *La Tribune Juive* has many advertisements for pensions for children. See also George Loinger and Katy Hazan, *Aux frontières de l'espoir* (Paris: Fondation pour la mémoire de la Shoah/Éditions Le Manuscrit, 2006), 42.

12. Downs notes that in 1910, 50 per cent of the children sent to *colonies* were placed in families; by 1936, this figure had dropped to 10 per cent. Laura Lee Downs, *Childhood in the Promised Land: Working-Class Movements and the Colonies de Vacances in France, 1880–1960* (Durham, NC: Duke University Press, 2002), 15–67.

13. As Erin Corber shows, the Œuvre israélite de séjours à la campagne also admitted non-Jewish children and had little emphasis on Jewish tradition, although after 1910 the meat was apparently kosher. There was no Jewish instruction or ritual and apparently a Christmas tree, which implies it hosted children during school vacations and not just in the summertime. Corber, "L'Esprit du Corps," 165.

14. Corber, "L'Esprit du Corps," 165.

15. More research is needed on the actors and practices surrounding Jewish youth in the interwar period. Loinger and Hazan, *Aux frontières de l'espoir*, 63–6.

16. Mémorial de la Shoah, Fonds Enfants CMLXVIII (1)6, Weitzmann, Walter. This became the Œuvre de Protection pour l'Enfance after the Second World War. CJDC, *Les enfants de La Guette*, 11.

17. This term refers to the French tradition of converting the former domiciles of the nobility into social welfare spaces. Samuel Boussion and Mathias Gardet (eds.), *Les châteaux du social: XIXe–XXe Siècle* (Paris: Beauchesne/Presses Universitaires de Vincennes, 2010).

18. See Chapter 4 on this initiative. It was initially called the "Internat de jeunes filles." For details on the Russian period of the school, see Olga Efimovsky, *Il était une fois . . . Brunoy . . . Quincy . . .* (Self-published, 1991).

19. Daniela Gauding, "La société pour la protection sanitaire des juifs en Allemagne," in Hobson Faure et al.(eds.), *L'Œuvre de secours aux enfants et les populations juives* 74–87.

20. *La Revue OSE*, June–July 1939, trans. from French.

21. Jaclyn Granick points out that despite what American Jewish funders hoped, disrupted family life and communal preferences led Jews in interwar Poland to embrace communal homes for orphans. Jaclyn Granick, *International Jewish Humanitarianism in the Age of the Great War* (Cambridge: Cambridge University Press, 2021). Sean Martin, "How to House a Child: Providing Homes for Jewish Children in Interwar Poland," *East European Jewish Affairs*, 45, no. 1 (2014), 26–41. Janusz Korczak, for example, established children's republics in the two Jewish orphanages he directed in Warsaw from 1912 to 1942. As a pediatrician, he may have been close to the Polish branch of the OSE (TOZ), after its reestab-

lishment in 1921. Liba Engel, "Experiments in Democracy: Dewy's Lab School and Korczak's Children's Republic," *The Social Studies* (May/June 2008), 117–21. On the TOZ, see Nadav Davidovitch, "La société pour la protection sanitaire des juifs (TOZ): Présence de l'OSE en Pologne entre les deux guerres," in Hobson Faure et al.(eds.), *L'Œuvre de secours aux enfants et les populations juives*, 62–73.

22. JDC-NY, AR 1933–1945, France, file 610, "Care for Refugee Children in France," January 3, 1939.

23. JDC-NY, AR 1933–1945, France, file 610, "Care for Refugee Children in France," January 3, 1939.

24. It appears that Trude Frankl was still alive, and apparently in a position to help OSE children, in June 1940. JDC-NY, file 610, file 131. Letter from Elise Stiassny to Dr. Elias and Trude Frankl, June 21, 1940.

25. USHMM, RG 17.017, Trude Frankl Report, April 1939, trans. from German.

26. Downs, *Childhood in the Promised Land*, 195–236. On the transnational networks that developed around education, see Zoe Moody, *Les droits de l'enfant: Genèse, institutionnalisation et diffusion (1924–1989)* (Neufchâtel: Éditions Alphil-Presses Universitaires Suisses, 2016), 61–83.

27. Downs, *Childhood in the Promised Land*, 201–2.

28. Juliette Pary, *Mes 126 Gosses* (Paris: Flammarion, 1938), 5–6. Trans. from French.

29. Pary, *Mes 126 Gosses*, 6.

30. Pary, *Mes 126 Gosses*, 6.

31. Anne Mendelssohn Weil, cited in Elisabeth Young-Bruehl, *Hannah Arendt: For Love of the World* (New Haven, CT and London: Yale University Press, 2004), 120.

32. USHMM, RG 17.017, Trude Frankl Report, April 1939, trans. from German.

33. Engel, "Experiments in Democracy"; Till Kössler, "Children in the Spanish Civil War," in Martin Baumeister and Stefanie Schüler-Springorum (eds.), *"If you tolerate this . . .": The Spanish Civil War in the Age of Total War* (Chicago, IL: Campus Verlag, 2008), 118–25.

34. Moisei Pistrak, *Les problèmes fondamentaux de l'école du travail* (Paris: Desclée de Brouwer, [1925] 1973). Pary was the sister of Nina Gourfinkel, who represented the World Jewish Congress in France during the Second World War. Nina Gourfinkel, *Aux prises avec mon temps: L'autre patrie* (Paris: Seuil, 1953). Samuel Boussion, Email correspondence, April 18, 2018.

35. Downs, *Childhood in the Promised Land*, 198. On children's republics after the Second World War, see Samuel Boussion, Mathias Gardet, and Martine Ruchat (eds.), *L'internationale des républiques d'enfants, 1939–54* (Paris: Anamosa, 2020).

36. The Bund (the General Jewish Labor Bund) emerged in 1897 in the Russian Empire. It embodied a commitment to socialism and asserted Jews' right to live as a protected minority in the diaspora. Among other goals, it sought to unite Jewish workers and encouraged the development of the Yiddish language.

37. Hazan, *Les orphelins de la Shoah*, 112; Papanek, *Out of the Fire*, 35.

38. On the Rothschild family's politics, see Herbert Lottman, *La Dynastie Rothschild* (Paris: Seuil, 1995), 221–39.

39. Lisa Gossels papers, The Children of Chabannes Transcripts, Interview with Lida Jablonski, 510. Marina Mintec, "Fonds Brauner: Répertoire numérique" (Master's Thesis, Université d'Angers, January 2008), 11.

40. This is most likely Wilhelm Anton Katz, born in Offenbach Germany on January 9, 1919, who received French nationality at the moment of the children's arrival

in March 1939 (revoked in March 1942). "Les dénaturalisés de *Vichy: Lettres J* à N, Répertoire méthodique établi par Thomas Lebée, Annie Poinsot et Bernard Raquin," https://www.siv.archives-nationales.culture.gouv.fr/siv/rechercheconsultation/consultation/ir/pdfIR.action?irId=FRAN_IR_057228, consulted May 20, 2021. One finds him in North Africa later in the war. "Les Eclaireurs israélites de France en Afrique du Nord pendant la guerre," Témoignage du Dr. Robert Shapiro (Rhino), commissaire régional EIF pour l'Afrique du Nord (Algérie, Tunisie, Maroc), 19 janvier 1997, http://le-scout.fr/blog/wp-content/uploads/2014/02/EIF_afrique_du_nord.pdf, consulted May 20, 2021. For more on the Katz family, see Renato Simoni, *Walter Katz: Un aviador al servicio de la Republica (1936–38)* (Rovira: Publicacions Universitat Rovira, 2020). See also Mémorial de la Shoah, Matzdorff Collection MDXXVIII, Box 1, Le Hôme de la Guette, Lida Jablonski, c.1968.

41. Lisa Gossels papers, The Children of Chabannes Transcripts, Interview with Lida Jablonski, 510.

42. His wife Lida states 1931 in an interview, but she seems to have been confusing his arrival date with her own arrival date in France from Latvia. Lisa Gossels private papers, Lisa Gossels papers, The Children of Chabannes Transcripts, Interview with Lida Jablonski, 510. All other sources on Jablonski state 1933: Hazan, *Les orphelins de la Shoah*, 113; Samuel Boussion, "À la croisée des réseaux transnationaux de protection de l'enfance: L'OSE et les communautés d'enfants de l'après-guerre," in Hobson Faure et al.(eds.), *L'Œuvre de secours aux enfants et les populations juives*, 184–205.

43. Hazan, *Les orphelins de la Shoah*, 113. See also his portrait in Sebastian Voigt, *Der jüdische Mai '68: Pierre Goldman, Daniel Cohn-Bendit und André Glucksmann im Nachkriegsfrankreich* (Göttingen: Vandenhoeck & Ruprecht, 2016), 163–82.

44. Dennis Shirley, *The Politics of Progressive Education: The Odenwaldschule in Nazi Germany* (Cambridge, MA: Harvard University Press, 1992), 134.

45. Anne Grynberg, "Précurseurs et Passeurs," Conference Presentation, Les Juifs de Russie et d'Union soviétique à Paris, 1881–1991, École des hautes études en sciences sociales, Paris, November 2008, 5. A trained biologist, Decroly sought to introduce the study of nature and scientific experimentation into school curricula, as well as hands-on learning.

46. On the diffusion of Adlerian psychology in the interwar period in the United States and France, see Olivier Brachfeld, *Inferiority Feelings: In the Individual and the Group* (London: Routledge, 2013), 73–93.

47. Zahra, *The Lost Children*, 101.

48. Ernst Papanek, "Contributions of Individual Psychology to Social Work," *American Journal of Individual Psychology*, 11, no. 2 (1955), 145.

49. Claude-Michel Brauner, "Alfred et Françoise Brauner par leur fils," Conference Presentation, Enfances en Guerre: Témoignages d'enfants sur la guerre, December 7–9, 2011, http://www.enfance-violence-exil.net/fichiers_sgc/BRAUNER.pdf, consulted June 19, 2018.

50. Rose Duroux and Célia Keren, "Retours sur dessins: Fred/Alfred Brauner 1938, 1946, 1976, 1991," in Rose Duroux and Catherine Milkovitch-Rioux (eds.), *Enfances en guerre: Témoignages d'enfants sur la guerre* (Geneva: L'Équinoxe/Éditions Georg, 2013), 100.

51. Yoram Mouchenik, "Les enfants dans la guerre: Entretien avec Alfred Brauner," *L'Autre: Cliniques, cultures et sociétés*, 11, no. 1 (2010), 12, trans. from French.

52. Duroux and Keren, "Retours sur dessins," 99–119; Yannick Ripa, "Naissance du dessin de guerre: Les époux Brauner et les enfants de la guerre civile espagnole," *Vingtième Siècle: Revue d'histoire*, 89, no. 1 (2006), 29–46; Rose Duroux and Catherine Milkovitch-Rioux (eds.), *J'ai dessiné la guerre: Le regard de Françoise et Alfred Brauner* (Clermont-Ferrand: Presses Universitaires Blaise Pascal, 2011).

53. Mouchenik, "Les enfants dans la guerre," 13, trans. from French.

54. "Mabel Irene Goldin," Abraham Lincoln Brigade Archives, http://www.alba-valb.org/volunteers/mabel-irene-goldin, consulted May 23, 2018. See her oral history, conducted by Esther Brown in 1991, https://findingaids.library.nyu.edu/tamwag/alba_audio_131/audio/nzs7hd00/, consulted August 7, 2024.

55. Mémorial de la Shoah, Matzdorff Collection MDXXVIII, Box 2, Minnie Engel Diary, c.1939–44.

56. Mémorial de la Shoah, Matzdorff Collection MDXXVIII, Box 1, Le Hôme de la Guette, Lida Jablonski, c.1968.

57. The many writings on the Brauners' work with Jewish children, including their own, are curiously silent on this question, suggesting that this topic remained taboo after the war. Alfred's maternal uncle, Erwin Wexberg, was secular but considered a Jew by Nazi officials and in postwar accounts. According to the Brauners' son, Françoise (i.e., Fritzi) attended a Protestant school. He also mentions that Françoise never saw her family again after leaving Austria. On Wexberg, see Nathan Koren, *Jewish Physicians: A Biographical Index* (Jerusalem: Israel University Press, 1973), 263; see also Ulrich Kümmel, *Erwin Wexberg: Ein Leben zwischen Individualpsychologie, Psychoanalyse und Neurologie* (Göttingen: Vandenhoeck & Ruprecht, 2010), 114; Brauner, "Alfred et Françoise Brauner par leur fils." The genealogical website Geni lists Françoise Brauner's mother, Mina Riesel, as having perished at Sobibór, https://www.geni.com/people/Mina-Riesel/6000000005405913003, consulted June 18, 2018.

58. Isaac Deutscher, *Non-Jewish Jew and other Essays* (s.l.: Oxford University Press, 1968); Leora Auslander, "The Boundaries of Jewishness or When is a Cultural Practice Jewish?," *Journal of Modern Jewish Studies*, 8, no. 1 (2009), 47–64. See also George Mosse, *German Jews Beyond Judaism* (Bloomington, IN: Indiana University Press, 1985), 55–71.

59. Lisa Silverman, *Becoming Austrians: Jews and Culture Between the Wars* (Oxford: Oxford University Press, 2012), 6. See also Yuri Slezkine, *The Jewish Century* (Princeton, NJ: Princeton University Press, 2004), 204–371.

60. Silverman, *Becoming Austrians*, 3–27; Judith Butler, *Gender Trouble: Feminism and the Subversion of Identity* (New York: Routledge, 1990), 134–41.

61. Dennis Shirley, *The Politics of Progressive Education: The Odenwaldschule in Nazi Germany* (Cambridge, MA: Harvard University Press, 1992), 64.

62. Mémorial de la Shoah, Matzdorff Collection MDXXVIII, Box 1, Le Hôme de la Guette, Lida Jablonski, c.1968. She was most likely referring to the Hungarian rabbinical student Georges Vadnai who intervened with the children for Passover in 1939 and later in La Bourboule, who was not, to my knowledge, "very liberal." Georges Vadnaï, *Jamais la lumière ne s'est éteinte: Un destin juif dans les ténèbres du siècle* (Lausanne and Paris: L'Âge d'Homme, 1999), 71, 77–8.

63. Papanek, *Elly und Alexander*, 79.

64. Papanek, *Out of the Fire*. The Papanek collection at the IISG (file B-8) has many documents showing his Jewish background: born in 1900, by 1927 he had corrected his religious identity to "*Konfessionslos.*"

65. Visual History Archive (VHA), USC Shoah Foundation Interview with George Papanek, interview 11978, February 11, 1996.

66. Papanek, *Out of the Fire*, 52; Interview with Gus Papanek, Lexington, July 16, 2015; VHA, USC Shoah Foundation Interview with George Papanek, interview 11978, February 11, 1996.

67. Papanek, *Elly und Alexander*, 71–3. Also on Papanek, see Jean-Christophe Coffin, "Ernst Papanek (1900–1973): Un pédagogue à l'épreuve de la violence," in Hobson Faure et al., *L'Œuvre de Secours aux Enfants et les populations juives*, 148–65; Hansen-Schaberg et al., *Ernst Papanek. Pädagogische und therapeutische Arbeit*.

68. VHA, USC Shoah Foundation Interview with George Papanek, interview 11978, February 11, 1996.

69. Papanek, *Out of the Fire*, 33–49. He may have been a relative of Dr. Alexander Lourié, Nathalie Lourié's late husband (see Chapter 3). This is not unlikely, since Nathalie Lourié mentions OSE in her correspondence.

70. Papanek, *Out of the Fire*, 35. In this, he echoes Rosa Luxemburg's famous 1917 statement: "I have no place in my heart for the ghetto: I feel at home in the entire world, wherever there are clouds and birds and human tears."

71. Mémorial de la Shoah, Matzdorff Collection MDXXVIII, Box 1, Le Hôme de la Guette, Lida Jablonski, c.1968, trans. from French.

72. Mémorial de la Shoah, Matzdorff Collection MDXXVIII, Box 1, Le Hôme de la Guette, Lida Jablonski, c.1968.

73. Papanek, *Out of the Fire*, 37–8.

74. Papanek, *Out of the Fire*, 52.

75. *L'Univers Israélite*, April 21, 1939, no. 31. According to one source, the Eaubonne home was opened in September 1939 and had 35 places available. USHMM, RG 11.001M, Russian Holocaust Foundation Files on the JDC Paris office, File 295, Letter from OSE Paris to JDC Paris, January 31, 1940. However, this contradicts the more reliable article in *L'Univers Israélite*, announcing the creation of the home in May 1939, with 60 places for orthodox children. *L'Univers Israélite*, June 9, 1939, no. 38.

Chapter 7

1. USHMM, RG 2007.421 Ruth Salmon Seltzer Papers, Folder 12, Heinz Löw diary, trans. from German by its author.

2. USHMM, USHMM, RG 17.017, Trude Frankl report, April 1939.

3. A version of the song can be found at https://www.youtube.com/watch?v=IVWPEB6nw00.

4. Ruth was not the only child to remember this tradition; when Ernst Valfer picked me up from the station, he immediately shared the same anecdote. Interview with Ruth, California, December 11, 2016; Interview with Ernst Valfer, Berkeley, December 13, 2016.

5. Carol Low Papers, Songs from the La Guette Reunion, 1999. The lyrics of "*Alles schweiget*" are the following: "*Alles schweiget, Nachtigallen; Locken mit süssen Melodien, Tränen im Auge, Schwermut im Herz.*" [All is silent, nightingales; Drawn in by sweet melodies, Tears in the eye, melancholy in heart.]

6. Joachim Schlör, *"Liesel, it's time for you to leave.": Von Heilbronn nach England. Die Flucht der Familie Rosenthal vor nationalsozialistischer Verfolgung* (Heilbronn: Stadtarchiv Heilbronn, 2015), Unpublished English excerpt, 2.

7. Schlör, *"Liesel, it's time for you to leave,"* 2; Carlos Sluzki, "Migration and Family Conflict," *Family Process*, 18, no. 4 (1979), 379–90.

8. Natalia Aleksiun, "Uneasy Bonds: On Jews in Hiding and the Making of Surrogate Families," in Eliyana Adler and Katerina Capova (eds.), *Jewish and Romani Families in the Holocaust and Its Aftermath* (New Brunswick, NJ: Rutgers University Press, 2021), 85–102; Patrick Cabanel, "Enfants juifs et mamans justes," in Jablonka, *L'Enfant-Shoah*, 113–28.

9. I build here on my analysis in Laura Hobson Faure, "Exploring Political Rupture Through Jewish Children's Diaries: Kindertransport Children in France, 1938–1942," *Journal of Modern European History*, 19, no. 3 (2021), 265–8.

10. Minnie Engel gave the diary to Alfred and Françoise Brauner. The Brauners published a small excerpt in Alfred and Françoise Brauner, *L'Accueil des enfants des survivants* (Paris: Cahiers du Groupement de Recherches Pratiques pour l'Enfance, 2014), 104–5. I used the entire journal, trans. from German by Jean-Pierre Randon.

11. YIVO, OTC, RG 1941, Folder 61. Heinz Lonnerstädter Diary, trans. from German by Art Kern.

12. USHMM, RG 2007.421 Ruth Salmon Seltzer Papers, Folder 12, Heinz Löw diary, trans. from German by Henry Low.

13. Email correspondence with Carol Low, May 27, 2022; Email with Carol Low and Michaela Raggam-Blesch, February 20, 2024.

14. USHMM, RG 2007.421 Ruth Salmon Seltzer Papers, Folder 12, Heinz Löw diary.

15. USHMM, RG 2007.421 Ruth Salmon Seltzer Papers, Folder 12, Heinz Löw diary.

16. Vadnaï states he performed the seder at the Château de la Guette and not the Château de Maubuisson, yet one group of children arrived at La Guette on March 15, 1939, before Passover. Vadnaï, *Jamais la lumière ne s'est éteinte*, 71; Archives départementales de Seine et Marne, M13184, Rapport du Maréchal des Logis Chef Quesney, commandant la brigade, sur l'arrivée de réfugiés israélites allemands à Villeneuve-Saint-Denis, 21 mars 1939.

17. Mémorial de la Shoah, Matzdorff collection MDXXVIII, Box 2, Minnie Engel diary, c.1939–1944, trans. from German.

18. YIVO, RG 1941, OTC, Folder 61, Heinz Lonnerstädter Diary.

19. USHMM, RG 2007.421 Ruth Salmon Seltzer Papers, Folder 12, Heinz Löw diary.

20. USHMM, Description of Photo 65499. In a later account, Bikales states his mother was responsible for finding him a place on a Kindertransport. Norbert Bikales Papers, "Kristallnacht and its Aftermath," November 10, 2014.

21. Norbert Bikales Papers, "Kristallnacht and its Aftermath," November 10, 2014.

22. Interview with Ernst Valfer, Berkeley, December 13, 2016.

23. Herzberg (with Stephan Lewy), *The Past Is Always Present*, 89. Stephan Lewy is one of the rare children to have been reunited with his parents in the United States.

24. Hirsch, *Home Is Where You Find It*, 84–5.

25. Erving Goffman's classic sociological study emphasizes the capacity of individuals ("performers" or "teammates") to negotiate everyday social situations with a certain set of strategies designed to portray their self or team in the best light. Erving Goffman, *The Presentation of Self in Everyday Life* (New York: Doubleday, 1959).

26. Brauner, *L'Accueil des enfants des survivants*, 89.
27. Mémorial de la Shoah, Matzdorff Collection MDXXVIII, Box 1, Minnie Engel Account, October 1987.
28. Interview with Herbert Feuerstein, New York, July 2015.
29. Telephone interview with Ernst Valfer, November 24, 2016.
30. The Talmud, Shavuot 39a.
31. See Denise Baumann's discussion of Jewish law as it applied to Jewish children after the Holocaust. Denise Baumann, *La mémoire des oubliés: Grandir après Auschwitz* (Paris: Albin Michel, 1988), 139–40.
32. Interview with Susi K., New York, July 2015.
33. Interview with Susi K., New York, July 2015.
34. Schuster, *Abraham's Son*, 70. Upon arrival in France, Schuster, along with the older Hirsch siblings, were sent to the École Maïmonide in Paris, where Marcus Cohn oversaw their schooling and care. Schuster had his bar mitzvah at this school.
35. Elfriede Schloss Papers, Letter from Isidor Marx to former children, Pessah April 1939. The letter can also be found in the Fritz Strauss Papers at the USHMM (RG 2015.533.3), Folder 2.
36. USHMM (RG 2015.533.3), Fritz Strauss Papers, Folder 2, Letters from Joseph Einhorn to Fritz Strauss, undated, trans. from German.
37. *Revue OSE*, March 1939, 29.
38. Zeitoun, *Histoire de l'OSE*, 139.
39. Mémorial de la Shoah, Matzdorff Collection MDXXVIII, Box 1, Le Hôme de la Guette, Lida Jablonski, c.1968, trans. from French.
40. Mémorial de la Shoah, Matzdorff Collection MDXXVIII, Box 1, Le Hôme de la Guette, Lida Jablonski, c.1968, trans. from French.
41. Brauner, *L'Accueil des enfants des survivants*, 89–97.
42. Mémorial de la Shoah, Matzdorff Collection MDXXVIII, Box 2, Minnie Engel Diary, c.1939–44, trans. from German.
43. Mémorial de la Shoah, Matzdorff Collection MDXXVIII, Box 2, Minnie Engel Diary, c.1939–44, trans. from German.
44. USHMM, RG 2007.421 Ruth Salmon Seltzer Papers, Folder 12, Heinz Löw diary, trans. from German.
45. USHMM, RG 2007.421 Ruth Salmon Seltzer Papers, Folder 12, Heinz Löw diary, trans. from German.
46. YIVO, OTC, RG 1941, Folder 61, Heinz Lonerstadter Diary.
47. Papanek, *Out of the Fire*.
48. Papanek, *Out of the Fire*, 117.
49. Alfred Brauner, *Ces enfants ont vécu la guerre: Les répercussions psychiques de la guerre moderne sur l'enfance* (Paris: Éditions sociales françaises, 1946), reprinted in CDJC, *Les enfants de La Guette*, 67–80; Brauner, *L'Accueil des enfants des survivants*, 98; E. Lochy, 'Alfred Brauner au Château de la Guette', International Conference Presentation, Enfances en Guerre: Témoignages d'enfants sur la guerre, Unesco, December 2011, http://www.enfance-violence-exil.net/fichiers_sgc/Lochy.pdf, consulted September 14, 2020; Mémorial de la Shoah, Matzdorff Collection MDXXVIII.
50. Alfred Brauner, *Ces enfants ont vécu la guerre*, 79, trans. from French.
51. Carol Low Papers, La Guette, 1939, Souvenir de la réunion pour les 60s, "République du Château de la Guette, Proclamée le 1er Mai 1939," 1999.

52. YIVO, OTC, RG 1941, Folder 61, Heinz Lonerstädter Diary. He states June 25, 1939. Minnie states early July. Other material from the period states May 1, 1939.
53. Mémorial de la Shoah, Matzdorff Collection MDXXVIII, Box 2, Minnie Engel diary, trans. from German.
54. The geographic origins of the children are listed in CDJC, *Les enfants de La Guette*, 82–7.
55. Mémorial de la Shoah, Matzdorff Collection MDXXVIII, Box 2, Minnie Engel Diary, c.1939–44, trans. from German.
56. Mémorial de la Shoah, Matzdorff Collection MDXXVIII, Box 2, Minnie Engel Diary, c.1939–44.
57. On his work in Spain, see Ripa, "Naissance du dessin de guerre," 29–46. Alfred Brauner, "Les répercussions psychiques de la guerre moderne sur l'enfance" (PhD Dissertation, Université de la Sorbonne, 1946). Published the same year as *Ces enfants ont vécu la guerre*.
58. Mémorial de la Shoah, Matzdorff Collection MDXXVIII, Box 1.
59. Tara Zahra mentions that Alfred Brauner noted the pedagogical utility of nationalism in his work with Spanish children. Zahra, *The Lost Children*, 57.
60. Paul Peter Porges, cited in the *Vienna Review*, https://en.wikipedia.org/wiki/Paul_Peter_Porges#cite_note-2, consulted December 17, 2021.
61. W.M. [Werner Matzdorff], "Esquisse d'une page d'histoire," in CDJC, *Les enfants de La Guette*, 17–18, trans. from French.
62. Mémorial de la Shoah, Matzdorff collection MDXXVIII, Box 1, Letter from Martin Axelrad to Werner Matzdorff, May 9, 1986, trans. from French. Later, he would become, like his educators, a Communist. He is the author of an anti-creationist thriller, *Dieu n'existe pas*. S.N., "Axelrad, Martin," *Le Maitron*, http://maitron-en-ligne.univ-paris1.fr/spip.php?article145639, consulted March 1, 2024.
63. Mémorial de la Shoah, Matzdorff Collection MDXXVIII, Box 2, Minnie Engel Diary, c.1939–44, trans. from German.
64. Brauner, *L'Accueil des enfants des survivants*, 98; Papanek, *Out of the Fire*, 107–8.
65. Interview with Eda Pell, Marin, December 11, 2016.
66. Papanek, *Out of the Fire*, 56.
67. Interview with Ernst Valfer, Berkeley, December 13, 2016.
68. Interview with Ernst Valfer, Berkeley, December 13, 2016.
69. Papanek, *Out of the Fire*, 58–63.
70. IISG, Ernst Papanek Collection, File F-22, Letter from Henny Marks to Ernst Papanek, August 1965.
71. Alessandro Portelli, "What Makes Oral History Different," in Robert Perks and Alistair Thompson, *The Oral History Reader* (London: Routledge [1979] 2006), 36.
72. Interview with Ernst Valfer, Berkeley, December 13, 2016.
73. Interview with Kurt Sonnenfeld, New York, July 15, 2015.
74. Interview with Kurt Sonnenfeld, New York, July 15, 2015.
75. Interview with Ernst Valfer, Berkeley, December 13, 2016.
76. Hanna Papanek was instrumental in preserving Papanek's archives by sending them to the International Institute for Social History in Amsterdam. She also published, with Inge Hansen-Schaberg and Gabriele Rühl-Nawabi, *Ernst Papanek. Pädagogische und therapeutische Arbeit: Kinder mit Verfolgungs-, Flucht- und Exilerfahrungen während der NS-Zeit* (Vienna: Böhlau Verlag, 2015).
77. Interview with Gitta and Renée Spindel, Santa Cruz, December 15, 2016.

Chapter 8

1. Elfriede Schloss Papers, Programme, Cirque Supermedrano, le plus grand du monde; 18. La Marche finale (undated, c. September 1939).
2. Papanek, *Out of the Fire*, 124.
3. Interviews, Elfriede Schloss and Ruth, December 2016.
4. Papanek, *Out of the Fire*, 25.
5. Susan Gross Solomon, "Silences secondaires et transmission: Les enfants survivants de la Shoah élevés dans les Maisons d'enfants juifs dans la France d'après 1945," in Hobson Faure, Pignot, and Rivière, *Enfants en guerre*, 389–411.
6. Here I build on Hobson Faure, "Exploring Political Rupture," 268–70.
7. USHMM, RG 2007.421 Ruth Salmon Seltzer Papers, Folder 12, Heinz Löw diary, trans. from German.
8. Mlle. Bernheim was most likely Josette Bernheim, head of Germaine de Rothschild's charitable works. Loinger and Hazan, *Aux frontières de l'espoir*, 65.
9. Loinger and Hazan, *Aux frontières de l'espoir*, 65.
10. Loinger and Hazan, *Aux frontières de l'espoir*, 54.
11. Loinger and Hazan, *Aux frontières de l'espoir*, 53–66.
12. Loinger and Hazan, *Aux frontières de l'espoir*, 67.
13. Mouchenik, "Les enfants dans la guerre," 14.
14. Mémorial de la Shoah, Matzdorff Collection MDXXVIII, Box 1, Le Hôme de la Guette, Lida Jablonski, c.1968.
15. Mémorial de la Shoah, Matzdorff collection MDXXVIII, Box 1, Letter from Martin Axelrad to Werner Matzdorff, May 9, 1986.
16. AN, F/7/16080, Letter from (illegible) to Monsieur Enriquet, Direction de la Police du Territoire et des Etrangers, December 1, 1939.
17. Mémorial de la Shoah, Matzdorff collection MDXXVIII, Box 1, Letter from Martin Axelrad to Matzdorff, May 9, 1986.
18. Mémorial de la Shoah, Matzdorff Collection MDXXVIII, Box 1, Le Hôme de la Guette, Lida Jablonski, c.1968.
19. CDJC, *Les enfants de La Guette*, 45.
20. USHMM, RG 2007.421 Ruth Salmon Seltzer Papers, Folder 12, Heinz Löw diary.
21. Diane Afoumado, *Exil impossible: L'errance des juifs du paquebot 'St.-Louis'* (Paris: L'Harmattan, 2005), 193–8. See also Weiss, *Mémoires d'une européenne*, 233–48; Papanek, *Out of the Fire*, 63–76.
22. USHMM, Russian Holocaust Foundation, JDC Collection File 354, List of *St. Louis* children in Union OSE homes. This list states that there were 27 children from the *St. Louis* in the OSE homes. This number is confirmed in a letter from the OSE to the CAR, reprinted in Afoumado, *Exil impossible*, 218–19. Hanna Papanek and others place this number at 60. Papanek, *Elly und Alexander*, 77.
23. Hanna Papanek states this was an Austrian branch of the Red Falcons. However, there was indeed a French branch of the Red Falcons. Downs, *Childhood in the Promised Land*, 198.
24. Papanek, *Elly und Alexander*, 66–7.
25. Papanek, *Elly und Alexander*, 66–7.
26. Papanek was interned in Domfront and then in Damigny (Orne, Normandy). Lilly Maier, *Auf Wiedersehen, Kinder!: Ernst Papanek, Revolutionär, Reformpädagoge und Retter jüdischer Kinder* (Vienna: Molden Verlag, 2021), 140.

27. Papanek, *Elly und Alexander*, 83–4.

28. Papanek, *Elly und Alexander*, 84.

29. On these terms, see Carrie Paechter, "Tomboys and Girly Girls: Embodied Femininities in Primary Schools," *Discourse: Studies in the Cultural Politics of Education*, 31, no. 2 (2010), 221–35.

30. Interview with Hanna Papanek, Lexington, MA, July 16, 2015.

31. Daniel Boyarin, *Unheroic Conduct: The Rise of Heterosexuality and the Invention of the Jewish Man* (Berkeley, CA: University of California Press, 1997).

32. Max Nordau, in 1898 at the second congress of the Zionist Organization in Basel, discussed the need to strive for *Muskeljudentum* as a solution to Jewish distress [*Juddennot*]. Patrick Farges, "'Muscle' Yekkes?: Multiple German Jewish Masculinities in Palestine/Israel after 1933," *Central European History* (special issue on 'Masculinities in the Third Reich'), 513, no. 3 (September 19, 2018), 466–87.

33. Sharon Gillerman, *Germans into Jews: Remaking the Jewish Social Body in the Weimar Republic* (Stanford, CA: Stanford University Press, 2009), 136–62. On *Bildung*, see Mosse, *German Jews*, 1–20.

34. Erin Corber, "Race, corps, et dégénérescence chez les Éclaireurs Israélites dans l'Entre-deux-guerres," *Archives Juives: Revue d'histoire des Juifs de France*, 50, no. 2 (2017), 55–75. As an example, see Loinger and Hazan, *Aux frontières de l'espoir*, 53–66.

35. Interview with Kurt Sonnenfeld, New York, July 15, 2015.

36. Interview with Gus Papanek, in the presence of Hanna Papanek, Lexington, July 16, 2015.

37. Interview with Ernst Valfer, Berkeley, December 13, 2016.

38. Fredrik Barth, *Ethnic groups and Boundaries: The Social Organization of Culture Difference* (Boston, MA: Little, Brown and Co., 1969), 9–38; Papanek, *Elly und Alexander*, 78.

39. Interview with Ernst Valfer, Berkeley, December 13, 2016.

40. Interview with Elfriede Meyer Schloss, San Diego, December 16, 2016. Aryanization and ghettoization in Frankfurt intensified after February 1940. "Frankfurt am Main. The City and the Holocaust," Holocaust Research Project, http://www.holocaustresearchproject.org/nazioccupation/frankfurt.html, consulted June 3, 2018.

41. The contemporaneous sources I have found cannot be considered representative. Furthermore, Heinz Löw's diary makes many allusions to his prime caretaker, his grandmother. USHMM, RG 2007.421 Ruth Salmon Seltzer Papers, Folder 12, Heinz Löw diary.

42. Dwork and Van Pelt, *Flight from the Reich*, 245–63.

43. Brauner, *L'Accueil des enfants des survivants*, 96–7.

44. Papanek, *Out of the Fire*, 107–8.

45. Censorship began as early as 1939. According to one source, postal service between France and Germany ended in 1940. CDJC, *Les enfants de La Guette*, 43. See also, "Le contrôle postal sous Vichy," Courriers de France et de Français durant la Seconde Guerre mondiale, http://ww2postalhistory.fr/Fr40_01_fr.php?cat=post40&activ=02, consulted June 12, 2018.

46. Dwork and Van Pelt, *Flight from the Reich*, 246–54. Some of this correspondence was collected and translated into French by Werner Matzdorff, whose own family benefited from Luz's generosity. Mémorial de la Shoah, Werner Marzdorff Collection MDXXVIII. See also forthcoming work by Deborah Dwork on Tante Elisabeth.

47. Mémorial de la Shoah, Marzdorff Collection MDXXVIII, Box 1, Tante Elisabeth to Hanna-Ruth Klopstock,1945; Box 2, Ursula Matzdorff journal, c.1942–1943; Dwork and Van Pelt, *Flight from the Reich*, 256.
48. Mémorial de la Shoah, Matzdorff collection MDXXVIII, Box 1, Letter from Elisabeth Luz to Annettli-Hanna –Ruth Klopstock, February 15, 1945.
49. USHMM, RG 2007.421, Ruth Salmon Seltzer Papers, Folder 12, Heinz Löw diary.
50. Ernst Papanek, "Children during Air Raids," *Progressive Education*, XIX, no. 3 (March 1942), 157–9; Ernst Papanek, "My Experiences with Children in War-time," *Trend, Quarterly Student's Journal of the New York School of Social Work, Columbia University*, 4, no. 1 (Fall 1942), 6–7. More generally, on the psychological turn, see Zarha, *The Lost Children*, 88–117.
51. Papanek, "Children during Air Raids," 159.
52. Interview with Werner Dreifuss, San Diego, December 16, 2016; Werner Dreifuss, *The Epitome of the American Dream: Memoirs of Werner Dreifuss* (Self-published, 2016), 20–7, 228.
53. Dreifuss, *The Epitome of the American Dream*, 228.
54. Interview with Hanna Papanek, Lexington, MA, July 16, 2015.
55. USHMM, RG 2007.421 Ruth Salmon Seltzer Papers, Folder 12, Heinz Löw diary.
56. USHMM, RG 2007.421 Ruth Salmon Seltzer Papers, Folder 12, Heinz Löw diary.

Chapter 9

1. Mémorial de la Shoah, Matzdorff Collection MDXXVIII, Box 1, Le Hôme de la Guette, Lida Jablonski, c.1968. In this chapter, I build on themes explored in Hobson Faure, "Exploring Political Rupture," 270–2.
2. JDC-NY, France, AR 1933–1945, File 610, Cable from Joseph Schwartz, February 3, 1941.
3. Conversation with municipal employee of La Bourboule, April 2014.
4. "Rothschilds Bring $1,000,000 in Gems: Notables and Jewels here from Europe on a Yankee Clipper," *The New York Times*, July 11, 1940.
5. Jablon, Quennouëlle-Corre, and Straus, *Politique et finance*, 57–8, 63–5.
6. JDC-NY, France, AR 1933–1945, File 610, Cable from Joseph Schwartz, February 3, 1941 states that the expenses of the home are being covered entirely by the Rothschild family still, but that help was requested from the JDC.
7. Downs, "Enfance en guerre," 413–48; Lindsey Dodd, "Wartime Rupture and Reconfiguration in French Family Life: Experience and Legacy," *History Workshop Journal*, 88 (2019), 134–52.
8. *La Revue OSE*, November 1939, 7–8. The JDC helped fund this activity.
9. Lemalet, "Les comités d'accueil," 87–104, especially 96.
10. According to Célia Bertin, they had a liaison during the occupation, around 1943. Bertin, *Louise Weiss*, 241, 320–5. Letters from Rucart from 1942 to 1945 can be found in the Louise Weiss collection, BNF, NAF 17812, 261–70.
11. Mémorial de la Shoah, Fonds Chevrier, CCLXXIII-9, Rapport sur l'assistance privée étrangère en France, November 5, 1939, by Felix Chevrier. See also Hazan, *Rire le jour, pleurer la nuit*, 14–15; "Chevrier, Félix [Chevrier Jules, Félix]," *Le Maitron*, March 2010, https://maitron.fr/spip.php?article79066, consulted July 18, 2023.

12. By October 1940, there were 6 Union OSE homes in the unoccupied zone. Archives d'État, UISE collection, 92.18.4, Union OSE report, October 1940. The larger figure of 14 takes into account those of other organizations, including the Éclaireurs Israélites de France and the Pouponnière. See Hazan and Klarsfeld, *Le sauvetage des enfants juifs pendant l'Occupation*, 19, 79–103.

13. Hazan, *Rire le jour, pleurer la nuit*, 14–15.

14. USHMM, RG-50.812.0041, Interview with Ruth Keller conducted by Lisa Gossels, https://collections.ushmm.org/search/catalog/irn538984, consulted June 18, 2018.

15. She does not state where the others were placed at this moment. Salomon et al., *Andrée Salomon, une femme de lumière*, 96.

16. Salomon et al., *Andrée Salomon, une femme de lumière*, 98. She does not provide their date of arrival in Clermont-Ferrand.

17. OSE headquarters archives, Lists.

18. Alice Freistadt-Lederer was born in 1902 and was listed on the Quincy boys' retroactive lists as one of their educators (OSE Archives-Headquarters). Her professional credentials can be found on her 1938 questionnaire for the Vienna Jewish Community, https://www.nli.org.il/ar/archives/NNL_CAHJP997011 250265805171/NLI#$FL196737637, consulted August 21, 2023.

19. Jacoby, *Davongekommen*, 70.

20. OSE Headquarters archives, folder De Monbrison, "Témoignage d'Eric Goldfarb," Nouvelles Racines, no. 50, Combs-la-Ville, 19–20.

21. Jacoby, *Davongekommen*, 70–1.

22. Herzberg, *The Past Is Always Present*, 90–3; Ralph Moratz, "Escape from the Holocaust," Blog, Chapter 6, https://ralphm1935.wordpress.com, consulted June 20, 2018.

23. Herzberg, *The Past Is Always Present*, 92.

24. OSE Headquarter Archives, Folder Monbrison, Letter from C. Peter Gossels to Francoise (sic) Blanchard, April 14, 1997. Interview with C. Peter and Werner Gossels and Stephan Lewy, Wayland, 2015.

25. I am currently annotating this manuscript for publication.

26. YIVO, GJCA casefile for Hans Stern.

27. Stephan Lewy papers, Hans Stern, "Children under Nazi Invasion Boots."

28. Annette Wieviorka describes this phase of the occupation well: "Those who arrive are Germans. They are young, beautiful, clean, well-shaven, well-dressed [. . .]. They commit no crime. They occupy, very simply, correctly." Annette Wieviorka, *Tombeaux: Autobiographie de ma famille* (Paris: Seuil, 2022), 189. More generally, see Michael Mann, "Were the Perpetrators of Genocide 'Ordinary Men' or 'Real Nazis'? Results from Fifteen Hundred Biographies," *Holocaust and Genocide Studies*, 14, no. 3 (2000), 331–66.

29. Stephan Lewy papers, Hans Stern, "Children under Nazi Invasion Boots," 29.

30. From Stephan Lewy's biography. Herzberg, *The Past Is Always Present*, 104.

31. Archives du Ministre des Affaires étrangères, Cabinet du Ministre, 24GMII/1, Letter from Cabinet civil du Maréchal Pétain to Louise Weiss, January 18, 1941; Bertin, *Louise Weiss,* 274–84.

32. Anna Toscano, *Michel Romanoff de Russie: Un destin français* (Paris: L'Harmattan, 2014), 53–69.

33. Mémorial de la Shoah, Christian de Monbrison collection, Account by Renée de Monbrison, 5.

34. Interview with C. Peter Gossels, Boston, July 17, 2015; Interview with Norbert Bikales, Livingston, New Jersey, July 10, 2015; Stephan Lewy papers, Hans Stern, "Children under Nazi Invasion Boots"; Eryk Goldfarb biography, USHMM, https://collections.ushmm.org/search/catalog/pa1149957, consulted June 20, 2018.

35. Alexandre Doulut's PhD shows that foreign and French Jews had a much higher survival rate in the unoccupied zone, especially foreign Jewish children, even after the full occupation of France in November 1942. Alexandre Doulut, "La déportation des Juifs de France: Changement d'échelle" (PhD Dissertation, Université Paris 1 Panthéon-Sorbonne, 2021), 369–87.

36. State Archives Geneva, UISE Collection, Folder 92.18.3, Handwritten note from Erna Magazier to Georges Thélin (UISE), November 22, 1940.

37. See the 1941 account of an older child from the group, Bernd Warschuer, which also states they were going to Limoges. Chabannes Diary, Mémorial de la Shoah, Chevrier Collection, CCLXXIII-9, Journal de Chabannes. La Pouponnière enabled organizations to evacuate Jewish children from French internment camps, such as Gurs. The parents, who remained in the camps, were deported. See Pierre Goetschel's documentary on the role of his grandfather, Gustave Goestchel, in La Pouponnière: L'héritage retrouvé.

38. State Archives Geneva, UISE Collection, Folder 92.18.3, Note from Erna Magazier to Georges Thélin (UISE), November 22, 1940. Stephan Lewy papers, Hans Stern, "Children under Nazi Invasion Boots," Mémorial de la Shoah, Chevrier collection CCLXXIII-9, contains notecards on each child, showing the date of their arrival in Chabannes.

39. Interview with Norbert Bikales, Livingston, July 10, 2015.

40. Interview with Norbert Bikales, Livingston, July 10, 2015.

41. Several of the younger children were sent to the Château de Chaumont. Moratz, "Escape from the Holocaust 1939," posted on May 17, 2015, https://ralphm1935. wordpress.com, consulted August 28, 2023.

42. See Corber, "L'Esprit du Corps" and Noémie Beltramo and Rudy Rigaut, "Des colonies de vacances juives au service de la régénération physique: L'exemple de la Colonie scolaire, 1927–1939," Archives Juives: Revue d'histoire des Juifs de France, 56, no. 1 (2023), 60–77.

43. Berta Romana Seidenstein, interviewed by Michaela Raggam-Blesch, Vienna, December 2015.

44. Berta Romana Seidenstein, interviewed by Michaela Raggam-Blesch, Vienna, December 2015.

45. IISG, Ernst Papanek Collection, File F-22, Letter from Ilsa Shellan to Ernst Papanek, April 16, 1967.

46. Afoumado, Exil impossible, 218–19.

47. Catherine Collomp, Résister au nazisme: Le Jewish Labor Committee, New York, 1934–1945 (Paris: CNRS Éditions, 2016), 99–112; Papanek, "Quatre enfants à Montintin," 386–402.

48. Telephone interview with Ernst Valfer, November 24, 2016.

49. Interview with Ruth, California, December 11, 2016.

50. Interview with Ruth, California, December 11, 2016.

51. The home had been set up by Rabbi Zalman Schneerson, who transferred it to the OSE in 1941. Hazan and Klarsfeld, Le sauvetage des enfants juifs pendant l'Occupation, 128–31.

52. USHMM, Susi Hilsenrath Warsinger Collection, RG 2000.127, Diary, trans. from German by Susan Hilsenrath Warsinger June 27, 1941.
53. Interview with Ruth, California, December 11, 2016.
54. Interview with Ruth, California, December 11, 2016.
55. Hirsch, *Home Is Where You Find It*, 43.
56. Interview with Susi Hilsenrath Warsinger, Washington, DC, June 6, 2014. See also a recording of her presenting at the US Holocaust Memorial, https://www.youtube.com/watch?v=u0r61JA07lA, consulted June 15, 2018.
57. USHMM, Susi Hilsenrath Warsinger Collection, RG 2000.127, Diary, July 28, 1941.
58. USHMM, Susi Hilsenrath Warsinger Collection, RG 2000.127, Diary, July 28, 1941.
59. USHMM, Susi Hilsenrath Warsinger Collection, RG 2000.127, Diary, June 30, 1941.
60. USHMM, Susi Hilsenrath Warsinger Collection, RG 2000.127, Diary, July 2, 1941.
61. USHMM, Susi Hilsenrath Warsinger Collection, RG 2000.127, Diary, July 6, 1941.
62. USHMM, Susi Hilsenrath Warsinger Collection, RG 2000.127, Diary, July 15, 1941.
63. Interview with Ernst Valfer, Berkeley, December 3, 2016.
64. Interview with Ernst Valfer, Berkeley, December 3, 2016.
65. Interview with Ernst Valfer, Berkeley, December 3, 2016.
66. Interview with Ernst Valfer, Berkeley, December 3, 2016.
67. Sluzki, "Migration and Family Conflict," 379–90.
68. USHMM, Susi Hilsenrath Warsinger Collection, RG 2000.127, Diary, July 15, 1941.

Chapter 10

1. He was head of the Jüdische Wirtschaftshilfe. C. Peter Gossels Papers, Charlotte Lewy Gossels Biography.
2. YIVO, German Jewish Children's Aid Collection (hereafter GJCA), RG 294, Werner Gossels Case File; Kaplan, *Between Dignity and Despair*, 50–73.
3. He was most likely sent to St Cyprien and transferred to Gurs. On expulsions from Belgium to France, see Sybil Milton and Frederick D. Bogin, *Archives of the Holocaust: An International Collection of Selected Documents. American Jewish Joint Distribution Committee, New York, Volume 10. Parts 1 and 2.* (New York and London: Garland Publishing, 1995), Document 158, Memorandum on the Situation of Jewish Refugees from Belgium in France, September 8, 1940, 789–90; Herman Van Goethem and Patricia Ramet (eds.), *Drancy-Auschwitz, 1942–1944: Les Juifs de Belgique déportés via la France* (Malines: Kazerne Dossin/VUBPress, 2015).
4. Interview with C. Peter Gossels, Boston, July 17, 2015; VHA, USC Shoah Foundation, C. Peter Gossels interview (37230), December 1, 1997.
5. YIVO, GJCA Collection, RG 294, Werner Gossels Casefile, Letter from Charlotte Lewy to Mrs. Gruenfeld, February 28, 1941.
6. VHA, USC Shoah Foundation, Interview with C. Peter Gossels, Boston, December 1, 1997.

7. In Berlin, Peter had attended a Jewish school for two years; Interview with C. Peter Gossels, Boston, July 17, 2015.
8. Letter from Onkle Fanti to his nephews, August 11, 1939, in C. Peter R. Gossels, *Letters from our Mother*, 77. This letter and all others from this book were trans. from German.
9. Letter from Charlotte Lewy to her children, February 11, 1940, in C. Peter R. Gossels, *Letters from our Mother*, 117.
10. Letter from Charlotte Lewy to her children, February 26, 1940, in C. Peter R. Gossels, *Letters from our Mother*, 121.
11. Letter from Charlotte Lewy to her children, December 2, 1940, in C. Peter R. Gossels, *Letters from our Mother*, 194.
12. According to the Yad Vashem victims' database, his deportation occurred from Berlin to the Piaski Ghetto in Poland. His place of murder is not listed. https://yvng.yadvashem.org/nameDetails.html?language=en&itemId=11522760&ind=1, consulted March 3, 1942.
13. Hazan, *Rire le jour, pleurer la nuit*, 50. Interview with Raïa J., Paris, May 9, 2017. Shannon Fogg points out that the children's homes were in fact beneficial to the local economy, leading to a positive perception of their presence. Shannon Fogg, *The Politics of Everyday Life in Vichy France: Foreigners, Undesirables, and Strangers* (New York: Cambridge University Press, 2009), 151–88.
14. One can read, in Peter's school notebook, "Child who learned French for two years. Excellent results. Intelligent child." L'institutrice Paillassou, Chabannes, August 2, 1941, reprinted in C. Peter R. Gossels, *Letters from our Mother*, 243.
15. VHA, USC Shoah Foundation, Interview with C. Peter Gossels, December 1, 1997.
16. Lisa Gossels and Dean Wetherell, *The Children of Chabannes*, Good Egg Productions, 1999 [DVD].
17. Letter from C. Peter Gossels to his parents, *Letters from our Mother*, 227. See French version of letter, 228–9.
18. Anne Grynberg, *Les camps de la honte: Les internés juifs des camps français, 1939–1944* (Paris: La Découverte, 1999), 81.
19. Grynberg, *Les camps de la honte*, 12.
20. Letter from C. Gossels to Dr. Lippmann, April 4, 1941, in C. Peter R. Gossels, *Letters from our Mother*, 217.

Chapter 11

1. Viviana Zelizer, *Pricing the Priceless Child: The Changing Social Value of Children* (Princeton, NJ: Princeton University Press, 1994), 3–21, 56–72, quote on 209.
2. Moody, *Les droits de l'enfant*, 126. More generally, see Paula Fass (ed.), *The Routledge History of Childhood in the Western World* (New York: Routledge, 2015).
3. In her study of the USCOM, Kathryn Close gives the figure of 309 children brought to the United States by the USCOM until August 1942. After this date, an additional 80 children were sent from Lisbon, most of whom had crossed from France into Spain illegally. Close, *Transplanted Children*, 27. After the war, OSE identified 253 children as its wards. In addition to these children, sponsored by the USCOM, some Jewish children benefited from the USCOM transports to

the United States, having obtained private sponsorship. These children are not included in the USCOM's statistics, which allows me to posit that approximately 280 were Jewish for the 1941–1942 period. Serge Klarsfeld, *French Children of the Holocaust: A Memorial* (New York: New York University Press, 1996), 102–4; Archives OSE-Headquarters, "Liste des enfants partis pour les États-Unis en 1941–1942," May 29, 1945.

4. Among the first to mention the evacuations was Maurice Davie in 1947. Likewise, USCOM commissioned a history of its work in 1953. There was a gap in the scholarship until 1980 when Hillel Kieval published a significant article on the question of the rescue of Jewish children in occupied France, making use of American and French archival resources. A decade later, historian Judy Tydor Baumel-Schwartz, the younger sister of two evacuees, published a book on the experiences of Jewish child refugees in the United States during the Second World War, touching on the evacuations from France. Maurice Davie, *Refugees in America: Report of the Committee for the Study of Recent Immigration from Europe* (New York: Harper and Brothers, 1947), 208–16; Close, *Transplanted Children*, 25–35; Kieval, "Legality and Resistance in Vichy France"; Baumel-Schwartz, *Unfulfilled Promise*, 83–8. Most recently, Deborah Dwork and Robert Jan. Van Pelt dedicated several pages to those they call the "USCOM Children": Dwork and Van Pelt, *Flight from the Reich*, 235–50.

5. To provide some examples: the OSE archives are held at this organization's head-quarters in Paris, at the Mémorial de la Shoah, and at the YIVO institute in New York. The USHMM has a copy of OSE records from the Mémorial de la Shoah but not the entire collection. The AFSC headquarters archives are located in Philadelphia, while the archives of its branch offices throughout France are also available at the USHMM in Washington, DC. USCOM archives are scattered throughout other collections, forcing historians to piece together parts of its history in the GJCA Collection at YIVO and the JDC archive.

6. On the role of OSE in the evacuations, see Hazan, "Le sauvetage des enfants juifs de France vers les Amériques," 481–93. Likewise, Sabine Zeitoun acknowledges other organizations, yet presents the Union OSE as the one responsible for selecting the children. Zeitoun, *L'Œuvre aux secours aux enfants (OSE)*, 137–45. On the USCOM, see Ostrovsky, "We Are Standing By"; Ron Coleman, "The US Committee for the Care of European Children (USCOM) and the Rescue of Children," USHMM Research Brief (unpublished), September 2015. On the AFSC, see Laura Gumpert, "Humble Heroes: How the American Friends Service Committee Struggled to Save Oswald Kernberg and Three Hundred Other Jewish Children from Nazi Europe" (Undergraduate Thesis, Haverford College, 2002). Most recently, Stephanie Corazza provided the most multifaceted analysis on occupied France, upon which I rely in the following chapters. Corazza, "The Routine of Rescue."

7. Alexis de Tocqueville, *De la démocratie en Amérique, textes essentiels: Anthologie critique par J.L. Benoît* (Paris: Pocket, 2007), 86–90.

8. Jonathan Sarna, *American Judaism: A History* (New Haven, CT and London: Yale University Press, 2004), 2–3; Jonathan Woocher, *Sacred Survival: The Civil Religion of American Jews* (Bloomington, IN: Indiana University Press, 1986), 22–62; Michael N. Dobkowski, *Jewish American Voluntary Organizations* (Westport, CT: Greenwood, 1986), 641–59.

9. Beth Wenger, *New York Jews and the Great Depression: Uncertain Promise* (New Haven, CT and London: Yale University Press, 1996), 136–65.

10. Henry Feingold, *A Time for Searching: Entering the Mainstream, 1920–1945* (Baltimore, MD: The John Hopkins University Press, 1992), 90–124; Jonathan Woocher, *Sacred Survival*, 34–5.

11. Baumel-Schwartz, *Unfulfilled Promise*, 15–16. It included the American Jewish Committee, the American Jewish Congress, and the B'nai Brith. The American Jewish Committee, established in 1906, mobilized the "uptown" elite with its discreet approach to defending Jews' civil rights. "Downtown Jews," as descendants of the late-nineteenth-century Eastern European migrations, usually more Zionist, left-wing, and working-class, preferred the more vocal American Jewish Congress.

12. Baumel-Schwartz, *Unfulfilled Promise*, 16. For a detailed account of the GJCA's creation, see Bat-Ami Zucker, *Cecilia Razovsky and the American Jewish Women's Rescue Operations in the Second World War* (London: Valentine Mitchell, 2008), 31–61.

13. Zucker, *Cecilia Razovsky*, 2–3.

14. Muncy, *Creating a Female Dominion*, 38–65.

15. After running the National Council of Jewish Women's Immigrant Aid Department from 1920 onward, Razovsky became associate director of the organization in 1932.

16. The NCC was created in 1934 at the suggestion of the State Department and James McDonald, High Commissioner for Refugees. While technically non-sectarian, the large majority of its funds came from the JDC. The NRS succeeded this organization in 1939 and provided an array of services to potential refugees. "Finding Aid, National Coordinating Committee for Aid to Refugees," YIVO Archives, http://www.yivoarchives.org/index.php?p=collections/controlcard&id=33738, consulted June 26, 2018; "National Refugee Service," YIVO Archives, http://www.yivoarchives.org/index.php?p=collections/controlcard&id=33739, consulted June 26, 2018. See also Genizi, *American Apathy: The Plight of Christian Refugees from Nazism* (Ramat-Gan: Bar-Ilan University Press, 1983), 286–98.

17. As Daniel Walkowitz points out, in the United States, social work had largely feminized by the 1930s. However, men remained in positions of power. Daniel J. Walkowitz, "The Making of a Feminine Professional Identity: Social Workers in the 1920s," *American Historical Review*, 95, no. 4 (1990), 1055.

18. This meant they would require a quota number. Baumel-Schwartz, *Unfulfilled Promise*, 51.

19. The Department of Labor reserved the right to request the posting of bonds to prevent the children from becoming public charges. Baumel-Schwartz, *Unfulfilled Promise*, 17; Zucker, *Cecilia Razovsky*, 33–8.

20. It is unclear whether this was stipulated in the law or simply a guideline, but what is clear is that Americans were uncomfortable with perceived racial mixing, which informed the policies of caring for children by members of their own faith. On the controversies of "mixed race" child adoption schemes, see Linda Gordon, *The Great Arizona Orphan Abduction*. Kathryn Close calls this policy an "American tradition": Close, *Transplanted Children*, 30. Judith Tydor Baumel states this is a law: Baumel-Schwartz, *Unfulfilled Promise*, 144. For placement guidelines, see Ron Coleman Papers, "Planning for Care of Children from Overseas seeking Refuge in the United States," *The Child*, 5, no. 1 (July 1940), 9–10; "Care of

Children Coming to the United States for Safety Under the Attorney General's Order of July 13, 1940," United States Department of Labor, Children's Bureau, Publication No. 268, 1941.

21. Baumel-Schwartz, *Unfulfilled Promise*, 51; Zucker, *Cecilia Razovsky*, 57.

22. Joseph P. Chamberlain, NCC chairman, a law professor at Columbia, cited in Zucker, *Cecilia Razovsky*, 46.

23. Corazza, "The Routine of Rescue," 73–4.

24. Baumel-Schwartz, *Unfulfilled Promise*, 51; YIVO, OTC Collection RG 1941, Folder 119, Email from Judy Tydor Baumel to Iris Posner, January 17, 2003.

25. As with the progressive women who staffed the Children's Bureau, they did not replace men but benefited from the new structure to create a "female dominion." Muncy, *Creating a Female Dominion*, 48–54.

26. Other board members included Dr. Solomon Lowenstein, Maurice Karpf, Harry Lurie, Isaac Asofsky, Joseph Hyman, Judge Nathan Perlman, Max Kohler, as well as Cheryl Wise; Zucker, *Cecilia Razovsky*, 54.

27. YIVO, GJCA Collection, RG 249, File 79, Note from Lotte Marcuse, April 17, 1941.

28. JDC, AR 1933–1945, Organizational Files: GJCA, File 236, Letter from JC Hyman to W. Haber, December 7, 1940.

29. Gordon, *The Great Arizona Orphan Abduction, 3–19*. I build here on Laura Hobson Faure "Jewish Children Refugees from Central Europe," 135–9.

30. Robert Bremner, "Other People's Children," *Journal of Social History*, 16, no. 3 (1983), 88; Sean Martin, "How to House a Child: Providing Homes for Jewish Children in Interwar Poland," *East European Jewish Affairs*, 45, no. 1 (2015), 29. On Jewish orphanages in the United States: Reena Sigman Friedman, "Founders, Teachers, Mothers and Wards: Women's Roles in American Jewish Orphanages, 1850–1925," *Shofar*, 15, no. 2 (1997), 21–42; Reena Sigman Friedman, *These Are Our Children: Jewish Orphanages in the United States, 1880–1925* (Waltham, MA: Brandeis University Press, [1994] 2002).

31. Zahra, *The Lost Children*, 72. More generally, Dagmar Herzog, *Cold War Freud: Psychoanalysis in an Age of Catastrophes* (Cambridge: Cambridge University Press, 2017).

32. Baumel-Schwartz, *Unfulfilled Promise*, 18; Ron Coleman Papers, "Care of Children coming to the United States for Safety under Attorney General's Order of July 13, 1940. Standards Prescribed by the Children's Bureau," 2.

33. Boris Bogin, *Jewish Philanthropy: An Exposition of Principles and Methods of Jewish Social Service in the United States* (New York: Macmillan Company, 1917), 160. In the aftermath of the First World War, American Jewish welfare standards were quickly aligning with the professionalizing trends in the larger field of American welfare. Especially during the Depression, social work offered progressive-minded American Jews stable employment and a needed refuge from increasing antisemitism. Herman D. Stein, "Jewish Social Work in the United States, 1654–1954," *American Jewish Yearbook*, 57 (1956), 2–98. Feingold, *A Time for Searching*, 152, 220.

34. Baumel-Schwartz, *Unfulfilled Promise*, 105–7, 146–50.

35. Haim Genizi, "New York Is Big: America Is Bigger: The Resettlement of Refugees from Nazism, 1936–1945," *Jewish Social Studies*, 46, no. 1 (1984), 61–72.

36. Baumel-Schwartz, *Unfulfilled Promise*, 18–19; Zucker, *Cecilia Razovsky*, 41–7.

37. For example, the 1921 quota for Poland was just under 6,000 individuals, whereas the quota for Germany was about 51,000. In 1929, Congress modified the quotas again, cutting the German quota to just under 26,000 immigrants annually, while the United Kingdom's was increased from 34,000 to 66,000. Barry Trachtenberg, *The United States and the Nazi Holocaust: Race, Refuge, and Remembrance* (London: Bloomsbury Academic, 2018), 19.

38. Naomi Cohen, *Not Free to Desist: The American Jewish Committee, 1906–1966* (Philadelphia, PA: Jewish Publication Society of America, 1972), 137–42.

39. Trachtenberg, *The United States and the Nazi Holocaust*, 20.

40. Perkins was the first woman to hold a cabinet-level position in the United States. Bat-Ami Zucker, "Frances Perkins and the German-Jewish Refugees, 1933–1940," *American Jewish History*, 89, no. 1 (March 2001), 35–59.

41. From 1937 to 1940, George Messersmith, as assistant secretary of State, had authority over the visa division. He was well-informed about the situation in Nazi Germany but preferred a conservative interpretation of visa regulations. Furthermore, visa policy was shaped by President Hoover's September 1930 decision to strictly apply the 1882 Immigration Act, which stated that any person "likely to become a public charge" (LPC Proviso) should be denied a visa. Anyone without a work contract or sufficient resources was required to submit two strong affidavits from friends or family. Richard Breitman and Alan M. Kraut, *American Refugee Policy and European Jewry, 1933–1945* (Bloomington, IN: Indiana University Press, 1987), 39–51, 56–62; Baumel-Schwartz, *Unfulfilled Promise*, 11–13.

42. Aristide R. Zolberg, *A Nation by Design: Immigration Policy in the Fashioning of America* (New York: Harvard University Press, 2006), 277.

43. Breitman and Kraut, *American Refugee Policy*, 57–8.

44. Richard Breitman and Allan J. Lichtman, *FDR and the Jews* (Cambridge, MA: Belknap Press, 2013), 316.

45. American Jewish Historical Society (AJHS), Kenworthy Papers, P-511, Box 2, Folder 10, "Present at meeting at Dr. Kenworthy's, December 18, 1938."

46. AJHS, Kenworthy Papers, P-511, Box 2, Folder 10, Meeting at My Home, December 18, 1938.

47. Including Katherine Lenroot, director of the United States Children's Bureau. See also Catherine Rymph, "American Child Welfare and the Wagner-Rogers Bill of 1939," *Jewish Historical Studies: A Journal of English-Speaking Jewry*, 51 (2019), 285–300.

48. Joyce Antler, "Justine Wise Polier," *Shalvi/Hyman Encyclopedia of Jewish Women*, 31 December 1999, Jewish Women's Archive, viewed on September 22, 2023, https://jwa.org/encyclopedia/article/polier-justine-wise.

49. More research is needed on Kenworthy and her personal motivation for this cause. Her religious affiliation is noted in AFSC Archives (Philadelphia), Box Comms and Orgs: American Jewish Committee to Open Road, Letter from Justine Wise Polier to Clarence Pickett, November 17, 1939.

50. AJHS, Kenworthy Papers, P-511, Box 3, Folder 10, Letter from Kenworthy to Pickett, December 8, 1938.

51. AJHS, Kenworthy Papers, P-511, Box 1, folder 4, Letter from Kenworthy to Johnson, June 16, 1939.

52. Genizi, *American Apathy*, 172.

53. Clarence Pickett, *For More than Bread: An Autobiographical Account of Twenty-Two Years' Work with the American Service Committee* (Boston, MA: Little, Brown and Co., 1953), 166–7.

54. AJHS, Kenworthy Papers, P-511, Box 2, Folder 10, Meeting at My Home, December 18, 1938.
55. AJHS, Kenworthy Papers, P-511, Box 2, Folder 10, Meeting at My Home, December 18, 1938.
56. AJHS, Kenworthy Papers, P-511, Box 2, Folder 10, Meeting at My Home, December 18, 1938.
57. AJHS, Kenworthy Papers, P-511, Box 2, Folder 10, Meeting at My Home, December 18, 1938.
58. AJHS, Kenworthy Papers, P-511, Box 2, Folder 11, Some notes, December 19, 1938.
59. Zelizer, *Pricing the Priceless Child.*
60. AJHS, Kenworthy Papers, P-511, Box 2, Folder 12, "Jan. 15, 1939."
61. AJHS, Kenworthy Papers, P-511, Box 2, Folder 12, "Jan. 15, 1939." According to Zolberg, there were about 525,000 self-identifying Jews and 292,000 individuals of Jewish descent in Germany in 1933. Zolberg, *A Nation by Design*, 272.
62. Michael Berkowitz, "Introduction: Breadth and Depth in the History of the Kindertransport and Beyond," *Jewish Historical Studies*, 51 (2019), xii.
63. AJHS, Kenworthy Papers, Box 2, Folder 13, Notes on Meeting in Marion Kenworthy's home, February 20, 1939.
64. Baumel-Schwartz, *Never Look Back*, 201. The fact that the archives of the sending institutions in Germany were lost makes this question difficult to explore. Curio, " 'Invisible' Children," 41–56; Paul Weindling, "The Kindertransport from Vienna: The Children Who Came and Those Left Behind," *Jewish Historical Studies*, 51 (2019), 16–32. Rose Holmes notes that "non-Aryan" children in Austria were selected by the AFSC. Her statistics (644 "non-Ayran" children) pertain to those sent to England. Rose Holmes, "A Moral Business: British Quaker Work with Refugees from Fascism, 1933–39" (PhD Dissertation, University of Sussex, December 2013), 130–48.
65. AJHS, Justine Wise Polier Collection (P-527), Folder 19, Letter from Eleanor Roosevelt to Justine Wise Polier, January 4, 1939.
66. Congressional Record, February 9, 1939, 1278, https://www.govinfo.gov/content/pkg/GPO-CRECB-1939-pt2-v84/pdf/GPO-CRECB-1939-pt2-v84.pdf, consulted June 26, 2018.
67. Goldstein, "Contesting the Categories," 94–5.
68. Baumel-Schwartz, *Unfulfilled Promise*, 55–6, 165; AJHS, Kenworthy Papers, P-511, Box 1, Folder 7, "Plan for the Care of German Refugee Children in the United States."
69. Dorothy Legaretta, *The Guernica Generation: Basque Refugee Children of the Spanish Civil War* (Reno, NV: University of Nevada Press, 1984), 179–83; Gloria Totoricagüena, "Historical Aspects to Political Identity in the New York Basque Community," http://www.euskonews.com/0234zbk/kosmo23402.html, consulted August 8, 2018; Donald Crosby, "Boston's Catholics and the Spanish Civil War: 1936–1939," *The New England Quarterly*, 44, no. 1 (1971), 96–9.
70. Breitman and Kraut, *American Refugee Policy*, 73; Rymph, "American Child Welfare," 297.
71. *Il Grido della Stirpe*, March 25, 1939, reprinted in the Congressional Record, April 21, 1939, https://www.govinfo.gov/content/pkg/GPO-CRECB-1939-pt4-v84/pdf/GPO-CRECB-1939-pt4-v84-15.pdf, consulted June 28, 2018.
72. This comment was published in Pierrepont Moffat's diary, which was published in 1956. Raphael Medoff, "American Jewish Responses to Nazism and the Holocaust," in Marc Lee Raphael (ed.), *The Columbia History of Jews and Judaism in America* (New York: Columbia University Press, 2008), 297.

73. Grainne McEvoy, "Family Unity, Child Refugees and the American Catholic Bishop's Response to the Wagner-Rogers Bill, 1939" (Working Paper, Boston College Center for Christian Jewish Learning, January 2015), 18–19.
74. Breitman and Lichtman, *FDR and the Jews*, 317; Baumel-Schwartz, *Unfulfilled Promise*, 30.
75. AFSC Archives, Phil., Comms and Orgs, American Jewish Committee to Open Road, The Non-Sectarian Foundation for Refugee children, Inc, Minutes, March 16, 1940.
76. AFSC Archives, Phil., Comms and Orgs, American Jewish Committee to Open Road, The Non-Sectarian Foundation for Refugee children, Inc, Minutes, March 16, 1940.
77. AFSC Archives, Phil., Comms and Orgs, American Jewish Committee to Open Road, The Non-Sectarian Foundation for Refugee children, Inc, Minutes, March 16, 1940; Letter from Owen Lovejoy to Clarence Pickett, April 16, 1940.
78. AFSC Archives, Phil., Comms and Orgs, American Jewish Committee to Open Road, Letter from Owen Lovejoy to Agnes King Inglis, May 16, 1940.
79. Rymph, "American Child Welfare." On Owen R. Lovejoy, see https://digital.jane-addams.ramapo.edu/items/show/2179, consulted October 4, 2023.
80. AFSC Archives, Phil., Comms and Orgs, American Jewish Committee to Open Road, The Non-Sectarian Foundation for Refugee children, Inc, Minutes of special meeting of directors, July 9, 1940; Genizi, *American Apathy*, 321–3.
81. AFSC Archives, Phil., Comms and Orgs, American Jewish Committee to Open Road, Letter from Clarence Pickett, September 23, 1940. USCOM was incorporated on July 3, 1940. Coleman, "The US Committee," 7.
82. Close, *Transplanted Children*, 79. We also see members from the New York School of Social Work, AFSC, as well as Jewish organizations, such as William Haber.
83. This term was coined by Churchill in 1946, yet it refers to a longer period, dating from the end of the nineteenth century.
84. Ostrovsky, "We Are Standing By," 230–50.
85. Ostrovsky, "We Are Standing By," 238.
86. JDC-NY, AR 1933–1944, Orgs: USCOM, File 343, General Memorandum 11, by Eric Biddle, October 26, 1940.

Chapter 12

1. Papanek, *Out of the Fire*, 217–18.
2. Rare are the historical accounts of rescue that take into account the difficulty Jews had convincing non-Jews to assist them. Ostrovsky's work on the USCOM, for example, praises the committee's rescue work without alluding to the tensions involved and without discussing the JDC's role. Ostrovsky, "We are Standing By," 239–44. This kind of difficulty, however, is a theme in many survivors' memoirs. On Poland, see Tec, *Dry Tears*, 35–40; On France, Françoise Frenkel, *Rien où poser sa tête* (Paris: L'Arbalète Gallimard, [1945] 2015).
3. Abraham J. Karp, *To Give Life* (New York: Schocken Books, 1981), 59–73; Marc Lee Raphael, *A History of the United Jewish Appeal* (Place unknown: Scholars Press, 1982).
4. In its first year, the United Jewish Appeal raised over $15 million, marking a huge increase from the total of $7 million collected in previous separate campaigns. Karp, *To Give Life*, 71.

5. On the history of the JDC, see Yehuda Bauer's three-part institutional history, including *My Brother's Keeper, American Jewry and the Holocaust: The Joint Distribution Committee, 1939–1945* (Detroit, MI: Wayne State University Press, 1981) and *Out of the Ashes: The Impact of American Jews on Post-Holocaust Jewry* (Oxford: Pergamon Press, 1989). On its role in France from 1933 to 1954, see Hobson Faure, *A "Jewish Marshall Plan."*

6. See Chapter 8 and, more generally, Afoumado, *Exil impossible.*

7. JDC-NY, AR 1933–1944, Orgs.: OSE, File 325, Report on the Central Board of the OSE Union, Fifth Conference 1937, by Gurvic, submitted to conference on August 28, 1937. This report states that JDC provided 23 per cent of its 1930 budget, and 22 per cent in 1936.

8. JDC-NY, AR 1933–1944, Orgs.: OSE, File 325, Memo from Katzki to Warburg, June 21, 1939.

9. JDC-NY, AR 1933–1944, France: Children, File 610, Cable (JDC Lisbon to NY); October 7, 1940, Memo to the US Children's Bureau, Washington, DC, September 30, 1940; YIVO, GJCA collection, RG 249, Folder 318, "One year in OSE's children's houses for refugees in France," by Ernst Papanek, March 1940.

10. OSE Archives (Headquarters), Tschenloff Collection, "Les tâches de l'OSE dans l'hémisphère occidental," by Leon Wulman, January 1946. This document states 1924, while a second report states 1925 and 1929. JDC-NY, AR 1933–1944, Orgs.: OSE, File 325, Report on the Central Board of the OSE Union, Fifth Conference 1937, by Gurvic, submitted to conference on August 28, 1937. There are multiple spellings of this individual's name (Gourvitch). I use the spelling Gurvic. JDC-NY, JDC News, December 15, 1944. The first delegation was composed of 18 doctors; JDC-NY, AR 1933–1944, Orgs.: OSE, File 325, J. Golub "OSE-Pioneer of Jewish Health," *Jewish Social Service Quarterly*, Vol. XIV, no. 4 (June 1938), reprinted with permission of the JDC, July 7, 1939. I first explored this question in Laura Hobson Faure, "Attentes européennes, réalités américaines: l'émigration des enfants juifs de l'œuvre de secours aux enfants de la France occupée vers les Etats-Unis," in Hobson Faure et al. (eds), *L'Œuvre de secours aux enfants et les populations juives*, 166–83.

11. In addition to Dr. Jack Golub and Ratnoff, M. Rosenau, E. Libman, A. Rongy. JDC-NY, AR 1933–1944, Orgs.: OSE, File 325, Report on the Central Board of the OSE Union, Fifth Conference 1937, by Gurvic, submitted to conference on August 28, 1937. On JDC and TOZ, see Granick, *International Jewish Humanitarianism*, 182–94; Jack Golub, "The JDC and Health Programs in Eastern Europe," *Jewish Social Studies*, 5, no. 3 (1943), 293–304.

12. The OSE was echoing the actions of its sister organization, ORT. JDC-NY, AR 1933–1944, Orgs.: OSE, File 325, Report on the Central Board of the OSE Union, Fifth Conference 1937, by Gurvic, submitted to conference on August 28, 1937; "Form American Committee to Sponsor OZE Health Work in Europe," JTA, May 29, 1929.

13. On February 17, 1938, for example, the American OSE Committee organized a meeting at Harmonie Club in New York City, attended by 65 physicians. A second meeting was planned at Dr. Golub's home at the end of February 1938 for 30–40 physicians. JDC-NY, AR 1933–1944, Orgs.: OSE, File 325, Letter from Rongy to Warburg, February 17, 1938; Letter from Golub to Hyman, February 18, 1938. A.J. Rongy was born in Lithuania and came to the US at the age of 15. "Funeral Services Today for Dr. A.J. Rongy; Died at Mt. Sinai Hospital at Age of 71," *JTA*, October 12, 1949. JDC-NY, AR 1933–1944, Orgs.: OSE, File 325, Letter from Golub to Hyman, February 18, 1938.

14. Established in 1904 by Jewish medical students, Phi Delta Epsilon considered itself non-sectarian. In 1928, it had 42 chapters and 3,500 members. "Non-sectarian Medical Fraternity Protests Discrimination Against Jews," *JTA*, December 26, 1928. See also "History, Phi Delta Epsilon," http://phide.org/history-2/, consulted September 25, 2018.
15. JDC-NY, AR 1933–1944, Orgs.: OSE, File 325, Letter from Hyman to Golub, February 17, 1938.
16. JDC-NY, AR 1933–1944, Orgs.: OSE, File 325, Letter from Hyman to Troper, January 12, 1939.
17. Dr. Laserson was sent by OSE in January 1939; Boris Pregel was sent in June 1939. JDC-NY, AR 1933–1944, Orgs.: OSE, File 325, Letter from Hyman to Troper, January 12, 1939. JDC-NY, AR 1933–1944, Orgs.: OSE, File 325, Letter from Henrietta Buchman JDC (NY) to Pregel, Tres. Union OSE France, July 7, 1939.
18. JDC-NY, AR 1933–1944, Orgs.: OSE, File 325, Letter from Henrietta Buchman JDC (NY) to Pregel, Tres. Union OSE France, July 7, 1939.
19. JDC-NY, AR 1933–1944, Orgs.: OSE, File 325, Letter from Henrietta Buchman JDC (NY) to Pregel, Tres. Union OSE France, July 7, 1939.
20. "3 Polish Jewish Leaders Allowed to Enter U.S. on 6-month Visas," *JTA*, October 29, 1939.
21. JDC-NY, AR 1933–1944, Orgs.: OSE, File 326, Letter from Leon Wulman to JDC, February 12, 1940.
22. JDC-NY, AR 1933–1944, Orgs.: OSE, File 326, Letter from Brutzkus and Gurvic to Golub, October 18, 1940.
23. JDC-NY, AR 1933–1944, Orgs.: OSE, File 326, Summary of meeting JDC NY (Leavitt) and Pregel, November 6, 1940. After a brief period of employment at JDC in 1929–1930, Moses Leavitt joined JDC in 1940 as general secretary. "Dr. Joseph C. Hyman Resigns After Quarter of a Century of Active Service with J.D.C.," *JTA*, January 13, 1947; JDC-NY, AR 1933–1944, Orgs.: OSE, File 326, Letter JDC (Moses Leavitt) to Charles F. Noyes Company, November 26, 1940.
24. JDC-NY, AR 1933–1944, Orgs.: OSE, File 326, Letter from Pregel and Rongy to JDC NY (Hyman), December 18, 1940. The committee was co-chaired by Dr. A.J. Rongy and Dr. Boris Pregel; Dr. Golub and Dr. Jedwabnik were vice-chairmen and Dr. Chaim Breyner served as treasurer.
25. JDC-NY, AR 1933–1944, Orgs.: OSE, File 327, Letter from Hyman to Leavitt, February 18, 1941.
26. JDC-NY, AR 1933–1944, Orgs.: OSE, File 327, Letter from Hyman to Leavitt, February 18, 1941. Hyman suggested $300, but $250 was provided per month, Letter from Buchman to Wulman, April 9, 1941.
27. JDC-NY, AR 1933–1944, Orgs.: OSE, File 327, Letter from Hyman to Leavitt, February 18, 1941.
28. Email correspondence with Catherine Collomp, April 19, 2012. On his difficulties escaping France, see IISG, Papanek collection, Folder A-7, Interview with Edward Linn, Transcript of tape 1.
29. Papanek, *Out of the Fire*, 199.
30. JDC-NY, AR 1933–1944, Orgs.: USCOM, File 343, Letter from Hyman to JDC Lisbon, November 18, 1940.
31. JDC-NY, AR 1933–1944, Orgs.: OSE, File 326, Report by Papanek to the American Committee of the OSE, December 26, 1940.

32. JDC-NY, AR 1933–1944, France: Children, File 610, Letter from Comité israélite (Guy de Rothschild) to Schwartz (Lisbon JDC), August 20, 1940.

33. JDC-NY, AR 1933–1944, France: Children, File 610, Letter from Schwartz to Troper, September 9, 1940.

34. JDC-NY, AR 1933–1944, France: Children, File 610, Letter from Troper to Schwarz, October 7, 1940.

35. "Rothschilds Bring $1,000,000 in Gems," *The New York Times*, July 11, 1940. See also Laura Hobson Faure, "Baroness Germaine de Rothschild."

36. JDC-NY, AR 1933–1944, France: Children, File 610, Letter from Germaine de Rothschild to Mr. Troper, July 20, 1940.

37. Rothschild Archive, Waddesdon Manor, JDR2/33/11, Letter from Germaine de Rothschild to Dorothy de Rothschild, January 15, 1941.

38. Rothschild Archive, Waddesdon Manor, JDR2/33/11, Letter from Germaine de Rothschild to Dorothy de Rothschild, undated.

39. Rothschild Archive, Waddesdon Manor, JDR2/33/11, Letter from Germaine de Rothschild to Dorothy de Rothschild, January 15, 1941, trans. from French.

40. Rothschild Archive, Waddesdon Manor, JDR2/33/11, Letter from Germaine de Rothschild to Dorothy de Rothschild, January 25, 1941, trans. from French.

41. The boys who came were students of the Philanthropic gymnasium in Frankfurt who boarded in a hostel run by Hugo and Lilli Steinhardt. Jon Nordheimer, "15 Who Fled Nazis as Boys Hold a Reunion," *The New York Times*, July 28, 1983.

42. Rothschild Archive, Waddesdon Manor, JDR2/33/11, Letter from Germaine de Rothschild to Dorothy de Rothschild, January 15, 1941, trans. from French.

43. University of Michigan, Bentley Historical Library, William Haber Papers, Box 20, Folder NRS 1941, "Summer Placement for Refugee children – 1941. A Report of the Committee on summer placement for refugee children." c.1941.

44. Rothschild Archive, Waddesdon Manor, JDR2/33/11, Letter from Germaine de Rothschild to Dorothy de Rothschild, April 28, 1941, trans. from French.

45. Papanek, *Out of the Fire*, 219.

46. Papanek, *Out of the Fire*, 217–28. JDC-NY, AR 1933–1944, Orgs.: OSE, File 326, Report by E. Papanek to the American Committee of the OSE, December 26, 1940. IISG, Papanek Collection, B-5, Ernst Papanek Agenda, 1940. The idea that Papanek was extremely active is supported by Jenny Masour-Ratner, *Mes vingt ans à l'OSE, 1941–1961* (Paris: Fondation pour la mémoire de la Shoah/ Éditions Le Manuscrit, 2006), 39–40.

47. IISG, Ernst Papanek Collection, B-5, Ernst Papanek agenda 1940. His agenda shows him meeting with Mr. Rosen on September 16 and Tropper [sic] on September 19.

48. Baumel-Schwartz, *Unfulfilled Promise*, 57.

49. Elsa Castendyck, "Refugee Children in Europe," *Social Service Review*, 13, no. 4 (December 1939), 587–601.

50. Susan Ware and Stacy Lorraine Braukman (eds.), *Notable American Women: A Biographical Dictionary, Completing the Twentieth Century* (Cambridge, MA: Belknap Press, 2004), 520.

51. JDC-NY, AR 1933–1944, Orgs.: OSE, Folder 326, Report by E. Papanek to the American Committee of the OSE, December 26, 1940.

52. AFSC Phil., Foreign Service, Refugee services, general to Cummington Hostel, 1940, US Committee folder, Cable from Pickett to Kershner, November 4, 1940.

53. USCOM papers used to be held at Marshall Field's business offices in Chicago. Since

this institution went out of business, some his papers on the USCOM were transferred to the Chicago History Museum (Series 2, subseries 4). I have accessed incomplete records at the YIVO's GJCA collection, the JDC archive in New York, and the AFSC archive in Phil. See the (now out-of-date) dissertation, David Nathan, "The United States Committee for the Care of European Children, 1940–1953: A History and Guide to the Records" (Master's Thesis, University of Massachusetts, 1983).

54. JDC-NY, AR 1933–1944, France: Children, File 610, Letter from M. Troper to J. Schwartz, October 7, 1940.

55. Steven Stoll, "Adele Rosenwald Levy, 1892–1960," Shalvi/Hyman Encyclopedia of Jewish Women, Jewish Women's Archive. https://jwa.org/encyclopedia/article/Levy-Adele-Rosenwald, consulted July 5, 2018. AJHS, Kenworthy Papers, P-511, Box 2, Folder 10, List Present, December 18, 1938 and January 15, 1939.

56. JDC-NY, AR 1933–1944, France: Children, File 610, Letter from JDC NY (Hyman) to JDC Lisbon, November 18, 1940.

57. Papanek, *Out of the Fire*, 224–7.

58. JDC-NY, AR 1933–1944, France: Children, File 610, Letter from M. Troper to J. Schwartz, October 7, 1940.

59. JDC-NY, AR 1933–1944, France: Children, File 610 JDC, Letter from JDC NY (J. Hyman) to JDC Lisbon, November 18, 1940.

60. AFSC Phil., Foreign Service, Refugee services, general to Cummington Hostel, 1940, US Committee folder, Letter to the Attorney General of the United States, July 20, 1940.

61. Genizi, *American Apathy*, 175.

62. Pickett, *For More than Bread*, 94.

63. JDC provided AFSC a grant of $2,500 in 1933 and $2,500 in 1934. Genizi, *American Apathy*, 174–5.

64. Pickett, *For More than Bread*, 133–4, 143; Genizi, *American Apathy*, 197–8.

65. Pickett does not date this request in his autobiography. The Assistant Secretary of State refused his offer. Pickett, *For More than Bread*, 140–1.

66. YIVO, OTC collection, RG 1941, Folder 119, Letter from Cecilia Razovsky to Morris Troper, August 1, 1939.

67. Pickett, *For More than Bread*, 143–4.

68. AFSC Phil., General files, Comms and Orgs, American Jewish Committee to Open Road, Letter from Executive secretary to Mr. Trager (American Jewish Committee), April 5, 1939; Letter from Samuel Scheiner to John Rich, March 7, 1940; Letter from Lillian Traugott to Samuel Scheiner, April 29, 1940.

69. The literature on antisemitism in the United States is too extensive to list here and under renewal. For a concise summary, see Henry Feingold, *A Time for Searching*, 1–34.

70. AFSC Phil., Foreign Service, Refugee services, general to Cummington Hostel, 1940, US Committee folder, Cable from Pickett to Kershner, November 4, 1940; Letter from B. Cloeren to Eric Biddle, November 26, 1940, containing Kershner's response.

71. YIVO, GJCA Collection, RG 249, File 318, Letter from JDC (Lillian Cantor) to Lotte Marcuse, November 25, 1940. "Mr. Hyman asked me to advise you that under no conditions are any of us to address letters to, or call up the US COMM, without clearing this through Dr. Haber, who has the direct contact with that Committee."

72. YIVO, GJCA Collection, RG 249, 318, Letter from J. Hyman to Eric H. Biddle, USCOM, November 18, 1940.

73. One can find two dates for its creation, October 1939 and the official date of May 1940. Susan Subak, *Rescue & Flight: American Relief Workers Who Defied the Nazis* (Lincoln, NE: University of Nebraska Press, 2010), 26–7.

74. On Sharp's work in Prague, see Brade and Holmes, "Troublesome Sainthood"; Subak, *Rescue & Flight*, 3, 40 and, more generally, 1–65. Subak states the USCOM asked Sharp to represent their work in Europe before her departure in June 1940, but, as seen above, the USCOM was not formally created until July 1940. See also Deborah Dwork, *Saints and Liars: The Story of Americans Who Saved Refugees from the Nazis* (New York: W.W. Norton & Co., 2025).

75. Cited in Coleman, "The US Committee," 10.

76. USHMM, Martha and Waiststill Sharp Collection, series 1.2, folder 4, telegram in French, September 5, 1940.

77. Archives départementales des Pyrénées Atlantiques, Série W, 1031 W 133: Organisation des soupes populaires [. . .], aides aux réfugiés et à des œuvres diverses, Rapport de l'Inspection générale des services de Police Administrative, Vichy, du 2 octobre 1940.

78. Children of Jewish backgrounds were included. Subak, *Rescue & Flight*, 61. Clement and Mercedes Brown were Catholic, and six of Pastor Edouard Theis's daughters, Protestants, were included. USHMM, 67.017, Sharp Collection, Series 3, folder 26, Questionnaire USHMM, 67.017, Sharp Collection, Series 1.2, box 2, Transport lists.

79. Costs for the evacuation were shared by USC, USCOM, and HIAS, the Jewish migration agency. Coleman, "The US Committee," 10; Subak, *Rescue & Flight*, 60–4. The USCOM stated in January 1941 that 16 children came with the Unitarian group, which reflects the number they sponsored. AFSC, General Files, Foreign Service, Refugee Services, Comms and Orgs, 1941, Report of the Executive Director to the Board of Directors, January 1941.

80. There may have been rivalry between the two organizations. Their relationship was not without conflict due to the USC's "patriotic stance" as opposed to Quaker neutrality. Genizi, *American Apathy*, 217.

81. JDC-NY, AR 1933–1944, France: Children, File 610, Cable from Lisbon, December 10, 1940. The same cable can be found in the AFSC Phil. archives, General files, Comms and Orgs, American Jewish Committee to Open Road.

82. JDC-NY, AR 1933–1944, France: Children, File 610, Letter from J. Hyman to C. Pickett, January 24, 1941. OSE's lists of children were also sent directly to Papanek and were found in the GJCA archives. YIVO, GJCA, File 318, A list sent directly from Gurvic to Papanek, January 27, 1941, of children to emigrate.

83. JDC-NY, AR 1933–1944, France: Children, File 610, Letter from John Rich (AFSC) to Joseph Hyman, January 28, 1941.

84. AFSC Phil., General Files, Foreign Service, Refugee Services, Comms and Orgs, 1941, Report of the Executive Director to the Board of Directors, January 1941.

85. AFSC Phil., General Files, Foreign Service, Refugee Services, Comms and Orgs, 1941, Report of the Executive Director to the Board of Directors, January 1941.

86. Elfriede Schloss Papers, Excerpt from AFSC archive, Letter from Marshall Field to Clarence Pickett, February 7, 1941.

87. Elfriede Schloss Papers, Excerpt from AFSC archive, Memorandum from USCOM to Howard Kershner (AFSC), February 7, 1941.

88. Elfriede Schloss Papers, Excerpt from AFSC archive, Memorandum from USCOM to Howard Kershner (AFSC), February 7, 1941.

89. Elfriede Schloss Papers, Excerpt from AFSC archive, Memorandum from USCOM to Howard Kershner (AFSC), February 7, 1941.
90. JDC-NY, AR 1933–1944, Orgs.: USCOM, File 343, Daily Memorandum 1, to Warburg from Evelyn Morrissey, February 18, 1941. Meeting with Miss Ingles (USCOM) and Troper, Hyman, and Leavitt.
91. AFSC Phil., General files 1941, Comms and Orgs, Selfhelp of emigrés from Central Europe to War resisters league, 1941, Recommendation of the sub-committee appointed pursuant to resolutions of the Board dated January 22, 1941 by Clarence Pickett, Louis Weiss and Alfred Whitman, February 25, 1941.
92. Coleman, "The US Committee," 11.
93. YIVO, GJCA, RG 249, File 290, Memo regarding USCOM – C. Razovsky March 13, 1941; Elfriede Schloss Papers, Letter from Allen Bonnell to James Vail AFSC, June 18, 1941.
94. USHMM, RG 1995.A.1218, Irene Arnold Unpublished Memoirs, October 1988. Her statement confuses several groups of children.
95. The debate was triggered by the publication of Arthur Morse, *While Six Million Died: A Chronicle of American Apathy* (London: Secker and Warburg, 1968).
96. Interview with Gus Papanek, Lexington, MA, July 16, 2015.
97. Papanek, *Out of the Fire*, 217.
98. Papanek, *Out of the Fire*, 217.
99. Papanek, *Out of the Fire*, 227.
100. Cited in Pickett, *For More than Bread*, 171.

Chapter 13

1. OHD, (1)20, Andrée Salomon interviewed by Haim Avni, 1963, trans. from French.
2. Éric Alary, "Les Juifs et la ligne de démarcation," *Cahiers de la Shoah*, 5 (2001), 13–49.
3. The geographic divisions that resulted from the armistice are much more complex than a simple two-zone scenario. The north-east of France was occupied yet under the jurisdiction of Nazi authorities in Belgium. The Italian zone, initially quite narrow, expanded to include Nice from November 1942 to September 1943. On the deportation process in each zone, see Alexandre Doulut, "La déportation des Juifs de France." See also Alary, "Les Juifs."
4. Published in the *Journal Officiel*, July 23, 1940. The majority of those who were denaturalized were Jews. Claire Zalc, *Dénaturalisés: Les retraits de nationalité sous Vichy* (Paris: Seuil, 2016).
5. Published in the *Journal Officiel*, October 18, 1940. On its origins, see Laurent Joly, "The Genesis of Vichy's Jewish State of October 1940," *Holocaust and Genocide Studies*, 27, no. 2 (2013), 276–98; Laurent Joly, *Vichy dans la "solution finale": Histoire du Commissariat général aux questions juives (1941–1944)* (Paris: Grasset, 2006), 75–100.
6. Published in the *Journal Officiel*, October 18, 1940. On its application, see Doulut, "La déportation des Juifs de France," 225–30.
7. See Laurent Joly, *L'État contre les Juifs: Vichy, les nazis et la persécution antisémite* (Paris: Grasset, 2018); on its implications for Jewish individuals, see Poznanski, *Les Juifs en France*.
8. Nicolas Mariot and Claire Zalc, *Face à la persécution: 991 Juifs dans la guerre* (Paris: Odile Jacob/Fondation pour la mémoire de la Shoah, 2010); Zalc and

Mariot, "Identifier, s'identifier: Recensement, auto-déclarations et persécution des Juifs de Lens (1940–1945)," *Revue d'histoire moderne & contemporaine*, 54, no. 3 (2007), 91–117.

9. The historiography has now reached the consensus that this decision was made prior to the January 1942 Wannsee conference, at which the "Final Solution" was confirmed and its logistics discussed. Peter Hayes, *Why?: Explaining the Holocaust* (New York: W.W. Norton & Co., 2017).

10. On communal divisions among French Jews, see Caron, *Uneasy Asylum* and Poznanski, *Les Juifs en France*. On the departures during this moment, considered the "golden window of opportunity," see Jennings, *Escape from Vichy*, 17–33. With the exception of Jennings' study, we have not significantly studied the emigration of Jews from occupied France in the 1940–1942 period.

11. OHD, (1)20, Andrée Salomon interviewed by Haim Avni, 1963.

12. Kieval, "Legality and Resistance in Vichy France," 345.

13. Here, I base my analysis on the American and French OSE archives, as well as the French AFSC collection held at the US Holocaust Memorial Museum, private papers, and the AFSC Philadelphia headquarters. I also rely on Stephanie Corazza's excellent dissertation, Corazza, "The Routine of Rescue," 38–103, and that of Kelly Palmer, "Humanitarian Relief and Rescue Networks in France, 1940–45" (PhD Dissertation, Michigan State University, 2010), 73–112.

14. Grynberg, *Les camps de la honte*, 41, 59.

15. In May 1940, women aged 17 to 56 from belligerent countries were also interned. In October 1940, two pieces of Vichy legislation allowed for the internment of foreign Jews and foreigners, passed on October 4 and 10, 1940, respectively.

16. Van Goethem and Ramet, *Drancy-Auschwitz, 1942–1944*.

17. Michael R. Marrus and Robert O. Paxton, *Vichy France and the Jews* (Stanford, CA: Stanford University Press, 1995), 66.

18. Grynberg, *Les camps de la honte*, 12.

19. Reed, *The Children of La Hille*, 53. See also Simon Collignon, "Les homes Bernheim et Speyer (1938–1940): Témoignages d'enfants réfugiés d'Allemagne et d'Autriche," *Les cahiers de la mémoire contemporaine*, 6 (2005), 21–67.

20. Reed, *The Children of La Hille*, 79.

21. He does not recall the actual date, but it is most likely after the October 4 or October 10 law. Henri Parens, *Renewal of Life: Healing from the Holocaust* (Rockville, MD: Schreiber Publishing, 2004), 34–5.

22. Parens, *Renewal of Life*, 22–61. See also Corazza, "The Routine of Rescue," 104–57.

23. OSE Headquarters Archives, Folder OSE-La Guette, Union OSE Report, January–June 1942. On evacuating children from the camps, see Zeitoun, *Histoire de l'OSE*, 264–72; Vivette Samuel, *Rescuing the Children: A Holocaust Memoir* (Madison, WI: University of Wisconsin Press, 2002), 50–6; Alice Resch Synnestvedt, *Over the Highest Mountains: A Memoir of Unexpected Heroism in France during World War II* (Pasadena, CA: Intentional Productions, 2005), 95–125.

24. Grynberg, *Les camps de la honte*, 228; Corazza, "The Routine of Rescue," 128. On the colonies, see Célia Keren, "Autobiographies of Spanish Refugee Children at the Quaker Home in La Rouvière (France, 1940): Humanitarian Communication and Children's Writings," *Cahiers de la Framespa*, 5 (2010), https://journals.open-edition.org/framespa/268, consulted March 4, 2024; Shannon Fogg, " 'Beaucoup de mères ne veulent pas se séparer de leurs enfants': Les limites de l'aide apportée

aux enfants par l'American Friends Service Committee dans la France de Vichy," in Hobson Faure, Pignot, and Rivière, *Enfants en guerre*, 195–213.

25. YIVO, American OSE Committee Collection, RG 494, Folder 1, Letter from J. Millner and L. Gurvic to Amerose, June 12, 1941. As of this date, a total of 296 children had been released from the internment camps. Around 200 were received in OSE homes, 50 in Quaker children's colonies and 50 in Secours Suisse homes.

26. AFSC provided food to 84,000 children and vitamins for 100,000 children in 1941 alone in France. Genizi, *American Apathy*, 201. See also forthcoming work by Shannon Fogg.

27. In collaboration with Louise Weiss, and as a gesture of thanks to France for its reception of the *St. Louis* refugees, JDC opened the Mimi Pinson Canteen in Paris, for destitute women and children. JDC-NY, AR 1933–1944, France: Children, File 610, Report of Mimi Pinson Kitchen, 81 rue Lepic, Paris by Mrs. Louise Weiss, president of managing committee, February 27, 1940.

28. Donald Lowrie, *The Hunted Children* (New York: W.W. Norton & Co., 1963), 45–50. He was forced to change employers to the World's Alliance YMCA in order to remain in France.

29. On this particular moment of panic and distress, see Varian Fry, *Surrender on Demand* (Boulder, CO: Johnson Books, [1945] 1997), as well as the novel by Anna Seghers, *Transit* (Paris: Éditions Autrement, [1944] 1995). More generally, see Julia Elsky, *Writing Occupation: Jewish Émigré Voices in Wartime France* (Palo Alto, CA: Stanford University Press, 2020).

30. He also represented the American Friends of Czechoslovakia, known as Czech Aid. Lowrie, *The Hunted Children*, 104.

31. OHD, 12 (47) Herbert Katzki interviewed by Yehuda Bauer, 1968.

32. Lowrie, *The Hunted Children*, 85.

33. OHD, 12 (47) Herbert Katzki interviewed by Yehuda Bauer, 1968.

34. USHMM, RG 50.030*337, Interview with Hebert Katzki, June 2, 1995. Katzki worked in banking until 1936. His first overseas assignment for JDC was in France, where he arrived in December 1939.

35. Lowrie, *The Hunted Children*, 87.

36. On JDC in France during the 1942–1944 period, see Laura Hobson Faure, " 'Guide and Motivator' or 'Central Treasury'?: The Role of the American Jewish Joint Distribution Committee in France, 1942–1944," in Jacques Sémelin, Claire Andrieu, and Sarah Gensburger (eds.), *Rescue Practices Facing Genocides: Comparative Perspectives* (London and New York: Hurst/Columbia University Press, 2011), 293–311 and Hobson Faure, *A "Jewish Marshall Plan,"* 23–39.

37. In spite of its importance, this group's work in France has, until recently, received little scholarly attention. Shannon Fogg, "Remembering the American Friends Service Committee's Wartime Aid," Conference Presentation, Society for French Historical Studies, March 2018. See also Keren, "Autobiographies"; Fogg, "The American Friends Service Committee and Wartime Aid to Families," 108–22; Palmer, "Humanitarian Relief," 73–112; Corazza, "The Routine of Rescue," 38–103.

38. Pickett, *For More than Bread*, 115.

39. Daniel Maul, "The Politics of Neutrality: The American Friends Service Committee and the Spanish Civil War, 1936–1939," *European Review of History: Revue Européenne d'histoire*, 23, no. 1–2 (2016), 94–5.

40. Howard E. Kershner, *The Menace of Roosevelt and His Policies* (New York: Greenberg, 1936).

41. USHMM, AFSC Collection, RG 67.007M, Box 60, Folder 55. Howard Kershner Diary, October 2 and November 7, 1939.
42. USHMM, AFSC Collection, RG 67.007M, Box 60, Folder 55. Howard Kershner Diary, November 5, 1939.
43. USHMM, AFSC Collection, RG 67.007M, Box 60, Folder 55. Howard Kershner Diary, February 19, 1941.
44. Palmer, "Humanitarian Relief," 87–8; Shannon Fogg, "American Quakers in France," Seminar talk in Nancy Green's seminar, École des hautes études en sciences sociales, January 30, 2018.
45. OHD, 12 (47) Herbert Katzki interviewed by Yehuda Bauer, 1968.
46. Lowrie, *The Hunted Children*, 83.
47. This included Mr. Stevenson, Helga Holbek, and Céline Rott. LBI, France concentration camp collection, AR 3987/MF 836, Nîmes Committee Minutes, December 10, 1940; Synnestvedt, *Over the Highest Mountains*, 89.
48. LBI, French concentration camp collection, AR 3987/MF836, Quakers file.
49. On February 14, 1941, Kershner wrote that it would be tragic to cancel the program now, cited in Corazza, "The Routine of Rescue," 61.
50. Elfriede Schloss Papers; Letter from Margaret Frawley to John Richardson (acting director of US COMM), March 12, 1941. The letter quotes a letter from Kershner from February 20, 1941.
51. JDC-NY, AR 1933–1944, Orgs.: USCOM, File 343, Memo 351, From Katzki to Lisbon, March 21, 1941.
52. USHMM, AFSC Collection, RG 67.007M, Box 60, Folder 55. Howard Kershner Diary, "Concerns to be Presented to Maréchal Pétain," January 8, 1941; see January 20, 1941 for account of their meeting.
53. USHMM, AFSC Collection, RG 67.007M, Box 60, Folder 55. Howard Kershner Diary, undated entry, Two Days with Maréchal Pétain.
54. USHMM, AFSC Collection, RG 67.007M, Box 60, Folder 55. Howard Kershner Diary, undated entry, Two Days with Maréchal Pétain.
55. USHMM, AFSC Collection, RG 67.007M, Box 60, Folder 55. Howard Kershner Diary, undated entry, Two Days with Maréchal Pétain. This piece is followed by diary entries on September 22 and 23, 1941, providing a similar, yet less polished, account of the same event.
56. Citations from Kershner's diary turn up in Clarence Pickett's autobiography. Pickett, *For More than Bread*, 171. Palmer, "Humanitarian Relief," 92.
57. USHMM, AFSC Collection, RG 67.007M, Box 57, Folder 3, Delegates' meeting, October 14, 1941.
58. His numbers on the internee population are grossly underestimated. Howard E. Kershner, "Defeated France Knows Only Hunger and Want," *The New York Times*, June 28, 1942; Palmer, "Humanitarian Relief," 82–3.
59. It is likely he did not write this piece, since he had returned to the United States by this date (he went back in late May or early June 1942); USHMM, AFSC Collection, RG 67.007M, Box 60, Folder 55. Howard Kershner Diary, Diary of Emergency Evacuation of Jewish Children, October 9, 1942.
60. Promotional film on AFSC aid, 1942, https://www.youtube.com/watch?v=l9aG_LbcQHA, consulted August 10, 2018.
61. USHMM, AFSC Collection, RG 67.007M, Box 57, Folder 3, Delegates' meeting, October 13, 1941.

62. Christopher Browning, "From Humanitarian Relief to Holocaust Rescue," *Holocaust and Genocide Studies*, 30, no. 2 (2016), 222.
63. Howard Kershner, *Quaker Service in Modern War* (New York: Prentice-Hall, 1950), 190.
64. Cited in Palmer, "Humanitarian Relief," 99.
65. Selfhelp of Émigres' leadership was both Christian and Jewish. Genizi, *American Apathy*, 329–31. See AFSC Phil., General files 1941, Comms and Orgs, File: Selfhelp of émigres from Central Europe to War Resisters League.
66. USHMM, AFSC Records, RG 67.007M, Box 57, Folder 3, Delegates' meeting, September 3, 1941.
67. AFSC Phil., General Files, Foreign Service, France: Marseilles correspondence Jan. to April to France Refund of unclaimed funds, 1941, File, Marseille letters May–August 1941, Letter from John Rich to Allen Bonnell (Marseille) on SelfHelp contribution to camps, July 23, 1941.
68. AFSC Phil., General Files, Foreign Service, France: Marseilles correspondence Jan. to April to France Refund of unclaimed funds, 1941, File, Marseille letters May–August 1941, Letter from John Rich to Allen Bonnell (Marseille) on SelfHelp contribution to camps, July 23, 1941.
69. USHMM, AFSC Records, RG 67.007M, Box 57, Folder 3, Delegates' meeting, September 3, 1941.
70. Grynberg, *Les camps de la honte*, 204.
71. The article not only mentioned the "heterogeneous populations" in the camps but also the "former Jewish population of Baden." "Misery and Death in French Camps. Thousands Interned Give Up Hope, Lacking Nearly All Decencies of Life," *The New York Times*, January 26, 1941.
72. Grynberg, *Les camps de la honte*, 245–8.
73. Peschanski, *La France des camps*, 238.
74. I visited the camp in 2021. The cemetery's restoration was financed by a German Jewish association from the Baden in the 1960s. Scott Soo, "Putting Memory to Work: A Comparative Study of Three Associations Dedicated to the Memory of the Spanish Republican Exile in France," *Diasporas: Histoire et sociétés*, 113 (2005), 109–20.
75. Palmer, "Humanitarian Relief," 97. As this book was going to print, I discovered Paul Moke's analysis of Kershner, which independently confirms my findings. Paul Moke, "AFSC and the Holocaust. Pathways of Conscience in Vichy France," *Quaker History*, 109 (2020), 8–14.
76. One must distinguish between the AFSC and the Religious Society of Friends. In the occupied zone, four Quakers from the Religious Society of Friends in Paris risked sending a letter to Xavier Vallat, head of Vichy's Commissariat général aux questions juives, to protest Vichy's treatment of Jews. YIVO, GJCA collection, RG 249, File 151, Copy of a Letter addressed by the Religious Society of Friends (Quakers) to Monsieur le Haut Commissaire aux questions juives, July 15, 1941.
77. Corazza, "The Routine of Rescue," 55–6.
78. Palmer, "Humanitarian Relief," 87, 98–100; Fogg, "American Quakers in France." Holbek's proactive work on behalf of Jewish rescue is detailed in Synnestvedt, *Over the Highest Mountains*.
79. Synnestvedt, *Over the Highest Mountains*, 79. According to one source, AFSC had a permanent resident in Gurs only in March 1943. LBI, AR 3987/MF 836, Quakers file, Report on Relief Activities of Secours Quaker in France (Based on

conversations with Helga Holbek), by Ross and Marjorie McClelland, October 1943. However, other sources show AFSC in Gurs in 1941. Synnestvedt, *Over the Highest Mountains*, 95–124.

80. Synnestvedt, *Over the Highest Mountains*, 105.

81. Synnestvedt, *Over the Highest Mountains*, 57–92.

82. The sources differ on the number expelled: 3,000 according to Alary, "Les Juifs," 17. On Weill and the AFSC, see Synnestvedt, *Over the Highest Mountains*, 81.

83. Persecution—and escape from it—is a major theme in the deeply seated commemorative traditions, established in the Middle Ages, of *selihot*, second Purims, and fast days. Yosef Hayim Yerushalmi, *Zakhor, Jewish History and Jewish Memory* (New York: Schocken Books, 1989), 31–52. On Salomon's religious views, one finds many photos of her with bare arms and uncovered hair. See also Zeitoun, *L'Œuvre de secours aux enfants*, 328; Weill, "Introduction," 33–73.

84. OSE Headquarters Archives, Andrée Salomon Papers, Letter from Isidor Marx to A. Salomon, April 2, 1945.

85. Letter from Frédéric Hammel to Andrée Salomon in Salomon et al., *Andrée Salomon*, 177–8. On Gamzon and the EIF, see Lee, *Pétain's Jewish Children*.

86. Georges Weill, Ruth Fivaz-Silbermann, and Katy Hazan, "Joseph Weill," http://www.ose-france.org/wp-content/uploads/2011/06/JOSEPHWEILL.pdf, consulted August 15, 2018. On the creation of the youth center, see Corber, "The Kids on Oberlin Street."

87. Poznanski, "A Methodological Approach," 1–39; YIVO, American OSE Committee Collection, RG 494, Folder 1, List of OSE collaborators (in early 1941). On the OSE's founders and their multiple border crossings, see Zalashik, "De l'est vers l'ouest."

88. YIVO, American OSE Committee Records, RG 494, Folder 1, Letter to Juli Davidovitch (i.e. Jules Brutzkus) to Joseph Millner, June 11, 1941.

89. OHD, 1(20), Andrée Salomon interviewed by Haïm Avni, 1963; Zeitoun, *L'Œuvre de secours aux enfants*, 348.

Chapter 14

1. YIVO, GJCA Collection, RG 249, Werner Gossels Casefile, Letter from Mrs. Gruenfeld to Mrs. Perlmutter, February 18, 1941. English version, trans. by Mrs. Gruenfeld.

2. AFSC Phil., General files 1941, Comms and Orgs, Selfhelp of emigres from Central Europe to War resisters league Administrative report of the Activities of the USCOM (February 22, 1941). On Dom Odo, see Nina Valbousquet, *Les âmes tièdes: Le Vatican face à la Shoah* (Paris: La Découverte, 2024), 82, 105.

3. This chapter independently confirms Stephanie Corazza's work and agrees with her argument that "rescue existed on a continuum with relief efforts, and that the involvement of American organizations and relief workers [. . .] shaped its scope and broader mandate." Corraza, "The Routine of Rescue," 38–103, quote on 43.

4. YIVO, American OSE Committee Collection, RG 494, Folder 1, Letter from Lourié and Gurvic to Amerose, January 20, 1941.

5. YIVO, American OSE Committee Collection, RG 494, Folder 1, Letter from Lourié and Gurvic, April 15, 1941: "Everything must be done to expedite the matter, and while it is not done all other questions must be put aside. The Government will help us here, and it is imperative that you get as many visas and passages as you can."

6. AFSC Phil., General files 1941, Comms and Orgs, Selfhelp of emigres from Central Europe to War resisters league, US Committee for the Care of European Children, Inc, Preliminary statement, Plan for evacuation of children from France in relation to the problem of securing admission of such children into the United States (undated).
7. Synnestvedt, *Over the Highest Mountains*, 71; Keren, "Autobiographies."
8. AFSC Phil., General files 1941, Comms and Orgs, File: Selfhelp of emigres from Central Europe to War resisters league, Memo from Frawley to Kershner, May 9, 1941; Corazza, "The Routine of Rescue," 56.
9. YIVO, American OSE Committee Collection, RG 494, Folder 1, Letter from Lourié and Gurvic, April 15, 1941. Mémorial de la Shoah, OSE collection, OSE (1)181, Letter from Allen Bonnell to James Vail, June 18, 1941.
10. AFSC Phil., General Files Foreign Service, England/France (relief in France, general reports) 1941, Undated Document from OSE appealing for emigration of adolescents, and those 16 and over; Corazza, "The Routine of Rescue," 59–60.
11. YIVO, American OSE Committee Collection, RG 494, Folder 1, Letter from Lourié and Gurvic, May 29, 1941. A total of five escorts accompanied the children. Elfriede Schloss Papers, AFSC excerpt, Letter from Philip Conrad to Mary Rogers, June 4, 1941.
12. YIVO, American OSE Committee Collection, RG 494, Folder 1, Letter from Lourié and Gurvic, May 19, 1941. Last-minute changes may have changed this composition slightly.
13. Elfriede Schloss Papers, Letter from AFSC France, most likely Philip Conrad to AFSC in Philadelphia, June 10, 1941.
14. Mémorial de la Shoah, OSE collection, OSE (1)182, transport list.
15. See Vivette Samuel's account of the departures, published in *Evidences* in the 1950s, reprinted in Salomon et al., *Andrée Salomon*, 117–18. On the resident social workers of the OSE and other humanitarian organizations, see Stephanie Corazza, "The Routine of Rescue."
16. Yad Vashem, O.9, 141, 6943, Ruth Lambert, Written testimony (letters to Uri), October 17, 1984. Lambert was alluding to the illegal border crossings over the Pyrenees that occurred from 1942 onward.
17. Elfriede Schloss Papers, Letter from Allen Bonnell to James Vail AFSC, June 18, 1941. Also found in AFSC Phil., General files, Foreign service, France, 1941, Individuals–Lindsley Noble to France internment camps.
18. AFSC Phil., General Files, Foreign Service, France: Marseilles correspondence Jan. to April to France Refund of unclaimed funds, 1941 Letter from Frawley to Allen Bonnell, July 18, 1941.
19. AFSC Phil., General files, 1941, Publicity to Comms and Orgs, Council on refugee aid. Morris Troper, "The everlasting mercy," delivered at the dinner of the USCOM at the Waldorf Astoria, September 10, 1941.
20. Isaac Chomski, "Children in Exile," *Contemporary Jewish Record*, 4, no. 5 (October 1941), 522–8, quote on 527. This was a publication of the American Jewish Committee.
21. Chomski, "Children in Exile," 528.
22. Ostrovsky, "We are Standing By," 240.
23. YIVO, GJCA RG 249, Folder 480.
24. Papanek, *Out of the Fire*, 235–7, quote on 237.
25. USHMM, Ruth Salmon Seltzer collection, Heinz Löw diary, "Till May 28, 1941," trans. from German.

26. YIVO, OTC Collection, Heinz Lonnerstädter Diary, June 7, 1941, trans. from German. On the politics of their arrival and reception in Lisbon, see Nadia Vargaftig, "Exils d'enfants: Lisbonne, ville d'accueil et de transit d'enfants juifs pendant et après la Seconde Guerre mondiale" (Master's Thesis, University of Paris 1, 2001). On Jewish youth in Lisbon, see Kaplan, *Hitler's Jewish Refugees*, 146–53.

27. Interview with Elfriede Schloss, San Diego, December 17, 2016.

28. YIVO, RG 494, Folder 1, Letter from Union OSE France (Lourié and Gourvitch/Gurvic) to American OSE Committee, January 20, 1941. I explore this in greater detail in Hobson Faure, "Attentes européennes, réalités américaines," 177–80 and "European Expectations, American Realities: The Immigration of Jewish Children from Occupied France to the United States, 1941–42," in Martine Gross, Sophie Nizard, and Yann Scioldo-Zürcher (eds.), *Gender, Families and Transmission in Contemporary Jewish Context* (Cambridge: Cambridge Scholars Publishing, 2017), 150–2.

29. YIVO, RG 494, Folder 1, Letter from Union OSE France to American OSE Committee, March 26, 1941.

30. Papanek, *Out of the Fire*, 221.

31. Zahra, *The Lost Children*, 99–117; Hobson Faure, "Jewish Child Refugees," 131–49; Genizi, "New York Is Big: America Is Bigger," 61–72.

32. Papanek, *Out of the Fire*, 228.

33. YIVO, American OSE Committee Collection, RG 494, Folder 1, Letter to Juli Davidovitch (Jules Brutzkus) from Joseph Millner, June 11, 1941.

34. YIVO, American OSE Committee Collection, RG 494, Folder 1, Letter from J. Millner and L. Gurvic to Amerose, June 12, 1941. The name of the rabbi has been changed to respect the wishes of "Ruth" to remain anonymous. The boy in question was not allowed a place on the transport.

35. YIVO, American OSE Committee Collection, RG 494, Folder 1, June 4, 1941, Union OSE to AFSC.

36. Elfriede Schloss Papers, Letter from Allen Bonnell to James Vail AFSC, June 18, 1941.

37. Elfriede Schloss Papers, Letter from Allen Bonnell to James Vail AFSC, June 18, 1941.

38. YIVO, GJCA Collection, RG 249, Folder 480, List of children who had to be hospitalized upon arrival. YIVO, American OSE Committee, RG 494, Folder 1, Letter from Union OSE to Amerose; July 23, 1941.

39. YIVO, GJCA Collection, RG 249, Folder 290, Letter to Allen Bonnell AFSC Marseille from Margaret Frawley, July 18, 1941.

40. AFSC Phil., General Files, Foreign Service France: Marseilles correspondence Jan. to April to France Refund of unclaimed funds, 1941, Letter from Frawley to Allen Bonnell, July 18, 1941.

41. Salomon recalls taking the children to the hospital to be combed to hide scabies. Zeitoun, *L'Œuvre aux secours aux enfants*, 354–5; Salomon et al., *Andrée Salomon*, 114–15.

42. YIVO, American OSE Committee Collection, RG 494, Folder 1, Letter Union OSE to Amerose, July 7, 1941.

43. YIVO, American OSE Committee Collection, RG 494, Folder 62, Letter from J. Brutkus to H. Kershner, June 17, 1941, Letter from J. Judkyn (AFSC) to J. Brutkus, June 18, 1941.

44. YIVO, Amerose, RG 494, file 194, Letter from A. Einstein to M. Field, June 25, 1941.
45. JDC-NY, AR 1933–1944, Orgs.: USCOM, File 343. Letter from Rosenwald Family Foundation to Marshall Field, USCOM, June 19, 1941.
46. AFSC Phil., General Files Foreign Service, England/France (relief in France, general reports) 1941, Letter from Executive Sec to Kershner, June 18, 1941. The initials CEP in the corner indicate this was sent by Clarence Pickett.
47. YIVO, GJCA Collection, RG 249, Letter from Margaret Frawley to Allen Bonnell AFSC Marseille, July 18, 1941.
48. AFSC Phil., General files 1941, Comms and Orgs, Selfhelp of emigres from Central Europe to War resisters league, cable, July 15, 1941, from AFSERCO (Phil.) to Marseille.
49. YIVO, GJCA Collection, RG 249, Folder 290, Letter to Allen Bonnell AFSC Marseille from Margaret Frawley (AFSC), July 18, 1941.
50. YIVO, GJCA Collection, RG 249, Letter to Allen Bonnell AFSC Marseille from Margaret Frawley (AFSC), July 18, 1941.
51. AFSC Phil., General Files, Foreign Service France: Marseilles correspondence Jan. to April to France Refund of unclaimed funds, 1941, Cable, July 18, 1941 Quakers Marseille from AFSERCO "age limit 16 at time issuance visa imperative [. . .] Recommend keep choice children under twelve as much possible including teen age group only where exclusion break family ties."
52. AFSC Phil., General Files Foreign Service France: Marseilles correspondence Jan. to April to France Refund of unclaimed funds, 1941, Letter 322, from M. Frawley to L. Nobel, July 28, 1941.
53. AFSC Phil., General Files Foreign Service France: Marseilles correspondence Jan. to April to France Refund of unclaimed funds, 1941, Cable from AFSCO (Phil.) to AFSC Marseille, July 28, 1941.
54. YIVO, American OSE Committee, RG 494, Folder 1, Letter from Louiré and Gurvic to Amerose, September 3, 1941. YIVO, GJCA, RG 249, File 481, Statistics on Second transport and transport lists.
55. YIVO, American OSE Committee, RG 494, Folder 1, Letter from Millner and Gurvic to Amerose, written between August 13 and 20, 1941.
56. USHMM, AFSC Records, RG 67.007M, Box 57, Folder 3, Delegates' meeting, August 22, 1941.
57. Corazza, "The Routine of Rescue," 62; USHMM, AFSC Records, RG 67.007M, Box 57, Folder 3, Delegates' meeting, August 18, 1941.
58. USHMM, AFSC Records, RG 67.007M, Box 11, Folder 27, Letter from Ross McClelland to Mary Elmes, September 8, 1941; Corazza, "The Routine of Rescue," 58.
59. USHMM, AFSC Records, RG 67.007M, Box 57, Folder 3, Delegates' meeting, August 18, 1941.
60. USHMM, AFSC Records, RG 67.007M, Box 57, Folder 3, Delegates' meeting September 3, 1941.
61. USHMM, AFSC Records, RG 67.007M, Box 10, Folder 20, Delegates' conference, October 10, 1941, cited in Corazza, "The Routine of Rescue," 81.
62. USHMM, AFSC Records, RG 67.007M, Box 11, Folder 27, Letter from Ross McClelland to Mary Elmes, September 8, 1941.
63. AFSC Phil., General files 1941, Comms and Orgs, File: Selfhelp of emigres from Central Europe to War resisters league, USCOM Letter from Robert Lang to Margaret Frawley, December 8, 1941.

64. AFSC Phil., General files 1941, Comms and Orgs, File: Selfhelp of emigres from Central Europe to War resisters league, Letter from P. Conrad (AFSC Lisbon) to Phil., September 10, 1941.
65. YIVO, American OSE Committe, RG 494, Folder 1, Letter from Union OSE to Amerose, October 6, 1941, trans. from French.
66. YIVO, American OSE Committee, RG 494, Folder 1, Letter from Union OSE to Amerose, October 12, 1941.
67. YIVO, American OSE Committee, RG 494, Folder 4, Letter from Union OSE to Amerose, November 26, 1941.
68. YIVO, American OSE Committee, RG 494, Folder 1, Letter from Union OSE to Amerose, March 22, 1941. As of June 1941, she was going to the OSE offices twice a week. YIVO, American OSE Committee, RG 494, Folder 4, Letter from Union OSE to Amerose, June 13, 1941.
69. YIVO, American OSE Committee, RG 494, Folder 4, Letter from Union OSE to Amerose December 9, 1941.
70. AFSC Phil., General files 1941, Comms and Orgs, File: Selfhelp of emigres from Central Europe to War resisters league, Letter from Lang to Pickett, October 21, 1941, citation from Lang to Frawley, November 26, 1941.
71. JDC-NY, AR 1933–1944, France: Children, File 610, Summary of French Text, Report on the Activities of the 3rd Management Office of the UGIF (Formerly OSE) for the months of March and April 1942, dated July 28, 1942. The number of children must likely includes homes of the French Jewish boyscouts and other Jewish organizations.
72. Yad Vashem, O.9, 141, 6943, Ruth Lambert testimony, Lettre à Uri, 1984, trans. from French.
73. AFSC Phil., General files 1941, Comms and Orgs, File: Selfhelp of emigres from Central Europe to War resisters league, Letter from Frawley to Lang, December 23, 1941.
74. AFSC, General Files Foreign Service Refugee services, Comms and Orgs, American Committee for Christian Refugees to YWCA 1942, Frawley to Lowry, January 7, 1942, Frawley to Lang, January 28, 1942.
75. Marjorie Miles McClelland (1913–1978) studied at Stanford University as an under-graduate and then did graduate work at the University of Cincinnati and Yale University in child psychology. She came to Europe with her husband Roswell in August 1940 and arrived in Marseille in August 1941. Roswell McClelland, "An Unpublished Chapter in the History of the Deportation of Foreign Jews from France 1942," https://portal.ehri-project.eu/units/us-005578-irn507327, consulted August 21, 2018.
76. USHMM, AFSC Records, RG 67.007M, Box 11, Folder 28, Letter from Majorie McClelland to Mary Elmes, April 8, 1942. I base my observations on the profiles written by the children themselves in Corsino Fernandez and Julian Llerandi (eds.), *We Came Alone: Stories of the Children Who Fled the Ravages of Two Wars and Came to America in Search of New Lives* (Self-published, 2006).
77. Corazza, "The Routine of Rescue," 87 and, more generally, 82–8.
78. YIVO, GJCA Collection, RG 249, Folder 290, Letter from Majorie McClelland, May 9, 1942.
79. AFSC Phil., AFSC, General Files Foreign Service Refugee services, Comms and Orgs, American Committee for Christian Refugees to YWCA 1942, Letter from M. McClelland, first page with date missing.
80. On their arrival in the US, see Papanek, *Out of the Fire*, 243. He claims they were auctioned off "like a slave market."

81. AFSC Phil., AFSC, General Files Foreign Service Refugee services, Comms and Orgs, American Committee for Christian Refugees to YWCA 1942, Letter from G. Kershner, August 11, 1942. See also Letter from Frawley to Lang, August 3, 1942 and from Frawley to Pickett and Vail, December 1, 1942.
82. YIVO, GJCA Collection, RG 249, Folder 290, Letter from Marshall Field to Mrs. Kahn, July 14, 1942.
83. Archives Ministère des Affaires étrangères, Vichy-Guerre, 1939–45, 1GMII/37, Amérique, USA.
84. This seems to include the trial evacuation in December 1940, organized by Martha Sharp, but does not include some 30 children who came on the transports with independent affidavits. Close, *Transplanted Children*, 27. In total, the USCOM brought 1,193 children to the United States from 1940 to 1943, from England and the Continent. This included 735 Protestant, 113 Catholic and 320 Jewish children, and the remainder were unaffiliated or from mixed marriages. Genizi, *America Apathy*, 327.
85. Klarsfeld, *French Children of the Holocaust*, 102–4.
86. Suzanne Spellen, "Walkabout: The Sausage King of Brooklyn, Part 3," Brownstoner, http://www.brownstoner.com/blog/2012/12/walkabout-the-sausage-king-of-brooklyn-part-3, consulted July 9, 2018.
87. Mary Lowenthal Felsteiner, *To Paint her Life: Charlotte Salomon in the Nazi Era* (Berkeley, CA: University of California Press, 1997), 132.
88. Salomon quoted in Felsteiner, *To Paint her Life*, 130.
89. USHMM, AFSC Records, RG 67.007M Box 57, Folder 3, Delegates' meeting, August 20, 1941, August 22, 1941. AFSC Phil., General files 1941, Comms and org, File: Selfhelp of emigres from Central Europe to War resisters league, Letter from Lang to Traugott, August 20, 1941. It appears they were not selected for the transport.
90. Felsteiner, *To Paint her Life*, 138. See also the account of one child, Valerie Kampf, discussed in Eliad Moreh-Rosenberg and Yehudit Shendar, "The Portrait and the Maiden," https://www.yadvashem.org/museum/art/articles/the-portrait-and-the-maiden.html, consulted January 12, 2024.
91. The Charlotte Salomon collection is now housed at the Jewish Museum of Amsterdam. They have found at least one of the Jewish children evacuated by Ottilie Moore. Email correspondence with Batya Wolff, March 31, 2016.
92. YIVO, American OSE Committee Records, RG 494, Folder 1, Emigration d'enfants, October 1941.
93. YIVO, GJCA Collection RG 249, Folder 187, Letter from Lotte Marcuse to Leon Wulman, August 25, 1941.
94. Herzberg, *The Past Is Always Present*, 100, 124.
95. YIVO, American OSE Committee Records, RG 494, Folder 19, Letter from Arthur Lewy to Amerose, January 2, 1942.
96. Eliyana Alder and Katerina Capkova (eds.). *Jewish and Romani Families in the Holocaust and its Aftermath* (New Brunswick, NJ: Rutgers University Press, 2020).
97. Interview with C. Peter R. Gossels, Boston, July 17, 2015.
98. USHMM, Selected Individual Files of Children Under the Care of the Œuvre de Secours aux Enfants, RG 43.113M, File 15, Claus and Werner Gossels, Letter from Max Gossels to Union OSE, March 10, 1941.
99. USHMM, RG 43.113M, File 15, Claus and Werner Gossels, Letter from Union OSE to Max Gossels, April 15, 1941.

100. USHMM, RG 43.113M, File 15, Claus and Werner Gossels, Letter Max Gossels to Union OSE, April 19, 1941.
101. Interview with C. Peter R. Gossels, Boston, July 17, 2015.
102. USHMM, RG 43.113M, File 15, Claus and Werner Gossels.
103. C. Peter Gossels, *Letters from our Mother*, 347–53; Kaplan, *Between Dignity and Despair*, 173–9.
104. YIVO, GJCA Collection, RG 249, Werner Gossels casefile, Letter from director of Sommers children's bureau to M. Marcuse, July 1, 1941.
105. YIVO, GJCA Collection RG 249, Werner Gossels casefile, Letter from Marcuse to Sampson, Sommers children's bureau, July 7, 1941.
106. YIVO, GJCA Collection, RG 249, Werner Gossels casefile, Letter from Marcuse to Sampson, September 11, 1941.
107. YIVO, GJCA Collection, RG 249, Werner Gossels casefile, Letter from Marcuse to Mrs. Maletz, October 6, 1941.
108. YIVO, GJCA Collection RG 249, Werner Gossels casefile, Letter from Marcuse to Dora Margolis, Jewish childcare association, Boston, January 20, 1942.
109. C. Peter Gossels Papers, Letter from Charlotte Gossels to Peter and Werner, November 10, 1941, trans. from German by C. Peter Gossels.
110. On the brothers once in the United States, see Hobson Faure, "Jewish Child Refugees from Central Europe," 145–9.
111. Fernandez and Llerandi, *We Came Alone*, 1.
112. Michael André Bernstein, *Forgone Conclusions: Against Apocalyptic History* (Berkeley, CA: University of California Press, 1994), 9–41.

Chapter 15

1. Letter from Karl to Papanek, reprinted in Papanek, *Out of the Fire*, 249.
2. Joly, *L'État contre les Juifs*, 89.
3. Joly, *L'État contre les Juifs*, 118–19. See also Zuccotti, *The Holocaust, the French and the Jews*, 102.
4. Several mothers remained behind, as well as "a handful of Red Cross volunteers." Zuccotti, *The Holocaust, the French, and the Jews*, 113–17.
5. Laurent Joly, *La Rafle du Vél d'Hiv: Paris, juillet 1942* (Paris: Grasset, 2022), 200–13. Each convoy is described in detail at Yad Vashem's "Transports to Extinction database." Convoy 20 included 530 children under sixteen, http://db.yadvashem.org/deportation/transportDetails.html?language=en&itemId=5092592, consulted August 22, 2018.
6. Joly, *La Rafle du Vél d'Hiv*, 70.
7. Their names were Margit Spira, Joséphine, Erna (and possibly Berta) Majzels, Herta Müller, Marguerite Gorlitz, and Lucie Lunenfeld. Their arrest and deportation dates can be found on Yad Vashem's Central Victims Database, with the exception of Berta Majzels, whose fate remains unknown. In addition four unaccompanied German sisters from Worms, Edith, Jenny, Frida and Cécile Becker, were deported from the orphanage.
8. Interview between Berta Romana Seidenstein and Michaela Raggam-Blesch, Vienna, December 2, 2015. On Jews of mixed heritage in Vichy France, see Laurent Joly, "La frontière entre 'judaïsme' et 'aryanisme:' Logique antisémite, contentieux juridique et pratiques bureaucratiques autour du classement des 'demi-juifs' en France occupée (1940–44)," *L'atelier du Centre de recherche histor-*

iques, 21 bis (2020), https://journals.openedition.org/acrh/10751?lang=en, consulted March 2, 2024.

9. The Reigner Telegram was written by World Jewish Congress representative Gerhart Riegner on August 8, 1942 and forwarded to Washington, DC several days later. The US State Department refused to disseminate the information without confirmation. Rabbi Stephen Wise received a copy in late August 1942 and released information in the press on November 23, 1942. Wyman, *The Abandonment of the Jews: America and the Holocaust, 1941–1945* (New York: Pantheon Books, 1984), 42–58.

10. Archives Ministère des Affaires étrangères, Vichy-Guerre, 1939–1945, 1GMII/37, Amérique, USA; JDC-NY, AR 1933–1944, France: Children, File 610, JDC Press Release, August 28, 1942.

11. Robert Paxton, 'Preface', in Marrus and Paxton, *Vichy France and the Jews*; Joly, *L'État contre les Juifs*, 218–25. According to Joly, France should be compared with Denmark, Slovakia, and Croatia because they had a similar form of Nazi occupation.

12. JDC-NY, AR 1933–1944, France: Children, File 610, "Les événements graves dont vous avez été les témoins continuent," Lazare Gurvic, August 13, 1942.

13. JDC-NY, AR 1933–1944, France: Children, File 610, "Les événements graves dont vous avez été les témoins continuent," Lazare Gurvic, August 13, 1942.

14. JDC-NY, AR 1933–1944, France: Children, File 610, Letter addressed to Dr. Schwartz by Dr. B. Tschlenoff, undated, trans. from German.

15. JDC-NY, AR 1933–1944, France: Children, File 610, Letter from Schwartz to Leavitt, August 26, 1942.

16. AFSC Phil., General Files Foreign Service Refugee services, Comms and Orgs, American Committee for Christian Refugees to YWCA 1942, Cable to Pickett from Marshall Field, September 3, 1942.

17. JDC-NY, AR 1933–1944, France: Children, File 610, Cable from Donald Lowrie to Lang USCOMM, September 18, 1942.

18. Staff members expressed some relief at Kershner's departure; USHMM, AFSC Records, RG 67.007M, Box 27, Folder 10, Helga Holbek to Marjorie McClelland, August 13, 1942. AFSC Phil., General Files Foreign Service Refugee services, Comms and Orgs, American Committee for Christian Refugees to YWCA 1942, Cable USCOM, May 29, 1942.

19. USHMM, AFSC Records, RG 67.007M, Box 27, Folder 10, Helga Holbek to Marjorie McClelland, August 13, 1942.

20. Its members included the Ecumenical council, YMCA and YWCA, the Catholic Church, Union internationale de secours aux enfants, Swiss Relief Organization for Emigrant Children, AFSC, Service social d'aide aux émigrants, and OSE. JDC-NY, AR 1933–1944, France: Children, File 610, "A Short meeting held today," August 14, 1942, trans. from French September 18, 1942. Yehuda Bauer states that the meeting was called by Union OSE's Boris Tschlenoff. Bauer, *American Jewry*, 259.

21. JDC-NY, AR 1933–1944, France: Children, File 610, Letter to James Vail from M. Leavitt, August 18, 1942.

22. USHMM, AFSC Files, RG 67.007M, Box 60, File 55, "American Friends Service Committee, Diary of Emergency Emigration of Jewish Refugee children," Starting October 6, 1942.

23. Milton and Bogin, *Archives of the Holocaust*, Letter from Joseph Schwarz to JDC NY, August 11, 1942, document 186, 929.

24. LBI, French concentration camp collection, AR 3987/MF836, Children File, "American Friends Service Committee, Diary of Emergency Emigration of Jewish Refugee children. Starting Oct 26, 1942." On the negotiations, see also Lowrie, *The Hunted Children*, 218–28. See also Bruce Hiatt's diary, which gives a daily assessment of his actions. AFSC Phil., General files, Foreign service, France, 1942. Hiatt replaced Kershner in September 1942.

25. JDC-NY, AR 1933–1944, France: Children, File 610, Notes of a discussion at a sub-committee meeting to consider organizational structure of USCOM and GJCA, September 21, 1942. These USCOM minutes show the assumption that almost all of the 1,000 children would be Jewish.

26. JDC-NY, AR 1933–1944, France: Children, File 610, Memorandum (JDC), September 4, 1942.

27. See, for example, the seven-page memo prepared by JDC for Mrs. David Levy, September 1942: JDC-NY, AR 1933–1944, France: Children, File 611.

28. JDC-NY, AR 1933–1944, France: Children, File 610, Statement by Mr. George L. Warren, September 14, 1942.

29. LBI, French concentration camp collection, AR 3987/MF836, Children File, "American Friends Service Committee, Diary of Emergency Emigration of Jewish Refugee children. Starting Oct 23, 1942"; "American Friends Service Committee, Diary of Emergency Emigration of Jewish Refugee children; Oct 26, 1942"; Minutes of Meeting re. Emigration of Jewish Refugee children, October 27, 1942.

30. JDC-NY, AR 1933–1944, France: Children, File 610, Records of statements and remarks made at Board Meeting of the USCOM, September 21, 1942.

31. Corazza, "The Routine of Rescue," 96–101.

32. LBI, France concentration camp collection, AR 3987/MF 836, Notes on conference at Vichy, October 16th, 1942 regarding Children's Emigration; Marrus and Paxton, *Vichy France and the Jews*, 266–8.

33. Corazza, "The Routine of Rescue," 40.

34. Marrus and Paxton, *Vichy France and the Jews*, 248.

35. There are multiple and contradictory accounts of this round-up concerning the time and date and the number arrested. I rely on Hazan, *Rire le jour, pleurer la nuit*, 63–9. However, other accounts can be found in the documentary *The Children of Chabannes*, by Lisa Gossels and Dean Wetherell. Their footage, donated to the USHMM, is now available online; Lisa Gossels generously provided me the transcripts of these interviews. For Lida Jablonski's account of the round-up, see USHMM, RG-50.812.0024, Interview with Lydia [sic] Jablonski by Lisa Gossels and Dean Wetherell, 1996–98. https://collections.ushmm.org/search/catalog/irn539006, consulted August 24, 2018.

36. Lisa Gossels Papers, Interview with Gert Alexander by Lisa Gossels and Dean Wetherell, 1996–98, 7.

37. Sarah L. Holloway, Louise Holt, and Sarah Mills, "Questions of Agency: Capacity, Subjectivity, Spatiality and Temporality," *Progress in Human Geography*, 43, no. 3 (2019), 458–77; Michel de Certeau, *L'invention du quotidien*, 1: *Arts de Faire* (Paris: Gallimard, 1990), 57–63.

38. USHMM, RG-50.812.0024, Interview with Lydia [sic] Jablonski by Lisa Gossels and Dean Wetherell, 1996–98, https://collections.ushmm.org/search/catalog/irn539006, consulted August 24, 2018.

39. There is a contradiction in the number of children arrested or deported. Hazan states that eight were arrested, three were liberated, and six were deported; Hazan,

Rire le jour, pleurer la nuit, 63–5. It is possible that Rolf Rothschild, who was indeed deported on Convoy 26, was not arrested during the round-up but individually. USHMM, RG-50.812.0024, Interview with Lydia [sic] Jablonski by Lisa Gossels and Dean Wetherell, 1996–98, https://collections.ushmm.org/search/catalog/irn539006, consulted August 24, 2018.

40. Yad Vashem, Trains to Extinction Database, Convoy 26, http://db.yadvashem.org/deportation/transportDetails.html?language=en&itemId=5092598, consulted August 29, 2018.

41. According to Gert Rosenzweig (later Jerry Gerard), this was Marjan Sztrum. Lisa Gossels Papers, Interview with Jerry Gerard for Children of Chabannes Film, 232. However, according to Katy Hazan, he became a slave laborer and wrote to his brother from Pless on September 19, 1942. Hazan, *Rire le jour, pleurer la nuit*, 46.

42. Lisa Gossels Papers, Interview with Jerry Gerard for Children of Chabannes Film, 232.

43. According to multiple sources cited by Hanna Papanek, the raid took place on August 26, 1942, although the time of the raid differs in the accounts. Papanek, *Elly und Alexander*, 156–61. However, one contemporaneous source states two raids occurred, on the nights of September 1–2 and 2–3. JDC-NY, AR 1933–1944, France: Children, File 610, Memo signed HKB (Henrietta Buchman, JDC), September 24, 1942. This is also suggested in the above-cited letter. Letter from Karl to Papanek, reprinted in Papanek, *Out of the Fire*, 249.

44. Papanek, *Elly und Alexander*, 156.

45. Laura Hobson Faure, Kindertransport to France Database (unpublished).

46. AFSC Phil., General Files Foreign Service Refugee services, Comms and Orgs: American Committee for Christian Refugees to YWCA 1942, Letter from Margaret Frawley to Robert Lang, March 17, 1942.

47. CDJC, *Les enfants de la Guette*, 52.

48. Norbert Bikales Papers, "*Un temps lumineux?* Some recollections of Chabannes," c.1999.

49. Her network was also known as the circuit spécifique-circuit B. Zeitoun, *L'Œuvre aux secours aux enfants*, 369–83.

50. Fouzi Ghlis, "Des enfants juifs dans les maisons de l'entre'aide d'hiver du Maréchal (1941–44)," in Hobson Faure et al.(eds.), *L'Œuvre de secours aux enfants et les populations juives*, 238.

51. Haïm Avni, "The Zionist Underground in Holland and France and the Escape to Spain," in Yisrael Gutman and Efraim Zuroff (eds.), *Rescue Attempts during the Holocaust: Proceedings of the Second Yad Vashem International Historical Conference. Jerusalem, April 8–11, 1974* (Jerusalem: Yad Vashem, 1977), 555–90; Pedro Correa Martín-Arroyo, "Europe's Bottleneck: The Iberian Peninsula and the Jewish Refugee Crisis, 1933–1944" (PhD Dissertation, London School of Economics, 2018), 233–80.

52. Hobson Faure, "European Expectations, American Realities," 143–57; Hobson Faure, "Jewish Child Refugees from Central Europe."

53. YIVO, OTC, Folder 65, Letter to Oswald Kernberg from his father, October 19, 1941.

Conclusion

1. Mémorial de la Shoah, Matzdorff Collection, Box 2. Ursula Matzdorff diary, c.1942–43, trans. from German.

2. Born in 1924, she was certainly on the list to be arrested in the August 26, 1942 round-up. She was aware of the danger. She stayed with her aunt and uncle, and then worked as a nanny. When she returned in early September, her aunt and uncle were gone, and she found herself alone. It was then that she tried to cross into Switzerland. After a few months in the Münchwilen refugee camp, Ursula was able to join Tante Elisabeth. She did not provide postwar testimony, having died in Israel in 1952. Mémorial de la Shoah, Matzdorff Collection, Box 2. Ursula Matzdorff Tagebuch. Dwork and Van Pelt, *Flight from the Reich*, 253–6.
3. At least three of the AFSC delegates were recognized as Righteous Among the Nations for their individual rescue work in the 1942–1944 period, including Mary Elmes, Alice Resch Synnestvedt and Holga Holbek. https://collections.yadvashem.org/en/righteous/4015287 and https://collections.yadvashem.org/en/righteous/4017147, consulted March 7, 1942; Cabanel, *Histoire des justes*, 171–5; Moke, "AFSC and the Holocaust," 17–19.
4. Andrieu, "Sauvetages dans l'Europe allemande," 1821–67, quote on 1821.
5. On the falsifications of the extreme right in France, see Laurent Joly, *La falsification de l'histoire: Éric Zemmour, l'extrême droite, Vichy et les Juifs* (Paris: Grasset, 2022).
6. Baumel-Schwartz, *Unfulfilled Promise*, 9.
7. Certeau, *L'invention du quotidien*, 57–63.
8. David Hollinger, "Communalist and Dispersionist Approaches to American Jewish History in an Increasingly Post-Jewish Era," *American Jewish History*, 95, no. 1 (2009), 1–32.
9. Elfriede Schloss Papers, Excerpt from AFSC archive, Memorandum from USCOM to Howard Kershner (AFSC), February 7, 1941.
10. OHD, Andrée Salomon interview with Haim Avni, 1963, trans. from French.
11. Muncy, *Creating a Female Dominion*.
12. For example, mass deportations required collaboration across borders. The establishment of Jewish councils (Judenrate) throughout Nazi-occupied Europe is yet another example of transnational persecution measures. Laurien Vanstenhout, *Between Community and Collaboration: Jewish Councils in Western Europe under Nazi Occupation* (Cambridge: Cambridge University Press, 2022).
13. Granovetter, "The Strength of Weak Ties: A Network Theory Revisited," 201–33.
14. Rebecca Erbelding uses these terms to describe the debate that began with Morse's accusatory text, Morse, *While Six Million Died*. Rebecca Erbelding, *Rescue Board: The Untold Story of America's Efforts to Save the Jews of Europe* (New York: Doubleday, 2018).
15. Moshe Gottlieb, *American Anti-Nazi Resistance, 1933–1941* (New York: Ktav, 1981); Collomp, *Résister au nazisme*.
16. Garbarini, "Diaries," 91–104 and, more generally, *Numbered Days*.
17. Lisa Moses Leff, *The Archive Thief* (Oxford and New York: Oxford University Press, 2015). On the looting and destruction of French archival holdings during the Second World War, see Cœuré, *La mémoire spoliée*.
18. The term 'palimpsests' is used by Keren, "Autobiographies." More generally, see Stargardt, "Children," 218–31; Manon Pignot, *Allons enfants de la patrie: Génération grande guerre* (Paris: Seuil, 2012).
19. Yad Vashem, O.9, 141, 6943, Ruth Lambert testimony, Lettre à Uri, 1984, trans. from French.
20. Saul Friedländer was among the first to address Holocaust Studies' intellectual isolation and singular development. Saul Friedländer, "Introduction," in Friedländer, *Probing the Limits*, 1–21.

21. An even greater number of Jewish children were not under the care of organizations. Their war years, spent in families and informal foster care, remain underdocumented by historians. Dwork, *Children with a Star*, 31–65.
22. Sluzki, "Migration and Family Conflict," 379–90.
23. Clifford, *Survivors*, 198–214; Arlene Stein, *Reluctant Witnesses: Survivors, Their Children, and the Rise of the Holocaust Consciousness* (Oxford and New York: Oxford University Press, 2014).
24. Friedländer was born in Prague, into a German-speaking Jewish family. Saul Friedländer, *When Memory Comes* (New York: Farrar, Straus & Giroux, 1979), 44–5.
25. The work on this topic is significant. On postwar therapeutic perceptions, see Clifford, *Survivors*, 38–57; for a psychological perspective, see Nathalie Zajde, "La thérapie des enfants: Entre psychologie et histoire," in Jablonka, *L'Enfant-Shoah*, 131–44.
26. Schuster, *Abraham's Son*, 198.
27. Parens, *Renewal of Life*, 92–3.
28. Beth B. Cohen, *Case Closed: Holocaust Survivors in Postwar America* (New Brunswick, NJ: Rutgers University Press, 2007), 94–114; Beth B. Cohen, *Child Survivors of the Holocaust: The Youngest Remnant and the American Experience* (New Brunswick, NJ: Rutgers University Press, 2018).
29. IISG, Ernst Papanek Collection, File F-22, Letter from Renée Eisenberg (née Spindel) to Ernst Papanek, July 11, 1956. Interviews with Renée and Gitta Spindel, Santa Cruz, December 15, 2016; Interview with Werner Dreifuss, San Diego, December 17, 2016.
30. Elfriede Schloss Papers, "We are Growing," c.1979. International Institute for Social History, Ernst Papanek Collection, File F-22, Letter from Henry Schuster "Heinz" to Dr. Lene Papanek, July 25, 1978.

Researching *Who Will Rescue Us?*

1. An exception: work on the Emergency Rescue Committee and the Jewish Labor Committee. Fry, *Surrender on Demand*; Collomp, *Résister au nazisme*. On Jewish rescue efforts in France: Lazare, *La Résistance juive en France*; Cohen, *Persécutions et sauvetages*; Zuccotti, *The Holocaust, the French, and the Jews*; Poznanski, *Les Juifs en France*.
2. An early example is John F. Sweets, *Choices Under Vichy: The French Under Nazi Occupation*. More recently: Fogg, *The Politics of Everyday Life in Vichy France*; Mariot and Zalc, *Face à la Persécution*.
3. As makes clear the recent study by Ruth Fivaz-Silbermann, *La fuite en Suisse: Les Juifs à la frontière franco-suisse durant les années de la "Solution finale"* (Paris: Calmann-Lévy, 2020).
4. Anne Grynberg and Denis Peschanski have briefly explored the work of the Comité de Nîmes. However, their work has not focused on the decision-making process in the United States. Grynberg, *Les camps de la honte*,194–6; Peschanski, *La France des camps*, 246–57. See also Bauer, *American Jewry*, 152–77, 235–65; Hobson Faure, "'Guide and Motivator' or 'Central Treasury'?," 293–311; Andrieu, "Sauvetages dans l'Europe allemande," 1821–67.
5. Nancy L. Green, *Repenser Les Migrations* (Paris: Presses Universitaires de France, 2002), 20.

6. Friedländer, *The Years of Extermination*, 24. Several French scholars have recently built upon Friedländer's approach. Claire Zalc and Tal Bruttmann (eds.), *Microhistories of the Holocaust* (New York: Berghahn Books, 2017), 1–13.

7. In a similar vein to Atina Grossman, *Jews, Germans and Allies: Close Encounters in Occupied Germany* (Princeton, NJ: Princeton University Press, 2007).

8. For example, in May 1940, the Ministère des Affaires étrangères destroyed a large part of its own archives on the eve of the Nazi occupation. Cœuré, *La mémoire spoliée*.

9. Alexandra Zapruder, *Salvaged Pages: Young Writers' Diaries of the Holocaust* (New Haven, CT and London: Yale University Press, 2002), 9.

10. According to Sonnert and Holton's study of 2,500 individuals who came to the United States as Central European refugee children (with their parents and unaccompanied), 89 per cent had returned to their country of origin at least once; one third had been back between 3 and 5 times. According to the authors "men showed a stronger interest, involvement or more frequent contacts with their country of origin." Gerhard Sonnert and Gerald Holton, *What Happened to the Young Children Who Fled Nazi Persecution* (New York: Palgrave, 2006), 99. More generally, see Anna Schenderlein, *Germany on their Minds: German Jewish Refugees in the United Sates and their Relationships with Germany, 1938–1988* (New York: Berghahn Books, 2020).

11. The authors note nonetheless that there was no "GI Bill effect" in their study. In fact, the veterans as a group had lower educational attainment. Sonnert and Holton, *What Happened*, 76–7, 141–4, 173–4.

12. I conducted 52 interviews, including multiple interviews with the same individuals and group interviews. OSE-USA helped me recruit individuals for the study through their newsletter. I also contacted some participants directly with the help of the OSE-USA co-presidents, Claudine Schweber and the late Jacques Fein, and then using the snowball method. While all of the children had been cared for at some point by OSE, some of my interviewees did not arrive in the United States until after the Second World War. With the exception of my initial question, "how did you end up in an OSE home?," and my closing question "do you consider yourself to be a Holocaust survivor?," I let the interviewee determine the shape and scope of the discussion, asking follow-up questions for clarity and to establish an overview of their life history. All interviews, unless otherwise stated, were recorded and transcribed. Beyond the insights they imparted to me, these individuals also granted me access, in many cases, to their personal papers and, more rarely, to their case files in the organizations that supervised their care. A case file on many children in this study exists in the French OSE archives in Paris, as well as in the GJCA collection at the YIVO Institute in New York, and occasionally in the AFSC archives, as well. To access them, one must obtain written permission from the individual or their descendants.

13. For a variety of reasons, the rate of survival in France was higher than in most countries, estimated at approximately 75 per cent. This rate should not be compared with other European countries, which had entirely different conditions during the Second World War, and is based on Klarsfeld's problematic approximation of the total number of Jews living in France on the eve of the war. Serge Klarsfeld, *Vichy Auschwitz: Le rôle de Vichy dans la Solution finale de la question juive en France, 1943–1944* (Paris: Fayard, 1985), 179. I am unable to provide clear figures for the number of Kindertransport children who were deported from

France and murdered in the Holocaust due to the fact that I do not have a definitive list of the children who arrived in France. However, I can state that at least 36 were deported to Nazi camps (3 of whom survived).

14. Garbarini, "Diaries," 91–104.
15. Garbarini, "Diaries," 94–5.
16. Garbarini, "Diaries," 102.
17. Garbarini, "Diaries," 91–104; Sharon Kangisser Cohen, *Testimony and Time: Holocaust Survivors Remember* (Jerusalem: Yad Vashem, 2014).
18. Writing in the early 1990s, Dwork's discussion of oral history shows a need to defend this practice. Browning also argued for the usage of testimony as a means of documenting what has been suppressed or unrecorded in written records. Shenker and Pollin-Galay have recently contributed to the scholarship by questioning how testimony is mediated. Dwork, *Children with a Star*, xxxiii–xlii; Christopher Browning, *Collected Memories: Holocaust History and Postwar Testimony* (Madison, WI: University of Wisconsin Press, 2003), 37–59; Noah Shenker, *Reframing Holocaust Testimony* (Bloomington, IN: University of Indiana Press, 2015); Hannah Pollin-Galay, *Ecologies of Witnessing: Language, Place, and Holocaust Testimony* (New Haven, CT and London: Yale University Press, 2018). See also Clifford, *Survivors*, 215–37.
19. Portelli, "What Makes Oral History Different," 32–42.
20. Rachel Einwohner, "Ethical Considerations on the Use of Archived Testimonies in Holocaust Research: Beyond the IRB Exception," *Qualitative Sociology*, 34 (2011), 415–30.
21. While grappling with this problem, I was confronted with an interesting test case that confirmed the ethical dilemma involving names: I wrote an article on two sisters from this study based on their case files and our oral history interview. Before submitting the article, I made the decision to show the sisters the article, in particular to ask their opinion about the name problem. The first version I showed them used false names, and I was surprised to find that both sisters agreed with my analyses and, with a few minor changes, said that I could use their real names. I then updated the article with their real names and sent it to them again. Suddenly, there were many problems with the article: the use of real names created many points of tension surrounding my analysis. After several months of discussion, we decided on the use of false names, which provided them privacy, and allowed me the capacity to delve into the more painful issues they raise. Laura Hobson Faure, "Siblings in the Holocaust and its Aftermath in France and the United States: Rethinking the 'Holocaust Orphan'?," in Adler and Capkova, *Jewish and Romani Families*, 103–14; Laura Hobson Faure, "Orphelines ou Sœurs?: Penser la famille juive pendant et après la Shoah en France et aux États-Unis," *20 & 21, Revue d'histoire*, no. 145 (January–March 2020), 91–104.
22. See Chapter 7.
23. Email from Ernst Valfer, September 5, 2018.

Bibliography

I. Archival Sources

United States

American Friends Service Committee Archives, Philadelphia

General Files
   Foreign Service, France, 1940
   Foreign Service, Refugee services, general to Cummington Hostel, 1940
   Comms and Orgs: American Jewish Committee to Open Road 1940
   Foreign Service, Refugee Services, Comms and Orgs, 1941
   1941: Publicity to Comms and Orgs Council on refugee aid, 1941
   Comms and Orgs: Selfhelp of emigres from Central Europe to War resisters league, 1941
   Foreign service France, Individuals–Lindsley Noble to France internment camps, 1941
   Foreign Service, England/France (relief in France, general reports), 1941
   Foreign Service/Refugee Services, Austria–France 1941
   Foreign Service France: Marseilles correspondence Jan. to April to France Refund of unclaimed funds, 1941
   Foreign Service Refugee services, Comms and Orgs: American Committee for Christian Refugees to YWCA 1942
   AFSC committees/publicity to Comms and Orgs Community Chests 1942
   Foreign Service England to France Paris Center 1942
   Foreign service, France, 1942

American Jewish Joint Distribution Archive, New York

AR 1933–1944 Organizations:
   OSE (325–9), GJCA (236–8), USCOM (343–5), AFSC (205–7)
AR 1933–1944, General:
   Children (610, 611, 612)

BIBLIOGRAPHY

Oral History archives:
  Herbert Katzki interview, 1976
  Joseph Schwartz interview, 1962

University of Michigan Bentley Historical Library

William Haber Papers

Center for Jewish History, New York

American Jewish Historical Society
  Marion Kenworthy papers (P-51)
  Justine Wise Polier papers (P-527)

YIVO Institute for Jewish Research
  American Committee of the OSE (RG 494)
  One Thousand Children Organization (RG 1941)
  German Jewish Children's Aid (RG 249)

Leo Baeck Institute
  France concentration camp collection (AR 3987/MF 836)
  Jonas Plaut Collection: Geschichte der Baruch-Auerbach'schen Waisen Erziehungs-
    Anstalten für jüdische Knaben und Mädchen in Berlin: anlässlich ihres
    hundertjährigen Bestehens, c.1940 (ME 503)

New York Public Library

The Ernst Papanek Papers
Various papers on the US Committee for the Care of European Children

United States Holocaust Memorial Museum

Peter Feigl Papers (1992.59)
American Friends Service Committee (RG 67.007M)
Werner Goldsmith Papers (RG-10.424)
Ruth Salmon Seltzer Papers (RG 2007.421)
Selected Individual Files of Children under the care of OSE (RG 43.113M)
Susan Hilsenrath Warsinger Papers (RG 2000.127)
Martha and Waitstill Sharp Collection (RG 67.017)
Archive of the Jewish Community of Vienna-Jerusalem Component Collection
  (RG 17.017)
Russian Holocaust Foundation, JDC Paris selected records (RG-11.001M—Fond
  722 Opis 1)
Oral Histories: Herbert Katzki, 1995 (RG-50.030*033); Lydia [sic] Jablonski
  (1996–1998) RG-50.812.0024; Ruth Keller RG-50.812.0041

BIBLIOGRAPHY

France

Public Archives

Archives Nationales–Pierrefitte-sur-Seine

André Philip Papers (625AP/1)
Georges Bonnet Papers (685AP/28)
Alfred and Françoise Brauner Papers (208AS XXII)
Archives on Refugees from Spain (AN, 20010221/1, 72AJ 2935)
Réfugiés Israélites, Commission Interministérielle (F/7/16079)
Interventions des associations en faveur des réfugiés allemands (F7/16080)

Archives du Ministère des Affaires étrangères

Série C. Administrative, Culte, Culte Israélite (27CPCOM/516-21)
Vichy-Guerre, Cabinet du Ministre 1940–1944
(24GMII/1, Amérique: 1GMII/33-37)

Archives diplomatiques, Nantes

Archives rapatriées de l'ambassade de France à Berlin, Coll. B, 1815–1939 (83PO/B)
Karlsruhe: Consulat 303PO/1/1-32

Archives départementales de la Creuse

René Castille and Alfred Bourdet Collection (147J)

Archives départementales du Bas-Rhin

Strasbourg, Orphelinat juif alsacien (100 J 8-10)
Archives du Consistoire Israelite du Bas-Rhin (2237W)
Direction générale des services d'Alsace-Lorraine (Valot), 1925–1940 (98AL: 394, 397 1/2)

Bibliothèque nationale de France

Louise Weiss Collection (NAF 17794)

Private Archives

Alliance israélite universelle

Central Committee Minutes, Paris, March 1938–June 1939
Paix et Droit, 1937–1939
Samedi, 1937–1939

Association du Consistoire israélite central

L'Univers Israélite, 1937–1939

BIBLIOGRAPHY

Mémorial de la Shoah

Œuvre de Secours aux Enfants Collection
Christian de Monbrison Collection (Fonds 975)
Communauté Israélite de Vichy (CMLV_955)
Werner Marzdorff Collection (MDXXVIII)
Félix Chevrier Collection (CCCLXXII)
Fonds Enfants (CMLXVIII)

Œuvre de secours aux enfants–Paris Headquarters Archives

Amerose Collection
Andrée Salomon Collection
Boris Tschenloff Collection
Château de Quincy: Programme educatif
Children's case files
Commemorative voyage to Chabannes, August 1988
Émigration des Enfants USA Collection
Lists for Chabannes, Montintin, La Guette, Quincy
Miscellaneous uncatalogued files
Christian de Monbrison Collection
Eighty-year OSE reunion, 1993
La Revue OSE, 1937–1939

USC Shoah Foundation, Visual History Archive, American University of Paris, France

C. Peter Gossels interview (37230, December 1, 1997)
George Papanek (11978, February 11, 1996)

Quaker Archives, Paris

H1–23: Minutes du Comité de Coordination 1940–1943, Secours quaker 1940–1945
16.34.44–16.35.59: Account by Eunice Clark Smith
16.38.04: Le Secours suisse dans le Sud de la France, 1939–1947
16.45.10: Documents on the work of the French Quakers during the Second World War

The United Kingdom

The Rothschild Archive, Waddesdon Manor

Correspondence Dorothy de Rothschild and Germaine de Rothschild (JDR2/33/11, JDR2/15/13, JDR2/51/7, JDR2/70/13)

The Wiener Holocaust Library

Walter Kaufmann, "Mes souvenirs," September 1942, unpublished manuscript 4248

365

BIBLIOGRAPHY

Germany

Jüdisches Museum Frankfurt

Various photos

Jüdisches Museum Berlin

Marianne Hirsch Diary

Switzerland

State Archives of Geneva

Union Internationale de Secours aux Enfants Collection (UISE)
Executive Committee minutes (92.1.10–92.1.13)
Country Files: Switzerland (92.33.15)
Country Files: France (91.18.2–91.18.32)

The Netherlands

International Institute for Social History (IISG), Amsterdam

Ernst Papanek Papers (ARCH01031)
Bruno Kurzweil Papers (ARCH02816)
Henry Jacoby Papers (ARCH00675)

Israel

Avram Harmon Oral History Division, Hebrew University of Jerusalem

12 (47) Herbert Katzki oral history by Yehuda Bauer, 1968
1(20) Andrée Salomon oral history by Haïm Avni, 1960, June 8, 1963
(27)28 Andrée Salomon oral history by Rivka Bannit, 1965

Yad Vashem

O.9, 141, 6943 Ruth Lambert testimony

II. Private Papers

Ruth Avokat Keller
Caprice Gracia Benrubi Adler
Norbert Bikales
Ron Coleman
Werner Dreifuss
Albert Erlebacher
Jacques Fein
Martin Glass (Gerard Glass)
Lisa Gossels
C. Peter Gossels

BIBLIOGRAPHY

Georges Grunwald (Hanna Eisfelder-Grunwald)
Stephan Lewy
Carol Low (Heinz Löw)
Raïa J.
Margot Gunther Jeremias
Hanna Kaiser Papanek
Jeannine Korman
Paulette Korsia Dorflaufer
Ninette Lavergne
Anne Levine
René Lichtman
Stephanie Lynn (Hilda Mann)
Gerald Mahler Watkins
Elfriede Meyer Schloss
Christian de Monbrison
Marion Oliner
Inge and Charles Roman
Claudine Schweber
Gitta Spindel Ryle
Ernst Valfer
Felice Z.

III. Oral History Interviews conducted by Author

1. Vera Nora, July 2012
2. Hanna Papanek, December 18, 2013
3. Susan (Susi) Hilsenrath Warsigner, June 2014
4. Paulette Korsia Dorflaufer, 2014
5. Norbert Bikales, July 10, 2015
6. Group interview: Inge Roman, Charles Roman, Stella Geller, Hanna Keselman, Norbert and Gerda Bikales, July 10, 2015
7. Caprice Adler (Gracia Benrubi), July 12, 2015
8. Herbert Feuerstein, July 13, 2015
9. Susi K., July 13, 2015
10. Felice Z. and Béate Z., July 14, 2015
11. Marion Orliner, July 14, 2015
12. Kurt Sonnenfeld, July 15, 2015
13. Gus Papanek, July 16, 2015
14. Hanna Papanek, July 16, 2015
15. C. Peter Gossels, July 17, 2015
16. Group Interview: Stephan Lewy, C. Peter Gossels, Werner Gossels (in the presence of their wives, Nancy and Elaine Gossels), July 17, 2015
17. René Lichtman, July 28, 2015
18. Eric Cahn, email interview, September 8, 2015
19. Ernst Valfer, email interview, June 6, 2016
20. Henri Parens, June 14, 2016
21. Christian de Monbrison, September 15, 2016
22. Margot Gunther Jeremias, September 26, 2016
23. Eda Pell, November 2016

24. Ernst Valfer, November 24, 2016
25. Anne Zimmer Levine, December 5, 2016
26. Christian de Monbrison, December 8, 2016
27. Eda Pell, December 11, 2016
28. Ernst Valfer, December 13, 2016
29. Renée Spindel Eisenberg and Gitta Spindel Ryle, December 15, 2016
30. Elfriede Schloss, December 17, 2016
31. Werner Dreifuss, December 17, 2016
32. Rabbi Keith Stern, January 13, 2017
33. Joan Stern Lorah, January 27, 2017
34. Eve Kugler, February 27, 2017
35. Christophe Moreigne, April 13, 2017
36. Peter Halban, April 18, 2017
37. Ninette Lavergne, April 22, 2017
38. Raia J., May 9, 2017
39. Lisa Gossels, May 19, 2017
40. Ninette Lavergne and Jacques Depomme, June 7, 2017
41. Ernst Valfer, September 14, 2017
42. Martin Glass, October 2, 2017
43. René Lichtman, October 28, 2017
44. Christian de Monbrison and Martin Glass, November 4, 2017
45. Martin Glass, November 4, 2017
46. Stephanie Lynn, October 8, 2018
47. David Findling, April 11, 2019
48. René Lichtman, December 7, 2021
49. Peter Halban, June 24, 2022
50. Joan Stern, July 23, 2022
51. Werner Gossels, December 16, 2022
52. Claude-Michel Brauner, January 9, 2023

IV. Published Primary Sources

Press Articles, 1938–1942 period

Jewish Telegraphic Agency (JTA)
L'Univers Israélite
La Tribune Juive
La Revue OSE
Paix et Droit
Neue Freie Presse
Samedi
The New York Times

Books and Varia

American Jewish Committee, *The Jews in Nazi Germany: A Factual Record of their Persecution by the National Socialists.* New York: American Jewish Committee, 1933.
Barrès, Maurice. *Les diverses familles spirituelles de France.* Paris: Émile Paul Frères, 1917.
Bogin, Boris D. *Jewish Philanthropy: An Exposition of Principles and Methods of Jewish Social Service in the United States.* New York: Macmillan Company, 1917.

BIBLIOGRAPHY

Bonnet, Georges. *Dans la tourmente: 1938–1948*. Paris: Fayard, 1971.

Brauner, Alfred. *Ces enfants ont vécu la guerre: Les répercussions psychiques de la guerre moderne sur l'enfance*. Paris: Éditions Sociales Françaises, 1946.

Brauner, Alfred, and Françoise Brauner. *L'Accueil des enfants survivants*. Paris: Cahiers du groupement de recherches pratiques pour l'enfance, 1994.

Brauner, Claude-Michel. "Alfred et Françoise Brauner par leur fils," 2011. http://www.enfance-violence-exil.net/fichiers_sgc/BRAUNER.pdf.

Castendyck, Elsa. "Refugee Children in Europe," *Social Science Review*, 13, no. 4 (December 1939), 587–601.

CDJC (ed.). *Les enfants de La Guette: Souvenirs et documents, 1938–1945*. Paris: Centre de Documentation Juive Contemporaine, 1999.

Close, Kathryn. *Transplanted Children: A History*. New York: The United States Committee for the Care of European Children, Inc., 1953.

Cord, Edith Mayer. *Becoming Edith: The Education of a Hidden Child*. New Mildford, NJ: Wordsmithy, 2008.

Dreifuss, Werner. *The Epitome of the "American Dream": Memoirs of Werner Dreifuss*. Self-published, 2016.

Efimovsky, Olga. *Il était une fois . . . Brunoy . . . Quincy . . .* Self-published, 1991.

Fernandez, Corsino, and Julian Llerandi (eds.). *We Came Alone: Stories of the Children Who Fled the Ravages of Two Wars and Came to America in Search of New Lives*. Self-published, 2006.

Fleg, Edmond. *Pourquoi je suis Juif*. Paris: Les Éditions de France, 1928.

Frenkel, Françoise. *Rien où poser sa tête*. Paris: L'Arbalète Gallimard, 2015.

Friedländer, Saul. *Quand vient le souvenir*. Paris: Seuil, [1978] 2008.

Friedländer, Saul. *When Memory Comes*. New York: Farrar, Straus & Giroux, 1979.

Fry, Varian. *Surrender on Demand*. Boulder, CO: Johnson Books, [1945] 1997.

Golub, Jack. "The JDC and Health Programs in Eastern Europe," *Jewish Social Studies*, 5, no. 3 (1943), 293–304.

Gourfinkel, Nina. *Aux prises avec mon temps: L'autre patrie*. Paris: Seuil, 1953.

Green, Eric. "The Loneliest Boy." https://archive.org/details/loneliestboy/page/n1/mode/2up.

Hammel, Frédéric Chimon. *Souviens-toi d'Amalek: Témoignage sur la lutte des Juifs en France (1938–1944)*. Paris: CLKH, 1982.

Hernandez, Elizabeth, *La Fondation Rothschild sous l'Occupation, 1939–1944*. Paris: Fondation de Rothschild, 2010.

Herzberg, Lillian Belinfante (with Stephan Lewy). *The Past Is Always Present*. Bloomington, IN: Archway Publishing, 2015.

Hirsch, Benjamin. *Home Is Where You Find It*. Self-published, 2006.

Hirschler, Alain. *Grand Rabbin Résistant: René Hirschler, 1905–1945, mon père*. Paris: Éditions Caractères, 2016.

Jablon, Robert, Laure Quennouëlle-Corre, and André Straus. *Politique et finance à travers l'Europe du XXe siècle: Entretiens avec Robert Jablon*. Brussels: P. Lang, 2009.

Jacoby, Henry. *Davongekommen, 10 Jahre Exil 1936–1946, Prag-Paris-Montauban-New York-Washington: Erlebnisse und Begegnungen*. Frankfurt am Main: Sendler Verlag, 1982.

Kanner, Amalia, and Eve Rosenzweig-Kugler. *Shattered Crystals*. Lakewood, NJ: CIS Publishers, 1997.

Kershner, H.E. "Defeated France Knows Only Hunger and Want," *The New York Times*, June 28, 1942.

———— *Quaker Service in Modern War*. New York: Prentice-Hall, 1950.

———— *The Menace of Roosevelt and His Policies*. New York: Greenberg, 1936.

Klüger, Ruth. *Refus de témoigner: Une jeunesse*. Paris: V. Hamy, 2005.

Kofman, Sarah. *Rue Ordener, Rue Labat*. Lincoln, NE: University of Nebraska Press, 1996.

Lambert, Raymond-Raoul. *Carnet d'un témoin, 1940–1943: Présenté et annoté par Richard Cohen*. Paris: Librairie Arthème Fayard, 1985.

Loinger, Georges, and Katy Hazan. *Aux frontières de l'espoir*. Paris: Fondation pour la mémoire de la Shoah/Éditions Le manuscrit, 2006.

Lowrie, Donald. *The Hunted Children*. New York: W.W. Norton & Co., 1963.

McClelland, Roswell. "An Unpublished Chapter in the History of the Deportation of Foreign Jews from France in 1942," https://portal.ehri-project.eu/units/us-005578 -irn507327.

Masour-Ratner, Jenny. *Mes vingt ans à l'OSE: 1941–1961*. Paris: Fondation pour la mémoire de la Shoah/Éditions Le Manuscrit, 2006.

Matzdorff, Werner. "Esquisse d'une page d'histoire," In CDJC (ed.), *Les enfants de La Guette*, 12–24. Paris: Centre de Documentation Juive Contemporaine, 1999.

Moratz, Ralph. "Escape from the Holocaust 1939," *Escape From The Holocaust 1939*, blog, n.d., https://ralphm1935.wordpress.com.

Mores, Marquis de. *Rothschild, Ravachol et Cie*. Paris, 1892.

Papanek, Ernst. "Children during Air Raids," *Progressive Education*, XIX, no. 3 (March 1942).

———— "Contributions of Individual Psychology to Social Work," *American Journal of Individual Psychology*, 11, no. 2 (1955).

———— "My Experiences with Children in War-Time," *Rend (Quarterly Students Journal, New York School of Social Work, Columbia University)*, 4, no. 1 (Fall 1942).

Papanek, Ernst, with Edward Linn. *Out of the Fire*. New York: Morrow, 1975.

Papanek, Hanna. "Exile or Emigration: What Shall We Tell the Children?," in Viktoria Hertling (ed.), *Mit Den Augen Eines Kindes: Children in the Holocaust. Children in Exile. Children under Fascism*, 220–36. Amsterdam and Atlanta: Rodopi, 1998.

———— "Men, Women, and Work: Reflections on the Two-Person Career," *American Journal of Sociology*, 78, no. 4 (1973), 852–72.

———— "Quatre Enfants à Montintin: Mémoire et Histoire, 1940–42," in Pascal Plas and Michel Kiener (eds.), *Enfances Juives: Limousin-Dordogne-Berry, terres de refuge, 1939–1945*, 386–402. Saint-Paul: Souny, 2006.

Papanek, Hanna, trans. Joachim Helfer and Peter Lösche. *Elly und Alexander: Revolution, Rotes Berlin, Flucht, Exil – eine sozialistische Familiengeschichte*. Berlin: Vorwärts-Buch Verl.-Ges, 2006.

Parens, Henri. *Renewal of Life: Healing from the Holocaust*. Rockville, MD: Schreiber Publishing, 2004.

Pary, Juliette. *Mes 126 Gosses*. Paris: Flammarion, 1938.

Pell, Joseph, and Fred Rosenbaum. *Taking Risks: A Jewish Youth in the Soviet Partisans and His Unlikely Life in California*. Berkeley, CA: RDR Books, 2004.

Piatigorsky, Jacqueline. *Jump in the Waves: A Memoir*. New York: St. Martin's Press, 1988.

Pickett, Clarence. *For More than Bread: An Autobiographical Account of Twenty-Two Years' Work with the American Friends Service Committee*. Boston, MA: Little, Brown and Co., 1953.

Reed, Walter W. *The Children of La Hille: Eluding Nazi Capture during World War II*. Syracuse, NY: Syracuse University Press, 2015.

BIBLIOGRAPHY

Rothschild, Germaine de. *Bernard Palissy et son école (Collection Édouard de Rothschild)*. Paris: Au pont des arts, 1952.

—— *Luigi Boccherini, sa vie, son œuvre*. Paris: Plon, 1962.

Rothschild, Guy de. *Whims of Fortune: The Memoirs of Guy de Rothschild*. New York: Random House, 1985.

Salomon, Andrée, Katy Hazan, Georges Weill, and Jean Salomon (eds.). *Andrée Salomon, une femme de lumière*. Paris: Fondation pour la mémoire de la Shoah/ Éditions Le Manuscrit, 2011.

Sands, Philippe. *East West Street: On the Origins of "Genocide" and "Crimes against Humanity."* New York: Penguin Random House, 2017.

Schuster, Henry D. "Kinder Transport," in Philip K. Jason and Iris Posner (eds.), *Don't Wave Goodbye: The Children's Flight from Nazi Persecution to American Freedom*, 20–3. Westport, CT: Praeger, 2004.

Schuster, Henry D., and Caroline A. Orzes. *Abraham's Son: The Making of an American*. Baltimore, MD: Publish America, 2010.

Schwab, Fanny. *Laure Weil: Sa vie, son œuvre*. Strasbourg: Home Laure Weil, 1969.

Seghers, Anna. *Transit*. Paris: Éditions Autrement, [1944] 1995.

Spire, André. *Quelques juifs et demi-juifs*. Paris: Grasset, 1928.

Stock, Ernest. *Tri-Continental Jew: A 20th Century Journey*. Mendele Electronic Books, 2015.

Stock, Ernest, Julie Stock, and Edward Timms. *Jugend auf der Flucht: Die Tagebücher von Ernst und Julie Stock*. Berlin: Metropol, 2004.

Synnestvedt, Alice Resch. *Over the Highest Mountains: A Memoir of Unexpected Heroism in France during World War II*. Pasadena, CA: Intentional Productions, 2005.

Tec, Nechama. *Dry Tears: The Story of a Lost Childhood*. Westport, CT: Wildcat Pub. Co., 1982.

Vadnai, Georges. *Jamais la lumière ne s'est éteinte: Un destin juif dans les ténèbres du siècle*. Lausanne and Paris: L'Âge d'Homme, 1999.

Weiss, Louise. *Ce que femme veut: Souvenirs de la IIIè République*. Paris: Gallimard, 1946.

—— *Mémoires d'une Européenne, Tome III (1934–1939)*. Paris: Payot, 1970.

—— *Souvenirs d'une enfance républicaine*. Paris: Denoël, 1937.

Wiesel, Elie. *La nuit*. Paris: Éditions de Minuit, 2007.

V. Secondary Sources

Abraham Lincoln Brigade Archives. "Mabel Irene Goldin." Abraham Lincoln Brigade Archives. http://www.alba-valb.org/volunteers/mabel-irene-goldin.

Adler, Eliyana, and Katerina Capkova (eds.). *Jewish and Romani Families in the Holocaust and its Aftermath*. New Brunswick, NJ: Rutgers University Press, 2020.

Adler, Jacques. *The Jews of Paris and the Final Solution: Communal Response and Internal Conflicts, 1940–1944*. New York and Oxford: Oxford University Press, 1987.

Adler-Rudel, Salomon. *Jüdische Selbsthilfe unter dem Naziregime, 1933–1939*. Tubingen: Mohr, 1974.

Afoumado, Diane. *Exil impossible: L'errance des juifs du paquebot "St.-Louis."* Paris: L'Harmattan, 2005.

Akoka, Karen. *L'asile et l'exil: Une histoire de la distinction réfugiés-migrants*. Paris: La Découverte, 2020.

Alary, Éric. "Les Juifs et la ligne de démarcation," *Cahiers de la Shoah*, 5 (2001), 13–49.

BIBLIOGRAPHY

Aleksiun, Natalia. "An Invisible Web: Philip Friedman and the Network of Holocaust Research," in Regina Fritz, Éva Kovács, and Béla Rásky (eds.), *Before the Holocaust had its Name: Early Confrontations of the Nazi Mass murder of the Jews*, 149–65. Vienna: New Academic Press, 2016.

——— "Uneasy Bonds: On Jews in Hiding and the Making of Surrogate Families," in Eliyana Adler and Katerina Capova (eds.), *Family in the Holocaust and Its Aftermath*, 85–102. New Brunswick, NJ: Rutgers University Press, 2021.

Aleksiun, Natalia, Raphael Utz, and Zofia Woycicka (eds.). *The Rescue Turn and the Politics of Holocaust Memory*. Detroit, MI: Wayne State University Press, 2023.

Andrieu, Claire. "Conclusion. Rescue, a Notion Revised," in Jacques Sémelin, Claire Andrieu, and Sarah Gensburger (eds.), *Resisting Genocide: The Multiple forms of Rescue*, 495–506. London: Hurst, 2011.

——— "Sauvetages dans l'Europe allemande," in Alya Aglan and Robert Frank (eds.), *1937–1947: La Guerre-Monde. Tome II, 1821–67*. Paris: Gallimard, 2015.

——— *Tombés du ciel: Le sort des pilotes abattus en Europe, 1939–1945*. Paris: Tallandier, 2021.

Antebi, Elizabeth. "Changer la femme pour changer l'homme: Le modèle des institutrices de l'Alliance israélite universelle," in Sonia Sarah Lipsyc (ed.), *Femmes et Judaïsme aujourd'hui*, 257–68. Paris: Éditions In Press, 2008.

Antler, Joyce. "Justine Wise Polier." Shalvi/Hyman Encyclopedia of Jewish Women. March 20, 2009. Jewish Women's Archive. https://jwa.org/encyclopedia/article/polier-justine-wise.

Arendt, Hannah. *À travers le mur, suivi par Notre fille de Martha Arendt*. Paris: Payot, 2017.

——— *Antisemitism: Part One of The Origins of Totalitarianism*. New York: Harcourt, Brace and World, [1951] 1968.

Auslander, Leora. "The Boundaries of Jewishness or When Is a Cultural Practice Jewish?," *Journal of Modern Jewish Studies*, 8, no. 1 (2009), 47–64.

Avni, Haïm. "The Zionist Underground in Holland and France and the Escape to Spain," in Yisrael Gutman and Efraim Zuroff (eds.), *Rescue Attempts during the Holocaust: Proceedings of the Second Yad Vashem International Historical Conference. Jerusalem, April 8–11, 1974*, 555–90. Jerusalem: Yad Vashem, 1977.

Barnett, Barbara. *The Hide-and-Seek Children: Recollections of Jewish Survivors from Slovakia*. Glasgow: Mansion Field, 2012.

Barth, Frederik. *Ethnic Groups and Boundaries: The Social Organization of Culture Difference*. Boston, MA: Little, Brown and Co., 1969.

Bauer, Yehuda. *American Jewry and the Holocaust: The American Jewish Joint Distribution Committee, 1939–1945*. Detroit, MI: Wayne State University Press, 1981.

——— *My Brother's Keeper: A History of the American Jewish Joint Distribution Committee, 1929–1939*. Philadelphia, PA: The Jewish Publication Society, 1974.

——— *Out of the Ashes: The Impact of American Jews on Post-Holocaust Jewry*. Oxford: Pergamon, 1989.

——— *Rethinking the Holocaust*. New Haven, CT and London: Yale University Press, 2001.

Baumann, Denise. *La mémoire des oubliés: Grandir après Auschwitz*. Paris: Albin Michel, 1988.

Baumel-Schwartz, Judith Tydor. "Gender and Family Studies of the Holocaust: The Development of a Historical Discipline," in Esther Herzog (ed.), *Life, Death, and Sacrifice: Women and Family in the Holocaust*, 21–40. Jerusalem: Gefen, 2008.

BIBLIOGRAPHY

———— *Never Look Back: The Jewish Refugee Children in Great Britain, 1938–1945*. West Lafayette, IN: Purdue University Press, 2012.

———— *Unfulfilled Promise: Rescue and Resettlement of Jewish Refugee Children in the United States, 1934–1945*. Juneau, AK: Denali Press, 1990.

Beltramo, Noémie, and Rudy Rigaut. "Des colonies de vacances juives au service de la régénération physique: L'exemple de la Colonie scolaire, 1927–1939," *Archives Juives: Revue d'histoire des Juifs de France* 56, no. 1 (2023), 60–77.

Berkovitz, Jay. *The Shaping of Jewish Identity in Nineteenth-Century France*. Detroit, MI: Wayne University Press, 1989.

Berkowitz, Michael. "Introduction: Breadth and Depth in the History of the Kindertransport and Beyond," *Jewish Historical Studies*, 51 (2019), 9–15.

Bernstein, Michael André. *Forgone Conclusions: Against Apocalyptic History*. Berkeley, CA: University of California Press, 1994.

Bertin, Célia. *Louise Weiss*. Paris: Albin Michel, 2015.

Birnbaum, Pierre. *Un mythe politique: La "République juive."* Paris: Fayard, 1988.

Blanc-Chaléard, Marie-Claude. *Histoire de l'immigration*. Paris: La Découverte, 2001.

Boussion, Samuel, and Mathias Gardet (eds.). *Les châteaux du social: XIXe–XXe siècle*. Paris: Beauchesne/Presses Universitaires de Vincennes, 2010.

Boussion, Samuel, Mathias Gardet, and Martine Ruchat (eds.). *L'Internationale des républiques d'enfants, 1939–54*. Paris: Anamosa, 2020.

Boyarin, Daniel. *Unheroic Conduct: The Rise of Heterosexuality and the Invention of the Jewish Man*. Berkeley, CA: University of California Press, 1997.

Boyarin, Jonathan. *Jewish Families*. New Brunswick, NJ: Rutgers University Press, 2013.

Brachfeld, Olivier. *Inferiority Feelings: In the Individual and the Group*. London: Routledge, 2013.

Brade, Laura, and Rose Holmes. "Troublesome Sainthood: Nicholas Winton and the Contested History of Child Rescue in Prague, 1938–1940," *History & Memory*, 29, no. 1 (2017), 3–40.

Breitman, Richard, and Alan Kraut. *American Refugee Policy and European Jewry, 1933–1945*. Bloomington, IN: Indiana University Press, 1987.

Breitman, Richard, and Allan J. Lichtman. *FDR and the Jews*. Cambridge, MA: Belknap Press, 2013.

Bremner, Robert. "Other People's Children," *Journal of Social History*, 16, no. 3 (1983), 83–103.

Brenner, Michael. *A Short History of the Jews*. Princeton, NJ: Princeton University Press, 2010.

Browning, Christopher. *Collected Memories: Holocaust History and Postwar Testimony*. Madison, WI: University of Wisconsin Press, 2003.

———— "From Humanitarian Relief to Holocaust Rescue: Tracy Strong Jr., Vichy Internment Camps, and the Maison des Roches in Le Chambon," *Holocaust and Genocide Studies*, 30, no. 2 (2016), 211–46.

Butler, Judith. *Gender Trouble: Feminism and the Subversion of Identity*. New York: Routledge, 1990.

Cabanel, Patrick. "Enfants juifs et mamans justes," in Ivan Jablonka (ed.), *L'Enfant-Shoah*, 113–28. Paris: Presses Universitaires de France, 2014.

———— *Histoire des justes en France*. Paris: Dunod, [2012] 2024.

———— *Juifs et protestants en France: Les affinités électives, XVIe–XXIe siècle*. Paris: Fayard, 2004.

Caestecker, Frank. "Children in Twentieth Century Europe Affected by War: Historical Experiences in Giving Them Refuge," in Ilse Derluyn (ed.), *Re-Member: Rehabilitation, Reintegration and Reconciliation of War-Affected Children*, 267–88. Cambridge: Intersentia, 2012.

Cairns, Lucille. "Jewish Children's Homes in Post-Holocaust France: Personal Témoignages," in Seán Hand and Steven T. Katz (eds.), *Post-Holocaust France and the Jews, 1945–1955*, 139–54. New York: New York University Press, 2015.

Caron, Vicki. *Between France and Germany: The Jews of Alsace-Lorraine, 1871–1918*. Stanford, CA: Stanford University Press, 1988.

——— "Louise Weiss," Shalvi/Hyman Encyclopedia of Jewish Women, June 23, 2021. Jewish Women's Archive. https://jwa.org/encyclopedia/article/weiss-louise.

——— "Loyalties in Conflict: French Jewry and the Refugee Crisis, 1933–1935," *Leo Baeck Institute Yearbook*, 36 (1991), 305–38.

——— *Uneasy Asylum: France and the Jewish Refugee Crisis, 1933–1942*. Stanford, CA: Stanford University Press, 1999.

Certeau, Michel de. *L'invention du quotidien*, 1: *Arts de faire*. Paris: Gallimard, 1990.

Charnow, Sally. *Edmond Fleg and Jewish Minority Culture in Twentieth-Century France*. Milton Park: Routledge, 2021.

Chouraqui, André. *L'Alliance israélite universelle et La Renaissance juive contemporaine (1860–1960): Préface de René Cassin*. Paris: Presses Universitaires de France, 1965.

Clifford, Rebecca. "Child Survivors, Generations and Memory in Post-1968 France," forthcoming.

——— *Commemorating the Holocaust: The Dilemmas of Remembrance in France and Italy*. Oxford: Oxford University Press, 2013.

——— "Families after the Holocaust: Between the Archives and Oral History," *Oral History Journal*, 46, no. 1 (Spring 2018), 42–54.

——— *Survivors: Children's Lives after the Holocaust*. London: Yale University Press, 2020.

——— "Who Is a Survivor?: Child Holocaust Survivors and the Development of a Generational Identity," *Oral History Forum. Forum d'Histoire Orale*, 37 (2017).

Cœuré, Sophie. *La mémoire spoliée: Les archives des Français, butin de guerre nazi puis soviétique (de 1940 à nos jours)*. Paris: Payot, 2007.

Cohen, Asher. *Persécutions et sauvetages: Juifs et Français sous l'Occupation et sous Vichy*. Paris: Éditions du Cerf, 1993.

Cohen, Beth B. *Case Closed: Holocaust Survivors in Postwar America*. New Brunswick, NJ: Rutgers University Press, 2007.

——— *Child Survivors of the Holocaust: The Youngest Remnant and the American Experience*. New Brunswick, NJ: Rutgers University Press, 2018.

Cohen, Boaz, and Rita Horvath. "Young Witnesses in the DP Camps: Children's Holocaust Testimony in Context," *Journal of Modern Jewish Studies*, 11, no. 1 (March 2012), 103–25.

Cohen, Naomi Weiner. *Not Free to Desist: The American Jewish Committee, 1906–1966*. Philadelphia, PA: Jewish Publication Society of America, 1972.

Cohen, Steven Martin, and Paula Hyman (eds.). *The Jewish Family: Myths and Reality*. New York: Holmes & Meier, 1986.

Cohen, Yolande. "Le Conseil national des femmes françaises (1901–1939)," *Archives Juives: Revue d'histoire des Juifs de France*, 44, no. 1 (2011), 83–105.

——— "Protestant and Jewish Philanthropies in France: The Conseil National des Femmes Françaises (1901–1939)," *French Politics, Culture and Society*, 24, no. 1 (2006), 74–92.

Coleman, Ron. "The US Committee for the Care of European Children (USCOM) and the Rescue of Children." Unpublished USHMM Research Brief. September 2015.

Collignon, Simon. "Les homes Bernheim et Speyer (1938–1940): Témoignages d'enfants réfugiés d'Allemagne et d'Autriche," *Les cahiers de la mémoire contemporaine*, 6 (2005), 21–67.

Collomp, Catherine. *Résister au Nazisme: Le Jewish Labor Committee, New York, 1934–1945*. Paris: CNRS Éditions, 2016.

Corazza, Stephanie. "The Routine of Rescue: Child Welfare Workers and the Holocaust in France." PhD Dissertation, University of Toronto, 2017.

Corber, Erin. "L'Esprit du Corps: Bodies, Communities, and the Reconstruction of Jewish Life in France, 1914–1940." PhD Dissertation, Indiana University, 2013.

———— "Race, corps, et dégénérescence chez les Éclaireurs Israélites dans l'Entre-deux-guerres," *Archives Juives: Revue d'histoire des Juifs de France*, 50, no. 2 (2017), 55–75.

———— "The Kids on Oberlin Street: Place, Space and Jewish Community in Late Interwar Strasbourg," *Urban History*, 43, no. 4 (2016), 581–98.

Correa Martín-Arroyo. "Europe's Bottleneck: The Iberian Peninsula and the Jewish Refugee Crisis, 1933–1944." PhD Dissertation, London School of Economics, 2018.

Courriers de France et de Français pendant la Seconde Guerre mondiale. "Le Contrôle Postal Sous Vichy." Courriers de France et de Français durant la Seconde Guerre mondiale. http://ww2postalhistory.fr/Fr40_01_fr.php?cat=post40&activ=02.

Crosby, Donald. "Boston's Catholics and the Spanish Civil War: 1936–1939," *The New England Quarterly*, 44, no. 1 (1971), 82–100.

Curio, Claudia. "'Invisible' Children: The Selection and Integration Strategies of Relief Organizations," *Shofar* 23, no. 1 (2004), 41–56.

———— "'Unsichtbare' Kinder. Emigration und Akkulturation von Kindern und Jugendlichen. Das Beispiel Kindertransporte 1938/39." PhD Dissertation, Technische Universität Berlin, 2005.

———— "Were Unaccompanied Children a Privileged Class of Refugees in the Liberal States of Europe?," in Frank Caestecker and Bernard Moore (eds.), *Refugees from Nazi Germany and the Liberal European States*, 183–4. New York: Berghahn Books, 2010.

Daltroff, Jean. "Fanny Schwab (1898–1991)." http://judaisme.sdv.fr/today/laurew/fanny.htm.

Davie, Maurice. *Refugees in America: Report of the Committee for the Study of Recent Immigration from Europe*. New York: Harper and Brothers, 1947.

Delpard, Raphaël. *Les enfants cachés*. Paris: J-C Lattès, 1993.

Denechère, Yves. "Les parrainages des enfants étrangers au 20ème siècle: Une histoire des relations interpersonnelles transnationales," *Vingtième Siècle: Revue d'histoire*, 126 (2015), 147–61.

Deroo, Delphine. *Les enfants de la Martellière*. Paris: Grasset, 1999.

Deutscher, Isaac. *Non-Jewish Jew and Other Essays*. S.l.: Oxford University Press, 1968.

Dobkowski, Michael N. *Jewish American Voluntary Organizations*. Westport, CT: Greenwood, 1986.

Dodd, Lindsay. "Wartime Rupture and Reconfiguration in French Family Life: Experience and Legacy," *History Workshop Journal*, 88 (2019), 134–52.

Doron, Daniella. "Feeling Familial Separation: Emotions, Agency, and Holocaust Refugee Youths," *Jewish Social Studies*, 28, no. 3 (2023), 1–30.

———— *Jewish Youth and Identity in Postwar France: Rebuilding Family and Nation*. Bloomington, IN: Indiana University Press, 2015.

Doulut, Alexandre. "La déportation des Juifs de France: Changement d'échelle." PhD Dissertation, Université Paris 1 Panthéon-Sorbonne, 2021.

Downs, Laura Lee. *Childhood in the Promised Land: Working-Class Movements and the Colonies de Vacances in France, 1880–1960.* Durham, NC: Duke University Press, 2002.

——— "Enfance en guerre: Les évacuations d'enfants en France et en Grande-Bretagne (1939–1940)," *Annales: Histoire, Sciences Sociales,* 2 (2011), 413–48.

Duroux, Rose, and Célia Keren. "Retours sur dessins: Fred/Alfred Brauner 1938, 1946, 1976, 1991," in Rose Duroux and Catherine Milkovitch-Rioux (eds.), *Enfances en Guerre: Témoignages d'enfants sur la guerre,* 99–119. Geneva: L'Equinoxe/ Éditions Georg, 2013.

Duroux, Rose, and Catherine Milkovitch-Rioux (eds.). *J'ai dessiné la guerre: Le regard de Françoise et Alfred Brauner* (Clermont-Ferrand: Presses Universitaires Blaise Pascal, 2011).

Dwork, Deborah. *Children with a Star: Jewish Youth in Nazi Europe.* New Haven, CT and London: Yale University Press, 1991.

——— *Saints and Liars: The Story of Americans Who Saved Refugees from the Nazis.* New York: W.W. Norton & Co., 2025.

Dwork, Deborah, and Robert Jan. van Pelt. *Flight from the Reich: Refugee Jews, 1933–1946.* New York: W.W. Norton & Co., 2012.

Ehetreiber, Christian, Heimo Halbrainer, and Bettina Ramp. *Der Koffer der Adele Kurzweil: Auf den Spuren einer Grazer jüdischen Familie in der Emigration.* Graz: CLIO-Verein f. Geschichts- u. Bildungsarbeit, 2001.

Einwohner, Rachel. "Ethical Considerations on the Use of Archived Testimonies in Holocaust Research: Beyond the IRB Exemption," *Qualitative Sociology,* 34 (2011), 415–30.

Elsky, Julia. *Writing Occupation: Jewish émigré Voices in Wartime France.* Palo Alto, CA: Stanford University Press, 2020.

Engel, Liba. "Experiments in Democracy: Dewy's Lab School and Korczak's Children's Republic," *The Social Studies* (May/June 2008), 117–21.

Epelbaum, Didier. *Les enfants de papier: Les Juifs de Pologne immigrés en France jusqu'en 1940.* Paris: Grasset, 2002.

Epstein, Simon. "Les Institutions israélites françaises de 1929–1939: Solidarité juive et lutte contre l'antisémitisme." PhD Dissertation, Université Paris 1, 1990.

Erbelding, Rebecca. *Rescue Board: The Untold Story of America's Efforts to Save the Jews of Europe.* New York: Doubleday, 2018.

Fabian, Ruth, and Corinna Coulmas. *Die deutsche Emigration in Frankreich nach 1933.* Munich: KG Saur, 1978.

Farges, Patrick. "'Muscle' Yekkes?: Multiple German Jewish Masculinities in Palestine/Israel after 1933," *Central European History,* 51, no. 3 (September 2018), 466–87.

Fass, Paula. *The Routledge History of Childhood in the Western World.* London and New York: Routledge, 2015.

Feingold, Henry. *A Time for Searching: Entering the Mainstream, 1920–1945.* Baltimore, MD: The John Hopkins University Press, 1992.

——— *Bearing Witness: How America and Its Jews Responded to the Holocaust.* Syracuse, NY: Syracuse University Press, 1995.

——— *The Politics of Rescue: The Roosevelt Administration and the Holocaust, 1938–1945.* New Brunswick, NJ: Rutgers University Press, 1970.

Felsteiner, Mary Lowenthal. *To Paint Her Life: Charlotte Salomon in the Nazi Era.* Berkeley, CA: University of California Press, 1997.

Fette, Julie. *Exclusions: Practicing Prejudice in French Law and Medicine, 1920–1945.* Ithaca, NY: Cornell University Press, 2012.

Fhima, Catherine. "Au cœur de la 'renaissance juive' des années 1920: Littérature et judéité," *Archives Juives: Revue d'histoire des Juifs de France*, 39, no. 1 (2006), 29–45.

Fivaz-Silbermann. *La fuite en Suisse: Les Juifs à la frontière franco-suisse durant les années de la "Solution finale."* Paris: Calmann-Lévy, 2020.

Fogg, Shannon. "American Quakers in France." Seminar talk in Nancy Green's seminar, École des hautes études en sciences sociales, January 30, 2018.

——— "Remembering the American Friends Service Committee's Wartime Aid." Conference Presentation at the Society for French Historical Studies, March 2018.

——— "The American Friends Service Committee and Wartime Aid to Families," in Lindsey Dodd and David Lees (eds.), *Vichy France and Everyday Life: Confronting the Challenges of Wartime, 1939–1945*, 107–22. London: Bloomsbury, 2018.

——— *The Politics of Everyday Life in Vichy France: Foreigners, Undesirables, and Strangers.* New York: Cambridge University Press, 2009.

Formaglio, Cécile. "Cécile Brunschvicg, femme, féministe, juive, face aux défis de l'intégration et de la neutralité religieuse," *Archives du Féminisme*, no. 9 (December 2005), 29–42.

——— *"Féministe d'abord": Cécile Brunschvicg (1877–1946).* Rennes: Presses Universitaires de Rennes, 2014.

Fraser Kirsh, Mary. "La politique de placement des enfants en Grande-Bretagne et en Palestine," in Ivan Jablonka (ed.), *L'Enfant-Shoah*, 51–66. Paris: Presses Universitaires de France, 2014.

Friedländer, Saul. "Introduction," in Saul Friedländer (ed.), *Probing the Limits of Representation: Nazism and the "Final Solution,"* 1–21. Cambridge, MA: Harvard University Press, 1992.

——— *Nazi Germany and the Jews, Volume One: Years of Persecution (1933–1939).* New York: HarperCollins, 1997.

——— *The Years of Extermination: Nazi Germany and the Jews, 1939–1945.* New York: HarperCollins, 2007.

Fuchs, Julien. *Toujours Prêts!: Scoutismes et mouvements de jeunesse en Alsace, 1918–1970.* Strasbourg: La Nuée Bleue, 2007.

Garbarini, Alexandra. "Diaries, Testimonies and Jewish Histories of the Holocaust," in Norman J.W. Goda (ed.), *Jewish Histories of the Holocaust: New Transnational Approaches*, 91–104. New York: Berghahn Books, 2014.

——— *Numbered Days: Diaries and the Holocaust.* New Haven, CT and London: Yale University Press, 2006.

Geertz, Clifford. *The Interpretation of Cultures: Selected Essays.* New York: Basic Books, 1973.

Genizi, Haim. *American Apathy: The Plight of Christian Refugees from Nazism.* Ramat-Gan: Bar Ilan University Press, 1983.

——— "New York Is Big: America Is Bigger: The Resettlement of Refugees from Nazism, 1936–1945," *Jewish Social Studies*, 46, no. 1 (1984), 61–72.

Gensburger, Sarah. "Bringing the State Back into Memory Studies: Commemorating the Righteous in France, 2007–20," in Natalia Aleksiun, Raphael Utz, and Zofia Woycicka (eds.), *The Rescue Turn and the Politics of Holocaust Memory*, 43–165. Detroit, MI: Wayne State University Press, 2023.

BIBLIOGRAPHY

———— *Les Justes de France: Politiques publiques de la mémoire*. Paris: Presses de Sciences Po, 2010.

Gigliotti, Simone, and Monica Tempian (eds.). *The Young Victims of the Nazi Regime: Migration, the Holocaust, and Postwar Displacement*. London: Bloomsbury Academic, 2016.

Gilbert, Martin. *The Boys: Triumph over Adversity: The Story of 732 Young Concentration Camp Survivors*. London: Phoenix, 1997.

————*The Righteous: The Unsung Heroes of the Holocaust*. London: Doubleday, 2002.

Gildea, Robert. "Jacques Sémelin and the French Recovery of Righteousness," *Shofar: An Interdisciplinary Journal of Jewish Studies*, 39, no. 2 (2021), 246–56.

Gillerman, Sharon. *Germans into Jews: Remaking the Jewish Social Body in the Weimar Republic*. Stanford, CA: Stanford University Press, 2009.

Goffman, Erving. *Asylums: Essays on the Social Situation of Mental Patients and Other Inmates*. New York: Random House, 1968.

———— *The Presentation of Self in Everyday Life*. New York: Doubleday, 1959.

Goldstein, Eric L. "Contesting the Categories: Jews and Government Classification in the United States," *Jewish History*, 19, no. 1 (2005), 79–107.

Gordon, Linda. *Heroes of Their Own Lives: The Politics and History of Family Violence, Boston 1880–1960*. New York: Penguin Books, 1989.

———— *The Great Arizona Orphan Abduction*. Cambridge, MA: Harvard University Press, 1999.

Gossels, Lisa, and Dean Wetherell. *The Children of Chabannes*. Good Egg Productions, 1999 [DVD].

Gottlieb, Moshe. *American Anti-Nazi Resistance, 1933–1941*. New York: Ktav, 1981.

Grange, Cyril. *Une élite parisienne: Les familles de la grande bourgeoisie juive (1870–1939)*. Paris: CNRS Éditions, 2016.

Granick, Jaclyn. *International Jewish Humanitarianism in the Age of the Great War*. Cambridge: Cambridge University Press, 2021.

Granovetter, Mark. "The Strength of Weak Ties: A Network Theory Revisited," *Sociological Theory*, 1 (1983), 201–33.

Green, Nancy L. *Repenser les migrations*. Paris: Presses Universitaires de France, 2002.

———— "To Give and to Receive: Philanthropy and Collective Responsibility Among Jews in Paris, 1880–1914," in Peter Mandler (ed.), *The Uses of Charity*, 197–226. Philadelphia, PA: University of Pennsylvania Press, 1990.

Greenspan, Henry. *On Listening to Holocaust Survivors: Recounting and Life History*. Westport, CT: Praeger, 1998.

Grendi, Edoardo. "Micro-analisi e storia sociale," *Quaderni Storici*, 12, no. 35 (1977), 506–20.

Gross, Martine, Sophie Nizard, and Yann Scioldo-Zürcher. *Gender, Families and Transmission in the Contemporary Jewish Context*. Cambridge: Cambridge Scholars Press, 2017.

Grossman Atina. *Jews, Germans and Allies: Close Encounters in Occupied Germany*. Princeton, NJ: Princeton University Press, 2007.

Grynberg, Anne. *Les camps de la honte: Les internés juifs des camps français, 1939–1944*. Paris: La Découverte, 1999.

———— "Précurseurs et Passeurs." Conference Presentation, Les Juifs de Russie et d'Union Sovietique à Paris, 1881–1991, École des hautes études en sciences sociales, Paris, November 2008.

———— "Un Kibboutz en Corrèze," *Les Cahiers du Judaïsme*, 30 (2011), 89–103.

Guedj, Jeremy. *Les Juifs de France et le nazisme, 1933–1939: L'histoire renversée*. Paris: Presses Universitaires de France, 2024.

Gumpert, Laura. "Humble Heroes: How the American Friends Service Committee Struggled to Save Oswald Kernberg and Three Hundred Other Jewish Children from Nazi Europe." Undergraduate Thesis, Haverford College, 2002.

Hammel, Andrea, and Bea Lewkowicz (eds.). *The Kindertransport to Britain 1938–39: New Perspectives*. Leiden: Brill, 2012.

Hansen-Schaberg, Inge, Hanna Papanek, and Gabriele Rühl-Nawabi. *Ernst Papanek. Pädagogische und therapeutische Arbeit: Kinder mit Verfolgungs-, Flucht- und Exilerfahrungen während der NS-Zeit*. Vienna: Böhlau Verlag, 2015.

Harris, Mark Jonathan. *Into the Arms of Strangers: Stories of Kindertransport*. Sabine Films, 2000 [Documentary].

Hayes, Peter. *Why?:Explaining the Holocaust*. New York: W.W. Norton & Co., 2017.

Hazan, Katy. "Le sauvetage des enfants juifs de France vers les Amériques, 1933–1947," in Hélène Harter and André Kaspi (eds.), *Terres Promises: Mélanges Offerts à André Kaspi*, 481–93. Paris: Publ. de la Sorbonne, 2008.

——— *Les Enfants de l'après-guerre dans les maisons de l'OSE*. Paris: OSE/ Somogy éditions d'art, 2012.

——— *Les Orphelins de la Shoah: Les maisons de l'espoir, 1944–1960*. Paris: Belles Lettres, 2000.

——— *Rire le jour, pleurer la nuit: Les enfants juifs cachés dans la Creuse pendant la guerre, 1939–1944*. Paris: Calmann-Lévy, 2014.

Hazan, Katy, and Serge Klarsfeld. *Le sauvetage des enfants juifs pendant l'Occupation, dans les maisons de l'OSE, 1938–1945*. Paris: OSE/Somogy éditions d'art, 2008.

Heim, Susanne. "Immigration Policy and Forced Emigration from Germany: The Situation of Jewish Children (1933–1945)," in Paul Shapiro (ed.), *Children and the Holocaust Symposium Presentations*, 1–18. Washington, DC: United States Holocaust Memorial Museum, 2004.

Herzog, Dagmar. *Cold War Freud: Psychoanalysis in an Age of Catastrophes*. Cambridge: Cambridge University Press, 2017.

Heywood, Colin. *A History of Childhood: Children and Childhood in the West from Medieval to Modern Times*. Cambridge: Polity Press, 2009.

Hirsch, Marianne, and Leo Spitzer. "Archives of Possibility: Photography, Memory, Memorialization." Presentation at the Holocaust Educational Foundation Summer Institute, Evanston, June 2017.

——— "School Photos and Their Afterlives," in Elspeth H. Brown and Thy Phu (eds.), *Feeling Photography*, 252–72. Durham, NC: Duke University Press, 2014.

Histrecmed. "Benjamin Weill-Hallé (1875-1958)." Histrecmed. http://www.histrecmed.fr/index.php?option=com_content&view=article&id=254:weill-halle-benjamin&catid=9.

Hobson Faure, Laura. *A "Jewish Marshall Plan": The American Jewish Presence in Post-Holocaust France*. Bloomington, IN: Indiana University Press, 2022.

——— "Attentes européennes, réalités américaines. L'émigration des enfants de l'Oeuvre de Secours aux Enfants de la France occupée vers les Etats-Unis, 1941–1942," in Hobson Faure et al. (eds.), *L'Oeuvre de Secours aux Enfants et les populations juives*, 149–66. Paris: Armand Colin, 2014.

——— "Baroness Germaine de Rothschild," in Shalvi/Hyman Encyclopedia of Jewish Women. Jewish Women's Archive, February 14, 2022. https://jwa.org/encyclopedia/article/rothschild-baroness-germaine-de

——— "European Expectations, American Realities: The Immigration of Jewish Children from Occupied France to the United States, 1941–42," in Martine Gross, Sophie Nizard, and Yann Scioldo-Zürcher (eds.), *Gender, Families and Transmission in Contemporary Jewish Context*, 143–57. Cambridge: Cambridge Scholars Press, 2017.

——— "Exploring Political Rupture Through Jewish Children's Diaries: Kindertransport Children in France, 1938–1942," *Journal of Modern European History*, 19, no. 3 (2021), 258–73.

——— "'Guide and Motivator' or 'Central Treasury'?: The Role of the American Jewish Joint Distribution Committee in France, 1942–44," in Claire Andrieu, Jacques Sémelin, and Sarah Gensburger (eds.), *Rescue Practices Facing Genocides. Comparative Perspectives*, 293–311. London and New York: Hurst/Columbia University Press, 2011.

——— "Jewish Child Refugees from Central Europe in France and the United States: Transnational Perspectives on their Care, 1938–1945," *European Holocaust Studies*, 5 (April 2024), 131–49.

——— "Un 'Plan Marshall juif': La présence juive américaine en France après la Shoah, 1944–54." PhD Dissertation, École des hautes études en sciences sociales, 2009.

Hobson Faure, Laura, Mathias Gardet, Katy Hazan, and Catherine Nicault (eds.). *L'Œuvre de Secours aux Enfants et les populations juives au XXe siècle: Prévenir et guérir dans un siècle de violences*. Paris: Armand Colin, 2014.

Hobson Faure, Laura, Manon Pignot, and Antoine Rivière (eds.). *Enfants en guerre: "Sans famille" dans les conflits du 20ème siècle*. Paris: CNRS Éditions, 2023.

Hollinger, David A. "Communalist and Dispersionist Approaches to American Jewish History in an Increasingly Post-Jewish Era," *American Jewish History*, 95, no. 1 (2009), 1–32.

Holloway, Sarah L., Louise Holt, and Sarah Mills. "Questions of Agency: Capacity, Subjectivity, Spatiality and Temporality," *Progress in Human Geography*, 43, no. 3 (2019), 458–77.

Holmes, Rose. "A Moral Business: British Quaker Work with Refugees from Fascism, 1933–39." PhD Dissertation, University of Sussex, December 2013.

Hyman, Paula. *From Dreyfus to Vichy: The Remaking of French Jewry, 1906–1939*. New York: Columbia University Press, 1979.

——— *Gender and Assimilation in Modern Jewish History: The Roles and Representation of Women*. Seattle, WA: University of Washington Press, 1995.

——— *The Emancipation of the Jews of Alsace: Acculturation and Tradition in the Nineteenth Century*. New Haven, CT and London: Yale University Press, 1991.

Jablonka, Ivan. *Histoire des grands-parents que je n'ai pas eus: Une enquête*. Paris: Seuil, 2012.

——— (ed.). *L'Enfant-Shoah*. Paris: Presses Universitaires de France, 2014.

Jason, Philip K., and Iris Posner (eds.). *Don't Wave Goodbye: The Children's Flight from Nazi Persecution to American Freedom*. Westport, CT: Praeger, 2004.

Jennings, Eric T. *Escape from Vichy: The Refugee Exodus to the French Caribbean*. Cambridge, MA: Harvard University Press, 2018.

Jockush, Laura. *Collect and Record!: Jewish Holocaust Documentation in Early Postwar Europe*. New York: Oxford University Press, 2012.

Joly, Laurent. *La falsification de l'histoire: Éric Zemmour, l'extrême droite, Vichy et les Juifs*. Paris: Grasset, 2022.

——— "La frontière entre 'judaïsme' et 'aryanisme': Logique antisémite, contentieux juridique et pratiques bureaucratiques autour du classement des 'demi-juifs' en

France occupée (1940–44)," *L'atelier du centre de recherches historiques*, 21 bis (2020), https://journals.openedition.org/acrh/10751?lang=en, consulted March 2, 2024.

———— *La Rafle du Vél d'Hiv: Paris, juillet 1942.* Paris: Grasset, 2022.

———— *L'État contre les Juifs: Vichy, les nazis et la persécution antisémite.* Paris: Grasset, 2018.

———— "The Genesis of Vichy's Jewish State of October 1940," *Holocaust and Genocide Studies*, 27, no. 2 (2013), 276–98.

———— *Vichy dans la "solution finale": Histoire du Commissariat général aux questions juives (1941–1944).* Paris: Grasset, 2006.

———— "Vichy, les Français et la Shoah: Un état de la connaissance scientifique," *Revue d'histoire de la Shoah*, 2 (2020), 13–29.

Kangisser Cohen, Sharon. "A Child's View: Children's Depositions of the Central Jewish Historical Commission (Poland)," in Sharon Kangisser Cohen, Eva Fogelman, and Dalia Ofer (eds.), *Children in the Holocaust and its Aftermath: Historical and Psychological Studies of the Kerstenberg Archive*, 43–61. Oxford: Berghahn Books, 2017.

———— *Testimony and Time: Holocaust Survivors Remember.* Jerusalem: Yad Vashem, 2014.

Kaplan, Marion A. *Between Dignity and Despair: Jewish Life in Nazi Germany.* New York: Oxford University Press, 1998.

———— *Hitler's Jewish Refugees: Hope and Anxiety in Portugal.* New Haven, CT and London: Yale University Press, 2020.

———— *The Making of the Jewish Middle Class: Women, Family and Identity in Imperial Germany.* Oxford: Oxford University Press, 1991.

Karol, Tammy. "Reunion Held for Recipients of Rothschild Aid," *The Canadian Jewish News*, August 11, 1983.

Karp, Abraham J. *To Give Life: The UJA in the Shaping of the American Jewish Community.* New York: Schocken Books, 1981.

Kaspi, André (ed.). *Histoire de l'Alliance israélite universelle de 1860 à nos jours.* Paris: Armand Colin, 2010.

Kerber, Linda. "Separate Sphere, Female Worlds, Woman's Place: The Rhetoric of Women's History," *Journal of American History*, LXXV (1989), 9–39.

Keren, Célia. "Autobiographies of Spanish Refugee Children at the Quaker Home in La Rouvière (France, 1940): Humanitarian Communication and Children's Writings," *Les Cahiers de Framespa*, 5 (2010), https://journals.openedition.org/framespa/268.

———— "L'évacuation et l'accueil des enfants espagnols en France: Cartographie d'une mobilisation transnationale (1936–1940)." PhD Dissertation, École des hautes études en sciences sociales, 2014.

Kertzer, David. *The Kidnapping of Edgardo Mortara.* New York: Knopf, 1997.

Kieval, Hillel J. "Legality and Resistance in Vichy France: The Rescue of Jewish Children," *Proceedings of the American Philosophical Society*, 124, no. 5 (1980), 339–66.

Klarsfeld, Serge. *French Children of the Holocaust: A Memorial.* New York: New York University Press, 1996.

———— *Vichy Auschwitz: Le rôle de Vichy dans la Solution Finale de la question juive en France, 1943–1944.* Paris: Fayard, 1985.

Koepp, Roy. "Holocaust Rescuers in Historical and Academic Scholarship," in Gerald Steinacher and Ari Kohen (eds.), *Unlikely Heroes: The Place of Holocaust Rescuers in Research ad Teaching*, 15–36. Omaha, NE: University of Nebraska Press, 2019.

Koren, Nathan. *Jewish Physicians: A Biographical Index*. Jerusalem: Israel University Press, 1973.

Körte, Mona. "Bracelet, Hand Towel, Pocket Watch: Objects of the Last Moment in Memory and Narration," *Shofar*, 23, no. 1 (2004), 109–20.

Kössler, Till. "Children in the Spanish Civil War," in Martin Baumeister and Stefanie Schüler-Springorum (eds.), *"If you tolerate this . . .": The Spanish Civil War in the Age of Total War*, 118–25. Chicago, IL: Chicago University Press, 2009.

Krohn, Helga. *Vor Den Nazis gerettet – Eine Hilfsaktion Für Frankfurter Kinder 1939 Schriftenreihe des Jüdischen Museums Frankfurt am Main Band 3*. Stuttgart: Jüdisches Museum Jan. Thorbecke Verlag, 1995.

Krondorfer, Björn (ed.). *Men and Masculinities in Christianity and Judaism: A Critical Reader*. London: SCM Press, 2009.

Kümmel, Ulrich. *Erwin Wexberg: Ein Leben zwischen Individualpsychologie, Psychoanalyse und Neurologie*. Göttingen: Vandenhoeck & Ruprecht, 2010.

Kushner, Tony. *Remembering Refugees Then and Now*. Manchester: Manchester University Press, 2006.

Laffitte, Michel. *Un Engrenage fatal: L'UGIF face aux réalités de la Shoah, 1941–1944*. Paris: Liana Lévi, 2004.

Laqueur, Walter. *Generation Exodus: The Fate of Young Jewish Refugees from Nazi Germany*. Hanover: Brandeis University Press, 2001.

Lazare, Lucien. *La Résistance juive en France*. Paris: Stock, 1987.

Lee, Daniel. *Pétain's Jewish Children: French Jewish Youth and the Vichy Regime, 1940–1942*. Oxford: Oxford University Press, 2014.

Leff, Lisa Moses. *Sacred Bonds of Solidarity: The Rise of Jewish Internationalism in Nineteenth-Century France*. Palo Alto, CA: Stanford University Press, 2006.

——— *The Archive Thief: The Man Who Salvaged French Jewish History in the Wake of the Holocaust*. Oxford: Oxford University Press, 2015.

Legaretta, Dorothy. *The Guernica Generation: Basque Refugee Children of the Spanish Civil War*. Reno, NV: University of Nevada Press, 1984.

Leglaive-Perani, Céline. "Donner au féminin: Juives philanthropes en France (1830–1930)," *Archives Juives: Revue d'histoire des Juifs de France*, 48, no. 2 (2015), 11–24.

Lemalet, Martine. *Au Secours des enfants du siècle*. Paris: Seuil, 1993.

——— "Les Comités d'accueil aux réfugiés et l'Œuvre aux Secours aux Enfants (1933–1939)," in Annette Wieviorka and Jean-Jacques Becker (eds.), *Justin Godart: Un homme dans son siècle (1871–1956)*, 87–104. Paris: CNRS Éditions, 2004.

Lemercier, Claire. "Analyse de réseaux et histoire de la famille: Une rencontre encore à venir?," *Annales de Démographie Historique*, 109, no. 1 (2005), 7–31.

Lewis, Mary D. *The Boundaries of the Republic: Migrant Rights and the Limits of Universalism in France*. Palo Alto, CA: Stanford University Press, 2007.

Lillie, Sophie. *Was einmal war: Handbuch der enteigneten Kunstsammlungen Wiens*. Vienna: Czernin, 2003.

Lipsyc, Sonia Sarah (ed.). *Femmes et Judaïsme aujourd'hui*. Paris: Éditions In Press, 2008.

London, Louise. *Whitehall and the Jews, 1933–1948: British Immigration Policy, Jewish Refugees and the Holocaust*. Cambridge: Cambridge University Press, 2000.

Lottman, Herbet. *La Dynastie Rothschild*. Paris: Seuil, 1995.

Maier, Lilly. *Auf Wiedersehen, Kinder!: Ernst Papanek, Revolutionär, Reformpädagoge und Retter jüdischer Kinder*. Vienna: Molden Verlag, 2021.

——— "Das Schicksal des Arthur Kern: Eine biographische Studie zu den französischen Kindertransporten." Master's Thesis, University of Munich, 2017.

Maitron. "Axelrad, Martin." *Le Maitron: Dictionnaire Biographique. Mouvement Ouvrier, Mouvement Social.* http://maitron-en-ligne.univ-paris1.fr/spip.php?article145639.

───── "Chevrier, Félix." *Le Maitron: Dictionnaire Biographique. Mouvement Ouvrier, Mouvement Social.* https://maitron.fr/spip.php?article79066.

Malino, Frances. "L'Émancipation des femmes," in André Kaspi (ed.), *Histoire de l'Alliance israélite universelle de 1860 à nos jours,* 263–93. Paris: Armand Colin, 2010.

───── "Prophets in Their Own Land?: Mothers and Daughters of the Alliance Israélite Universelle," *Nashim,* 3 (2000), 56–73.

Malinovitch, Nadia. *French and Jewish: Culture and the Politics of Identity in Early Twentieth-Century France.* Liverpool: Littman Library of Jewish Civilization, 2007.

───── "From the Muslim World to France and North America: A Transnational History of the Students and Teachers of the Alliance Israélite Universelle after 1945." Habilitation à diriger des recherches, Université de Paris, 2021.

Mann, Michael. "Were the Perpetrators of Genocide "Ordinary Men" or "Real Nazis"?: Results from Fifteen Hundred Biographies," *Holocaust and Genocide Studies,* 14, no. 3 (2000), 331–66.

Marin, Juliette. " 'Et je crois qu'il faudra encore beaucoup d'années pour arriver à l'égalité': L'engagement des femmes d'origine juive dans la bienfaisance féministe en France (1895–1939)." Master's Thesis, Université Paris 1 Panthéon-Sorbonne, 2024.

Mariot, Nicolas, and Claire Zalc. *Face à la persécution: 991 Juifs dans la guerre.* Paris: Odile Jacob/Fondation pour la mémoire de la Shoah, 2010.

Marrus, Michael R., and Robert O. Paxton. *Vichy France and the Jews.* Stanford, CA: Stanford University Press, 1995.

Martin, Sean. "How to House a Child: Providing Homes for Jewish Children in Interwar Poland," *East European Jewish Affairs,* 45, no. 1 (2014), 26–41.

Maul, Daniel. "The Politics of Neutrality: The American Friends Service Committee and the Spanish Civil War, 1936–1939," *European Review of History: Revue Européenne d'histoire,* 23, no. 1–2 (2016), 82–100.

Maurel, Chloé. "Yvonne Hagnauer et la Maison d'enfants de Sèvres (1941–1970)," *La Revue de l'enfance irrégulière,* no. 10 (2008), 161–79.

McAuley, James. *The House of Fragile Things.* New Haven, CT and London: Yale University Press, 2021.

McEvoy, Grainne. "Family Unity, Child Refugees and the American Catholic Bishop's Response to the Wagner-Rogers Bill, 1939." Working Paper. Boston College Center for Christian Jewish Learning, January 2015.

Meaux, Lorraine de. *Une grande famille russe, les Gunzburg: Paris-Saint-Pétersbourg, XIXe–XXe siècle.* Paris: Perrin, 2018.

Medoff, Raphael. "American Jewish Responses to Nazism and the Holocaust," in Marc Lee Raphael (ed.), *The Columbia History of Jews and Judaism in America,* 291–312. New York: Columbia University Press, 2008.

Michel, Virginie. "L'action médico-sociale de l'OSE à Paris dans les années trente," *Archives Juives: Revue d'histoire des Juifs de France,* 39, no. 1 (2006), 110–24.

Michlic, Joanna B. (ed.). *Jewish Families in Europe, 1939–Present: History, Representation, and Memory.* Waltham, MA: Brandeis University Press, 2017.

───── "Mixed Lessons from the Holocaust: Avoiding Complexities and Darker Aspects of Jewish Child Survivors' Life Experiences," *Journal of the History of Children and Youth,* 17, no. 2 (2024), 272–86.

————— "'The War Began for Me After the War': Jewish Children in Poland, 1945–1949," in Jonathan C. Friedman (ed.), *The Routledge History of the Holocaust*, 484–99. London: Routledge, 2012.

Milton, Sybil, and Frederick D. Bogin. *Archives of the Holocaust: An International Collection of Selected Documents. American Jewish Joint Distribution Committee, New York, Volume 10. Parts 1 and 2.*. New York: Garland Publishing, 1995.

Mintec, Marina. "Fonds Brauner: Répertoire numérique." Master's Thesis, Université d'Angers, 2008.

Moke, Paul. "AFSC and the Holocaust. Pathways of Conscience in Vichy France," *Quaker History*, 109, no. 2 (2020), 1–30.

Monti, Angelina. *Das Herz einer Mutter (My Yiddishe Mama): Angelina Monti*, n.d. https://www.youtube.com/watch?v=IVWPEB6nw00 [Video].

Moody, Zoe. *Les droits de l'enfant: Genèse, institutionnalisation et diffusion (1924–1989)*. Neufchâtel: Éditions Alphil-Presses Universitaires Suisses, 2016.

Moore, Bob. *Survivors: Jewish Self-Help and Rescue in Nazi-Occupied Europe*. Oxford and New York: Oxford University Press, 2010.

Moreh-Rosenberg Eliad and Yehudit Shendar. "The Portrait and the Maiden." https://www.yadvashem.org/museum/art/articles/the-portrait-and-the-maiden.html.

Morse, Arthur D. *While Six Million Died: A Chronicle of American Apathy*. London: Secker and Warburg, 1968.

Mosse, George. *German Jews Beyond Judaism*. Bloomington, IN: Indiana University Press, 1985.

Mouchenik, Yoram. "Les Enfants dans la guerre: Entretien avec Alfred Brauner," *L'Autre: Cliniques, cultures et sociétés*, 11, no. 1 (2010), 10–17.

Muncy, Robyn. *Creating a Female Dominion in American Reform, 1890–1935*. Oxford: Oxford University Press, 1994.

Nathan, David. "The United States Committee for the Care of European Children, 1940–1953: A History and Guide to the Records." Master's Thesis, University of Massachusetts, 1983.

Nicault, Catherine. "Dans la tourmente de la Seconde Guerre mondiale, 1939–1944," in André Kaspi (ed.), *Histoire de l'Alliance israélite universelle de 1860 à nos jours*, 295–330. Paris: Armand Colin, 2010.

————— "L'accueil des Juifs d'Europe centrale par la communauté juive française," in Karel A. Bartosek, Réné Gallissot, and Denis Peschanski (eds.), *De l'exil à la résistance: Réfugiés et immigrés d'Europe centrale en France, 1933–1945*, 53–59. Saint-Denis Paris: Presses Universitaires de Vincennes Arcantère, 1989.

————— "L'émigration de France vers la Palestine, 1880–1940," *Archives Juives: Revue d'histoire des Juifs de France*, 41, no. 2 (2008), 10–33.

Noiriel, Gérard. *Réfugiés et sans-papiers: La république et le droit d'asile, XIX–XXe Siècle*. Paris: Hachette, 1998.

Nordheimer, Jon, "15 Who Fled the Nazis as Boys Hold a Reunion," *The New York Times*, July 28, 1983.

Novick, Peter. *The Holocaust in American Life*. Boston, MA: Houghton Mifflin, 1999.

Ofer, Dalia. "Cohesion and Rupture: The Jewish Family in the East European Ghettos during the Holocaust," *Studies in Contemporary Jewry*, 14 (1988), 143–65.

Ofer, Dalia, and Lenore J. Weitzman (eds.). *Women in the Holocaust*. New Haven, CT and London: Yale University Press, 1998.

Oliner, Samuel P. "The Unsung Heroes in Nazi Occupied Europe: The Antidote for Evil," *Nationalities Papers* XII, no. 1 (Spring 1984), 129–36.

Oliner, Samuel P. and Oliner, Pearl. *The Altruistic Personality: Rescuers of Jews in Nazi Germany.* New York: The Free Press, 1988.

Ostrovsky, Michal. "'We Are Standing By:' Rescue Operations of the United States Committee for the Care of European Children," *Holocaust and Genocide Studies*, 29, no. 2 (Fall 2015), 230–50.

Otto, Rienhard. *Wie haste det jemacht?: Lebenslauf von Hanna Grunwald-Eisfelder.* Soltau: Schultze Hermann, 1992.

Paechter, Carrie. "Tomboys and Girly Girls: Embodied Femininities in Primary Schools," *Discourse: Studies in the Cultural Politics of Education*, 31, no. 2 (2010), 221–35.

Paldiel, Mordecai. *Diplomat Heroes of the Holocaust.* Jersey City, NJ: Ktav, 2007.

——— *Saving One's Own: Jewish Rescuers during the Holocaust.* Lincoln, NE: University of Nebraska Press, 2017.

Palmer, Kelly. "Humanitarian Relief and Rescue Networks in France, 1940–45." PhD Dissertation, Michigan State University, 2010.

Parisis, Jean-Marc. *Les inoubliables.* Paris: Flammarion, 2014.

Paxton, Robert O. "Jews: How Vichy Made it Worse," *The New York Review of Books*, March 6, 2014.

Peck, Abraham J. *The German-Jewish Legacy in America, 1938–1988: From Bildung to Bill of Rights.* Detroit, MI: Wayne State University Press, 1989.

Pénard, Étienne. "Le 'peuple du livre' à l'épreuve du 'judaïsme du muscle': Les communautés juives de France et le sport (fin XIXe–1948)." PhD Dissertation, Université Rennes 2, 2020.

Penslar, Derek J. *Shylock's Children: Economics and Jewish Identity in Modern Europe.* Berkeley, CA: University of California Press, 2001.

Perrot, Michelle. "Féminisme," in. Duclert and P. Simon-Nahum (eds.), *Les événements fondateurs: L'Affaire Dreyfus*, 132–9. Paris: Armand Colin, 2009.

Peschanski, Denis. *La France des camps: L'internement de 1938 à 1946.* Paris: Gallimard, 2002.

Pignot, Manon. *Allons enfants de la patrie: Génération Grande Guerre.* Paris: Seuil, 2012.

Pine, Lisa. "Gender and the Family," in Dan Stone (ed.), *The Historiography of the Holocaust*, 364–82. London: Palgrave Macmillan, 2004.

Pistrak, Moisei. *Les problèmes fondamentaux de l'école du travail*, edited by P. Rey-Herme. Paris: Desclée de Brouwer, 1973.

Pollin-Galay, Hannah. *Ecologies of Witnessing: Language, Place, and Holocaust Testimony.* New Haven, CT and London: Yale University Press, 2018.

Portelli, Alessandro. "What Makes Oral History Different?," in Robert Perks and Alistair Thompson (eds.), *The Oral History Reader*, 2nd edn., 32–42. London: Routledge, 2006.

Poujol, Catherine. "Les débuts de l'Union libérale israélite (1895–1939): Le pari de moderniser le Judaïsme français," *Archives Juives: Revue d'histoire des Juifs de France*, 40, no. 2 (2007), 65–81.

Poznanski, Renée. "A Methodological Approach to the Study of Jewish Resistance in France," *Yad Vashem Studies*, XVIII (1987), 1–39.

——— *Être Juif en France pendant la Seconde Guerre mondiale.* Paris: Hachette, 1994.

——— *Repenser la Résistance des Juifs en France.* Forthcoming.

——— "Women in the French-Jewish Underground: Shield-Bearers of the Resistance?," in Dalia Ofer and Lenore J. Weitzman (eds.), *Women in the Holocaust*, 234–52. New Haven, CT and London: Yale University Press, 1998.

Raphaël, Freddy. *Les Juifs d'Alsace et de Lorraine de 1870 à nos jours*. Paris: Albin Michel, 2018.

Raphael, Marc Lee. *A History of the United Jewish Appeal*. Place unknown: Scholars Press, 1982.

Revel, Jacques (ed.) *Jeux d'échelles: La Micro-analyse à l'expérience*. Paris: Gallimard, Seuil, 1996.

Ripa, Yannick. "Naissance du dessin de guerre: Les époux Brauner et les enfants de la guerre civile espagnole," *Vingtième Siècle: Revue d'histoire*, 89, no. 1 (2006), 29–46.

Rochefort, Florence. "Dreyfusisme et Femmes Nouvelles," in Vincent Duclert and Perrine Simon-Nahum (eds.), *Les événements fondateurs: L'Affaire Dreyfus*, 174–84. Paris: Armand Colin, 2009.

Rodrigue, Aron. *French Jews, Turkish Jews: The Alliance Israélite Universelle and the Politics of Jewish Schooling in Turkey, 1860–1925*. Bloomington, IN: Indiana University Press, 1990.

Roseman, Mark. *Lives Reclaimed: A Story of Rescue and Resistance in Nazi Germany*. New York: Metropolitan Books, 2019.

Rosenberg, André. *Les enfants dans la Shoah: La déportation des enfants juifs et tsiganes de France*. Paris: Les Éditions de Paris, 2013.

Rymph, Catherine. "American Child Welfare and the Wagner-Rogers Bill of 1939," *Jewish Historical Studies: A Journal of English-Speaking Jewry*, 51 (2019), 285–300.

Samuel, Vivette. *Rescuing the Children: A Holocaust Memoir*. Madison, WI: University of Wisconsin Press, 2002.

Samuels, Maurice. *The Right to Difference: French Universalism and the Jews*. Chicago, IL: University of Chicago Press, 2016.

Sarna, Jonathan. *American Judaism: A History*. New Haven, CT and London: Yale University Press, 2004.

Schenderlein, Anna. *Germany on their Minds: German Jewish Refugees in the United States and their Relationships with Germany, 1938–1988*. New York: Berghahn, 2020.

Schlör, Joachim. *"Liesel, it's time for you to leave.": Von Heilbronn nach England. Die Flucht der Familie Rosenthal vor nationalsozialistischer Verfolgung*. Heilbronn: Stadarchiv Heilbronn, 2015.

Schor, Ralph. *L'antisémitisme en France pendant les années trente*. Brussels: Éditions Complexe, 1992.

Scott Weaver, Meredith. "Lobbyists and Humanitarians: French Jewish Activism in Interwar Strasbourg, Nice, and Paris, 1919–1939." PhD Dissertation, University of Delaware, 2012.

———— "Republicanism on the Borders: Jewish Activism and the Refugee Crisis in Strasbourg and Nice," *Urban History*, 43, no. 4 (2016), 599–617.

Sémelin, Jacques, Claire Andrieu, and Sarah Gensburger (eds.). *Resisting Genocide: The Multiple Forms of Rescue*. London: Hurst, 2010.

Sewell, William. *Logics of History: Social Theory and Social Transformation*. Chicago, IL: University of Chicago Press, 2009.

Shenker, Noah. *Reframing Holocaust Testimony*. Bloomington, IN: Indiana University Press, 2015.

Shirley, Dennis. *The Politics of Progressive Education: The Odenwaldschule in Nazi Germany*. Cambridge, MA: Harvard University Press, 1992.

Silverman, Lisa. *Becoming Austrians: Jews and Culture between the World Wars*. Oxford: Oxford University Press, 2012.

Simmons, Erica. *Hadassah and the Zionist Project*. Lanham: Rowman & Littlefield, 2006.

Simoni, Renato. *Walter Katz: Un aviador al servicio de la Republica (1936–1938)*. Rovira: Publicacion URV, 2020.

Slezkine, Yuri. *The Jewish Century*. Princeton, NJ: Princeton University Press, 2004.

Sluzki, Carlos. "Migration and Family Conflict," *Family Process*, 18, no. 4 (1979), 379–90.

Sommer, Robert. "René Hirschler." http://judaisme.sdv.fr/histoire/rabbins/hirschl/hirschl.html.

Sonnert, Gerhard, and Gerald Holton. *What Happened to the Young Children Who Fled Nazi Persecution*. New York: Palgrave, 2006.

Soo, Scott. "Putting Memory to Work: A Comparative Study of Three Associations Dedicated to the Memory of the Spanish Republican Exile in France," *Diasporas: Histoire et Sociétés*, 113 (2005), 109–20.

Spellen, Suzanne. "Walkabout: The Sausage King of Brooklyn, Part 3." Brownstoner, June 12, 2012. https://www.brownstoner.com/history/walkabout-the-sausage-king-of-brooklyn-part-3/.

Stargardt, Nicholas. "Children," in Peter Hayes and John K Roth (eds.), *The Oxford Handbook of Holocaust Studies*, 218–31. Oxford: Oxford University Press, 2010.

——— *Witnesses of War: Children's Lives under the Nazis*. New York: Vintage Books, 2007.

Stauber, Roni. *Laying the Foundations for Holocaust Research: The Impact of the Historian Philip Friedman*. Jerusalem: Yad Vashem, 2009.

Stein, Arlene. *Reluctant Witnesses: Survivors, Their Children, and the Rise of the Holocaust Consciousness*. Oxford: Oxford University Press, 2014.

Stein, Herman D. "Jewish Social Work in the United States, 1654–1954," *American Jewish Yearbook*, 57 (1956), 2–98.

Stoll, Steven. "Adele Rosenwald Levy, 1892–1960." Shalvi/Hyman Encyclopedia of Jewish Women. February 27, 2009. Jewish Women's Archive. https://jwa.org/encyclopedia/article/Levy-Adele-Rosenwald.

Stone, Dan. *The Historiography of the Holocaust*. Houndmills: Palgrave Macmillan, 2004.

Strauss, Herbert A. *Jewish Immigrants from the Nazi Period in the USA, Volume One*. New York: K.G. Saur, 1979.

Subak, Susan Elisabeth. *Rescue & Flight: American Relief Workers who Defied the Nazis*. Lincoln, NE: University of Nebraska Press, 2010.

Sweets, John F. *Choices Under Vichy: The French Under Nazi Occupation*. New York: Oxford University Press, 1986.

Tocqueville, Alexis de. *De la démocratie en Amérique, textes essentiels: Anthologie critique par J.L. Benoît*. Paris: Pocket, 2007.

Topographie-der-Shoah. "Odyssee jüdischer Heimkinder." http://www.topographie-der-shoah.at/kinderheime.html.

Toscano, Anna. *Michel Romanoff de Russie: Un destin français*. Paris: L'Harmattan, 2014.

Totoricagüena, Gloria. "Historical Aspects to Political Identity in the New York Basque Community." http://www.euskonews.com/0234zbk/kosmo23402.html.

Trachtenberg, Barry. *The United States and the Nazi Holocaust: Race, Refuge, and Remembrance*. London: Bloomsbury Academic, 2018.

Trivellato, Francesca. "Microhistoria/Microhistoire/Microhistory," *French Politics, Culture, and Society*, 33, no. 1 (2015), 122–34.

Underwood, Nick. *Yiddish Paris: Staging Nation Community in Interwar France.* Bloomington, IN: Indiana University Press, 2022.

USHMM. "Eryk Goldfarb Biography." https://collections.ushmm.org/search/catalog/pa1149957.

———— *First Person 2017: Susan Warsinger.* https://www.youtube.com/watch?v=u0r61JA07lA [video]

Valbousquet, Nina. *Les âmes tièdes: Le Vatican face à la Shoah.* Paris: La Découverte, 2024.

Van Goethem, Hermann, and Patricia Ramet (eds.). *Drancy-Auschwitz, 1942–1944: Les Juifs de Belgique déportés via la France.* Malines: Kazerne Dossin/VUBPress, 2015.

Vanstenhout, Laurien. *Between Community and Collaboration: Jewish Councils in Western Europe under Nazi Occupation.* Cambridge: Cambridge University Press, 2022.

Vargaftig, Nadia. "Exils d'enfants: Lisbonne, ville d'accueil et de transit d'enfants juifs pendant et après la Seconde Guerre mondiale." Master's Thesis, Université Paris 1 Panthéon-Sorbonne, 2001.

Vickery, Amanda. "Golden Age to Separate Spheres?: A Review of the Categories and Chronology of English Women's History," *The Historical Journal,* 36, no. 2 (1993), 383–414.

Vilmain, Vincent. "Les Femmes juives françaises face à l'émancipation," *Archives Juives: Revue d'histoire des Juifs de France,* 48, no. 2 (2015), 4–10.

Vincler, Jeanne. *Communautés juives en péril: Alsace-Lorraine, 1933–39.* Metz: Serpenoise, 2010.

Voignac, Joseph. *Juive et républicaine: l'École Maïmonide.* Paris: Éditions l'Antilope, 2022.

Voigt, Sebastian. *Der jüdische Mai '68: Pierre Goldman, Daniel Cohn-Bendit und André Glucksmann im Nachkriegsfrankreich.* Göttingen: Vandenhoeck & Ruprecht, 2016.

Waldinger, Roger. *The Cross-Border Connection: Immigrants, Emigrants and Their Homelands.* Cambridge, MA: Harvard University Press, 2015.

Walkowitz, Daniel J. "The Making of a Feminine Professional Identity: Social Workers in the 1920s," *American Historical Review,* 95, no. 4 (1990), 1051–75.

Ware, Susan, Stacy Lorraine Braukman, and Radcliffe Institute for Advanced Study (eds.). *Notable American Women: A Biographical Dictionary Completing the Twentieth Century.* Cambridge, MA: Belknap Press, 2004.

Webb, Chris, and Terry Nichols. "Frankfurt am Main: The City and the Holocaust." Holocaust Education and Archive Research Team. http://www.holocaustresearch-project.org/nazioccupation/frankfurt.html.

Weber, Klaus. "La philanthropie des Rothschild et la communauté juive de Paris au XIXè siècle," *Archives Juives: Revue d'histoire des Juifs de France,* 44, no. 1 (2011), 17–36.

Weill, Georges. "Andrée Salomon et le sauvetage des enfants juifs (1933–1947)," *French Politics, Culture & Society,* 30, no. 2 (2012), 89–112.

———— "Introduction," in Andrée Salomon, Katy Hazan, Georges Weill, and Jean Salomon (eds.), *Andrée Salomon, une femme de lumière,* 33–73. Paris: Fondation pour la mémoire de la Shoah/Éditions Le Manuscrit, 2011.

Weill, Georges, Ruth Fivaz-Silbermann, and Katy Hazan. "Joseph Weill." http://www.ose-france.org/wp-content/uploads/2011/06/JOSEPHWEILL.pdf.

Weill, Joseph. "Laure Weil, 1875–1952." http://judaisme.sdv.fr/today/laurew/biog.htm.

Weinberg, David H. *A Community on Trial: The Jews of Paris in the 1930s*. Chicago, IL and London: University of Chicago Press, 1977.

Weindling, Paul. "The Kindertransport from Vienna: The Children Who Came and Those Left Behind," *Jewish Historical Studies*, 51 (2019), 16–32.

Wenger, Beth S. "Jewish Women and Volunteerism: Beyond the Myth of Enablers," *American Jewish History*, 79, no. 1 (1989), 16–36.

———— *New York Jews and the Great Depression: Uncertain Promise*. New Haven, CT and London: Yale University Press, 1996.

Werner, Michaël, and Bénédicte Zimmermann. "Beyond Comparison: Histoire Croisée and the Challenge of Reflexivity," *History and Theory*, 45, no. 1 (2006), 30–50.

———— (eds.). *De la comparaison à l'histoire croisée*. Paris: Seuil, 2004.

Wieviorka, Annette. *L'ère du témoin*. Paris: Pluriel, 2013.

———— *Tombeaux: Autobiographie de ma famille*. Paris: Seuil, 2022.

Woocher, Jonathan. *Sacred Survival: The Civil Religion of American Jews*. Bloomington IN: Indiana University Press, 1986.

Wyman, David S. *Paper Walls: America and the Refugee Crisis, 1938–1941*. Amherst, MA: University of Massachusetts Press, 1968.

———— *The Abandonment of the Jews: America and the Holocaust, 1941–1945*. New York: Pantheon Books, 1984.

Yerushalmi, Yosef Hayim. *Serviteurs du roi et non serviteurs des serviteurs*. Paris: Allia, 2011.

———— *Zakhor, Jewish History and Jewish Memory*. New York: Schocken Books, 1989.

Young-Bruehl. *Hannah Arendt: For Love of the World*. New Haven, CT and London: Yale University Press, 2004.

Zahra, Tara. *The Lost Children: Reconstructing Europe's Families after World War II*. Cambridge, MA: Harvard University Press, 2011.

Zajde, Nathalie. "La thérapie des enfants cachés: Entre psychologie et histoire," in Ivan Jablonka (ed.), *L'Enfant-Shoah*, 131–44. Paris: Presses Universitaires de France, 2014.

Zalc, Claire. *Dénaturalisés: Les retraits de nationalité sous Vichy*. Paris: Seuil, 2016.

———— "Des réfugiés aux indésirables: Les pouvoirs publics français face aux émigrés du IIIe Reich entre 1933–1939," in Éric Guichard and Gérard Noiriel (eds.), *Construction des nationalités et immigration dans la France contemporaine*, 259–73. Paris: Presses de L'Ecole normale supérieure, 1997.

———— "Les pouvoirs publics et les émigrés du IIIe Reich en France de 1933 à 1939: Problèmes d'identité." Master's Thesis, Université de Paris-VII, 1993.

Zalc, Claire, and Tal Bruttmann (eds.). *Microhistories of the Holocaust*. New York: Berghahn Books, 2017.

Zalc, Claire, and Nicolas Mariot. "Identifier, s'identifier: Recensement, auto-déclarations et persécution des Juifs de Lens (1940–1945)," *Revue d'histoire moderne & contemporaine*, 54, no. 3 (2007), 91–117.

Zapruder, Alexandra (ed.). *Salvaged Pages: Young Writers' Diaries of the Holocaust*. New Haven, CT and London: Yale University Press, 2002.

Zeitoun, Sabine. *Histoire de l'OSE: De la Russie tsariste à l'occupation en France, 1912–1944: L'Œuvre de secours aux enfants, du légalisme à la résistance*. Paris: L'Harmattan, 2012.

———— *L'Œuvre de secours aux enfants (OSE) sous l'occupation en France*. Paris: L'Harmattan, 1990.

Zelizer, Viviana A. *Pricing the Priceless Child: The Changing Social Value of Children.* Princeton, NJ: Princeton University Press, 1994.

Zolberg, Aristide R. *A Nation by Design: Immigration Policy in the Fashioning of America.* New York: Harvard University Press, 2006.

Zuccotti, Susan. *The Holocaust, the French, and the Jews.* New York: Basic Books, 1993.

Zucker, Bat-Ami. *Cecilia Razovsky and the American-Jewish Women's Rescue Operations in the Second World War.* London: Valentine Mitchell, 2008.

——— "Frances Perkins and the German-Jewish Refugees, 1933–1940," *American Jewish History,* 89, no. 1 (2001), 35–59.

Index